The Reconstruction of Resurrection Belief

Peter Carnley's previous publications

The Structure of Resurrection Belief (1987)
The Yellow Wallpaper and Other Sermons (2000)
Reflections in Glass (2004)
A Kind of Retirement (2016)
Resurrection in Retrospect (2019)

The Reconstruction of Resurrection Belief

Peter Carnley

CASCADE *Books* • Eugene, Oregon

THE RECONSTRUCTION OF RESURRECTION BELIEF

Copyright © 2019 Peter Carnley. All rights reserved. Except for brief quotations in critical publications or reviews, no part of this book may be reproduced in any manner without prior written permission from the publisher. Write: Permissions, Wipf and Stock Publishers, 199 W. 8th Ave., Suite 3, Eugene, OR 97401.

Cascade Books
An Imprint of Wipf and Stock Publishers
199 W. 8th Ave., Suite 3
Eugene, OR 97401

www.wipfandstock.com

PAPERBACK ISBN: 978-1-5326-6754-1
HARDCOVER ISBN: 978-1-5326-6755-8
EBOOK ISBN: 978-1-5326-6756-5

Cataloguing-in-Publication data:

Names: Carnley, Peter, author.

Title: The reconstruction of resurrection belief / Peter Carnley.

Description: Eugene, OR: Cascade Books, 2019. | Includes bibliographical references and index.

Identifiers: ISBN 978-1-5326-6754-1 (paperback). | ISBN 978-1-5326-6755-8 (hardcover). | ISBN 978-1-5326-6756-5 (ebook).

Subjects: LCSH: Jesus Christ—Resurrection. | Theology.

Classification: BT482 .C371 2019 (print). | BT482 (ebook).

Scripture quotations are from the New Revised Standard Version Bible, copyright © 1989 National Council of the Churches of Christ in the United States of America. Used by permission. All rights reserved worldwide

Manufactured in the U.S.A.   06/04/19

In memory of my
theological mentors and research supervisors

John Hick
(20 January 1922—9 February 2012)

and

Dennis Nineham
(27 September 1921—9 May 2016)

What a privilege.

Contents

Preface | ix
Acknowledgments | xiii
Abbreviations | xiv

1. Resurrection and the Ecclesial Experience of the Raised Christ | 1
2. The Nature of Faith | 30
3. The Object of Faith | 57
4. Paul and Stoicism | 73
5. Faith and the Senses | 100
6. The Presence of a Person | 123
7. Faith and Freedom, Ambiguity and Doubt | 141
8. Faith as Remembering and Knowing | 170
9. A Veridical Memory? | 197
10. A Uniquely Referring Memory | 223
11. The Resurrection of the Body | 242
12. A Little More Platonic Light | 269
13. Belief and Behavior | 289
14. Postscript | 304

Bibliography | 313
Author Index | 327
Subject Index | 331

Preface

THIS BOOK IS UNASHAMEDLY a work of systematic theology. By contrast with the focus of New Testament Studies, it is less concerned with historical and exegetical issues pertaining to the interpretation of ancient texts and more concerned to address the constructive work of articulating an understanding of Christian faith in the Resurrection of Christ for today.

New Testament scholars naturally concentrate on the meaning of the texts, and on what went on *behind* the texts, including an understanding of the originative events that produced them. The controlling interest, for example, might be on the nature of the oral processes of the transmission of the traditions about Jesus prior to the production of the first written Gospels, or on what went on in the mind of Saint Paul in writing to the various communities around the Mediterranean with which he had to do. The systematic theologian, by contrast, is more interested, not so much in what lies *behind* the texts as in what goes on in *front* of them. He or she has the task of articulating a coherent statement of faith in the service of the church of today as it seeks to clarify its theological understanding in the context of an increasingly secularized world of scientific materialism.

Obviously, the systematic theologian has necessarily to keep an eye on what current New Testament scholarship has to say specifically about the traditions relating to faith in Jesus' Resurrection; but the reception of the insights of the past concerning the nature of resurrection faith necessarily involves their re-interpretation in the only language we have—the language of contemporary use. And this is not to mention the need to understand the historical tradition of resurrection faith in the light of the contemporary epistemological and cosmological knowledge of the modern world. In the process of the reception of ancient traditions of faith those insights themselves are therefore inevitably changed as we make them our own—in some respects ever so slightly, and in other respects somewhat more dramatically.

We have always to remember that the first generation of Christian believers inhabited a world that was radically different from our own. Theirs was the thought-world of Second Temple Judaism that was informed by a somewhat melodramatic apocalyptic imagination relating to the End of the world. This was entirely different from contemporary fears of humanly produced catastrophe, whether by nuclear holocaust or the irreparable consequences of global warming. In addition they were immersed in a Hellenistic cultural environment that by the fist century had become extraordinarily mixed. In philosophical terms this was a world that was characterized by an amalgam of an inherited Stoic approach to ethical issues with an increasing interest in Platonic epistemological categories. From a contemporary perspective, we can see that Stoicism was on the way out while Platonism was once again coming into dominance. Hence, we speak of it today as the eclectic world of Middle Platonism.

Clearly, this was a world very different from our own. We are no longer Stoics or Middle Platonists in any real sense, let alone in the highly specific way that first-century Christians might have been. Today, the basic insights of Plato do not feed into the thought-world of popular culture in the way they were unwittingly absorbed and presupposed in the first century. As we reconstruct resurrection belief in our own language, we will work in epistemological terms, not in the light of Plato but, much more likely, in the light of Wittgenstein.

While appreciating the importance of Stoic and Platonic thought-forms for understanding Paul, we are therefore faced with articulating an epistemology of faith in the language of today, with as much logical coherence as we are capable of producing. Inevitably, this means using not only the language but the philosophical and cosmological presuppositions of today.

The basic raw experience that triggers the response of faith may be essentially the same across time insofar as it has to do with the same eternal and changeless religious Object, the transcendent and invisible God, and, in the case of Resurrection faith, with the Raised Christ "seated at God's right hand" (in some sense of this expression). In other words, in faith our concerns still focus upon the same heavenly reality to which the concrete experience of Christ's "life-giving Spirit" continues to point and bear witness. However, as we make the language of the New Testament our own, and as we inevitably bring a different interpretative grid to the understanding of it, the original insights of the first Christians cannot fail to become *uniquely ours*. Even though we may incorporate much of the same inherited New Testament language into our own interpretation and articulation of the experience of faith, the exact meaning content assigned to that inherited language will necessarily be somewhat different from that of our theological forebears. In the context of a contemporary world-view, we cannot avoid re-interpreting it; we are alert to the "fallacy of direct transference." This means that, if something is lost in translation, quite a deal will also inevitably be added in the same process.

Not least, as we articulate our faith today, we face the challenge of explaining how it might be possible for people in the twenty-first century to claim, not only an acquaintance with the "life-giving Spirit" of the Raised Christ as the animating Spirit of the Christian community, but how it is possible to identify that Spirit *as* the presence today of the now glorified and exalted Raised *Jesus* by reference to a historical person who lived some two thousand years ago. This will necessarily also involve us in the task of explaining how it is possible for some people to come to faith, so as to claim an acquaintance with the presence of the Raised Christ, while others do not. Surely few today will be unquestioningly content simply to imagine that some receive "the gift of faith" from God, while others for some inexplicable reason are cruelly deprived of it. In other words, we have to face the challenge of outlining an epistemology of faith that is capable of explaining the apparent ambiguity of the divine disclosure and the accompanying religious freedom that allows some to come to the decision of faith, while others obviously feel entirely comfortable in following alternative this-worldly pursuits.

In addition, we have to come to terms with the apparent universal "availability" of the Raised Christ, whose presence is the subject matter of our knowledge claims in faith, not just in one place, but in principle in any and all places at the same time. Only so can Christians claim to know themselves to be "in Christ" and members of "the Body of Christ" when they are called together into communities of faith today wherever in the world they may happen to find themselves.

This book therefore not only endeavors to understand St Paul in his Jewish Second Temple context and in the Hellenistic context of Middle Platonism; at best this would represent only half of the present theological challenge. In addition we have to address the systematic re-construction of resurrection belief in the context of our own world and in thought-forms that are meaningful today. Only so may we then be in a position to address questions of truth.

As with the production of the companion volume to this, *Resurrection in Retrospect*, I am very grateful to a number of key people who, since its beginning in 2010, have all helped in one way or another to bring this project to fruition: I am enormously grateful to the then President of the General Theological Seminary in New York, Lang Lowry, and the Interim Dean at the time, Bishop Peter Lee, for inviting me to come out of retirement to teach Systematic Theology at the General Theological Seminary of The Episcopal Church from 2010 to 2013. Likewise, I am grateful to the members of the Systematic Theology classes in those years for their keen enthusiasm and serious dedication to the task not only of wrestling with the complexities thrown up by the New Testament resurrection traditions, but of facing the challenge of producing a systematically coherent statement of faith in the Resurrection of Christ for the church today. I also appreciate the seriousness with which the Adult Education classes of the Episcopal Parish of St. Peter, Morristown, New Jersey, engaged with essentially the same issues between 2014 and 2015, and I especially wish to thank those who attended to the practical logistics relating to this exercise, especially the Reverend Janet Broderick, for being prepared to hire an aged antipodean stranger, and Mikael and Beth Salovaara, and Constance Silverman, who ensured that our "home away from home" was made so comfortable.

PREFACE

In more recent times I have been very grateful for the local encouragement and support of the Warden of John Wollaston Theological College in Perth, Gregory Seach, along with my friends David Wood and Susan Maushart. I am especially grateful to Luke Hoare who has been prepared to spend so much of his time on the painstaking and careful work of copy editing and checking references towards the end of the process. To convert something essentially British into the format of the *Chicago Manual of Style* is no mean accomplishment. For this help I am enormously appreciative.

In relation to the final phase of producing these two books, I wish to express my thanks to Dr. K. C. Hanson and the constantly helpful staff at Wipf and Stock for their obvious dedication to the achievement of excellence in their work. The production of this book and of *Resurrection in Retrospect* at the same time, was a big ask, to which they responded with no apparent sense of pressure; it has been a pleasure to deal with people of such obvious professional competence, infused with palpable generosity of spirit and care.

In and through all this, my loving wife Ann has been a constant support. Almost certainly, I would not have persisted with such a mammoth commitment without her patience and encouragement. Given that, for most of the last decade, she has lived with me despite the constant distraction of the theology of the Resurrection, I know she will now at last appreciate not having to ask "What are you thinking about?" quite so often. I promise that our next years together will be much more relaxed as we enjoy life and behave in the manner of the retired couple we really are.

Meanwhile, I am very grateful to God for the opportunity of being able to tackle some sustained thinking about this most important subject matter of Christian theology, and for all those who, often without being aware of it, have so generously helped and supported me in the course of it.

+Peter Carnley
East Fremantle, Western Australia
10 September 2018

Acknowledgments

Every effort has been made to trace and acknowledge copyright holders of material reproduced in this book. The publisher apologizes for any omissions that may remain and, if notified, will ensure that full acknowledgments are made in a subsequent edition.

Abbreviations

ExpT	*Expository Times*
JSNT	*Journal for the Study of the New Testament*
JSNTSup	Journal for the Study of the New Testament Supplement Series
JTS	*Journal of Theological Studies*
LCL	Loeb Classical Library
PG	Patrologia Graeca
RSG	N. T. Wright, *The Resurrection of the Son of God*. London: SPCK, 2003 (re-issued 2017)
SBT	Studies in Biblical Theology
TDNT	*Theological Dictionary of the New Testament*. 10 vols. Edited by Gerhard Kittel and Gerhard Friedrich. Translated by Geoffrey W. Bromiley. Grand Rapids: Eerdmans, 1964–76
WUNT	Wissenschaftliche Untersuchungen zum Neuen Testament

1

Resurrection and the Ecclesial Experience of the Raised Christ

THE THEOLOGY OF THE Resurrection of Jesus Christ falls into two broad categories. The first is comprised of the work of those who are anxious to prove "that it happened." In other words, there are those who believe that Christ's Resurrection should be handled retrospectively as a historical event of the past, just like any other event of human history. Access to the knowledge of it is gained by relying upon the historical reason and the techniques of critical historical research. B. F. Westcott in the nineteenth-century, and Wolfhart Pannenberg in the twentieth-century, for example, are among the most notable proponents of this kind of approach.[1] More recently, an outstanding example has also been provided by N. T. Wright, whose monumental book, *The Resurrection of the Son of God*,[2] is in fact the reigning paradigm of this kind of methodological commitment. Wright has mounted a confidently aggressive attempt to prove the occurrence of Christ's Resurrection purely as a historical event, which, he says, is open to public examination by any right thinking person "of any persuasion."[3]

Then, second, there are those who are not at all convinced about the viability of this kind of historical approach, and turn instead to the handling of the Resurrection essentially as a mystery of God with an uncompromisingly transcendental character. James D. G. Dunn, for example, expresses his discomfort with attempts to handle the Resurrection of Christ purely as a historical event, given the strength of the New Testament witness to the fact that it was from the first understood as a going from this world of historical time to the timeless eternity of God. A leaving of history to sit "at the right hand of the Father" hardly qualifies as a historical event. As Dunn rightly says, "'resurrection' almost by definition is an exit from history and so not properly speaking "historical.'"[4] Though the reported verbal precipitate of the human

---

1. See Westcott, *The Gospel of the Resurrection*, 1866; Pannenberg, *Jesus—God and Man*, 1968.
2. Wright, *The Resurrection of the Son of God*, 2003 (re-issued 2017). Hereafter *RSG*.
3. *RSG*, 21.
4. See Dunn's response to Stephen Davis, in *Memories of Jesus*, 320.

perception of its occurrence is certainly open to historical enquiry, such an "event" is itself not amenable to critical historical research.

In the nineteenth-century R. W. Macan pointed out, in response to B. F. Westcott's approach to an understanding of the Resurrection as an event of historical time of the kind that might be appropriated by the public exercise of the historical reason, that dogmatic judgments and faith commitments were already involved and, in fact, necessarily presupposed, in attempts to handle the New Testament evidence relating to the Resurrection of Jesus even as a historical event.[5] This caused Westcott to revise his language and to talk of the "revelation" of the Raised Christ by contrast with something accessible by reason alone.[6] In much twentieth-century theology, a similar appeal was also made to the category of revelation in the face of a perceived disenchantment with the capacity of all historical research ever to come up with fixed and certain conclusions. In the twentieth-century, as theologians sought to identify a "storm-free area" (*sturmfreies Gebiet*) for the commitment of faith that was independent of the shifting sands of historiographical research, the central theological interest came to focus exclusively on a religiously significant content with a transcendent and revelatory character. This was a primary motivation for both Karl Barth and Rudolf Bultmann, in different ways, to eschew a reliance on the historical reason and to base their understanding of faith on the category of the revelation of the Word of God. Hence, the surpassing popularity of the great twentieth-century "Word theologies" of Barth and Bultmann, whose joint efforts ensured that, today, the claim that the Raised Christ is encountered as a reality of present experience is most likely to be grounded in the hearing of what is understood to be his "living Word."

In the case of Barth, this outcome was achieved by pursuing a kind of "middle distance" reading of the New Testament witness, in which potential believers were invited to discern the "Word of God" within the words of the scriptural texts. The concern was in the judgment of faith to isolate and appropriate the objective content of the historical revelation of the Word of God in Christ, to which the Word of Scripture was said to bear witness. Bultmann, on the other hand, took the opposite course of insisting that the objectifying language of the New Testament witness had to be so proclaimed as to be heard as a revelatory "Word of address," which precipitated a revised existential self-understanding in the hearer. By having the New Testament witness de-objectified, which Bultmann famously spoke of as "demythologizing," the hearer was said thereby to grasp a new self-identity in faith, now as a creature under the Creator, or as an obedient disciple of Jesus Christ by appropriating the saving effect of his Cross. The hearing of this "Word of address" thus warranted Bultmann's celebrated declaration that Jesus had been "raised into the kerygma" so as to be met anew in the "Word-event" of the church's proclamation Sunday by Sunday.

---

5. See Macan, *The Resurrection of Jesus Christ* (1877).
6. Westcott, "The Resurrection of Christ" (1877), and *Revelation of the Risen Lord* (1881).

It was in large part in reaction to the heavy reliance on faith alone of these Word theologies of the previous generation that Wolfhart Pannenberg pursued his attempt in the late 1960s to revive a reliance on human reason so as to prove the occurrence of the Resurrection as a historical event of the past. Since then, there have been a number of studies, however, that have demonstrated the inadequacies of Pannenberg's attempted historical proof.[7] On the other hand, in the companion volume to this,[8] I have endeavored to demonstrate the failure, at almost every turn of argument, of N. T. Wright's historical "proof" in *The Resurrection of the Son of God* of 2003.[9]

Sometimes, non-historical approaches at once humbly acknowledge the limitations not just of the historical reason, but even the limitations of the capacity of human language to talk reasonably about the Resurrection in a literal matter-of-fact, clear and distinct kind of way. Those of this view are therefore constrained to rely upon the category of faith as the essential avenue of approach to it, and openly acknowledge the shortfall between religious experience and the capacity of finite language adequately to speak of it. Dunn himself speaks of "The Metaphor of Resurrection."[10] It is ultimately a mystery that defies attempts even to describe it in clear and distinct literal language. Indeed, sometimes at least, even those who are concerned to affirm the historical nature of the Resurrection as an event of space and time are prepared to acknowledge this aspect of "resurrection language." Wolfhart Pannenberg, for example, admits that the Resurrection "is so absolutely unique that we have no other name for this than the metaphorical expression of the apocalyptical expectation" (of Second Temple Judaism).[11] However, he insists that "Only the *name* we give to the event is symbolic, metaphorical, but not the reality of the event itself . . . In this sense, the resurrection of Jesus is an historical event, an event that really happened at that time."[12] This immediately raises

---

7. See my own discussion of the valiant attempts of both Westcott and Pannenberg to prove the occurrence of the Resurrection using the historical reason in Carnley, *The Structure of Resurrection Belief*, 29–95; also, Coakley, "Is the Resurrection a 'Historical' Event?"

8. Carnley, *Resurrection in Retrospect: A Critical Examination of the Theology of N. T. Wright*.

9. Cranfield, "The Resurrection of Jesus Christ," 390, concludes that "while the discovery of the dead bones of Jesus would indeed, as C. K. Barrett has rightly maintained, conclusively disprove the church's doctrine of the Resurrection and utterly destroy Christian faith, no amount of scientific historical-critical or other scholarly activity can prove conclusively that the Resurrection is true." The reference to C. K. Barrett here is to his *Commentary on the First Epistle to the Corinthians*, 344. While the first part of this proposition may be questionable, given that it presupposes a particular understanding of what a resurrection from the dead might involve that seems very problematic because it is so similar to a mere physical resuscitation or revivification, the second affirmation may certainly claim our assent.

10. The title of the concluding section of Dunn, *Jesus Remembered*.

11. Pannenberg, "Did Jesus Really Rise from the Dead?" 135. See also, Pannenberg, *Jesus—God and Man*, 98: ". . . . the possibility exists in reconstructing the course of events of speaking not only of visions of Jesus' disciples but also of appearances of the resurrected Jesus. In doing so, one speaks, then, just as the disciples themselves, in metaphorical language." Jesus "could only be experienced and designated by an extraordinary mode of experience, the vision, and only in metaphorical language."(99).

12. Pannenberg, "Did Jesus Really Rise from the Dead?" 135: "Resurrection" in literal terms means

an issue about the priority of questions of meaning over questions of truth: it is at the outset difficult to prove the occurrence of an event when exactly what happened is hidden behind a symbolic or metaphorical image.

Very often, those unconvinced about the capacity of critical historical research to prove the occurrence of the Resurrection of Christ think instead of faith as a religious commitment based upon the perception of what is identified as "the presence of the Raised Christ" in one form or another. For example, in the biblical tradition it is possible to begin an examination of Christ's Resurrection through what is reported to have been a concrete acquaintance with his "life-giving Spirit" (as in Paul's reference in 1 Cor 15:45). In St. John's Gospel, this kind of encounter is spoken of as an engagement with Christ's "abundant Spirit" or "Spirit without measure" (John 3:34). The revelatory and transcendent quality of it notwithstanding, in the context of an essentially empirical experience this means that it makes an appeal to faith as a kind of knowing in the present, rather than to the historical reason with its inescapable focus upon the past.

Thus, the theology of the Resurrection has wavered broadly between these two quite different methodological approaches. My own view is that the valiant attempts of those who have set out to prove the occurrence of the Resurrection of Christ purely as a historical event by relying on the historical reason and the techniques of critical historical research are doomed to failure. Richard Swinburne, in *The Resurrection of God Incarnate*, is more forthright: he proffers the view that attempts to prove the occurrence of the Resurrection by appeal to reason alone, without a prior faith in God, are in fact irrational.[13] His thesis is that resurrection faith only becomes viable on the basis of a pre-existing belief in God and the miraculous power of God to act within history, even in a way that might appear contrary to the accepted laws and regularities of nature with which historians usually work.

This does not mean that those who set out to handle the Resurrection essentially as a "mystery of God" that is revealed to faith do not face considerable challenges. Not least, they must embrace the task of articulating a coherent epistemology of faith (*fides*) capable of grounding a response of trust (*fiducia*). This is because, in logical terms, one must first know that the one in whom trust is placed is trustworthy; it would clearly be irrational to trust the untrustworthy. Indeed, reports of the resurrection of Adolf Hitler or Joseph Stalin would not be received as "good news." To welcome the news of the Resurrection of Jesus as "good news" we must necessarily know

---

"a standing up again."

13. Swinburne, *The Resurrection of God Incarnate*, 3: "New Testament scholars sometimes boast that they inquire into their subject matter without introducing any theological claims. If they really do this, I can only regard this as a sign of deep irrationality on their part."

something about *him*. And, very importantly, there is a need to explain how it is even possible to identify what is claimed to be known in faith *as* the actual living presence today of the historical Jesus of Nazareth who lived in Palestine in the first-century. After all, Christian resurrection faith only makes sense if the one claimed to be known by acquaintance in faith today is the very one whose remembered words and works are celebrated in the New Testament records. How is such an identity judgment to be justified? Even the identification of the "living Word" as a Word discerned *within* the words of Scripture, or as a "Word of address" personally heard to have been delivered by the Raised Jesus, seems somewhat arbitrarily made in the theologies of Karl Barth and Rudolf Bultmann.[14] A good deal of attention will therefore be turned to these epistemological questions in the following chapters of this book.

In the face of the admitted evidential shortfall that dictates that it is impossible to prove the occurrence of the Resurrection purely as a historical event of the past, it will therefore be necessary to grapple with these unresolved epistemological and ontological issues relating to the perception of the Christ of faith, and how this might connect with the "Jesus of history." This will involve us in the reconstruction of resurrection belief with as much logical coherence as can be mustered, while all the time acknowledging the unavoidable constraints imposed by the surpassing mystery of the acts of God.

The same kind of fundamentally different approaches to the theology of the Resurrection that has led to the polarization of views between those who approach it retrospectively as a historical event of the past, and those who see it in more transcendental terms as a mystery of God that may be perceived by faith even in the present, may also be detected in the historical discussion of some of Paul's most characteristic phraseology relating to the implications of his faith claims. These have to do specifically with his many attempts to describe the impact of his claim to perceive and know the continuing presence of the Spirit of the Raised Christ, and his own new-found status along with others in their shared participation in the life of faith and worship within the Christian community.

Historically, there has been a protracted theological discussion of the precise meaning, for example, of Paul's references to the church as "the Body of Christ," and also of his intended meaning in the associated use of his characteristic phrase, "in Christ." From one point of view, Paul's references to the "Body of Christ" are sometimes said to refer simply to the historical reality of "a body of people" who share a commonly held belief in Christ. In this case, when Paul speaks of the church as the "Body of Christ," his language is understood to amount to little more than a figure of

---

14. See the discussion of the element of "arbitrariness" in the theologies of both Barth and Bultmann in Carnley, *Structure of Resurrection Belief*, chapter 3.

speech. It is simply a metaphorical image used in reference to the corporate identity of the Christian church itself as a historical and social entity. This follows a characteristic Stoic use of the metaphor of "a body." Seneca spoke in a similar way, for example, when he described the civic arrangement of the State metaphorically as "a body," in much the same way as we still speak today of the State as "the body politic." The Stoics also regularly spoke metaphorically of the cosmos as a "body" with a divine "world soul." This kind of language is found in Philo at around the same time as Paul, and a little later also in Plutarch.[15] In this case, Paul may be understood to have meant simply that the church is in certain respects also *like* a body. His references may be said to refer to the way in which the baptized corporately constitute "a body of people" who share a common faith "in Christ," or who understand themselves to belong together "to Christ." In a sense, this suggests a historical body of people who are even in some way independent of Christ himself, who might even be assumed to be located somewhere else, quite apart from him though at least notionally related to him. In this case, Paul's words "you are the Body of Christ," could therefore simply mean "you are an earthly body of people who have intentionally made a commitment to follow Christ" . . . and little more than that. In this sense, the church as "the Body of Christ" may be understood as a straightforward historical phenomenon.

However, Paul's references to the "Body of Christ" also sometimes appear to speak not just of an earthly and historical reality, but of a more elevated kind of incorporation into an actual transcendental or heavenly reality. This is most noticeably the case in 1 Cor 12:12–27 and 1 Cor 6:15. Instead of being understood as a metaphor designed to refer to the church as a body of people, the concept of the "Body of Christ" has also therefore been interpreted in more relational terms which stress a shared corporate connection of an ontological kind, *to* the Raised Christ himself through some kind of incorporation by baptism and the gift of his Spirit into his very own heavenly life. Far from just being a metaphor, or figurative "manner of speaking," references to "the Body of Christ" thus point to the actual incorporation of the community of baptized believers, through the gift of his Spirit, into the transcendental reality *of* the personal life of the Raised Christ himself.[16] In this case, the Raised Christ is understood to inhabit his Body, the church, as a kind of "corporate personality."[17] Clearly, at the very least such

---

15. See for example, Seneca in *Epistle* 95.52: "We are limbs of a great body"; Philo speaks of the integration of many parts of a nation into a fellowship "as though it were a single body" (*Exposition of the Law*, iii.131), and Plutarch in *Philopoemen* viii.2, speaks of the making of the people of the Peloponnese "into a single body."

16. Robinson, *The Body: A Study in Pauline Theology*, is the classic paradigm of the denial that Paul's language is merely metaphorical.

17. Notions of "corporate personality" in the ancient world are now somewhat out of fashion. See Robinson, "The Hebrew Conception of Corporate Personality"; and Rogerson, "The Hebrew Conception of Corporate Personality." However, a positive view is expressed by Johnson, "Hebrew Conceptions of Kingship," in *Myth, Ritual and Kingship*," and *Sacral Kingship in Ancient Israel*; also Wedderburn, "Paul's Use of the Phrase 'In Christ,'" 97, n.52.

a proposal invites the exercise of the theological imagination in association with the essentially religious commitment of faith.

In a similar way, the discussion of the characteristically Pauline phrase, "in Christ," has oscillated between those who have held that it is used by Paul with a this-worldly orientation, and those who have insisted that it brings with it an otherworldly reference. Some have argued, for example, that the logical behavior of this phrase is entirely parallel to that of the image of the "Body of Christ" insofar as it simply refers metaphorically to the baptized, viewed corporately as "members of the church." This, for example, at least at first sight, appears to be what is expressed by the use of the phrase "in Christ" when in Rom 16:7 Paul greets his kinsfolk, Andronicus and Junia, who, he says, were "in Christ before [he] was."[18] In other words, Paul can be interpreted here to mean little more than "you were baptized members of the church before me" or "you came to faith in Christ before me." In this case, the phrase "in Christ" is roughly equivalent to saying that somebody has been admitted to membership of a crew "*in* the College rowing squad."

In this case, the meaning of the phrase "in Christ" suggests that a purely locative understanding is what Paul may have had in mind. Instead of being conscious of being located *in* a particular geographical place, Paul's over-riding sense of belonging to Christ, and of his own participation in the inclusive Jewish/Gentile community of the church, meant that he was more conscious of being "in Christ" than "in Palestine," or "in Greece," or wherever. In other words, what is expressed in shorthand by the use of the phrase "in Christ" is not much more than simply a sense of being a member of the church. The baptized are said to be "in Christ" in the sense that they corporately "belong to Christ" in a purely theoretical sense. In this case, the phrase "in Christ," like references to the church as "the Body of Christ," seems to be little more than a "manner of speaking," a way of referring to a historical belonging together in the church as a single community of people, all of whom are united by a common faith commitment *to* Christ and to one another. It seems in this case that those said to be "in Christ" belong together to Christ in an entirely notional sense, with "Christ" being seen as objectively separate from them, or even over-against them. In this case a history of the Christian church might be written as though the church were a social reality essentially like any other human community, group, or club.

On the other hand, in a way that is also parallel to the discussion of Paul's meaning in his references to "the Body of Christ," it has been equally popular in discussions of the phrase "in Christ" over the last couple of generations for theologians to argue that it, at least sometimes, appears to have a more transcendental reference. In this case, the phrase "in Christ" is much more than a figure of speech; rather, it has to be interpreted in more ontic terms to connote an incorporation by a kind of participation through the gift of the Spirit in the actual heavenly life of the Raised Christ understood as a transcendental divine reality. Instead of referring to

---

18. Rom 16:7.

a notional belonging *to* Christ together with others in the Christian community, it is as though it has to do with a kind of spiritual belonging through incorporation into the living, heavenly reality *of* Christ himself. In other words, it may be argued that it appears to signal a more intimate personal connection *with* Christ himself by sharing corporately in his transcendental personality. Once again, this is something that is perceived though faith.[19]

In an early flurry of interest in Paul's use of the phrase "in Christ" that was triggered in the first quarter of the twentieth-century by Adolf Deissmann and Wilhelm Bousset, followed by Albert Schweitzer, it became popular to speak of this as a kind of "mysticism." Schweitzer spoke of Paul's sense of belonging, not just to the church as an earthly and historical institution, but to something super-earthly and eternal. Whether we should today be inclined to employ such a "catch-all" concept as "mysticism," we rightly note the emphasis on the essentially religious experience of inter-personal *communion* with Christ as a fundamental point of entry for approaching Paul's understanding of this aspect of the implications of the Resurrection.

The theological discussion of Paul's use of the phrase "in Christ," along with theme of the "Body of Christ" in Paul's theology, has therefore oscillated historically between these two polarities: at one level we are able to talk about the experience of a historically observable community of human people; at another level we are being introduced to a less obvious, but no less real, purported acquaintance with an inner or hidden spiritual reality which is understood in faith to give this human community its cohesion and identity. J. A. T. Robinson who (famously) denied that Paul was simply speaking metaphorically only of a human community when he used the image of "the Body of Christ,"[20] has in large part been responsible for setting the terms of the ensuing debate. Early in this discussion, C. F. D. Moule entered upon a very careful and painstaking analysis of Paul's language,[21] with a view to judging whether we are dealing with one of these interpretations of Paul's words rather than the other, by addressing specifically the question of whether his language is to be understood as metaphorical or more than metaphorical. Moule himself came to the view that while many of Paul's references to "the Body of Christ" seem in fact to be metaphorical references to the church simply as a historically observable "body of people" who happen to believe in Christ, other references (though in his view a minority of them) certainly appeared to point to something more than just a metaphor. In doing so, Moule was clearly signalling the

---

19. A seminal discussion of this may be found in Moule, *The Origin of Christology*, 47–89.

20. Robinson, *The Body* (1952).

21. In *The Origin of Christology*, chapter 2: "The Corporate Christ." This has since been surpassed, especially by James D. G. Dunn's survey of this aspect of Paul's theology in *The Theology of Paul the Apostle* (1998), chapter 5, sec. 15: "Participation in Christ"; especially 15.1: "Christ mysticism."

need to exercise some caution before accepting Robinson's thesis unreservedly. At the end of the day, he thus tended to opt for *both* a metaphorical usage and something that was, if not exactly literal, more than metaphorical.

It should not be a surprise to find that the logical behavior of Paul's language about membership of the "Body of Christ," and his use of the phrase "in Christ," is very similar. Being "in Christ," and belonging as a member of the "Body of Christ" through being made one community in the Spirit "by baptism into Christ," appear to be more or less synonymous ways of referring to the same experienced reality. Indeed, there is not only an observable similarity of expression between Paul's phrase "in Christ" and his references to the church as the "Body of Christ," for he actually brings the two expressions together himself. In Galatians 3:27, he says "many of you as have been baptized into Christ have put on Christ" and in the next verse, the baptized therefore are said to become "one *in* Christ Jesus." In this inclusive community, there are thus "many members in one body";[22] they "are one body in Christ," for "in Christ... though many," they "form one body."[23] This is the same inclusive community that Paul describes in Galatians 3:28, in which there are declared to be no divisions based on ethnic differences, or social distinctions, or inter-personal divisions based on gender inequality. However, it is important to underline that this belonging "in Christ" as members together of the "Body of Christ" depends not upon their own good intentions and determined effort, so much as upon their incorporation into an organic whole by a common sharing in the life of Christ through the gift of his Spirit. The perception of this is obviously a judgment of faith.

It is in many ways unfortunate that this historical and somewhat unresolved discussion has tended to center around these two opposing sides of the debate as polar opposites. Certainly, it is as though the task of adjudicating between those who have aligned themselves on either side of this dispute is a matter of either/or. Perhaps, however, it should be approached somewhat more *apophatically* as a matter of neither/nor. It is surely clear, for a start, that the church cannot be "the Body of Christ" in a narrow literal sense, for a community of people cannot literally be identical to the physical and material body of Jesus that could have been encountered somewhere along the road between Galilee and Jerusalem in the first-century. However, nor is it just a mere metaphor. For it does not just mean that, when used in reference to the church and its relation to the Easter Jesus, it must therefore simply be a figure of speech. In other words, when, as an apparent metaphor it is unpacked in more prosaic and literal specification, it does not just signal "a group of people" who happen to

22. Rom 12:4.
23. Rom 12:5.

share a common faith in Christ. Hence J. A. T. Robinson insisted that we are dealing with much more than a mere metaphor.

Among the most notable of those who have pursued a course similar to Robinson, Ernst Käsemann also forthrightly rejected the possibility that Paul was speaking only metaphorically. Käsemann clearly demonstrated the importance of Paul's references to the church as the "Body of Christ" to the understanding of the essentially transcendental dimensions of his ecclesiology.[24] He pointed out that this entails that Paul's ecclesiological interest cannot be separated from an understanding of the "life-giving Spirit" of the Raised Jesus, whose presence was perceived in faith as the inner constitutive element of the church's life. Indeed, Paul's references to the "communion of the Spirit," and "living in the Spirit,"[25] and to membership of the "Body of Christ," and being "in Christ," appear to be different ways of speaking about the same experienced transcendental reality. He was thus speaking not just figuratively but in an ontic way, in an attempt to communicate his understanding of the essentially spiritual inner reality that was constitutive of the very being of the church and its entirely unique identity.

To Paul's mind, for example, the gift of the Spirit of the Raised Christ to the community of the baptized *makes* the church into a single body; it is the Spirit that creates an inclusive and reconciled community of love and peace, comprised of both Jews and Gentiles who previously were only too self-consciously aware of being humanly separated. Given Paul's clear understanding of the constitutive role of the Spirit in *making* the church into a single body, the phrase "communion of the Spirit" is the other side of the penny of "the Body of Christ." In other words, the church is the Body of Christ only because it is understood to be animated by his "life-giving Spirit." In Rom 8:2, Paul speaks of this as "the Spirit of life in Christ Jesus." Certainly, for Paul the resulting historical achievement of reconciled human unity among Jews and Gentiles is not just the product of human effort and resolve. It is the product of the creative activity of God.[26] In 1 Cor 12:12–27, for example, it is made clear that it is Christ's life-giving Spirit that allows Christ himself to be thought of in terms of a kind of "inclusive Person": to be joined to him by baptism in his Spirit is to become part of one body: "in one Spirit we were all baptized into one body—Jews or Greeks, slaves or free—and all were made to drink of one Spirit" (1 Cor 12:13). A little later in the same chapter of 1 Corinthians, Paul says: "Now you are the body of Christ and individually members of it."[27] This repeats a sentiment expressed earlier in the epistle, in 1 Cor 6:15: "Do you not know that your bodies are members of Christ?" Other passages suggest that the "glorious body" of the Raised Christ is somehow antecedent to the transformation of the lowly bodies of the baptized that are being fashioned to be like his body (e.g., Phil 3:21). That body appears not just to be a community of believers considered separate

---

24. Käsemann, *Perspectives on Paul*, 102–21.
25. 2 Cor 13:13; Gal 5:16–25; Rom 8:1–17; 1 Thess 4:1–18.
26. 1 Cor 12:18, 24.
27. 1 Cor 12:27.

from Christ, but the actual Body *of* Christ, almost as though it were the manifestation in physical form in space and time *of* an already existing, but otherwise hidden, heavenly and eternal personal reality. These references do not seem just to refer to a body of Christians as a corporate entity described metaphorically as "the Body of Christ," but not actually constitutively related to him in some kind of ontological way. In other words, being "found in him" (Phil 3:9) does not appear to be just a way of talking about being found "in the Church."

Instead of being just a trope or piece of figurative speech, it seems incontestable that, when Paul used this language he was not speaking speculatively or abstractly, but concretely and descriptively of an experienced reality that, in faith, he was struggling to interpret and understand. Moreover, it could only be understood theologically—i.e., from the perspective of his faith in the God who had "raised Jesus from the dead." Given that the Spirit that was understood to be constitutive of the life of the church so as to make it a single body, was also understood to have been received "from heaven" as a divine gift, we are immediately invited therefore to inhabit the world of theological discourse. As in all theological discourse, primitive descriptions, such as of the religious experience of participating in the life of the community of the baptized through the gift of the Spirit, naturally transcended a purely literal form of words and their inherited meanings. The inner spiritual texture of the community life of the church is described by Paul as the inter-personal "communion of the Spirit," and as a uniquely specific kind of love, the "love of God that has been poured into our hearts" through the gift of the Holy Spirit.[28] In Rom 15:30 he also speaks of "the love of the Spirit."

Given its transcendental point of origin, the perceived giftedness of its arrival was, also for Luke, like "a sudden rushing wind,"[29] or "a flame like fire,"[30] and so on. However, insofar as this language appears to be metaphorical, it is language that is not reducible to a simple, clear, and distinct this-worldly specification. If it appears to be metaphorical, it is somehow more than just metaphorical, for it seems clear enough that this language was used to refer to, and describe, a concretely experienced reality with which the first believers claimed to be acquainted in the life of the community of faith. In this way, it was much more than a mere figure of speech.

This means that both the references to the church as "the Body of Christ" and Paul's use of the phrase "in Christ" are neither simply literal nor simply metaphorical. Paul was not just appealing to a simile or trope; rather, he was using this language to refer to something else again, for it is language that has ontic implications. We do better to assess Paul's use of these forms of words by appealing to what Wittgenstein

---

28. Rom 5:5.
29. Acts 2:2.
30. Acts 2:3.

spoke of as "a family resemblance" among a group of loosely related uses of the same terms. The challenge is to come to grips, as best we can, with the cash value of what Paul actually had in mind when he used this somewhat idiosyncratic participative language, not just in relation to its verbal antecedents as pointers to an inherited messianic meaning content, but in its descriptive use in relation to the church, and what was experienced in concrete terms that grounded its faith and inspired its worship. Admittedly, this means that the epistemology of the faith-claim that provides the occasion for the use of this language cries out to be spelled out in detailed terms. What kind of knowing is this? And what is the more precise nature of the "Spirit of Christ" that is claimed to be known in faith? Not least, we have to face the challenge of giving an account of how what it pointed to could have been concretely perceived in faith in such a way that some came to identify it and claim to know it as the Spirit of the Raised Jesus Christ. In addition we must seek to explain how it was that some came to make such claims while others did not.

What is already clear is that, if the idea of "the Body of Christ" is important for understanding Paul's ecclesiology, then this ecclesiological understanding is also an important pointer, both to the manner of the post-Easter presence of the Raised Christ as a "life-giving Spirit," and to the nature of its perception as an important element of the church's resurrection faith. But, by a similar token, the Resurrection of Christ cannot be understood without thinking of the church as the vehicle through which the Raised Christ continues to make himself available to faith by the gift of his presence as its distinctive "life-giving" or "abundant" Spirit. This, after all, is why the church is appropriately spoken of as "his Body." If this sounds circular, it is constitutively circular. It is almost as though it were an analytic or necessary truth: just as it is not possible in ordinary language to think of a "bachelor" without thinking of "an unmarried male human being,"[31] so it is not possible to think of the Christian church just as a community of human people professing a shared set of beliefs, without reference to the actual presence of the Raised Christ as the "life-giving Spirit" that it claims is constitutive of its life.

Paul's ecclesiology thus has implications for an understanding of the transcendent being of the Raised Christ himself and of the manner in which he makes himself available to human people so as to facilitate their apprehension of his presence in faith. These are not just two entirely separate and contingently related matters. We come to an ontological understanding of what is implied in resurrection faith about

---

31. I acknowledge that the term "bachelor" has a more technical sense as "one who aspires to knighthood," or as "one who has received a primary degree in a modern university" (who may even be a woman). Hence the specification of "ordinary language" here simply to illustrate the nature of an analytic truth.

the being of the Raised Christ on the basis of what it is that is actually said to have been experienced when Paul speaks of the church as "the Body of Christ," or when he uses the phrase "in Christ."[32]

The rich complexity of what Paul appears to be trying to express, with its double reference to the historical reality of the church as a community of faithful people on one hand, and the constitutive presence of the other-worldly reality of "the Spirit of Christ" on the other, goes some way towards explaining how it is that Paul's words have triggered such a sustained and unresolved division of opinion. Because what Paul described had, not just a concrete experiential and historical reference that might be appropriated through the exercise of reason, but also a transcendental and eschatological reference that is perceived in faith, the church as "the Body of Christ" may be understood simultaneously as a community of people within historical space and time, *as well as* having its being and identity by participation in the transcendent life of the Raised Jesus. Despite the tendency of the historical debate to think in terms of an either/or, this must necessarily be handled as a both/and, or perhaps better, at least in the first instance, as a neither/nor. For the recognition that Paul's language is not purely literal, but at the same time that it is not just metaphorical in the sense of being simply figurative, but that it has ontic implications, is a positive gain.

If Paul's language about the church and its nature describes the earthly reality of a community of people and, at the same time, when viewed from the perspective of faith, points to the manner of its being brought into existence by the heavenly and transcendent agency of the Spirit that is constitutive of the distinctive inner texture of its life, then the perception in faith of the Raised Christ is not conceived in entirely individualistic terms, but in terms of the *Totus Christus*: Christ-with-his-own. The experienced reality of the communion of the church, in which we understand ourselves as persons in relation to others and not just as individuals, cannot be divorced from our understanding in faith of the presence of the living Spirit of the Raised Christ that makes us all one Body. As John Zizioulas says "a pneumatological constitution of Christology implies, from the standpoint of ontology, the understanding

---

32. The similarity with the traditional ontological argument for the existence of God may be helpful: One cannot think of God without thinking of God as existing, for God by definition is that than which nothing greater can be conceived. Because an existing God is greater than a non-existing God, God is thus thought of as existing not contingently but necessarily. He cannot really be thought of without being thought of as existing (Anselm's discovery). This does not mean that because one can think of God then God exists, for logical possibilities do not entail actual possibilities. It simply means that one cannot *think* of God without thinking of him as existing. Likewise, one cannot think ontologically of the church without thinking of its constitution by the presence of the Raised Christ as its "life-giving Spirit," and vice versa. The ontic implications of Paul's ecclesiology entail that one cannot think of the life-giving presence of the Raised Christ himself without thinking of the manner in which he makes himself available to faith in the life of the church: his presence is the animating Spirit of "the Body of Christ."

of Christ, not in terms of individuality which affirms itself by distancing itself from other individualities, but in terms of personhood which implies a particularity established in and through *communion*."[33] In other words, Zizioulas is making the point that, just as in order to be a person (as distinct from a human individual who is understood in separation from others), one must be involved in inter-personal give-and-take *with* others, so the person of Christ must be understood in relation to the Father; and, in the communion of the church, in relation to those who in faith respond to him. A person, as distinct from an individual, is in this sense one who addresses another and who can expect a similar response. Thus to be a human person, made in the image of God, as distinct from the rest of animal creation, is to be addressed by God and to respond prayerfully in worship. But to think of the Raised Christ as a person, and not just in individualistic terms, is to think it terms of his relation with those whom he calls to himself, and who respond in faith by baptism into his Spirit. In this way, the *personal* presence of the Raised Christ and the constitution of the church go hand in hand.

This means that, while contemporary New Testament theology wrestles to discern the meaning of what was going on *behind* the first-century texts of the early Christian witness to Christ, using exegetical tools and the techniques of critical historical research, it is important to the theological enterprise to attend also to what goes on *in front* of the texts. The reality of the actual experience of faith among those who look at those texts enquiringly as a source of inspiration today, and most importantly, the experience of those who are exposed to the hearing of those texts by their rehearsal in their liturgical consummation, has also to be brought to the interpretation of the texts themselves. Insofar as the baptized now know the animating Spirit of the communion of the church, and claim to identify it in faith *as* the personal Spirit of the Raised Christ, theology must pass beyond exegesis, and its commitment to the methodology of critical historical research, to the theological realism of constructing an epistemology of faith for today.

Among other things, this means that we do not just face the theological challenge of interpreting Paul and his words in a purely retrospective kind of way. The continuing importance of Paul's "participative'" language is that it is still meaningfully used, and provides us with the interpretative tools with which to order and come to terms with our own contemporary experience of faith. As Christians today we, no less than Paul himself and the first generation of Christians, also claim to be "in Christ" and "members of the Body of Christ," and when we do so we are quite certain that we mean what we say and are not merely using apparently metaphorical language as nothing more than a figure of speech. The theological task, therefore, is to interpret our own living Christian experience as much as it is to interpret the meaning of Paul's words in Scripture: in expressing our faith we thus speak not just out of Scripture, but also out of our own concrete experience of participating in the life and worship of the eschatological

---

33. Zizioulas, *Being as Communion*, 182.

community. The primary focus of the theological enterprise is therefore not just textual but contextual in this sense. This means that Scripture and experience become two mutually inter-interpretative entities. It is clear, therefore, that Christ's Resurrection cannot simply be handled retrospectively, only as an event of past historical time. Violence is done to our capacity to bear witness to it if we do.

How we are today to understand the specific contours of the experience of faith in the Raised Christ that Paul seeks to describe in the "participative" language of being "in Christ" or a member of the "Body of Christ," is itself, however, also a somewhat unresolved matter of theological dispute. In his seminal study of 1892, G. A. Deissmann grappled with the notoriously complex issue of just what could be meant by one personality being somehow "in" another. In fact, he famously argued that it was a linguistic impossibility to couple the Greek preposition *en* ("in") with a personal name, for it was impossible for one person to be somehow "inside" another.[34] Deissmann therefore judged it to be an entirely incomprehensible phrase, except as a way of speaking of a person's continuing "influence." However, this hardly does justice to what Paul appears to have been endeavoring to communicate. After all, a person's "influence" may live on for many years after his or her death, so long as a memory is kept alive. But it is difficult to read Paul without a much more realist sense of sharing in the objective and transforming *presence* of the living Christ. If the Raised Christ had "become a life-giving Spirit,"[35] or "the Spirit of life in Christ Jesus,"[36] and if that Spirit was understood as a gift that now dwelt *in them*,[37] then Christ himself dwelt (in some sense of "dwelt") in them.[38] As a result, given faith in his Resurrection from the dead, Paul, and those whom he brought to faith, could somehow now understand themselves to dwell *in Christ*, just as through the Spirit, he dwelt *in them*.[39] Clearly, something more was intended than living in a wake of a person's influence.

In the same tradition as Deissmann, Rudolf Bultmann, in his quest to make some contemporary sense of Paul's apparently mystical or "participative" language, set aside any suggestion that the personality of Christ somehow "magically" replaces the

---

34. See Deissmann, *Paul*, 297. His original insights are found in his 1892 Habilitationsschrift, *Die neutestamentliche Formel 'in Christo Jesu' untersucht*.

35. 1 Cor 15:45.

36. Rom 8:2.

37. Rom 8:9.

38. Rom 8:10.

39. Despite this apparent equation of "Christ" and "Spirit," there is a distinction in the regular use of "Christ" and "Spirit" insofar as Christian believers are most often referred to as being "in Christ," while the Spirit is usually said to be "in Christian believers," rather than vice versa. In one sense, this appears to be an intentionally deliberate New Testament datum, even if it is a distinction that is not always consistently drawn. However, for present purposes, I shall treat them as roughly equivalent ways of speaking of the same concrete experience.

mentality of the Christian believer by a kind of direct transference. Bultmann noted for example, as against some kind of magical transfer, that Paul himself indicated that he nevertheless expected human individuals to will and to decide things for themselves in the course of their own historical lives. Receiving the Spirit does not mean receiving "a mysterious power working with magical compulsion."[40]

In was in his quest for a more acceptable alternative to what he spoke of, somewhat derogatively, as these "primitive cosmological and magical views," that Bultmann appealed to contemporary existentialist philosophy. He thus re-interpreted Paul to mean that what was achieved in the decision of faith was a kind of revised "self-understanding." Among those who have taken issue with Bultmann, E. P. Sanders is one notable theologian who clearly saw the danger of using contemporary existentialist categories as a way of achieving a modernizing re-interpretation of Paul: "Being one Body and one Spirit with Christ is not simply living out a revised self-understanding . . ." Rather than modernize Paul, Sanders was at pains to understand Paul from within the context of Palestinian Judaism: "It seems to me best to understand Paul as saying what he meant and meaning what he said: Christians really are one body and Spirit with Christ . . ."[41] Sanders therefore argued, against Bultmann, that Paul's participative language refers not to "an *individual* and *subjective* experience" but to "a *collective* and *objective* event."[42] Nevertheless, Sanders found the precise meaning of Paul's language elusive: "What does this mean? How are we to understand it?" He pleaded, "We seem to lack a category of 'reality'—real participation in Christ, real possession of the Spirit,—which lies between naïve cosmological speculation and belief in magical transference on the one hand and a revised self-understanding on the other." Sanders confessed that while he did not have a new category of perception to propose, "This does not mean, however, that Paul did not have one."[43] Just what it means to be "in Christ," and to participate in the "life-giving Spirit of Christ" in faith, and to "live by the Spirit" as living members of the "Body of Christ," thus remained for him unresolved.

More recently Troels Engberg-Pedersen has similarly acknowledged that what Paul understood by participation in Christ on the part of Christian believers was probably "very reified," and that it "looks as if it is very far from constituting a real option for us."[44] Indeed, while admitting that "this whole way of thinking fits well into the ancient thought world," it is also one that "we cannot take over."[45] Even so, it seems incontestable that Christians continue to speak of their "membership of the

---

40. Bultmann, *Theology of the New Testament*, 1:336.
41. Sanders, *Paul and Palestinian Judaism*, 458.
42. Sanders, *Paul and Palestinian Judaism*, 458.
43. Sanders, *Paul and Palestinian Judaism*, 523.
44. Enberg-Pedersen, *Paul and the Stoics*, 27.
45. Enberg-Pedersen, *Paul and the Stoics*, 296.

Body of Christ," and of being "in Christ," in such a way as to suggest that it nevertheless does continue to be meaningful.

How, then, may we take some tentative steps so as to move towards the resolution of this issue? Given the difficulties attaching to a contemporary existentialist or phenomenological appropriation to Paul's language, it has instead become fashionable among New Testament scholars to focus on the conceptual *background* of Paul's use of participative language. The focus of interest has turned to the exploration of the *verbal* sources of the "in Christ" phraseology.[46] While this language is said to have been used in response to the Resurrection, there has been a tendency for this discussion to become airborne in a way that does not touch down therefore in religious experience. Thus, the concept of "participation" tends to be explained theologically by exploring its verbal origins, with the result that Paul is presented primarily as one who dealt in abstract theological terms, at the expense of seeing him in religious terms as a person of faith who grappled to describe a new-found experience of Christ. In this way, the role of the Spirit in achieving "incorporation" into Christ, or in explaining an ontic participation "in Christ," tends to be minimized. In one way this is understandable, for it might be thought that it "makes more sense" simply to stick with the verbal antecedents of Paul's language rather than to probe the hidden mysteries of his experience of faith. Indeed, it is this latter, of course, to which Bultmann and Sanders (and Deissmann before them) reacted so negatively. It is, as a consequence, somewhat out of fashion to focus upon the praxis of faith and worship to explain Paul's use of incorporative or participative language, yet the predominance of Paul's recourse to the impact of the Spirit, not as an idea, but as a concrete, empirically perceived reality of his post-Easter experience, compels us to do so.

The first thing to be said is that, even though Sanders is in a sense right in insisting on the collective and objective nature of what Paul refers to by using his participative language, it cannot be thought to be *exclusively* public and objective. Paul's language of "participation in Christ" also impacts subjectively upon members of the community as individual persons. For example, when Paul speaks of the behavioral obligations of those who are "in Christ," or members of the "Body of Christ," he conceives this as an outcome of their possession of the Spirit, and of "living in the Spirit." This applies to living as morally responsible individual persons as much as persons-in-community with others. They are to behave in a manner appropriate to their relation to Christ that

---

46. See the carefully considered discussion of Hewitt and Novenson, "Participationism and Messiah Christology in Paul."

is established by the gift of the Spirit. When Paul reminds those to whom he wrote his various letters of the relation to Christ that was established by their baptism into Christ and the gift of the Spirit, he thus went on in the parenetic passages of his letters to exhort them to live moral lives appropriate to this new-found relationship with Christ. But what he has in mind is clearly not just their corporate behavior as a community of people; they have a responsibility to live by what we would call today "community standards" but *as* individuals. This becomes very clear, for example, when Paul points out that a person of faith cannot be joined to Christ and also to a harlot.[47] This would be entirely inappropriate to an individual's belonging to Christ. Likewise, he is speaking to individuals when he lists the misbehaviors of the unrighteous who as a consequence will not inherit the Kingdom of God in 1 Cor 6:9–11.[48]

On the other hand, while Paul was clearly conscious of belonging to the Raised Christ, and of participating in the life of the Spirit along with others in the communion of the church, this was not at the expense of his own individual experience of faith and the behavioral norms that he understood to be required of him personally. Indeed, the collective and objective face of this experience cannot be understood in separation from his own subjective and individual experience of faith and its obligations. When he speaks of his own behavior, for example, he is clear to take responsibility for his own individual shortcomings, while attributing the good that he does to "Christ" *in* him; "It is no longer I who live but Christ in me."[49] Moreover, when he speaks in Galatians of the original revelation which triggered his faith and missionary activity as an apostle, he speaks of the revelation of Christ "in" him.[50] This can only have been an individual experience. While many, connecting this Galatians reference to his Damascus Road experience, insist that he really means that the revelation was made "to" him,[51] it remains a fact that he actually has in mind some kind of inner subjective experience at this point.

Among those who have tried to run this kind of argument, N. T. Wright, for example, is entirely unconvincing when he attempts to slide by the awkwardness of Paul's reference to God's "revelation of his Son *in* him," rather than "*to* him," by first suggesting that Paul is intent upon drawing out another emphasis here, so that "we cannot deduce anything from this word ("in") about the exact type of experience (ordinary seeing, or "seeing" in the heart)."[52] But then on the very next page, after bringing this Galatians passage into conformity "as a partial parallel" with 1 Cor 15:3–11, Wright actually does deduce what Paul actually meant after all: "Paul is making the

---

47. 1 Cor 6:15.

48. See also Gal 5:21: "I warn you, as I warned you before, that those who do such things shall not inherit the kingdom of God."

49. Gal 2:20.

50. Gal 1:16.

51. As, in fact, in the NRSV translation of this passage.

52. *RSG*, 379.

point that Jesus the Messiah has been revealed *to* him"!⁵³ It might have been more prudent to bring Galatians 1:16 into association with its "partial parallels" elsewhere in Galatians. For example, in Galatians 2:20, where Paul unequivocally declares that "Christ lives in me," and Galatians 4:6: "God has sent forth the Spirit of his Son *into* your hearts." It is clear that for Paul there is a sense in which Christ was indeed revealed *in* him and not only *to* him.⁵⁴

However, we can appreciate the discomfort of Wright and others of similar mind at this point. When this Pauline talk of the revelation of the Raised Christ *in* him, and as a consequence, of Christ being *in* him and of the Spirit being *in* him, is brought into association with his repeated use of the phrase "in Christ," we hear the echo of Adolph Deissmann's original declaration that this language is meaningless: for how can one person somehow be inside another? This is not to mention Bultmann's forthright rejection of what is imagined to be some kind of "magical transfer" by the implant of the personality of Christ into the lives of Christian believers by the gift of the Spirit.

We can also readily appreciate why this was deemed by Sanders, following Bultmann, also to be unacceptable, even though he was self-consciously aware that he had no alternative conceptual suggestion with which to replace it. Having (somewhat uncritically) embraced Bultmann's categorical dismissal of any suggestion that Paul might be thinking of a sort of "participation" with any kind of objective realism in the life of Christ and of the Spirit, but at the same time perceiving the inadequacy of modernizing Paul by re-interpreting his words in terms of modern existentialist categories, Sanders had nowhere else to go.

Certainly, in scriptural terms, the use of "participative" language in speaking of the post-Easter experience of the primitive Christian community persists as an unresolved challenge to would-be interpreters of Paul. This is not language, moreover, that was peculiar to Paul. For St. John, no less than Paul, also uses this kind of language, apparently assuming its capacity to communicate something meaningful. For example, in Jesus' farewell discourse in John 17, where John points to the need for the disciples to be one as Christ and the Father are one, the evangelist goes on to represent Jesus as praying: "As you, Father, are *in* me and I am *in* you, may they also be *in* us."⁵⁵ It may well be, of course, that John was not unaware of the Pauline precedent for this; certainly, it may be seen as John's amplification of the Pauline theological inheritance.

---

53. *RSG*, 390. My italics.

54. Likewise, when Paul in Gal 2:2 speaks of going "up by a revelation" to check out the Gospel he preached to the Gentiles with the Jerusalem leaders, this is unlikely to have been an outwardly visible revelatory appearance, but an inner conviction, somewhat akin to what Aquinas spoke of as "an angelic thought."

55. John 17:21.

Given the difficulties that Deissmann and Bultmann raised about the more precise meaning of Paul's participative language, not to mention what it could possibly mean for us today, it is understandable that the more recent phase in this quest has therefore taken a more linguistically focused turn. New Testament scholars, with N. T. Wright exercising a prominent leading role, have been content to explain the conceptual antecedents of Paul's use of this participative language. Wright, for example, has argued that the verbal source of the phrase "in Christ" is to be found in the *idea* of "incorporative messiahship" which Paul inherited from the traditions of Second Temple Judaism. This is said to have had its roots already in the text of 2 Samuel 19:43 and 20:1, where the destiny of the people of Israel is understood to be inextricably involved in the fortune or fate of the person of the king.[56] However, while Wright was able to cite analogous phrases, there is no actual precedent in the tradition of the use of the phrase "in the Messiah" to make a direct connection with Paul's "in Christ" language. More recently, in *Paul and the Faithfulness of God* (2013), Wright revised these notions by pointing to the inherited Second Temple hope of the corporate resurrection of all Israel, which the Raised Christ was understood by Paul and the first Christians to have anticipated. Somehow, the destiny of all the people of God was in this way to be found by anticipation *in him*.

In a similar quest for the verbal antecedents of Paul's language, A. J. M. Wedderburn has pointed to an analogy between Paul's "in Christ" phrase and Abraham as a representative figure.[57] Nils A. Dahl has gone further than this by arguing that in Galatians 3:14 Paul actually uses the phrase "in Christ" to replace "in your seed" of the Abrahamic tradition in a way that presupposes a messianic interpretation of "the offspring of Abraham."[58]

However, while these somewhat speculative suggestions exhibit enormous ingenuity, it has to be admitted that a good deal of guess-work is involved. Moreover, this entire debate tends to focus upon Paul's theological understanding, and its linguistic underpinning, at the expense of an appreciation that Paul was first a person of faith who was faced with the challenge of interpreting and explaining what had happened in his own recent *experience*, not to mention the continuing experiences of those to whom he wrote. While many of those who have quickly moved into an exposition of his theology have espoused their own commitment to what is described as a "critical realism" in their interpretation of the New Testament texts, there is a curious tendency to idealism in the current debate. A neo-Collingwoodian quest to "think the thoughts" of the *dramatis personae* of history[59] takes over at the expense of an epistemological realism which seeks to identify what it actually was in early Christian

---

56. Wright, *The Climax of the Covenant: Christ and the Law in Pauline Theology*, 46–47.
57. Wedderburn, "Paul's Use of the Phrase 'In Christ,'" 91.
58. Dahl, *Studies in Paul: Theology for the Early Christian Mission*, 130–31.
59. Collingwood, *The Idea of History*, represented history as an art rather than a science, that is said to involve the unapologetic idealism of "thinking the thoughts" of people in the past.

experience that gave rise to language which was designed in the first instance to describe it and to talk about it.

Paul's participative language, not just his use of the image of membership of the Body of Christ, and the phrase "in Christ," but of the related phrases "in the Lord" and "in the Spirit" (not to mention the linguistic reversals of these phrases—"Christ in us" (used at least sometimes by Paul)—and (more often) "the Spirit in us"), are also relevant to this discussion. To retreat into the verbal antecedents of Paul's use of the phrase "in Christ," as a way of explaining it as an expression of "Paul's messianism," is surely only half of the story. The other half has to do with the actual experience of faith, and the perception of the manner in which Christ's presence was apprehended and appropriated, that made recourse to that language not just as abstractly meaningful, but *realistically and descriptively* appropriate.

Whatever the verbal sources of Paul's "in Christ" phrase, the occasion of its use is quite another matter. It is of course always admitted by those in the current phase of this debate that the Resurrection of Christ was the "trigger" of Paul's recourse to this kind of language. However, the Resurrection as an event of the historical past is not to be divorced from the continuing experience of his presence. Apart from what the title "Christ" may have originally meant in terms of "incorporative" notions of messiahship, it was used also not just referringly, in the context of Paul's theological reflection on the significance of Jesus' Resurrection understood as a happening of the past, but also identifyingly, in faith claims to denote and describe an actual experience. Clearly, Paul's use of the phrases "in Christ," "in the Lord," and "in the Spirit," pointed to an objective, concretely given, and corporately shared, *experienced* reality.

Certainly, sometimes Paul speaks also of being "in the Spirit," or of being "in the Lord,"[60] in a way that appears to be roughly equivalent in experiential terms to the phrase "in Christ." In all likelihood, Paul used all these phrases without intending to signal any really significant differences in terms of what they were intended to denote. He may have varied his expression for little more than stylistic reasons. However, that said, while his more characteristic language is to say that believers are "in Christ," it is more characteristic of him to say that the Spirit is "in them" rather than that they are "in the Spirit." On the other hand, while he characteristically speaks of believers being "in Christ," he is less likely to be found speaking of Christ "in them," even though on some occasions he certainly does so, particularly in reference to himself, when he speaks of "Christ *in* me." Given these distinctions, instead of speaking of Paul's "participative language"

---

60. As for example in Phil 4:2: "I beg Euodia and Syntyche to be unanimous in the Lord." Or Philm 20: "let me have this benefit from you in the Lord." In Rom 16 the phrase "in the Lord" outnumbers "in Christ" (seven to four times). This is probably theologically inconsequential. For all practical purposes the phrases seem synonymous.

as an undifferentiated conglomerate, generically categorized as a kind of "mysticism," we will here therefore proceed by first considering those references where Paul speaks of Christ or the Spirit being "in him," rather than vice versa. The pressing question is whether we can avoid being forced into some kind of semi-magical transference which suggests one person somehow being within another, or whether we can make something of this that might have been acceptably meaningful for Paul, and perhaps in a way that remains a real option for us today. To further this discussion we may therefore have to break out of the circle of historical/exegetical interpretation of Paul's theology to do some constructive systematic theology.

Fortunately, this is not the first time that the Christian Church has had to grapple with this kind of issue. We have some shoulders on which to stand in the hope of seeing a little further. In the seventh century, Maximus the Confessor noted that in the prayers of Jesus in the Garden of Gethsemane there appeared to be a difference between Jesus' desires and those of the Father. While some argued at the time (and as it eventually turned out, unsuccessfully) that Jesus possessed two natures but only one will (*monothelitism*),[61] Maximus proposed that, as there are two natures in Christ, there must also be two wills, a divine will and a human will (*dyothelitism*). Though Jesus could be understood to have exercised a mind and will in his historical life which belonged to his human nature, and which was expressed in his human assent to the apparent will of God the Father in Gethsemane ("not my will but thy will be done"), his divine nature expressed a second will, the divine will of the Word Incarnate *in* him, which willed the salvation of humanity. Though Maximus suffered most terribly for this during the time of the ascendency of the *monothelite* party—by having both hands cut off to prevent him from writing, and his tongue cut out to prevent him from speaking and teaching, followed by his exile for treason and eventual death—he was subsequently vindicated at the Third Council of Constantinople (AD680–81). The wisdom of this Council was to endorse the *dyothelite* position that Maximus had earlier articulated and for which he had been ostracized. It thus became orthodox dogma,[62] and Maximus was honored with the status of "Confessor," having suffered in defense of the orthodox faith. Against *monothelitism*, the dogma of *dyothelitism* was promulgated as "the faith of the apostles, the faith of the fathers, and the faith of the orthodox."

Briefly put, Maximus saw that the historical Jesus exercised a human will in the course of his historical life. Thus, in his historical existence he exercised a will that desired food and drink when he was hungry and thirsty, which his divine nature did not need. More importantly, his human will was also exercised in his acts of

61. Monothelitism affirmed that the will of Christ is single; namely a divine will.
62. See Pelikan, *Christian Tradition*, vol. 2, 71.

obedience to the Father "even unto death"; thus he, as a historical human individual, willed and acted for the salvation of humanity. His decision in the Garden is therefore a proper human decision of his human willing. In this, his willing is exactly as ours. However, Maximus saw that the historical particularity of Jesus' human willing coincides with an eternal, and changeless will, which he harmoniously shared with the Father and the Holy Spirit. This also wills the salvation of humanity. It was not thinkable that there could be any kind of conflict between these two wills in terms of their objects. Thus, the Third Council of Constantinople affirmed that there were "two natural wills in Christ," but not "two natural wills that are contrary to each other." Christ's human or natural will (*to physikon thelema*—meaning "conforming to his human nature") was thus said to be ontologically distinct from the divine will ("conforming to his divine nature") but, as a deliberative will (*to gnomikon thelema*), it was functionally identical with the divine will. In his historical life, Jesus thus expressed a human will and activity that was perfectly coincidental with the eternal will that was natural to his divine nature. It was thus the exercise of his human will when he determined to offer his life in perfect obedience to his divine mission, willing humanly and in time, just as God also wills, though unchangeably and eternally, the salvation of humanity. This divine will was in fact an eternal and unchanging will shared by the unitary divine nature of the three hypostatic identities of the Trinity, while Christ's human will was unique to him and was exercised in the course of his historical life in a particular space and at a particular time.

In the person of the incarnate Christ, there were thus two natural wills (one according to each nature), and natural actions flowing from them, but in one single agent who was committed to one single and undivided purpose. For Maximus, the human reconciliation with God won by Christ was thus the divine will and action of God, but also the human will and action of the human Jesus.

Now the principle that was operative at the Third Council of Constantinople, that "having recognized two natures, a divine and a human, one must recognize two wills," may be brought to the illumination of the scriptural tradition. When viewed through this lens, we are alerted to some aspects of Paul's language that otherwise are easily overlooked. When Paul spoke of the "participation" of human believers, not just in a human reality of a "body of like-minded people," but in an essentially divine reality created by the gift of the divine Spirit of the vindicated and glorified Christ (so that this called for intentional human behavior that was in accord with the will of God), we can see that he was entering an arena in which what was called for was in fact a "co-incidence of willing." It was necessary to will and to act humanly in the historical living out of life, though in accordance with the eternal divine will of God, and not just of God the Father, but also in accordance with the revelation of God in Christ. Hence, in Rom 12:2 he exhorted the Christians of Rome "not to be conformed to this world but to be transformed by the renewing of your minds, so that you may discern what is the will of God." Clearly, in acting in accordance with decisions of their own will they were to do the will of God.

Moreover, when Paul held up the earthly pattern of Christ as a model for believers in Philippi to emulate, he thus naturally spoke of the need to have "the mind of Christ" in them: "let this mind be *in* you that was *in* Christ Jesus."[63] Likewise, in speaking of the "things of God" in 1 Cor 2, and of the difficulty of knowing the mysteries of God, he declared in a self-consoling and celebratory way: "But we have the mind of Christ."[64] And when Paul spoke of his own moral tussle, he was clearly able to identify his own defective human willing and the disappointing action that ensued from it, by contrast with the willing he identified as the mind and will of Christ *in* him, to which he sometimes referred simply as Christ "in him," and the far more acceptable action that ensued from it: "It is no longer I who live , but Christ lives *in* me."[65] Having the Spirit-informed mind and will of Christ was thus understood to require an appropriate standard of behavior, to "live in the Spirit" by doing the will of God *in* Christ Jesus.

The coincidence of the operation of wills, a divine will and a human will, in Paul's understanding of things is well illustrated also in 1 Cor 9:16–17 where Paul confesses to his sense of obligation to act in accordance with the will of God to preach the gospel. In this, he says, he is not just acting in accordance with his own will; the preaching of the gospel, in other words, is not just his own "bright idea." Rather, it is because of the moral pressure of the operation of the will of God *in him*, which he experiences as something laid upon him as a necessity. It not entirely of his own will, which he could discharge with a smug sense of self-congratulation, but something demanded of him: woe, if he does not act accordingly! Equally, it cannot be an occasion for boasting, but simply for obedience.

It is in this light that we are able to understand something of what Paul had in mind when he said, in Galatians 1:16, that God was pleased "to reveal his son *in me*." It is a mistake to try to bring this into conformity with an understanding of Paul's Damascus Road experience understood purely as an objectively visual encounter or "meeting" by insisting that what he really meant was that Christ was revealed *to* him. This is why Paul is not to be understood by drawing upon an alleged "interpretative parallel" found in 1 Cor 15:8, as N. T. Wright somewhat arbitrarily insists.[66] As important as the revelation *to* him on the Damascus Road was, it does not stand alone. Equally as real for Paul

---

63. *Phil* 2:5.

64. *1 Cor* 2:16. Explicitly in relation to this text, Maximus says: ". . .this does not come to us through the loss of our own intellectual power: nor does it come to us as a supplementary part added to our intellect: nor does it pass essentially and hypostatically into our intellect. Rather, it illumines the power of our intellect with its own quality and conforms the activity of our intellect to its own. In my opinion the person who has Christ's intellect is he whose intellection accords with that of Christ and who apprehends Christ through all things." *Writings,* "Two Hundred Texts on Theology and the Incarnate Dispensation of the Son of God written for Thassalios," Second-century, Text 83.

65. *Gal* 2:20.

66. *RSG*, 380.

is the subsequent presence of the Raised Christ though the medium of the Spirit, and the insistent experience of the revelation of Christ *in* Paul's life, as in the lives of other believers to whom God has also sent "the Spirit of his son."

There is absolutely nothing "magical" about this, any more than there is about a contemporary awareness among willing and acting humans, who, in the living out of their historical lives, inwardly discern and respond to the moral pressure to do what is interpreted in faith to be the eternal and unchangeable "mind and will *of God.*" There is no suggestion of the direct *transfer* of a divine personality into a human personality so as somehow to eliminate the need for human decision-making. Still less does this involve just a self-contained matter of revised self-understanding, like holding one's own breath. Rather, what is involved is the harmonious engagement of a human will as it is exercised in historical time with what is perceived to be the timelessly eternal divine will of God in "a coincidence of willing."

The one is expressed, both individually and together corporately, in word and deed in the historical and episodic incidents of life, and the other is the will of the eternal Word of God. Thus, humanly to will goodness, justice, and love such as expressed in the other-regarding service of others and to do it, is to do the will of God whose unchangeable and eternal desire for humanity is in faith understood to be goodness, justice, and love of the specific kind revealed in the life of Jesus, the servant of others. It is perfectly understandable that Paul spoke of the revelation of Christ "in him," and continued to speak both of the active operation of Christ "in him" and of "the Spirit in him." It was the same basic insight that led John Henry Newman to speak of the apprehension of the will of God in Christ through the inner voice of conscience, which he identified as the inwardly discerned "aboriginal Vicar of Christ" in him.[67] Likewise, though admittedly without the flourish of Newman's christological colouring, Immanuel Kant observed:

> Two things fill the mind with ever new and increasing admiration and reverence, the more often and more steadily one reflects on them: *the starry heavens above me and the moral law within me.*'[68]

There is nothing magical about this.

Even so, it is one thing for Paul to speak of the revelation of the moral pressure of the divine will of Christ *in* him, or the Spirit *in* him, and to exhort the Philippians to have the mind of Christ "*in* them," or to speak at length about the operation of the Spirit "*in*" the lives of the faith communities over which he continued to exercise a pastoral

---

67. Newman, *Letter to the Duke of Norfolk*, Sec. 5.248; *The Genius of John Henry Newman*, 263–64. Also, 5.247: "the voice of God in the nature and heart of man."
68. Kant, *Critique of Practical Reason*, 5.162.

interest. It is yet another thing again for him to speak of believers themselves being "in Christ," or "in the Lord," and "living in the Spirit," or being members of the "Body of Christ," for this is to suggest a more outwardly public and objectively perceivable aspect of their shared religious experience.

Given that this "outward and visible" face of being "in Christ," or being members of the "Body of Christ," offers itself to be perceived and appropriated in faith today, there are some fundamental things to be said. First, it seems difficult to avoid the conclusion that for Paul the experience of being "in Christ" or "in the Lord" was the result, not just of creative theorizing, but of the actual concrete experience of the gift of the Spirit to the baptized. As was argued in the companion volume to this,[69] early christological language was not just the product of Paul sitting in a corner and deductively "working out" some bright ideas. Rather, it was a much more spontaneous verbal response to the inductively discerned nature of the post-Easter reality with which he in faith had to do. As "the Spirit of life in Christ Jesus" was actually encountered, and known constitutively forming the inter-personal communion of the community of believers, it at the same time established a kind of relation with the Raised Jesus of a kind that was understood to be entirely unique and divinely significant. For, as we shall see below, while it was in some ways similar to the all-pervading and life-giving intelligible "warm-breath" (or *pneuma*) of contemporary Stoicism, that was understood to have its source in a divine celestial fire, Paul understood the Spirit fundamentally as a self-giving love that had its (no less heavenly) source in the Raised and exalted Christ "at the right hand of the Father." Indeed, the perceived "Spirit *of Christ*" in turn established a relation not just with the Raised Christ, but also with God through Christ. This indicates that the life-giving Spirit of the Raised Christ was experienced in such a way as to allow it to be understood to have originated from a privileged divinely exalted place. With the interpretative help particularly of Psalm 110, this is the place to which Jesus was believed to have gone, so as then to allow his Spirit to flow from this point of origin into the earthly lives of the early Christian believers, thus to become the experienced Object of their continuing faith claims, and the ground of their future hope. The suggestion is therefore that apart from the *verbal* sources of Paul's participative language in the traditions of Second Temple Judaism, the concrete experience of being incorporated by the gift of the Spirit into the life and love of Christ itself prompted the descriptive use of this kind of language. Apart from expressing a *meaning content* of a messianic kind that was inherited from the verbal traditions of Second Temple Judaism, in a very real sense these early christological claims were an attempt to express, describe, and account for a transcendental aspect of the first believers' actual continuing Easter experience. In other words, the very manner of the Raised Jesus' diffused presence through the gift of his Spirit already itself indicated something of his divine identity and status.

---

69. Carnley, *Resurrection in Retrospect*, chapter 8.

It is today a commonplace to acknowledge that, insofar as the use of the phrases "in Christ" or "in the Lord" suggests that believers understood themselves to participate in an "inclusive, all-embracing presence," the transcendent Raised Christ was clearly "beginning to be described in terms appropriate to nothing less than God."[70] In other words, the transfer of language originally designed to relate to God, and for reference to living in the all-embracing presence of God, appears to have been made, as a direct consequence of his Resurrection and exultation, to apply to the Raised Christ. In general terms, this is a characteristic of all the primitive christological claims, but it becomes particularly poignant in relation to the understanding of what Paul meant when he spoke of being "in Christ" or "in the Lord."[71]

Paul was therefore able to assure the Romans that what was most characteristic of their newly transformed lives was that they had to do, not just with "the Spirit of Christ," but with "the Spirit of God." Indeed, Paul appears to have had no qualms in identifying the experienced reality of the Spirit either as "the Spirit of God" or as "the Spirit of Christ."[72] Paul speaks of the transcendent quality of the experience of the Spirit among those "in Christ" when he speaks in the same breath of "the love of Christ" and, significantly, of "the love of God which is *in* Christ Jesus." Indeed, in chapter 8 of *Romans*, from which these last quotations come, he uses this language as though it were interchangeable. Apparently, this variant form of words describing "the love of Christ" or "the love of God" is designed to refer to the very same concretely experienced reality, where the word "same" is understood in a numerical rather than just a comparative sense. The experience of being "in Christ" was apparently understood as being in some way coincidental with being in the divine presence of the love of God in Christ. In other words, Paul's intention appears to have been to identify a specific kind of life-transforming love that was defined, not only in the historical life of Jesus and his obedience even unto death on the Cross (as remembered in Phil 2), but found in the continuing life of the post-Easter community of the baptized as the life giving Spirit that was constitutive of the Christian *koinonia*.

Moreover, while it is clearly a mistake to homogenize the traditions of the New Testament in a way that destroys its rich theological diversity, this kind of language is not peculiar to Paul. Within its variety, there is an impressive unity of thought in relation to some very basic issues. The tendency to speak of the Raised Christ in language

---

70. Moule, *Origin of Christology*, 53.

71. Basil of Caesarea was perhaps the first to draw dogmatic conclusions with regard to the status and dignity of the Son and of the Holy Spirit, by noting the parallels between the use of the same preposition "in," in relation also to God the Father. Basil points out that in the Old Testament "it says, that '*in* God we shall do valiantly,'" (*Psalm* 108:13); and Paul says ". . . *in* God who created all things"; while Paul and Timothy to the church of the Thessalonians speak of it as being ". . . *in* God our Father" (2 Thess 1:1), and so on. See Basil of Caesarea, *On the Holy Spirit* 5.11.

72. Rom 8:9.

that formerly was used of God is one of them. In the deutero-Pauline Epistle to the Ephesians, the Raised and glorified Christ, like God, is also understood to enjoy a cosmic presence: he "fills all things."[73] At the very least, this suggests that as a consequence of the Resurrection, the Raised and glorified Christ becomes like God insofar as God is the reality, as Luke says, "in whom we live, and move and have our being."[74] If it is understandable that in Ephesians the Raised Christ, like God, is understood to enjoy a cosmic presence, John likewise talks of individuals being together *in* one interpersonal communion analogous to the interpersonal communion of the Son with the Father. An assimilation of the Raised and exalted Christ with the all-embracing presence of the Father is expressed in a way that resonates with Paul's participative "in Christ" language, when John has Jesus pray that his disciples "may become perfectly one" as Christ himself and the Father are one: "As you, Father, are *in* me and I am *in* you, may they also be *in* us."[75] Indeed, references to one person being "in" another abound in Jesus' farewell discourse in John 17. The challenge before us is to explain how this language may continue in meaningful use today.

This brings me to the second fundamental point, that may now be made. When it comes to talk of the perception of "the Spirit," and specifically of "the Spirit of life in Christ Jesus," while there has been a great deal of discussion of the biblical imagery associated with the experience of the divine Spirit,[76] discussions of the epistemology presupposed in claims to know the Spirit, not to mention the ontological issue of what kind of reality it is that is being talked about, are few and far between. Indeed, while much New Testament theology has for so long been content to work within the essentially historical and highly speculative parameters set by the future oriented eschatological framework inherited from Second Temple Judaism, insofar as Paul made claims *to know* and to have to do with a reality objective to himself, recourse to a presupposed epistemology, even if of a broadly popular kind, was inevitable. In other words, it is clear enough that a good deal of Paul's reflection about the nature of faith, and especially about its behavioral demands in the interim of waiting for the return of Christ and the advent of the Eschaton, also presupposed some basic philosophical considerations of an epistemological and ontological kind that need to be unpacked and more clearly understood.

Clearly, it has been a mistake simply to side step these kinds of question by simply categorizing Paul's participative language as a kind of "mysticism," shrugging one's shoulders, and then moving on. Insofar as resurrection faith is grounded in experience,

---

73. Eph 4:10.
74. Acts 17:28.
75. John 17:23–26.
76. As *ruach*—wind, flame of fire, and so on.

it involves claims to know the continuing cosmic presence of Christ through the medium of the gift of his Spirit. In this case, the outline shape of a presupposed epistemology of faith asks to be brought to the surface of our awareness.

As we move towards a consideration of the epistemological implications of primitive Christian faith claims, it is pertinent to note that, while in the past this aspect of Paul's thought has tended to be spoken of generically as a kind of "mysticism" (largely following Albert Schweitzer), this kind of language may profitably be avoided. Instead, we might note that Paul's use of this participative language simply raises a set of questions concerning the epistemological and ontological assumptions presupposed by it.[77] In other words, we are justified in asking questions about the latent philosophical assumptions that were operative in the use of this language and that are as a consequence reflected in it. In describing the experience of faith and the gift of the Spirit, which led Paul, for example, quite naturally to speak of being "in Christ" or being "in the Lord," his unavoidable epistemological presuppositions will naturally entail some significant ontological outcomes. But first, we need to spend a little time exploring the outline shape of resurrection faith itself.

---

77. I am therefore deliberately trying to avoid talk of Paul's "Christ mysticism." As James D. G. Dunn has rightly observed, this kind of language has "overtones of intense individualistic preoccupation in contemplation of or even absorption into the divine" that are unnerving to those who recognize the "irreducibly corporate and social character of Christianity." *The Theology of Paul the Apostle*, 415.

2

The Nature of Faith

ATTEMPTS TO PROVE THE occurrence of the Resurrection as a historical event necessarily tend, as a matter of course, to concentrate on the narratives of the later Gospels of Luke and John with their alleged "massive physical detail."[1] These narratives are said to report somewhat matter-of-fact encounters in which the Raised Christ eats with his disciples,[2] and even offers the (in principle) tactile possibility of being physically examined.[3] It is understandable that such concretely physical details are found attractive in the quest to handle the Resurrection purely as a factual and observable historical event.

However, if the redaction criticism of these texts through the second half of the twentieth-century is correct in contending that these very details represent a development of an original tradition under the apologetic pressure to express and defend Easter faith, either in the face of nagging doubts from within the community of faith or hostile criticism from without, then perhaps we may profitably return to the earlier Easter narratives of Mark and Matthew as possible indicators of a more historically authentic original tradition. In the quest to prove the occurrence of the Resurrection as a historical event, these Gospels tend to be over-looked, not so much in relation to the empty tomb tradition, of course, but at least with regard to the appearances of the Raised Christ. In the historical discussion both of the nature of the appearances to the first witnesses, and about the nature of the seeing and perceiving that was implicitly associated with them, these earlier narratives of Mark and Matthew tend to be assigned a place of diminished importance for a number of reasons. Mark's Gospel is unfortunately almost always left entirely out of account, because it ends abruptly with the flight of the women from the empty tomb, leaving it without an appearance narrative of any kind. Despite the directive of the angel to "go and tell Peter and the others to go into Galilee," for there they would "see" (*opsesthe*) the Raised Christ, the women are said to have fled from the tomb and to have told

---

1. A phrase of Stephen Davis in "'Seeing' the Risen Jesus."

2. As when he "was at the table" with the travelers en route to Emmaus in *Luke* 24:30, or with the fishermen disciples at the beach breakfast in Galilee in John 21:13.

3. As in John's "doubting Thomas" story in John 20:24–29.

nobody, "for they were afraid."[4] *Mark* has no appearance narrative at all. Because, unlike the other Gospels, Mark does not end with a narrative of an appearance, it tends to be assumed that Mark has nothing at all to tell us either about the nature of the first appearances or the nature of faith. The historian's disinterest is thus understandable. But, as we shall see, this may be a mistake.

In Matthew's narrative of the somewhat enigmatic appearance of an apparently glorified and exalted Jesus on the mountain in Galilee, as if "from heaven,"[5] theological considerations tend to overwhelm the narrative to the point where the factuality of the kernel of the episode tends to recede into obscurity. Though Matthew does at least have an appearance narrative, this narrative is heavy-laden with Matthean phraseology, and is theologically conditioned by Matthew's over-riding emphasis on the Great Commission to universal mission.[6] As a consequence, the priority accorded the appearance narratives of Luke and John, given the attempted materializing clarity provided by their provision of more graphic physical detail, especially for those who are intent upon handling the appearance as a historically provable event, is perfectly understandable. However, the fact that the Easter narratives of Mark and Matthew are without much of the "massive physical detail" found in the later appearance narratives of Luke and John, may turn out to be much more positively helpful to a systematic theology of Easter faith than may at first be imagined. Indeed, it may yet be that Mark and Matthew are repositories of an earlier, more original tradition. In this case, they may prove capable of providing us with the more promising material with which initially to work.

Commentators regularly assume that Mark's omission of a narrative account of an appearance in Galilee can be explained either by conjecturing that Mark did not manage to finish his Gospel for some reason that is unknown to us,[7] or else by supposing that his finished Gospel once actually did end with an appearance narrative originally written by him, but unfortunately that ending has long since been lost.[8] Alternatively, it might even be conjectured that Mark was himself skeptical about the reality of the Resurrection and the actual meaning of the story of the empty tomb, and so deliberately left things unresolved. In this case, he may be said to have included the report that he

---

4. Mark 16:8.

5. Where he is understood to claim "all authority in heaven and on earth" (Matt 28:18).

6. Matt 28:19–20.

7. Some conjecture that he suddenly died, leaving the work incomplete. Others suggest that he came to a martyr's end.

8. See Metzger, *Textual Commentary*, 126, n.7: "Three possibilities are open: (a) the evangelist intended to close his Gospel in this place; or (b) the Gospel was never finished; or, as seems most probable, (c) the Gospel accidentally lost its last leaf before it was multiplied by transcription."

had received about the discovery of the empty tomb, but left its meaning hanging in the air by failing to spell out an Easter appearance in narrative form.

This last explanation is very unlikely. In the body of the Gospel, particularly in the "plain" or "open" teaching of its second half,[9] Mark in fact includes many anticipatory references to the Resurrection. The famous three-fold prediction of the passion (in Mark 8:31, 9:31 and 10:32–34) is also a three-fold prediction of the Resurrection as well, for in each case the foreboding cloud of the coming passion and death is followed by the promise that on the third day he would be raised.[10] Indeed, in addition to references to the Resurrection of Jesus in the form of these anticipatory promises in the second half of the Gospel, there are others apparently conceived in retrospect, as in the case of the affirmation, obviously after the event, that "the stone which the builders rejected has become the head of the corner; this was the Lord's doing and it is amazing in our eyes" (Mark 12:10–11). In addition, Mark indicates Christ's own resurrection belief at Mark 9:9; 12:18–27; 13:26–7; and 14:28. Clearly, Mark writes explicitly from the perspective of resurrection faith.

Not least among these references to the Resurrection is a statement in *Mark* 16:6, just a few verses before the end of the Gospel. Embedded in the explanatory announcement of the angel at the tomb are the words: "He is not here; he is *risen*."[11] So the indications are that Mark certainly believed in Jesus' Resurrection, even if he did not express it in the form of a detailed appearance narrative. The possibility that the lack of an appearance narrative is to be explained by his own misgivings or skepticism about the meaning of the empty tomb story does not need to be taken seriously. The absence of an appearance narrative at the end of his Gospel can hardly be explained by appeal to the notion that he found the story of the empty tomb so enigmatic that he himself doubted the Resurrection.

But what of the suggestion that Mark either did not complete his Gospel, or else completed it, but that its original ending, allegedly containing an appearance narrative, has been lost? A whole generation of eminent New Testament scholars in the first half of the twentieth-century debated this possibility with vigor. By-and-large, that debate hinged on what was said to be the "impossible grammar" of Mark's ending, which employs the verb *ephobounto* ("they were afraid") followed by the preposition *gar* ("for"), which was said to leave the narrative awkwardly unresolved.[12]

---

9. See Mark 8:32. This is by contrast with his teaching by parables in the first half of the Gospel.

10. See parallels at Matt 12:40, 27:63; Luke 24:6–7, 46; John 2:20–22, 11:25.

11. See also Mark 8:38, 9:9, 12:18–27, 35–37, 13:26–27, 14:28, 58, 62.

12. An exquisitely succinct and balanced account of the discussion of the ending of Mark's Gospel will be found in Nineham, *Saint Mark*, 439–42. F. C. Burkitt, in *Two Lectures on the Gospels* (1901), 28, declared: "That the Gospel was originally intended to finish at verse 8 is quite inconceivable." H. B. Swete in *The Gospel according to St Mark* (1898), 399, had thought it "improbable" rather than "inconceivable." A. E. J. Rawlinson in *St. Mark* (1925), 268, suggested that "on any reasonable view," the Gospel could hardly have ended with the words "for they were afraid." Rawlinson was impressed by Streeter's conjecture that Mark's ending had simple been "torn off": "At Rome in Nero's days a variety

Westcott and Hort actually printed their texts of Mark's Gospel with a semi-colon at the end of 16:8 followed by asterisks to indicate that the ending was missing! Others hankered after an appearance narrative to bring Mark into line with Matthew, Luke, and John.[13] This was the position eventually taken up by Rudolf Bultmann in *The History of the Synoptic Tradition* in 1931,[14] and by C. E. B. Cranfield in his *Gospel according to Saint Mark* in 1959.[15]

Though the possibility of a now lost ending seems to be seriously entertained by N. T. Wright,[16] I think these suggestions, though they have in fact enjoyed very wide speculative popularity, need no longer be taken with any more seriousness than the hypothetical and very problematic contention that Mark was perplexed and skeptical about the meaning of the empty tomb. Since the work of Julius Wellhausen in 1903, followed by a number of British New Testament scholars in the 1930s,[17] a growing number of more recent commentators[18] have helped us to the conclusion that Mark actually intended his Gospel to end exactly where it does end at 16:8, with the flight of the awestruck women and their silence. The view that the grammar dictates the necessary resort to a theory of a lost ending has been resoundingly answered. For a start, the alleged impossibility of a sentence ending with the preposition *gar* ("for") has been shown to be a definite possibility, numerous precedents having been found in Greek literature, and not least in the Septuagint.[19] St. Mark's own use of short sentences with *gar* is also identified as a feature of his style of writing.[20] This has pulled the rug from under the celebrated attempt to promote the theory of Mark's alleged "lost ending" on the basis of grammar alone.

However, apart from the fact that none of the hypothetical explanations of Mark's failure to provide an appearance narrative carried sufficient weight to make them credible, Mark's own concluding text itself renders the lost ending theory entirely improbable. The words of Mark 16:8 concerning the failure of the women to follow the directive of the angel, and their awestruck silence, do not themselves lead on naturally to a sequential narrative of the kind that is said either to have been intended but never written, or actually written but lost. In other words, a narrative story about the

---

of 'accidents' were by way of occurring to Christians and their possessions."

13. See Streeter in *The Four Gospels*, 333–60: "The Lost Ending of Mark."

14. Bultmann, *History of the Synoptic Tradition*, 285.

15. Cranfield, *Gospel according to Saint Mark*, 470; and "St Mark 16.1–8," 398–414.

16. Wright, *Who Was Jesus?* 85, where he says Mark's Gospel was "quite possibly truncated at both ends."

17. Notably Creed, "The Conclusion of the Gospel according to Saint Mark"; and Lightfoot, *Locality and Doctrine in the Gospels*; and Lightfoot, *The Gospel Message of St Mark*.

18. For example, Kümmel, *Introduction to the New Testament*, 71, quoting the support of Lightfoot, and a substantial list of English and German scholars, including E. Lohmeyer and Marxsen. More recently, John Fenton has returned to this issue: "The Ending of Mark's Gospel."

19. In Gen 18:15 and 45:3. See also, Menander's *Dyscolos* 437–438.

20. See Lightfoot's analysis in *Locality and Doctrine in the Gospels*, chap. 1.

disciples being in Galilee, in the belief that there they would see the Raised Christ, does not follow logically as a sequential episode from the statement about the silence of the women. Rather, these very words cut off the possibility that there ever was such an appearance narrative, either contemplated as an unfulfilled intention of Mark, or actually written but now lost. It is no surprise that both Matthew and Luke therefore omit this statement about the women remaining silent, as a matter of literary necessity, apparently for this very reason. Matthew makes no mention of the women telling no one. His inclusion of an appearance narrative in Galilee therefore follows on from the directive to go into Galilee, on the assumption that this message *was* delivered to the disciples. Luke, on the other hand, explicitly says that the message was delivered,[21] thus preparing the way for Peter to run to the tomb in Jerusalem.[22] And then Luke's narrative goes on to say that "on the same day" the travelers on the Road to Emmaus encountered the Raised Jesus.

Clearly, despite the alleged awkwardness of the grammar, in literary terms the text of Mark 16:8 itself suggests that there never was an appearance narrative attached to the end of Mark's Gospel similar to that later found in Matthew, Luke, and John. Nor did Mark plan to provide one. Mark's Gospel simply ends where Mark intended it to end.

In this case, Mark's intention may be explained in a number of ways. R. H. Lightfoot, following E. Lohmeyer,[23] imagined that "Galilee" could be understood as the "place of revelation," and that the directive to "Go into Galilee" was meant to prepare the disciples, not for an appearance to confirm the meaning of the empty tomb, but for the *parousia*, the eschatological return of the Raised Lord in glory as the vindicated Son of Man. Lohmeyer argued that the use of the future tense for "you will see him" (*opsesthe*) suggested an eschatological kind of "seeing." In this case, Mark could write no narrative account of this precisely because it was yet to happen! Credibility was loaned to Lightfoot's view by Mark's anticipatory remarks in Mark 13:26 and 14:62, which already employ the same Greek verb (*opsesthe*) in reference to the seeing of the Son of Man in glory. To this, Willi Marxsen added the contextual relevance of the advance of the Roman troops on Jerusalem around the time that Mark was writing.[24] Wars and rumors of wars signal the coming doom. Galilee therefore becomes the place to which believers are to go from Jerusalem for the hitherto concealed Raised

---

21. Luke 24:9.

22. Luke 24:12.

23. Lohmeyer, *Galiläa und Jerusalem*, 10–14; See also, *Das Evangelium des Markus*, 355–56, and Lightfoot, *Locality and Doctrine in the Gospels*, 61, 65 and 73, though Lightfoot seems to back away from this in *The Gospel Message of St Mark*, 95–96 and 106–16.

24. Marxsen, *Mark the Evangelist*, 89.

Jesus to reveal himself in all his glory at the Eschatological End. Norman Perrin also added his name to the view that the absence of an appearance narrative in Mark may be explained by the fact that Mark anticipated the *parousia*, and that this is what the disciples were to await in Galilee.[25]

Despite this, however, there is nothing impossible about the use of *opsesthe* in relation to a resurrection appearance, as opposed to a reference to the glorification of Christ at the Eschatological End. Not only is this verb (if in different tenses) used by Paul in 1 Cor 9:1 of his seeing of the Raised Christ; it is also used in the same kind of context in Matt 28:17, and in John's resurrection narratives in John 20:18, 25, and 29. Matthew certainly understood Mark's use of *opsesthe* to mean a resurrection appearance.[26] An Easter appearance in Galilee therefore has a greater claim on our attention as the best explanation of Mark's intention than the possibility of the *parousia* in Galilee at the End Time.[27]

Christopher Evans has forcefully argued,[28] also, that it is more likely that what was to happen in Galilee was the re-assembly of the flock under the leadership of the shepherd, rather than his appearance at the End of the world.[29] The disciple/leader motif in Mark 10:32, when Jesus went ahead of his disciples *"in the way,"* and reinforced by blind Bartimaeus as the paradigm of the true disciple who sees clearly and follows Jesus *on the way*,[30] gives added credence to Evans's proposal. The point is that it is not necessary to think of this as though Jesus literally walked ahead on the road to Galilee; nor did he *precede* the disciples in the sense of marching ahead of them and being there already in a temporal sense when they arrived. Christopher Evans has demonstrated that in *Mark*, the Greek verb *proagein* never simply means "precede" in a temporal sense. Rather, the motif of the shepherd and the flock provides the clue for appreciating the importance of relationality: the functional identity of the shepherd is established only in relation to a flock, and the flock in turn receives its identity and integrity through the work of the shepherd. *Proagein* appears again in Mark 16:7, with the angel telling the women that the Raised Christ is "going before" the disciples into Galilee. However, this suggests that the Raised Christ "goes before" the disciples, not in the temporal sense of preceding them and being there first, but in the sense of

---

25. Perrin, The Resurrection Narratives, 28–30.

26. Matt 28:7 and 10.

27. Daniel Smith speculates that Mark actually suppressed the tradition of appearances in Galilee in the interests of representing the empty tomb story as indicating essentially an "absence" rather than a future appearance. See *Revisiting the Empty Tomb*, 93–4. This problematic theory of Smith is discussed in *Resurrection in Retrospect*, chapter 5.

28. Evans, "I will go before you into Galilee."

29. This follows earlier suggestions of both Johannes Weiss and E. C. Hoskyns who, apparently independently, came to the conclusion that *proagein* in Mark 14:28 should be read in conjunction with Mark 10:32, where without doubt it means "to lead" rather than to precede. See Weiss, *Die Schriften des Neuen Testaments*, 197, and Hoskyns, "Adversaria Exegetica."

30. Mark 10:52.

being *with* the flock, as if "ahead" of it *as its leader*. The imagery of the flock and the shepherd, so much associated with the verb *proagein* in Mark, thus echoes the prophecy of Zechariah that is put on the lips of Jesus in Mark 14:27: "You will all fall away; for it is written 'I will strike the shepherd and the sheep will be scattered.'" A more natural reading of the directive of the angel in *Mark* 16:7 therefore suggests that what is envisaged in Galilee is therefore a re-grouping and rendezvous of the disciples, with the Raised Christ once again as the leader of the community. Clearly, Mark is already giving us some implicit clues as to the nature of the appearance of the Raised Christ as this would be experienced in Galilee.

Also, it has to be remembered that Mark wrote after Paul. Paul's letters make it clear that a tradition of appearances of the Raised Christ was not only already a set element of the broader Christian tradition, but was in fact itself a necessary prelude to the hoped-for *parousia*. Within the biblical tension of promise and fulfillment, the resurrection appearances, and the continuing experience of the presence of the Raised Christ through the medium of his Spirit, were interpreted as the promise, the down payment or first fruits, of future fulfillment in the form of the triumphant return of Christ and the outpouring of the Spirit on all flesh. Without the concrete experience of resurrection, the eschatological hope for fulfillment to come would become, not hope, but mere wishful thinking. For logical reasons, therefore, without resurrection appearances of some kind, the move from the story of the empty tomb to the hope of seeing the returning Christ of the *parousia* in Galilee becomes a difficult thesis to defend. Belief in the *parousia* pre-supposes resurrection belief based on experiences of appearances. Why then is there no appearance narrative at the end of Mark's Gospel?

More recently, it has been held that Mark's primary intention in narrating the empty tomb story without an appearance narrative was to present an account of the *disappearance* of Jesus' body, thereby suggesting that its inexplicable absence from the tomb was the result of an "assumption into heaven," similar to the Jewish tradition of the assumption of Enoch in Gen 5:24, and of Elijah in 2 Kgs 2:1–13, and the extra-canonical story of the assumption of Moses. Daniel Smith (apparently following Adela Yarbro Collins) has contended, for example, that this kind of "assumption into heaven," rather than a resurrection, is what Mark had in mind in narrating the story of the discovery that the tomb was empty. An "assumption tradition" based on the empty tomb story is in this way contrasted with a "resurrection tradition" based upon the tradition of appearances.

Apart from the biblical precedents for assumptions into heaven, Smith argues this thesis on the basis of alleged literary parallels with other assumption stories of notable figures in the Greco-Roman world, such as the assumptions of two of the most popular heroes of antiquity, Heracles and Achilles, and also of Romulus in the myth of the foundation of Rome.[31] In the case of Heracles, for example, Apollodorus says that "While the pyre was burning, it is said that a cloud passed under Heracles and with a peal of thunder wafted him up to heaven."[32] In addition to these popularly held beliefs in assumptions, there are the sporadic accounts from time to time of an imperial apotheosis.

Unfortunately, Smith's thesis of the occurrence of Greco-Roman stylistic influences in Mark's telling of the empty tomb story is not without its difficulties.[33] Curiously, Smith himself even acknowledges that the tradition of Jesus' death, burial and resurrection actually differs from the assumption stories of the surrounding Greco-Roman culture in the significant respect that there is no suggestion that Jesus did not die. But unfortunately this does not deflect him from portraying the meaning of the empty tomb in terms of an assumption rather than a death, burial, and resurrection. Moreover, we have already noted the many allusions to Jesus' coming death and resurrection in the text of Mark's Gospel, especially in the thrice-repeated predictions of the second half. More importantly, in the case of Jesus there is no suggestion elsewhere in the tradition that he somehow avoided death by being assumed into heaven. Indeed, the passion and death is surely central to the Christian Gospel. Jesus' Resurrection is clearly understood to have followed his death, and was therefore interpreted as a victory over death. In this respect, the alleged parallels with stories of the assumptions or apotheoses of popular figures or emperors in the ancient world does not really hold up.

On the other hand, Smith's argument relies heavily on placing a very weighty burden of significance on the "he is not here" and "you will not see me" phraseology found in Mark 16:6 and in Matt 23:37–39 and Luke 13:34–35.[34] Whether this kind of phraseology can be made to apply so narrowly as only to suggest an assumption into heaven, but not a death and resurrection, seems problematic. The suggestion that Mark developed this alleged "disappearance theory" also has to contend with the fact that the tradition of appearances, rather than a tradition of a disappearance, enjoys a much more secure rooting in the early Christian confession of faith and its proclamation, starting with the kerygmatic summary that Paul indicates he himself had originally received in 1 Cor 15. Indeed, even the story of the empty tomb itself points to the fundamental importance of the Easter appearances insofar as the words of the angel at the tomb actually interprets the tomb's emptiness as having been caused by Jesus' Resurrection. After announcing "He has been raised, he is not here," the angel then directs

---

31. Collins, "The Empty Tomb in the Gospel according to Mark," especially 130–31; and Collins, *Mark*, 791–93. See also, Smith, *Revisiting the Empty Tomb*, 53–61.

32. Apollodorus, 2, 7, 7.

33. See the earlier work of Danove, *The End of Mark's Story* (1993) and the discussion of the Collins/Smith theory of disappearance and assumption in O'Collins, Believing *in the Resurrection*, 17–19, 55–59, and 83–84.

34. Smith assigns these statements of Matthew and Luke to the hypothetical document Q (Q13:34–35). By this strategy, the suggestion can be made that the earlier source, Q, points to a belief in assumption based on the disappearance of Jesus' body.

the women to go and tell Peter and the disciples to go into Galilee for "there they will see him." This text points ahead to an appearance in Galilee in a way that is inimical to the theory that Mark simply had a disappearance to heaven in mind.

There is clearly a New Testament emphasis on the exultation and glorification of the Raised Christ, which certainly resonates with the idea of an assumption into heaven. But whether this comes from the tradition of assumptions in the ancient world seems very problematic. For, very importantly, Smith does not seem to have taken sufficient note of the fact that there is concrete scriptural evidence, as distinct from the reliance on parallels and similarities found in Greco-Roman culture, which indicates that, in the early Christian apologetic, appeal was made to concrete references from within Jewish religious culture itself in order to interpret and explain what had happened to the Crucified and Raised Jesus. The book of *Daniel* and the *Psalms* in particular were mined by early believers for references that might throw light on what had happened in their recent experience, and also to suggest that an element of prophetic foreknowledge had actually been fulfilled. It is clear that *Psalm* 16 was drawn upon to explain that Jesus' body had been saved from corruption in the grave by translation through death to immortality. And, very importantly, the enthronement Psalm 110: "Sit at my right hand till I make your enemies your footstool" was repeatedly used, sometimes possibly in tandem with Daniel 12,[35] to explain not only the heavenly destination of the Raised Jesus, now exalted "at God's right hand," but to indicate his vindication by God and his identity as God's Son. This also established the basis of the promise of his eventual return in triumph to reveal the eschatological implications of all this.[36] In 1 Cor 15:27 Paul also references Psalm 8:6—"God put all things into subjection under his feet"—with the same general purpose in mind.

It is significant that Smith only makes scant and passing reference to Psalm 110:1 and Psalm 8:6, and generally underestimates the role played by these texts in early Christian apologetic, while over-emphasizing alleged parallel allusions in the surrounding Greco-Roman culture. We can appreciate the relevance of Smith's emphasis on the "other worldly" realism of the orientation of religious thought in the surrounding culture of Middle Platonism, and the similarities and resonances of Jesus' vindication and triumph expressed in images of heavenly exaltation at "God's right hand," with Greco-Roman stories of assumption and the apotheosis of historical heroes and emperors. At least this keeps well clear of the suggestion that the mind-set of Second Temple Judaism was closeted in some kind of hermetically sealed compartment, far away from all foreign influences of this kind. We can take the point that speculative religious thought is no respecter of ethnic and national boundaries, certainly not boundaries that were yet to be drawn, such as those put in place only after the First World War. We can agree that when environmental cultural influences seem to be impacting upon the Jewish tradition, account must be taken of them;

---

35. See Acts 2:24–36 and 1 Cor 15:25.
36. See Lindars, *New Testament Apologetic*, 45–51.

however, it is quite another thing to argue that particular themes and motifs found in Greco-Roman culture *fully* account for certain elements found in the Gospels, even when no explicit inter-textual references or even reasonably clear allusions from the literature of the surrounding Hellenistic culture are to be found in the New Testament empty tomb story. This is particularly so when Israel's own Scriptures already provide adequate inter-textual warrants for these same themes and motifs. Certainly, we cannot underestimate the hermeneutical role played by Judaism's own religious texts in early Christian apologetic. The actual textual evidence suggests that these alone were sufficient to ground the tradition that Jesus, having been raised from the dead, had been exalted into heaven at God's right hand, even without recourse to Greco-Roman assumption stories. Whether resonances from the surrounding culture somehow supported these ideas or aided the reception of them, particularly among Gentiles as they heard the Easter proclamation, is one thing; that the surrounding culture is the source of those ideas is another. It is even a bridge further to argue, as Smith does, that originally a tradition of Jesus' assumption that was based on contributing factors from the surrounding culture was somehow drawn up in rivalry over against a competing tradition of Jesus' Resurrection based upon the appearance narratives. Even if Smith acknowledges that both traditions were eventually integrated, we are justified in thinking that this is a conjectural step too far.

The contention that in narrating the story of the empty tomb Mark presents what is essentially a disappearance—an assumption to heaven, or an apotheosis analogous to other instances from the culture of the Greco-Roman world—appears therefore to be unjustifiably over-developed by Smith. Indeed, the parallels are probably more obvious between the assumption of Heracles and Luke's account of the Ascension of the Raised Jesus into heaven, rather than to the story of the empty tomb.[37]

That said, there is certainly an element of heavenly exaltation that is part and parcel of the notion of resurrection, as distinct from a mere resuscitation and restoration to this world, and sometimes this is stressed elsewhere in the New Testament Easter traditions without any reliance on a tradition of appearances. The focus on exaltation, for example, is true of Phil 2 where Jesus' death is followed by a declaration of his exaltation by God, without mention of a resurrection appearance. The Epistle to the Hebrews, with its concentration on the heavenly intercession of the exalted Christ, likewise omits mention of resurrection appearances. Also noteworthy is 1 Timothy 3:16, where Jesus is said to have been "manifested in the flesh, justified in the Spirit, . . . and taken up in glory" after having been seen only by angels.

Of these, the classic example is the early creedal statement or Christ-hymn quoted by Paul in Phil 2:5–11 where the crucified Jesus, as the lowly self-effacing servant

---

37. An earlier discussion of the influence of the assumption of Heracles focused on parallels with Luke's two accounts of the Ascension (Luke 24:51 and Acts 1:9–11). See Rose, "Heracles and the Gospels." Though, generally speaking, Rose resists the thesis that there are close parallels between the story of Heracles and the Gospels, he admits that "There is a certain resemblance between the accounts of the two ascensions" (124).

who is obedient even unto death, is said in a radical reversal of fortune simply to have been vindicated by being "highly exalted" by God. The by-passing of any specific reference to the Resurrection, or to a resurrection appearance, in this passage in favor of moving straight into talk of the heavenly exaltation and vindication of the Crucified One, and the confession of his Lordship over all things is surely not to be passed over lightly. Indeed, the presentation of the Resurrection of the crucified lowly servant by an immediate appeal to the notion of his vindication and exaltation by God, without reference to the tradition of appearances, is worthy of consideration as a matter of some theological significance. Not least, this poses a challenge to the view of N. T. Wright that Easter faith *must* be understood to involve, not a going to heavenly glory, so much as a return to this world of the Christ who is then involved in mundane "meetings" with the disciples.

More importantly, this lack of specific interest in mentioning resurrection appearances in this early tradition quoted by Paul, brings us back to the Gospel of Mark and its ending. In theological terms Mark stands in very close association with this early precedent quoted by Paul in Philippians, chapter 2.[38] Certainly, Mark's systematic portrayal of Jesus as a messiah of a specific kind, a lowly servant figure as against the messiah anticipated by the Jews who might be said by contrast to have reckoned messianic God-likeness in terms of coercive power, echoes the servant Christology of this early creedal statement or hymn. Can it be a matter of coincidence that Paul's silence about the resurrection appearances in Phil 2:5–11, to the point of acquiescing in the move straight from crucifixion to vindication and exaltation, is actually being echoed in Mark's apparently intentional reluctance to provide his readers with an appearance narrative?

If Mark did not intend to communicate a story of a disappearance involving an assumption into heaven, and if he did actually believe in the Resurrection, as has already been argued, then the question now becomes one about the nature of resurrection faith. What is entailed about the nature of faith in Mark's failure to spell out an appearance narrative? If Mark intended that his Gospel should end at 16:8 with the statement that the women told nobody of the discovery of the empty tomb, with no interest at that point in narrating an appearance story, then by a paradox this may be of more significance to our understanding of the actual nature of the appearances of the Crucified and Raised Christ and of the nature of faith than we might imagine. While scholars like Stephen Davis and N. T. Wright focus attention on the alleged "massive physical detail" of the much later narrative traditions of Luke and John, the fact that Mark maintains an almost absolute silence should be

---

38. It is not surprising that their thought is not far apart, for of all the New Testament writers, Mark and Paul, writing about ten years apart, stand in close temporal proximity.

accorded an equal importance. Despite the failure of most discussions of the resurrection appearances to draw any positive conclusion from Mark's silence, it may itself be of enormous significance not just to our understanding of the manner of the Raised Christ's "appearing," but to the understanding of the Galilean location of the first appearances, and to a contemporary understanding of the nature of the human perception or "seeing" of him in faith as well.

The first thing to note about Mark's silence is that, as a supremely sophisticated author in literary terms,[39] his primary intention may simply be to raise a question in the minds of his readers: "What does the emptiness of the tomb mean?" It is a question reminiscent of that expressed by the disciples in the boat at the stilling of the storm: "Who then is this that even the wind and the sea obey him?"[40] Mark does not spell out an answer on that occasion. Rather than tell us, his readers must answer it for themselves. Likewise, he does not spell out the answer to the question raised by the discovery of the empty tomb either. In relation to our question about the nature of the Easter appearance of the Raised Jesus, his reticence about spelling out a detailed resurrection narrative means that Mark quite intentionally "shows but does not tell." The fact that the women say nothing about the tomb's emptiness means that neither therefore does Mark himself, who thus takes us on an entirely *apophatic* journey into Galilee.

Anybody who has attended a modern course in creative writing will immediately discern the meaning of "showing but not telling," but let me explain what I mean in relation to Mark. Mark obviously wrote his Gospel to be read, rather than with any consciousness that he was providing a chronicle of information that would one day be used as evidence to be tortured into answering questions put to it by those pursuing critical-historical research. After all, the discipline of historiographical research of this kind really only began to flourish in the middle of the nineteenth-century. When Mark's Gospel is simply received as a literary composition that was initially intended to be read, the story of the empty tomb as Mark uses it, without appending a narrative of an appearance of the Raised Christ, simply confronts the reader with an unresolved mystery and raises a question.[41] What does this mean? As Markus Bockmuehl puts it: "Mark deliberately enhances the suspense of the resurrection message at the tomb by continuing his customary secrecy theme and projecting the Easter reality into the reader's present."[42] If the emptiness of the tomb means resurrection from the dead,

---

39. I think an enormous injustice is done to St Mark by H. A. Guy in *The Origin of the Gospel of Mark* (1954), 162, where the ending of his Gospel is said to result from the fact that it is the work of an "unpolished writer." Mark's Greek at 16:8 may be inelegant, but as the originator (as far as we know) of the literary form of a gospel, and as the church's first systematic theologian, he has given us a Gospel which speaks of complex literary skill and unsurpassed theological sophistication.

40. Mark 4:41.

41. As was pointed out in Carnley, *Structure of Resurrection Belief*, 364–68.

42. Bockmuehl, "Resurrection," 105.

it therefore also means that we readers may encounter the Raised Christ. If so, the question is where and how?

Richard Bauckham has pointed out that the fact that Mark stops telling his story at Mark 16:8 "is not the end of the story." Quoting J. L. Magness, Bauckham goes on to say that "Absence from the text is not necessarily absence from the story."[43] This is because readers already know what is to follow, for they know that Jesus has predicted not only his suffering and death but his rising again after three days (Mark 8:31, 9:31, and 10:32–34), and indeed, quite explicitly, that after he is risen they will see him in Galilee (Mark 14:28). The message of the angel in Mark 16:7 simply reminds them of this. In this way Mark is said to employ the narrative device of "open closure," or "suspended ending,"[44] whereby readers "are left to imagine for themselves how the rest of the story will proceed."[45] Morna Hooker in her commentary on Mark's Gospel, similarly observed that ". . . the vital question is not whether Peter and his fellow disciples finally grasped the truth . . . but whether we, reading Mark's words, are prepared to hear the angel's message and follow Jesus into Galilee on the path of discipleship."[46] Hooker therefore raises the question that perhaps "Mark is inviting us to make our own response?"[47] In this way, the absence of an appearance narrative is accounted for by appeal to contemporary "reader-response" theory, according to which the author and the reader both contribute to the final outcome: the absent appearance narrative gives way to allow for "the beginning of discipleship."[48]

While to this point we can agree with Hooker and Bauckham's contention that for Mark's readers "the story after the end of Mark is one in which they themselves are involved,"[49] it is a mistake to think that this involvement is just a matter of "imagining themselves within the story."[50] Nor is the reader simply challenged with the question of whether he or she will follow Jesus into Galilee in the way of discipleship, with Galilee standing for "the place of discipleship." Somehow, to cast Mark in the mold of working with contemporary "reader response" theory is to over-modernize him.[51] Moreover, we have to remember that in the ancient world most people would not

---

43. Bauckham, *Gospel Women*, 293, quoting Magness, *Sense and Absence*, 121.

44. Bauckham, *Gospel Women*, 294, citing respectively Marguerat, *La Première Histoire de Christianisme,* 309, and Magness, *Sense and Absence*, 22 and passing references.

45. Bauckham, *Gospel Women*, 294.

46. Hooker, *St. Mark*, 392.

47. Hooker, *St. Mark*, 393.

48. Hooker, *St. Mark*, 394. Witherington, *The Gospel of Mark*, 442, makes a similar point: "True discipleship is only possible after Easter when the full significance of the life, death, and resurrection of Jesus can be known."

49. Bauckham, *Gospel Women*, 294.

50. Bauckham, *Gospel Women*, 294.

51. Nineham, *Saint Mark*, 442, quoting an article by W. L. Knox in the *Harvard Theological Review*, 35 (942) 13–23, warns against attributing Mark with "a degree of originality" which just happens to "suit the technique of a highly sophisticated type of modern literature."

have possessed a copy of Mark's Gospel and many would not have been literate. Most would not have been "readers" of his Gospel; instead they would have been hearers. The normative circumstance for the hearing of the Gospel would have been at a public gathering at which it is possible that the whole Gospel may even have been read in one sitting. If Christopher Bryan is right, this exercise would have taken about seventy minutes.[52] We know from the Acts incident in which the sleepy boy named Eutychus fell from the window[53] that Paul's long-winded preaching and talking made for quite extended gatherings well into the night, and we can conjecture that once the Gospels were written the reading of them would have led into worship, almost certainly a Eucharistic celebration. In this context, those who heard the reading of Mark's Gospel would not just have been invited to "imagine" the rest of Mark's story for themselves. Rather, the hearing of the story of the discovery of the empty tomb would have pointed forward to the possibility of encountering the concrete presence of the Raised Jesus in the breaking of bread. In other words something more is involved than "imagining" the end episode in the story. This would be to opt for a kind of idealism, whereas what the empty tomb points hearers towards is the theological realism of actual encounter with the Raised Christ in faith. Following the insights of Catherine Pickstock, we are invited to consider the possibility that hearers are involved not just in an idealistic imagining, but in an objective realism precipitated by the "liturgical consummation" of written material.[54] In other words, the mode of the involvement of the hearers of the story does not take the form of "imagination" as in "reader response" theory, so much as faith—the recognition in faith of the real presence of the Raised Christ, the continuing equivalent of the original Galilee experience of "seeing" the Raised Christ to which the angel at the tomb pointed the first believers.

When the first disciples were advised to "Go into Galilee" in the belief that there they would "see" the Raised Christ, something more was intended by the angel's directive than that "You should return home" or "Go back to your former occupation as fishermen." Though we would not want to rule out the possibility that the Raised Christ might become known as his presence was perceived within the dynamics of family life or within the co-operative enterprise of a workplace, this is probably not what was primarily meant by "Go into Galilee, there you will see him." Rather, Galilee is significant as the "place of mission" where the good news would be proclaimed of the inauguration of a Kingdom in which both Jews and Gentiles would be gathered together in one inclusive

---

52. Bryan, *Resurrection of the Messiah*, Kindle loc. 882. The reckoning of the David Suchet Audio Bible suggests it might take 80 to 90 minutes.

53. Acts 20:9.

54. Catherine Pickstock, *After Writing*, chap. 1. See also Dewey, "The Gospel of Mark as Oral/Aural Event"; Shiner, *Proclaiming the Gospel*; and especially Ong, *The Presence of the Word*, chap. 4; and Ong, *Orality and Literacy*, 31–77.

community under the shepherding leadership of the Raised Christ. Matthew makes this quite explicit in Matt 4:15, quoting the prophecy of Isaiah 9:1 in relation to the honoring of Galilee as the place of divine visitation and renewal.

J. Schreiber attempted to demonstrate[55] that Mark also understood Galilee as a place of ethnic diversity which included within it such places as Tyre and Sidon, Gerasa, Decapolis, Bethsaida, and Caesarea Philippi. Reginald Fuller has argued, in response to this suggestion, that Mark does not actually locate any of the places mentioned by Schreiber in Galilee. They are only at best "contiguous with" Galilee. This means, he believes, that, for Mark, Galilee is not the place where Gentiles are to be evangelized, but the place from which the mission to the Gentiles is to originate.[56] However, this is probably to put too fine a point on the purpose behind Mark's location of the promised resurrection appearance in Galilee as a geographical area.

It can be argued that Galilee had a long-standing reputation for its multi-culturalism,[57] and that this was what Mark had in mind in placing the directive "Go into Galilee" on the lips of the angel in Mark 16:7. This reputation is explicitly expressed in Matt 4:15, where the region is referred to as "Galilee of the Gentiles." It was fertile ground for the proclamation of the gospel of human inclusiveness wrought by the gift of the Spirit of God that overcomes all ethnic divisions (not to mention divisions based upon social status or gender difference).

Very understandably, Christopher Evans, following his teacher Hoskins, made much of Galilee as a symbol of the "place of mission" in a worldwide sense. If he was correct, Galilee may be taken not just as a geographical area, even with a reputation for multi-culturalism and ethnic diversity, but as a symbol of the Gentile world. The directive to "go into Galilee" is thus a commission to enter upon God's mission to the world, not just to Jews only but also to Gentiles—God's mission understood in a universalist sense. As Evans says: "In this mission, Jesus is known as the universal Lord."[58] While this is implicit in Mark rather than being spelled out, Matthew, by contrast, in his appearance narrative, is at pains to make this very explicit: Matthew ensures that in his account of Jesus' historical life and ministry, Jesus' mission is initially confined to the Jews; at Easter this becomes a universal mission to "go and baptize, and teach all nations" in the wider world.[59]

---

55. Schreiber, "Die Christologie des Markus."

56. Fuller, *The Formation of the Resurrection Narratives*, 62.

57. Judg 1:30, 33; Joel 4:4; Isa 8:23, 9:1; 1 Macc 5:21.

58. Evans, *Resurrection and the New Testament*, 81.

59. Matt 28:19. Generally speaking, the Gospel of Matthew is strongly Jewish in tone. Matthew's concern to confine the mission of the historical Jesus to Jews is found in Matt 10:5–8, and 15:24. However, the possibility of a mission with a universal scope is indicated in Matt 13:38 where "the field is the world" and in Matt 12:18–21: "on his name shall the Gentiles hope." Matt 24:14 repeats the focus of Mark 13:10 on a future mission to "all nations." What is clear is that Jesus' Resurrection universalizes the mission.

THE NATURE OF FAITH

However, an emphasis on the universal and inclusive nature of Christ's mission is not, of course, entirely new to Matthew: already in Mark it is a Syro-phoenician woman who is presented as the first to come to faith,[60] and at the end of the Gospel it is a foreigner, a Roman soldier at the foot of the Cross who declares the divine Sonship of the crucified one.[61] More importantly, Mark makes it clear that Israel's failure was to live to itself and not to make the Temple a house of prayer *"for all nations,"*[62] a phrase that Mark includes in the story of the casting out of the thieves from Temple, but which is omitted (almost certainly quite deliberately) from Matthew's version of the same story.[63] In this case, it is congruent with Mark's understanding of the mission of Jesus for Galilee, with its the multi-cultural reputation as an area of mixed ethnicity, to become the symbolic place where the Raised Jesus "goes before" (*proagein*) as the leader of the Easter community in a mission that includes both Jews and Gentiles. As we have seen, the same verb is used in Mark 14:28 of the shepherd who "goes before," as in the continuation of the shepherd-sheep metaphor of Mark 14:27, but this time he "goes before" them so as to be with them as their leader in universal mission. This eschatological gathering of the flock with the Raised Jesus as their leader contrasts with Jesus' lament of *Mark* 6:34 when he was "moved with compassion" because the people were "as sheep not having a shepherd."

Norman Perrin inclined to the view that the directive of the angel of Mark 16:7, which repeats a promise of Jesus himself ("After I am raised up I will go before you into Galilee"),[64] may in fact be read at two different levels: "On the one hand it moves at the historical level of the physical/geographical references to Jesus in Galilee, while on the other hand it moves at the symbolic level of a series of references to the experience of Christians, in the name of Jesus in the Gentile world."[65] Given the post-resurrection situation, however, Perrin tended to opt for "a symbolic reference" as "the more natural," adding that "these references may be taken to be references to Jesus leading his disciples into the Gentile world. It is in the Gentile world of the church's mission that they will see him."[66]

Readers/hearers of St Mark's Gospel may thus understand this advice of the angel in the sense that the place where the Raised Christ will be seen is not just a specific geographical area. Rather, if Galilee is also symbolic of the arena of mission, it means that wherever the mission initiated by the Raised Christ is prosecuted he will be present as leader; and this is a mission in which hearers of Mark's Gospel are all participants

---

60. Mark 7:29.
61. Mark 15:39.
62. Mark 11:17.
63. This phrase is almost certainly deleted by Matthew in his concern to keep Jesus' mission focused among the Jews until it is universalized with a focus on all nations of the world at Easter.
64. Mark 14:28.
65. Perrin, *The Resurrection Narratives*, 29.
66. Perrin, *The Resurrection Narratives*, 30.

wherever they are located. As Christopher Evans puts it: "At this point of the universal mission, the gospel of Jesus Christ which Mark sets out to write catches up with his readers who are themselves part of it."[67] They are, however, not invited just to be "imaginative" as in reader response theory. Rather, they are alerted to the possibility of faith, for there in the field of the church's mission "they will see him."

Austin Farrer once explained the absence of an ending to Mark's Gospel, in the sense of the absence of a narration of an appearance of the Raised Jesus, on poetic grounds. More specifically, his literary sensibility drew attention to the fact that the absence of a resurrection narrative can be appreciated by taking note of what Farrer described as corresponding "structural rhythms discernable elsewhere in the gospel."[68] It is understandable that New Testament scholars take a particular interest in grammatical and exegetical matters, and that those committed to a critical-historical analysis of the texts naturally concentrate on an attempted historical reconstruction of "what happened." But, in a sense, this fails to see the wood for the trees; by contrast a literary reading/hearing of *Mark* uncovers the theologically structured rhythms created by the church's first systematic theologian.

For example, contemporary readers and hearers of St Mark's Gospel also hear the directive of the angel to the women "Go into Galilee, there you will see him." It is as though those words are spoken to us, "over the shoulders of the women" as it were.[69] Those who hear are in a sense directed to "go into Galilee" as the arena of mission, with eyes peeled so as in faith to "see" the Raised Christ. In this way, the empty tomb story continues to effect its intended Marcan purpose: it confronts those who hear it with an apparently inexplicable mystery, but at the same time it raises the possibility of faith. This is not therefore just a possibility for those first-century witnesses who are said to have discovered the tomb empty, but for all who, repeatedly through the ages, read the story or hear it read, including those in the twenty-first-century.

Mark, who as far as we know invented the narrative form of a gospel, wrote so as to proclaim something about the true nature of the messianic identity of Jesus, and about the nature of true discipleship consequent upon seeing clearly the precise nature of that messiahship. Mark so structured his presentation of the traditions he had received as to make these specific points. At the same time, Mark's structuring of the material with which he worked communicates something about the nature of resurrection faith. The rhythm of the life of faith and discipleship as Mark presents it across his Gospel as a whole involves, at least in the first instance, the challenge to see and perceive the point of Jesus' parabolic teaching and healing miracles. As Mark presents

---

67. Evans, *Resurrection and the New Testament*, 81.
68. Farrer, *A Study in St Mark*, chapter vii.
69. To use the very felicitous phrase of Fenton, "The Ending of Mark's Gospel," 6.

this material in three sequences, Jesus' hearers are three times shown to be blind to his message, including not just Scribes and Pharisees,[70] but members of Jesus' own family,[71] and then even the inner circle of his close friends and disciples.[72] Three times his identity and the purpose of his mission is misunderstood: people remain blind. Then, very significantly, Mark narrates a miraculous coming from blindness to sight in the story of the man who sees by stages.[73] This highlights the way in which the truth of parables gradually dawns, and insights into Jesus' true identity are similarly by stages discerned in his healing ministry. All the while, Jesus' messianic identity is kept secret by Mark until the time comes to disclose exactly what kind of messiah Jesus actually is; otherwise it is only too easy to call him "messiah," but to get it wrong.

In the second half of the Gospel, the content of Jesus' "plain" or "open" teaching[74] about the true nature of his messiahship is arranged also in three sequences, each commencing with a prediction of the passion,[75] followed on each occasion by misunderstanding. First, there is the blindness in the misunderstanding of Peter,[76] then of the disciples who argue about status on the road,[77] and then James and John who ask for exalted places in the Kingdom.[78] In each of these sequences there is then a call to see clearly what kind of messiah Jesus really is and to take up the Cross as a true disciple.[79] It is at this very point that Mark pertinently places yet another story of the giving of sight to the blind. This time it is the story of Bartimaeus, who miraculously sees and then follows Jesus "in the way,"[80] thus becoming the paradigm of the true disciple. The "way" is, of course, the "way of the cross," and Mark's passion narrative immediately follows. Thus Bartimaeus, in the miracle of faith, sees clearly the nature of Jesus' messiahship and is then able to "take up the cross" and follow *in the way*.

All through his Gospel, Mark presents the coming to faith as a kind of seeing. Sight is given to the blind, for only those who have eyes to see clearly grasp the true nature of Jesus' messiahship, and are able to follow him in the same way, as his true disciples. This means following in the lowly way of the Cross. Then, as a consequence of Easter, this rhythm of *seeing and following* in the way of the Cross then continues beyond the Cross with Peter and the other disciples being directed to "go into Galilee," with the promise that there they will "see" the Raised Christ who as shepherd/leader

70. Mark 3:22.
71. Mark 6:1–6.
72. Mark 8:14–21.
73. The giving of sight to the unnamed man by stages in Mark 8:22–26.
74. Mark 8:32.
75. Mark 8:31, 9:31, and 10:32–34.
76. Mark 8:32–33.
77. Mark 9:32–33. It may be significant that some translations have "on the way."
78. Mark 10:37–38.
79. Mark 8:34, 9:35–50, and 10:42–45.
80. Mark 10:52.

once again "goes before" the flock-in-mission. In other words, it is a matter of *"seeing and following"* in the Gospel story up till Jesus' death, and then after it, as a consequence of the Resurrection, it is a matter of *"following and seeing"*: "Go into Galilee, there you will see him."

There is thus quite deliberately no ending to Mark's Gospel in the form of an appearance narrative, because, in a sense, that would close off far too many possibilities. Rather, the ending has to be written by people of faith in all successive ages. As true disciples, the baptized all "Go into Galilee," pursuing the Christian mission in the world, alert and prepared for an encounter with the Raised Jesus as leader and shepherd of the flock. For readers and hearers of Mark's Gospel, "Galilee," whether in the first-century or the twenty-first, thus continues to be understood less as a geographical place and more as a symbol of the arena of the mission of God in Christ. With the angel's direction "Go into Galilee," it is as though Mark is saying to his readers of whatever age: "Go out on mission, love one another, serve one another, see clearly what kind of messiah Jesus is and follow in the same way, live in trusting faith as true disciples, take up your cross and follow him."[81] The directive to the "true disciple" is to follow in the lowly way of the Crucified One, who came not to be served but to serve. It involves being other-regarding rather than self-regarding, being prepared to be last rather than first, helping the poor and disadvantaged, caring for the distressed, the lonely and the unloved, the homeless and the refugee. It involves restoring the sick to health, comforting those who mourn, and all the while, entering more deeply into the communion of God by breaking bread together so as to be a radically inclusive community of all nations of people.[82] Those who "do this in remembrance of him," in other words, "Go into Galilee" and prosecute the Christian mission, trusting in the promise delivered by Mark's angel/messenger that there "you will see him."

What is implicit about the nature of faith and discipleship in the silence of Mark's ending is spelled out and made explicit in the earliest actual appearance narrative we have, in Matt 28. If Mark "shows but does not tell," then Matthew more than compensates for this omission by telling us what happened in Galilee. There, the Raised Christ appears to the assembled disciples on the mountain "to which Jesus had directed them," but now he is revealed from heaven as the exalted and vindicated One, claiming "all authority in heaven and earth." In this way Matthew's narrative account of an appearance of the Raised Christ demonstrably explains the meaning of the empty tomb. However, even here there is no concentration of attention on any alleged "massive physical details" of Jesus bodily appearance such as we find in the later gospels of Luke and John. Indeed, in this final concluding tableau of Matthew's Gospel, by contrast

---

81. As did Bartimaeus, as the paradigm of the true disciple.
82. Mark 11:17 and 7:26–29.

with the narratives of the later gospels, physical tokens are apparently of no interest in the recognition of the presence of the Raised Christ. There is no invitation to inspect hands or feet or side. There is no breaking of bread, or eating of broiled fish and honeycomb. Rather, the emphasis is on the mission of the church to the world. Having seen the Raised Jesus, his disciples are in turn sent into the entire world on mission with the words of the Great Commission, and, very importantly, with the promise "I am with you always to the close of the age."[83]

The one who promised to "go before you into Galilee" now promises to be present in the on-going future mission of the church in all the world, as its exalted leader, and that mission is explicitly said to involve the making of disciples of all nations, through a ministry of baptizing, and teaching.[84] The Raised Christ is clearly presented as one whose presence may in principle be perceived in some way by faith in every age, and so "to the close of the age." As contemporary believers read the appearance narrative of Matt 28, they may therefore understand themselves to be part of that same continuing mission in which Christ promises always to be present. But as in Mark, Matthew does not go on to spell out in detail the nature of the seeing and perceiving of that promised presence.

Nevertheless, the promise of the Raised Christ to be with his disciples "to the end of the age" at least raises the notional possibility that knowledge claims might certainly be made in faith today. Matthew assures his readers that the Raised Christ will be with them always, and therefore in principle always available to be perceived and known, apparently in some kind of concretely objective and experiential way. In this case, it might reasonably be assumed that the promised presence of the Raised Christ may in principle be perceived and known not merely by description, but "seen" and known in a personal and relational way by acquaintance. This is by contrast with the prospect of only being able to claim to know *about* something abstract and verbally descriptive that is purported to have occurred long ago in the past. The epistemological question for today is therefore: exactly how is the promised continuing presence of the Raised Christ with his disciples perceived and known? The challenge of providing an epistemology of faith will be addressed in future chapters of this book. For the present, it is sufficient to note that, other than this intimation of the possibility of the knowing of the Raised Christ always "to the end of the age," Matthew does not take us much further than to make explicit the angelic promise of Mark: that the Raised Christ would "go ahead" of his disciples into Galilee, as their shepherd-leader in mission, and from there into the whole world.

---

83. Matt 28:20.

84. Baptizing in the threefold name of Father, Son, and Holy Spirit, and "teaching obedience to all Jesus has commanded."

Leslie Houlden, in a small but enormously important book,[85] has pointed up both the similarities and the differences between the respective treatments of the passion and resurrection narratives of Mark and Matthew, and particularly between what he believes is their resulting quite different approaches to the nature of faith. His point is that, whereas Mark is more than content to leave issues quite unresolved, with questions hanging in the air, Matthew ties off all the threads and fills in the gaps left by Mark, in a programmatic quest to ensure that there is no evidential short-fall that might inhibit resurrection belief. As a result, Matthew's redaction of the gospel material is not so much a misunderstanding of Mark as a deliberate attempt to "correct" Mark's "style of faith" in a way that, as far as Houlden is concerned, is thoroughly unhelpful.

The omission of an appearance narrative after Mark 16:7 is said by Houlden to be of a piece with Mark's firm insistence that Jesus taught by parables in a way that was "open ended, leaving much to the hearer" (Mark 4:1–34, especially v. 12).[86] As we have seen, there is a sense in which this is certainly the case. Indeed, it could likewise be argued that the theme of the messianic secret in the early chapters of Mark's Gospel is also a literary strategy, which raises the question of Jesus' identity (Who is this?) without providing an answer. However, Houlden then goes on to argue that the "ethos of faith which Mark so carefully creates"[87] is one of "self-abandonment to a mysterious divine initiative with consequences yet to be seen, not a judgment concerning a set of plain happenings."[88] In other words, Houlden's contention is that Mark's understanding of faith is one in which believers come to a commitment "on the basis of sheer trust, as opposed to well-based evidence or alleged knowledge."[89] This attributes to Mark an uncompromisingly non-cognitive approach to faith.[90]

Implicit in this thesis is an assumption that faith for Mark is a matter of making a freestanding commitment of trust (*fiducia*) without the felt need for justifying grounds. "We are simply *required* to trust."[91] Mark, says Houlden, is an author who invites a response of trusting faith but who "takes no trouble to give us grounds for doing so."[92] The absence of an appearance narrative is therefore said to be typical of Mark's reluctance to fill in the gaps. Instead, he intimates the possibility of faith in the Resurrection of Jesus but that is all. By leaving the empty tomb unexplained and without an appearance

---

85. Houlden, *Backward into Light*.

86. Houlden, *Backward into Light*, 63.

87. Houlden, *Backward into Light*, 64.

88. Houlden, *Backward into Light*, 56.

89. Houlden, *Backward into Light*, 56.

90. Houlden opted for a similar approach to faith in *Connections*, 150–53, were faith is said to be a judgment based upon "Jesus' whole presence and career" with the Resurrection then taking its place "as an ikon of the fact, inescapably involved in faith, that this Jesus is the focus of hope and life." The Resurrection becomes a graphic "demonstration of the victory of God in Christ."

91. Houlden, *Backward into Light*, 56.

92. Houlden, *Backward into Light*, 56. Thus we are invited to "sheer trust, as opposed to well-based evidence or alleged knowledge."

narrative upon which the judgment of faith might be based, Mark, in other words, lays the ground for a non-cognitive approach to faith as a form of voluntarism: faith really becomes a decision of will, a risk, unsupported by justifying grounds.

By contrast, Houlden explains that Matthew "fills in" the gaps left by Mark's "intimations." At Matthew's hands, Mark's "intimations" are said to become persuasive "demonstrations" in a way that (unfortunately, to Houlden's mind) undermines the notion of a genuinely trusting faith. Instead, Matthew's agenda is to foreclose on alternative explanations of what transpired in the days following Jesus' crucifixion and burial, almost so as to make the conclusion that Jesus was raised from the dead inevitable. The possibility of the clandestine removal of his body from the grave, for example, is countered by Matthew's account of the appointment of guards whose presence is designed to make sure that theories of a grave robbery become untenable. The perplexity of the women who in Mark wonder about how they are going to remove the stone from the tomb, is in a sense answered by Matthew by ensuring that Mark's angel messenger becomes an active agent of rock-removal. The angel descends with a flash accompanied by an earth tremor so as to make sure that we are left in no doubt about the divine portent of the Easter Event, and then the angel rolls away the stone before the women's eyes and even sits on it. The tomb is thereby revealed to be empty; the suggestion being that Jesus had somehow already vacated the tomb, even without the need to roll the stone away. It cannot be that he simply revived and walked out of it in a way that would have been possible had the stone already been removed when the women arrived . . . and so on. In this way Matthew systematically deals with objections to resurrection belief by closing off other possible explanations of the evidence. For Houlden, Matthew therefore becomes the villain who, after failing to get Mark's point about the alleged non-cognitive nature of faith as an unsubstantiated venture of trust, presents the Jesus story in a defensively apologetic way that diminishes its original freestanding voluntarism.

As additional evidence of the legitimacy and propriety of Mark's "non-cognitive" approach to faith, Houlden cites the understanding of faith as "the conviction of things not seen" (Heb 11:1), and even the Pauline "we walk by faith, not by sight" (2 Cor 5:7).[93] He also cites John 20:29: "Blessed are those who do not see yet believe." However, as we shall see, I think it is a complete mistake, both to read these texts as evidence for adopting an entirely non-cognitive approach to faith, and to read Mark in association with them. Unfortunately, I think Houlden pushes the alleged Marcan understanding of faith much further than the evidence will in fact warrant. While Mark does not describe an actual resurrection appearance, but simply allows the story of the empty tomb to raise the possibility of faith, this does not necessarily invite a purely voluntaristic view of faith. In other words, it is not that Mark is a proto-Kierkegaardian who invites us to the "venture of faith" understood as a risk, a leap into the dark. Mark is not in the business of making a virtue out of a commitment without rational support,

---

93. Houlden, *Backward into Light*, 63.

as though the believer is cut adrift "over seventy thousand fathoms." On the contrary, the angel's promise in Mark 16:7 is to "Go into Galilee, *there you will see him.*" Mark quite explicitly points towards the possibility of a cognitive experience. Even if Mark does not spell out the details of this experience of "seeing," it does not necessarily follow that he intends to suggest that nothing will be seen in faith in Galilee at all! Rather, the clear suggestion is that some kind of objective and cognitively perceived encounter with the Raised Jesus is going to eventuate. Likewise, Jesus' teaching in the obscure form of parables and riddles, and Mark's theme of the messianic secret (involving the withholding of Jesus' messianic identity in a way that prompts the question "Who is this?") is only pursued until it is appropriate for the specific nature of that identity to be more clearly disclosed and known. This "with-holding" of Jesus' identity in the first half of the Gospel has to be matched by the positive content of Jesus' "plain teaching" of the second half about the true nature of his messiahship. This delivers positive and explicit content to be known and appropriated in faith as the cognitive basis of true discipleship.

Likewise, for Mark the future seeing of the Raised Christ is also cognitively important, even if he is reluctant to describe a paradigm case by providing us with a narrative description of an appearance. Apart from his desire only to intimate, to "show and not to tell," so as to allow believers the autonomy and freedom to come to faith for themselves, the nature of the object of faith itself may also be taken into account as a reason for his reticence. It is at least thinkable that Mark is reluctant to provide a specific descriptive pattern or verbal paradigm of an appearance for fear of suggesting that all future experiences of seeing and knowing the presence of the Raised Christ in faith must somehow conform to it. Likewise, after narrating the doubting Thomas story, St. John, for a similar reason, pulls back from the suggestion that the seeing of Jesus implicit in that story, along with the implicit possibility of touching his crucifixion wounds, is to be understood as being in any way normative for faith. It is a story about the naturalness of doubt, not a paradigm of the nature of faith. It is those who do *not* see in precisely that kind of way, who are said to be blessed.[94]

At this point, it is also pertinent to note, that already, at the beginning and at the end of his Gospel, Mark has identified Jesus as the "Son of God."[95] It is not unthinkable that the appearance "from heaven" of the resurrected and glorified Son of God was conceived by Mark after a manner akin to human attempts to perceive and describe God as God is; that is to say, in a manner that is beyond description in words. There is, for example, a sense in which the appearance of the Raised Christ must be ineffable, and essentially "other" than *any* purely literal account that might be given of it. In this sense, Mark's

---

94. John 20:29.
95. Mark 1:1 and 15:39.

presentation of the story of the empty tomb, leaving it as an unexplained mystery, and his apparent reluctance to describe an appearance of the Raised Son of God are of a piece. Mark's reluctance to rush in where angels fear to tread, by succumbing to the temptation of trying to encapsulate the knowing appropriate to faith in a specific form of words, speaks of a nascent *apophatic* awareness of the limitations of language to encapsulate something that surpasses all understanding. It is not Mark's intention to suggest that nothing is known in faith at all; rather his reticence may be explained as a response to the awareness that mere words are inadequate to encapsulate what by definition is beyond words. The non-cognitive option suggested by Houlden is thus not the only way of explaining Mark's narrative reticence.

On the contrary, to admit that cognitive experience is often beyond the human capacity to express it in mere words does not entail, of course, that nothing is ever known. We certainly can claim to know things by actual acquaintance in cognitive experience, even if our ability to express this in words leaves us floundering. Clearly, something cognitively objective may be "seen" and known, and at the same time be beyond description in a few well chosen words.[96] By the same token, the knowing appropriate to faith is not a blind risk just because it is in a sense "beyond words." In fact, in matters of religious cognition, attempts verbally to describe the Object of the experience are always in danger of being interpreted in an over-literal, even fundamentalist kind of way, of such a kind that they are milked of any sense of transcendent mystery.[97] We do no service to the theological sophistication of Jewish thinkers of the South-Eastern Mediterranean, from at least Eudorus of Alexandria onwards, through to the great achievement of Philo in the first-century, and on to Albinus, if we underestimate their appreciation of the limitations of language. Mark is to be placed in this trajectory of theological sophistication.[98]

Furthermore, I do not think it necessary to set up such an antithesis between Matthew and Mark in the way Houlden thinks important, as though Matthew got Mark entirely wrong. Specifically in relation to the nature of faith, it is equally possible to see Matthew as one who built upon Mark by drawing out the implications of Mark's silence; whether Matthew destroys Mark's alleged understanding of the nature of faith is another matter. Houlden's over-emphasis on Mark's silence to the point where he interprets it as the outline of an approach to faith entirely without cognitive content, means that he fails to give sufficient importance to the fact that, while Matthew's own appearance narrative itself ends with Jesus' promise to be "present always" with his disciples, till the end of the age, Matthew gives no specific indication of exactly how

---

96. The taste of lychees is but one example.

97. This is as true of ordinary every day experience as much as of specifically religious experience, as, for example, in the case of the verbal challenge of describing precisely the taste of lychees or the aroma of a new vintage wine.

98. Eudorus, Philo, and Albinus may be regarded as the architects of the high orthodoxy of the *apophatic* way, by ensuring that divinely perceived reality is always understood to be beyond mere verbal description.

this "being with" is to be understood either. Exactly how Christ's promised continuing presence is to be perceived and known is left unexplained. In terms of its detailed outworking Matthew also leaves this open-ended. However, this does not mean that the venture of faith will be entirely without content and independent of justifying cognitive grounds. Like Mark, Matthew points to a more realist possibility of faith as a kind of knowing, even if he does not spell this out verbally either. Jesus simply promises to be "with" his disciples in mission and then leaves the fulfillment of this promise to be experienced by them.

The other New Testament statements cited by Houlden that, on the face of it, might appear to express a voluntaristic understanding of faith must also be processed with the exercise of some caution. For example, the understanding of faith as "the conviction of things not seen" in Heb 11:1, and even the Pauline statement that "we walk by faith, not by sight" in 2 Cor 5:7, are not necessarily to be interpreted non-cognitively. Though the object of the author of Hebrews' conviction that the Raised and exalted Christ was in heaven, eternally pleading the sacrifice of self-giving love, is obviously unseen, it is not necessarily arrived at as a free-standing decision of will without justifying grounds. It is not, in other words, an entirely groundless conviction. Rather, what is "unseen," and envisioned only imaginatively, is grounded in the post-Easter Christian experience of faith as a kind of concrete knowing of the Raised Christ. For, even if the focus of Hebrews is on the heavenly intercession of the Raised Christ, faith in the Resurrection is presupposed. It is not necessarily implied that resurrection faith itself is automatically understood as an entirely voluntaristic commitment without an objective point of reference, or that it is lacking in a cognitive grounding. Likewise, for Paul, the knowing appropriate to faith is confessed to be partial and incomplete, or even somewhat ambiguous, but it remains nevertheless a kind of "seeing" or knowing *of* something. His statement that "we walk by faith and not by sight" has to be balanced by the affirmation that something *is* positively perceived in faith—the life-giving Spirit of the Raised Christ is the guarantee or first-fruits of increased awareness to come. Even if it is not necessarily known with the clarity of sight in exactly the way the material and physical objects of this world are known, the Spirit is for Paul nevertheless something that is objectively perceived in faith. As we shall see in the next chapter, the Spirit is an all-pervading reality with which Paul has to do. It may be known partially and incompletely, like "a reflection in a mirror," as Paul puts it, and "not face to face"; nevertheless faith does see and perceive *something*. Paul is not guilty of promoting a non-cognitive voluntarism in his approach to faith, and there is no reason to believe that this was Mark's intention either.

The importance of this is, that in purely logical terms, one must have some positive cognitive basis before embarking on a self-involving venture of trust, if only for the obvious reason that one must know at least something about a person on which to base a judgment of trustworthiness before proceeding to place one's trust in them. It would be irrational to trust the untrustworthy. This is why in classical theology faith as knowledge (*fides*) is always logically prior to faith as trust (*fiducia*). It is first necessary to know something about the person in whom one places one's trust. This means that Christian faith is never just a blind decision of will, a kind of leap in the dark. That would be to mistake faith for wishful thinking. Rather, trusting faith is based upon an understanding of God's revealed nature as one who is faithful to his promises, and therefore, as trustworthy. An entirely blind "leap in the dark" can never be rationally justified; hence the importance of the theme of the faithfulness of God, as expressed, for example, in the covenantal convictions of the Hebrew-Christian tradition. Likewise, in order to place one's trust in the Resurrected Jesus one must have grounds for believing him to be alive and trustworthy.[99]

I do not therefore myself subscribe to non-cognitive views of faith, either as the style of faith that Mark intended to promote, or still less as an option that commends itself as a rationally viable possibility for the understanding of faith today. Rather than come to resurrection faith purely as a risk on the basis of the evidence of the empty tomb alone, it would be more prudent to suspend judgment. This story may raise a mysterious possibility, but a rational judgment of faith dictates the need of other additional justifying grounds. Hence, a systematic theology of resurrection faith must take the appearances tradition, and in Mark's case, the angel's directive to "Go into Galilee" and his promise that 'there you will see' the Raised Christ, with utmost seriousness.

While it is true that Mark "intimates but does not demonstrate," in the sense that he does not spell out an Easter appearance in narrative form, the kernel of a cognitive ground for faith is nevertheless contained within the angel's promise. This means we do not *just decide* to have faith in the face of a lack of evidence. This promise—the promised possibility of "seeing" the Raised Christ in the Galilee of the church's mission—contains the possibility of a concrete experience of encounter with the Raised One. Mark does not therefore offer us an approach to faith without taking the "trouble to give us grounds for doing so." Rather, we are invited to embark upon the venture of faith after discovering those grounds for ourselves. Given the finite limitations of human reasoning,[100] and the ultimate mystery of the incomprehensibility and descriptive unknowability of God, who is always beyond humanly construed images of him,

---

99. Wolfhart Pannenberg, rightly pointed out that "the motif that faith must remain a risk is problematic" (*Jesus—God and Man*, 109). He noted that, while this motif "is widespread in contemporary theology" "the essence of faith is destroyed where it appears as an unfounded risk" (110). Though Pannenberg does not elaborate, he might well have pointed out that Easter faith must have grounds upon which it is based, otherwise it is no more than an exercise in wishful thinking. Certainly, Pannenberg asserted that "The ground of faith must be as certain as possible."

100. After H. L. Mansel's Bampton Lectures, *The Limits of Religious Thought* (1859).

it does not come as a surprise that the Raised Christ of resurrection faith cannot be caught in the conceptual net of finite images of him either. Indeed, if we try to contain the reality of his presence in our images of him, he, "passing through the midst of them," will always "go his way."

For Mark, the way of Christ is initially the Way of the Cross which true disciples pick up and follow after him into the Galilee of the church's mission: his promise is that there they will in faith "see" him. We therefore today face the challenge of having to trace the outline contours of this "seeing" and knowing upon which our resurrection faith is based.

3

The Object of Faith

Primitive Christian faith and hope were purportedly grounded in a set of original historical experiences on the basis of which it was affirmed that the crucified Jesus had been raised from the dead and had "appeared" to various apostolic witnesses. However, though the very first witnesses to the Resurrection spoke enthusiastically of their apprehension of these visionary appearances, there is no suggestion that experiences of a similar kind continued as the basis of on-going Christian faith and hope.[1] Nor is it possible to say that summary lists of the appearances, let alone detailed narratives reporting them such as we find in the later Gospels, always featured as essential elements of the primitive Easter proclamation. The epistles of St. Paul, for example, make it abundantly clear that, while Paul obviously on occasion reminded the members of the communities that he had originally founded of the tradition of the appearances as an important feature of his original proclamation to them (as in the classic example of the early kerygmatic summary in 1 Cor 15:5–8), on other occasions the datum of the appearances does not feature in what Paul has to say about the essentials of the Gospel at all.

When Paul reminds his addressees of the good news of what God had accomplished in Christ, he instead often speaks of the Christ Event in elided terms, sometimes without so much as mentioning the appearances. In his summary of the content of the Gospel at the beginning of *Romans*, for example, the key elements of the good news are stated as "the Gospel of God concerning his Son who was descended from David according to the flesh and was declared to be Son of God with power according to the Spirit of holiness by resurrection from the dead, Jesus Christ our Lord."[2] Apart from the absence of any explicit reference to the tradition of the appearances here, we should note Paul's positive mention of the role of the "Spirit of holiness" in his understanding of the way in which the Resurrection of Christ was accomplished. As we shall see, this reference to the Spirit in relation to resurrection faith signals a sustained Pauline preoccupation and interest.

---

1. Indeed, St. John is at pains positively to point out that it is those who have *not* enjoyed experiences of seeing of the concrete kind that answered the skepticism of the doubting Thomas who are blessed (John 20:29).

2. Rom 1:3–4.

The omission of any explicit mention of the tradition of the appearances, or even of the bare occurrence of the Resurrection itself, is also noteworthy in the very early hymn quoted by Paul in Phil 2. Here, there is no mention of the subsequent gift of the Spirit either, but, significantly, the first believers clearly understood that it was from the exalted heavenly place to which Jesus had been raised, which is mentioned in Phil 2:9–11, that the gift of his Spirit had been distributed to people of faith. This is explicitly expressed in the deutero-Pauline epistle to the Eph 4:8: "When he ascended on high he led captivity captive, and he gave gifts to men." Even if this is not directly from Paul's own hand, these are the same "spiritual gifts" as are mentioned by Paul himself in 1 Cor 12.[3] It is because the raised and exalted Jesus is where he is that the Spirit is experienced in the life of the Church. As Barnabas Lindars put it: "There is an integral connection between his place in heaven and the gift of the Spirit."[4]

In Paul's letter to the Galatians, the crucifixion and the gift of the Spirit are explicitly linked as the defining events of the Gospel, without mention of the appearances. Here Paul was content to speak, once again obviously in elided terms, of these two sequential and inter-related events, this time implying the Resurrection as the necessary pre-condition of the receipt of the Spirit, but without actually mentioning it explicitly, and certainly without bothering to highlight the tradition of the first appearances.[5] Instead, Paul's original proclamation is said to have put Jesus' crucifixion "before their eyes,"[6] as a consequence of which in faith (as distinct from "works of the law") they were said to have been simultaneously freed from sin, and "supplied" by God with the Spirit.[7]

We have the sense here that the Spirit is not just an abstract or imagined reality that Paul brought before the mind's eye of the Galatians, as in the case of the historically remembered crucifixion, but a more concretely experienced and continuing reality with which they were actually acquainted. This descriptive summary of the Christ Event and its appropriation in faith obviously once again presupposes the Resurrection (and exaltation to heaven for that matter), for the living Spirit of Christ could be received and known in faith only as a consequence of his Resurrection from the dead.[8]

---

3. See Barnabas Lindars' useful discussion of this in *New Testament Apologetic*, 51–53. Behind this idea of the gift of the Spirit from heaven is Ps 68:19 (Eng. 18), which is also quoted in Acts 2:33. Though the *Psalm* text as we have it has "you receive gifts," the Targum paraphrase of this verse from Ps 68 has "you *gave* gifts to the children of men," rather than "receive" which is the reading witnessed to also in Eph 4:8. Lindars explains this textual modification by reference to a possible form of the Hebrew text that was available both to the Targum and the author of Ephesians, which had "gave" instead of "received," so as to defend the view that *Psalm* 68:19 was the origin of the language of "the gift of the Spirit."

4. Lindars, *New Testament Apologetic*, 55.

5. Gal 3:1–5.

6. Gal 3:1.

7. Gal 3:5.

8. A point clearly made by Calvin, *Institutes of the Christian Religion*, II.16. xiv–cv: "as regards his divine presence, we have Christ always: as regards his bodily presence, it was truly said to the disciples,

However, neither the actual Resurrection as a past historical event, nor the original appearances to the first witnesses, are explicitly mentioned.

Paul's over-riding concern in Galatians is to contrast the new order of God's righteousness, secured by trusting faith in the Raised Christ, with the futility of seeking righteousness through "works of the law." After all, a righteousness achieved by living a life of compliance to the Jewish law was available only to Jews. By contrast, the experience of the Spirit, which Jewish and Gentile Galatians jointly shared, has superseded the old order of sin and the flesh governed by the law. It is clear enough that to Paul's mind it is not that the Spirit is distributed as some kind of a reward of faith, but rather that access to it and to God through it, is by faith and not "works of the law." In fact, in Galatians faith and Spirit, *pistis* and *pneuma*, are interwoven in a kind of contrapuntal fugue to form a sustained theme. Given the apparent fundamental importance of the continuing experience of the Spirit in Paul's understanding of faith, it is not a surprise that the original tradition of the appearances to the *first* witnesses is in this way passed over altogether.

Rather than focusing on the Resurrection of Christ as a historical event in its own right, Paul therefore regularly pre-supposes its occurrence, or refers to it in an instrumental sense. Its occurrence is assumed as the necessary condition for the continuing gift of the Spirit of Christ. But the logic of this statement also runs in the reverse direction: if the living Spirit of Christ was understood to have been perceived and known through faith, in the contemporary experience of those to whom he wrote, then the suggestion is that Christ *must* have been raised. In other words, the living experience of the Galatians themselves who, as a consequence of the gift of the Spirit now walked in newness of life, itself attested to the truth that Christ was raised.[9] Indeed, Paul's argument is that in Christ "the blessings of Abraham" have come to Gentiles no less than to Jews, for to Gentiles and Jews alike "the promise of the Spirit" is received "through faith."[10] This phrase is correctly translated as "the promise *of* the Spirit" despite the preference of many translations to opt for "the promised Spirit"—as though the Spirit is itself already the fulfillment of God's promise.[11] As we shall see below, it is more consistent with Paul's usage elsewhere to understand him to mean that the Spirit that is received through faith is to be interpreted proleptically as itself

---

Me you have not always. For a few days the Church had him bodily present. Now, she apprehends him by faith, but sees him not by the eye.... Hence it is immediately added, that he 'sits at the right hand of God the Father' ... You see to what end he is so seated—namely, that all creatures both in heaven and earth should reverence his majesty, be ruled by his hand, do him implicit homage, and submit to his power."

9. This follows the pattern of Paul's argument in 1 Cor 15:17: "If Christ has not been raised, your faith is futile and you are still in your sins." Likewise, the logical implication is "if your faith is valid and you actually know the life of the Spirit and are no longer in your sins, then Christ must have been raised."

10. Gal 3:14.

11. See for example, the NEB.

the promise of what is yet to come at the Eschaton. Thus, the experience of the Spirit appropriated through faith was the ground of hope rather than the fulfillment of hope. In any event, my point is that Paul privileges talk of the experience of the Spirit to the point where it inevitably assumes an importance for both faith and hope that in a sense puts the tradition of the appearances into eclipse.

A great deal has been said about the mutually supportive inter-relation of the evidence of the empty tomb and the appearances insofar as one interprets the other—the empty tomb is often said to be a pointer to the nature of the resurrected body, and the appearances in turn are represented as being of such a concrete and physical kind as to entail that the tomb must have been left entirely empty. This is not to be compared, however, with the importance of Paul's concentration of attention upon experience of the Spirit as the continuing object of faith, over against either the story of the empty tomb or the narrative tradition of the appearances. The experience of the "life-giving Spirit" that was received as a gift "from heaven" implied that the Resurrection must have occurred; for Christ must have been exalted for the Spirit to be experienced as it was. By contrast, from Paul's point of view the empty tomb therefore ranks no mention at all, and references to the appearances tradition are few.

Some generations after Paul, Luke ensured that his readers were in no doubt about the importance of the role of the Spirit in the origins of faith: in Acts 5:32 he has Peter declare that it was not just the apostolic band of first believers that were witnesses to the Resurrection of the crucified Jesus, for the Holy Spirit "whom God has given to those who obey him" was also a palpable "witness to these things."

This concentration of attention on the experience of the presence of the Spirit means that, as I originally argued in 1987 in *The Structure of Resurrection Belief*, the Pauline tradition amply demonstrates that early faith and hope were "not exclusively traced back to a visionary experience of the past." Rather, Paul's exposition of the nature of faith and hope "is regularly traced back, not to an experience or vision of the bodily Jesus of some kind, but to the continuing presence of the Spirit of Christ."[12] The operative word here is "exclusively," for there are clearly some occasions when Paul does return to the tradition of the original appearances. Nevertheless, the overwhelming thrust of Paul's talk focuses on the importance of the experience of the presence of the Spirit of Christ as the continuing basis of faith and hope: the experience of the Spirit of Christ is the *object* of faith and the *ground* of hope.

Perhaps it is not surprising that N. T. Wright, in his monumental work, *The Resurrection of the Son of God*, takes exception to this contention, for Wright himself is anxious to give priority to the tradition of the empty tomb and the appearances in his attempt to prove the occurrence of the Resurrection as a historical event. This means that the

---

12. Carnley, *Structure of Resurrection Belief*, 249.

importance of the experience of the Spirit for an understanding of the make-up of Christian faith and hope is effectively neutralized.

Almost as though in a sneak preview to Wright's express concern to allocate priority to the historical evidence of the appearances and the empty tomb as the basis of faith to the exclusion of any role for the continuing presence of Christ through the medium of the Spirit, Wolfhart Pannenberg was likewise anxious to place a similar reliance on the historical reason alone. Like Wright, Pannenberg was also wedded to an approach to post-Easter faith and hope that was grounded exclusively upon an understanding of the resurrection as a historical event of the past. Unfortunately, in doing so Pannenberg had to pass over the contention of Ernst Käsemann that for Paul the Spirit was "the basis of the post-Easter imminent expectation."[13] Pannenberg opted instead to base faith and hope on an attempted historical proof of the resurrection by appeal to the evidence of the appearances and the empty tomb. Even so, the opinion of a New Testament scholar of Käsemann's stature was not easily set aside. Pannenberg therefore equivocated in the face of Käsemann's emphasis on the importance of the concrete experience of the Spirit as the ground of faith and hope, by at least hinting that the historical evidence constituted by the traditions of the appearances and empty tomb did not stand alone: thus he conceded that the "possession of the Spirit is not the only and ultimate ground of the imminent expectation."[14]

Wright countenances no such concession. He alleges, for starters, that no grounds were offered in *The Structure of Resurrection Belief* in support of the view that early Christian faith and hope were regularly sheeted back to an experience of the Spirit of Christ. Then, second, he insists that no grounds *could* in fact have been offered in support this contention, given his own argument (as he presents it in chapters 5, 6 and 7 of *The Resurrection of the Son of God*)[15] that faith and hope must be understood as responses to the occurrence of the Resurrection understood as a historical event of the past that he believes is firmly secured by the evidence of the empty tomb and appearances. Curiously, Wright seems to have forgotten that in these very chapters of *The Resurrection of the Son of God*, on the "Resurrection in Paul," he himself makes regular appeal to Paul's references to the Spirit in his own descriptions of Paul's understanding of resurrection faith and hope. Indeed, Wright can hardly avoid mention of Paul's emphasis on the eschatological role of the Spirit, both originally in the Resurrection of Jesus,[16] and in relation to the future resurrection of all the righteous faithful at the End

---

13. Pannenberg, *Jesus—God and Man*, 114, n. 134.

14. Pannenberg, *Jesus—God and Man*, 114, n. 134. Elsewhere in this same work Pannenberg acknowledges, following Ingo Hermann (*Kyrios und Pneuma*, 144), that "all 'genuine,' theologically pregnant statements about the Spirit in the principal Pauline letters are Christologically stamped" (*Jesus—God and Man*, 171). "Thus the Spirit is the pledge of the Christian resurrection hope (II Cor. 1:22), the firstfruits of the coming salvation (Rom. 8:23)" (115).

15. *RSG*, 373, n. 169.

16. *RSG*, 245.

Time, not to mention the continuing role of the Spirit that, as Wright himself says, was "even now at work to anticipate and guarantee that final event."[17]

Nevertheless, he is apparently reluctant to concede that the experience of the Spirit had an *originative* cognitive role in resurrection faith and hope. This is probably because he purports to establish the historicity of the Resurrection exclusively on the basis of the evidence of the appearances and the empty tomb: "When we ask the early Christians themselves what had occasioned this belief," he writes, "their answers home in on two things: stories about Jesus' tomb being empty, and stories about him appearing to people, alive again."[18] Unfortunately, this judgment is entirely fanciful. It clearly cannot apply to St. Paul who does not so much as mention the empty tomb in his own expressions of faith, let alone "home in on it"; nor can we say with confidence that it applies to the communities whose faith Paul describes, for when he writes to them about the nature of their faith it is also without ever mentioning the empty tomb. On the other hand, as we have just noted, even Paul's kerygmatic summaries of the appearances are few, and certainly are not cited exclusively or left to stand alone, either as the object of early faith or the ground of hope. By contrast, Paul's allusions to the importance of the experience of the Spirit of the Raised Christ recur over and over again. As Troels Engberg-Pedersen aptly remarks: the Spirit is "a concept that—as soon as one has spotted it—appears to be everywhere in Paul."[19]

It is not insignificant that Paul's theology of the Spirit appears to have been inherited by John, who in fact expands upon it and develops it as a fundamental theological theme of his Gospel. In a sense, John's *Gospel* is the Gospel of "he whom God has sent," who both "utters the words of God" and "gives the Spirit without measure."[20] The crucial Pauline theme of the gift of the Spirit to the baptized is filled out by John at John 3:5–8 where he has Jesus say:

> Truly, truly, I say to you, unless one is born of water and the Spirit, he cannot enter the kingdom of God. That which is born of the flesh is flesh, and that which is born of the Spirit is spirit. Do not marvel that I said to you, "You must be born again." The wind blows where it wishes, and you hear its sound, but you do not know where it comes from or where it goes. So it is with everyone who is born of the Spirit.

The First Epistle of John fills out the nature of the quality of the experience of the Spirit as a "divine love" that is known by the baptized in faith when he says:

> . . . the love of God was made manifest among us, that God sent his only Son into the world, so that we might live through him. In this is love, not that we have loved God but that he loved us and sent his Son to be the propitiation for

---

17. *RSG*, 373.
18. *RSG*, 686.
19. Engberg-Pedersen, *Cosmology and Self in the Apostle Paul*, 14.
20. John 3:34.

our sins. Beloved, if God so loved us, we also ought to love one another. No one has ever seen God; if we love one another, God abides in us and his love is perfected in us.[21]

Moreover, 1 John underlines the significance of this love as the perceived object known in the continuing response of faith when he says: "And by this we know that he *abides* in us, by the Spirit whom he has given us."[22] This is important enough for him to repeat in 1 John 4:13: "By this we know that we abide in him and he in us, because he has given us of his Spirit."

N. T. Wright's aversion to the possibility that on-going faith and hope might be grounded in the continuing experience of the Spirit of Christ is understandable. Given his own insistence on handling the Resurrection only as an event of the historical past in which the body of Jesus, now said to have been rendered materially and physically incorruptible, is alleged to have been restored to *this* world, and his claim that this is secured by the evidence of the empty tomb and the tradition of appearances, any role that the Spirit may have as an epistemic object in the make-up of faith is almost automatically eliminated. Clearly, for Wright, this past event, understood in this precise way, and made the subject of historical investigation, assumes an exclusive importance. Once understood as a historical event whose occurrence is said to have been proved by the exercise of the historical reason alone, this event then becomes the basis for an understanding of the nature of faith and hope as second order responses that are subsequent to it and dependent upon it. While the Resurrection itself is said to be proved by historical reasoning, faith judgments are then said to relate to the role and good purposes of God in it, and also to the consequential status and identity of Jesus as Messiah and Lord, whose return in glory is therefore awaited at the Eschaton.

These judgments of faith and hope are said to issue from the Resurrection understood as an event whose occurrence is allegedly proved by historical research based upon the evidence of the empty tomb and the appearances alone. But this means that the continuing experience of the Spirit in this case becomes a kind of add-on to "anticipate and guarantee" their hope while their faith judgments are therefore said to be independently secured by appeal to the empty tomb and appearances.

As a consequence, as Wright articulates his understanding of things in *The Resurrection of the Son of God*, the Spirit has no role as an objective datum in the response of faith. Understandably, when he came to an extended treatment of the theme of the Spirit a decade later in his subsequent volume, *Paul and the Faithfulness of God* (2013), it is Paul's "theology of the Spirit" rather than the actual experience of the Spirit as the object of faith and the ground of hope that is of interest to him.[23] As Larry Hurtado has recently perceptively observed: "Wright focuses on the conceptual content 'pneu-

---

21. 1 John 4:9–12.
22. 1 John 3:24.
23. Wright, *Paul and the Faithfulness of God*, 709, under the heading "Paul's Theology," 709–28.

matology," leaving the specifics of the phenomena in question somewhat vague."[24] For Wright, the Spirit becomes the subject matter of a theme of Paul's *theology* rather than the perceived object of Paul's religious experience and continuing faith.

While Wright naturally has confidence in his own powers of historical argument as he employs them in the chapters of *The Resurrection of the Son of God* to which he refers,[25] we may nevertheless prefer to rely upon the epistles of St. Paul himself regarding the fundamental importance (or otherwise) of the continuing experience of the Spirit of Christ for an understanding of the actual content of early Christian faith and hope. So let us return again to the words of St. Paul.

At the beginning of Romans, though the need for faith is not explicitly mentioned, it is implied as the appropriate response to being "called to belong to Jesus Christ" (Rom 1:6). This "belonging to Christ" is spelled out in terms of Paul's description of the life of the community of faith and the sharing of the Spirit of Christ (Rom 8:9). In the very next verse (Rom 8:10), he makes it clear that through the Spirit of Christ the believer has access to Christ *himself*. The Spirit is, as it were, the personal fluid extension of the Raised Christ, just as it is generally understood as the fluid extension of God.[26] This is entirely congruent with Paul's affirmation in *1 Cor* 15:45 that as a consequence of the Resurrection, Christ, the Second Adam, "has become a life-giving Spirit." In Rom 8:2 Paul speaks, apparently, of the same experienced reality as "the Spirit of life in Christ Jesus." Clearly, in Paul's mind it is the continuing reality of the Raised Christ as Spirit in whom the Romans are to place their trusting faith so as steadfastly to maintain both their relational belonging to him and a standard of behavior appropriate to that belonging. This is what he contrasts also in Galatians with an attempt to access the righteousness of God by "works of the law." Instead, Paul speaks of the life of faith[27] as a life lived to God, in which "through the Spirit" and by faith Christians eagerly wait for the hope of righteousness,[28] for those who "walk according to the Spirit,"[29] and who are "led by the Spirit,"[30] and "live by the Spirit," and "keep in step with the Spirit,"[31] will inherit God's Kingdom. Clearly, the Resurrection of Christ is presupposed, but faith and hope are grounded

---

24. Hurtado, "YHWH's Return to Zion," 424.
25. Chapters 5, 6, and 7 of *RSG*.
26. See Lindars, *New Testament Apologetic*, 57: "In all these Pauline passages the fluid notion of the Spirit as an outflow from God is retained, though it is through the mediation of the exalted Jesus."
27. Gal 2:20.
28. Gal 5:5.
29. Gal 5:16.
30. Gal 5:18.
31. Gal 5:25.

in the concrete experience of the living Spirit of Christ. Indeed, even N. T. Wright himself concedes, "Galatians does not mention the Resurrection explicitly."[32] Even in a passage (*Gal* 4:1–7), which Wright believes is one of "the most crucial passages in the whole letter,"[33] the idea of the inheritance of sons (and daughters) is secured by the concretely experienced fact that God has given "the Spirit of his Son into your hearts." It is through this possession of the Spirit they cry "Abba Father" and know themselves to be inheritors of God's Kingdom.

It is also clear from Paul's letters to the various communities that he founded, and in which he continued to take a keen pastoral interest, that their faith is not just a matter of the propositional belief *that* Jesus *had been* raised from the dead. In other words, in encouraging his early converts to continue steadfast in resurrection faith until the Day of Christ's return, Paul does not just exhort them to continue in a propositional belief verbally formulated by the *first* witnesses, as though faith were simply a matter of giving assent at second hand to experiences originally enjoyed by others. In other words, Paul does not describe the faith of those he addresses in his letters as though it were just a stammering repetition of an abstract verbal judgment that the first witnesses had themselves originally based on their experiences of appearances (nor even of the empty tomb, which Paul nowhere even mentions).

Even when Paul cites his own original experience of seeing the Raised Christ, it is often not to offer it to others as a datum for their faith, as in 1 Cor 15:8, so much as to bolster his own claim to apostolic status, as for example in 1 Cor 9:1 where appeal is made apparently to the Damascus Road appearance in order to warrant his commission to deliver the Gospel to the Gentiles. Likewise, in Galatians when Paul speaks of his Damascus Road experience, it is not to offer it as an experience to which others were then invited to give their assent, so much as to make the point that he had received the Gospel as a revelation directly from Christ himself, and not from human hands or at second-hand as a tradition passed on to him from others.[34] On occasions when he does remind them of the basics of their own faith, Paul regularly called the members of these communities to remain relationally faithful to the Raised Christ *himself*, and in their self-understanding to see themselves as belonging to him. Rather than *remind* them of the Raised Christ's original appearances to others, or even to himself, Paul therefore regularly, and at length, talked of the continuing living Spirit of Christ of which they were *themselves* witnesses. This is clearly described as something with which they had direct acquaintance; it was no second-hand experience, but something they could perceive and continue to claim to know themselves at first hand. Then, on

---

32. *RSG*, 224.
33. *RSG*, 221.
34. Gal 1:1, 11–12.

the basis of their continuing perception in faith of the presence of the Spirit among them, Paul's regular pattern of argument in his dealings with these communities is to exhort them to continue to love one another in the fellowship (*koinonia*) of the Spirit. They are to behave in a manner appropriate to their newfound relation to Christ, until the Day of his return. After encouraging them first to celebrate their common faith and their sharing in the same Spirit, he thus regularly goes on to call the members of these communities to live by a standard of moral behavior appropriate to their belonging to the Raised Christ, secured through their possession of his Spirit. It is thus this concrete experience of life within the community of faith informed by the presence of the Spirit of Christ that issued in Paul's ethical exhortations.

Generally speaking, Paul's letters to the early faith communities with which he had to do are therefore comprised of passages in which we find material that is *descriptive* of faith and hope on one hand, and, on the other, ethically *prescriptive* material outlining the style of life that this faith commitment demands. In the prescriptive material, Paul is clearly concerned with the implications of faith and hope for practical behavior in the living of life well. Thus, ethical exhortation (*parenesis*) in which he strongly urges believers to behave in a manner appropriate to their adherence to Christ makes up a significant proportion of his communications to them. But it is equally clear that this ethically prescriptive material is grounded in the description of the new life of faith and hope that God had made available to them through the Christ Event. This crucial Event is, however, rarely just described as an event of the past, to which they are urged to give a purely notional assent; instead, it is described as a continuing event or, better, a temporally extended state of affairs in which they themselves were active participants. Paul is at pains to exhort them to remain cognitively aware of this in faith and steadfastly committed to it in forward-looking hope.

In 1 Thess 4:8, for example, where God is described as "giving his holy Spirit" to them, it is clear that Paul thinks of this as a continuous, on-going phenomenon in the life of the community of faith. This fundamental emphasis of Paul is reflected also in the deutero-Pauline epistle to the Colossians, where the faithful whose "love in the Spirit" is said to have been reported to him by Epaphras, are exhorted to "continue securely established and steadfast in the faith" and not to shift in "the hope promised by the Gospel."[35] Clearly, both faith and hope have to be sustained through time, pending the final eschatological return of Christ. But this further entails that the gift of the Spirit is also understood as a continuous, concretely experienced and temporally extended feature of the life of the community of the baptized until the return of the Lord. Their faith and hope is described, in other words, not just in terms of assent to abstract propositional beliefs focused on the Resurrection, merely remembered as an event of the past, or even on the Spirit as a once-given occurrence of the historical past, but in terms of their concrete knowing *of* Christ's diffused presence through the gift of his Spirit in their life together. It is not a thing of the past to which they are invited to

---

35. Col 1:23.

look back, but an object of contemporary and continuing experience. Paul constantly reminds those to whom he wrote, therefore, of the new relation to God in Christ that had been brought into being among them. It is this new order of human being that, by the righteousness of God, was now shared and enjoyed by both Gentiles and Jews together without distinction.

While they all entered this new order by the decision of faith, as distinct from fulfilling "works of the law" (which could apply more exclusively and specifically only to Jews), their continuing shared life in Christ was secured by their common on-going possession and apprehension in faith of the operation of the Spirit in their lives. In much of Paul's descriptive writing out of which he develops his *parenetic* material, he thus reminds his addressees of the life-transforming significance of the Spirit as the continuing object and support both of their faith and their hope.

The ultimate fulfillment of eschatological hope effected by the greater outpouring of the Spirit also ultimately includes the resurrection of the bodies of those of faith, for just as Jesus was raised through the power of "the Spirit of holiness," so at the Eschaton the same Spirit could be relied upon to transform the bodies of all faithful believers into conformity with the glorious resurrection body of Christ himself. In other words, it was anticipated that the same Spirit of God that had worked so powerfully in him would effect the fulfillment of the resurrection hope of all believers. Thus, their awareness of the transformative impact of the Spirit already in their lives provided the assurance that the same Spirit would ultimately transform them into raised heavenly or pneumatic bodies of the kind Paul wrestles so earnestly to envisage and describe in 1 Cor 15. We will return to the question raised here about the nature of the resurrection body in a future chapter. For the moment, it is sufficient to make the connection between this aspect of the future Christian hope with the perception in faith of the active agency of God's Spirit in Christ.

Clearly, as Paul describes the on-going faith of the primitive Christian communities, it involved not just believing *that* Jesus *had* been raised from the dead, or even *that* he had appeared to certain witnesses, but instead it involved a relational knowing *of* Christ through the agency of his living Spirit. The initial commitment of trusting faith, in which they attached themselves to Christ at the point of entry into the Christian community by baptism, initiated their continuing experience of sharing in the Spirit. As a consequence of their being called into the community of faith by the Gospel, their perception of the Spirit of Christ through faith thus became not only the continuing cognitive object of their faith, but the ground and warrant of their eschatological hope.

Paul quite explicitly makes the logical connection between faith on one hand and hope on the other transparently clear, and in doing so his appeal to the presence of the Spirit is, once again, a quite fundamental datum. In 2 Cor 1:22, Paul speaks of God's giving of the Spirit as a "first installment" or "guarantee" (*arrabōn*); clearly, the reality of the Spirit that is concretely experienced through faith is interpreted as itself the promise of more to come. This echoes what we have already seen in *Galatians* 3:14: the blessing of Abraham, now shared by both Jews and Gentiles in the reconciled unity that issues from the receipt of the Spirit through faith, in turn constitutes the promise of future fulfillment. Clearly, the receipt and perception of the humanly unifying Spirit through faith, grounds the eschatological hope for a greater fulfillment to come. The importance of this is that it means that the Christian hope is not just a matter of wishful thinking, but is a genuine hope that is cognitively grounded in and justified by, the concrete experience of the Spirit that is apprehended by faith.

This idea of the Spirit as a guarantee of what is to come is repeated in 2 Cor 5:5. In a passage about the resurrection hope to the effect that "what is mortal may be swallowed up by life," Paul declares that "He who has prepared us for this very thing is God, who has given us the Spirit as a guarantee."[36]

In Romans, essentially the same sentiment is rehearsed again. In faith Paul affirms his perception of the gift of the Spirit: "God's love has been poured into our hearts through the Holy Spirit who has been given to us" (Rom 5:5). Then, in Rom 8:23, the same eschatological reference is implied as we have seen in 2 Cor 5:5, though this time the idea of the Spirit as a first installment or guarantee is replaced by the metaphor of the '"first-fruits" of a future harvest. The first ripe fruit of the harvest is to be interpreted in faith as a promise of future fulfillment in the form of a greater harvest to come, which once again thus becomes the object of Christian hope.

Clearly, the perception in faith of the presence of the Spirit in the life of the community of those baptized into Christ is the ground of the eschatological hope of a future "outpouring of the Spirit on all flesh."[37] By entering the life of the faith community, a continuing acquaintance with the reality of the Spirit, as the cohesive and unifying inner texture of its life, assumed a dual importance: as the object of their faith, which in logical terms then grounded their eschatological hope.

The same logical dynamic underpins Paul's discussion of faith, hope and love in 1 Cor 13. Here his cognitive talk of a partial seeing in faith as though perceiving a reflected image "dimly in a mirror" promises clarity of sight, "face to face," in the future. When "the perfect comes,"[38] then Paul says he will know no longer partially, but "fully, even as I have been fully known."[39] Clearly, the perception in faith of the presence of Christ in the form of the Spirit of love poured out in the life of the community, even if it is partial, in turn becomes the ground of forward looking hope. Indeed, it is *because* the perception of it is partial and incomplete as it is experienced

---

36. See also Eph 1:13–14.
37. Joel 2:28, as quoted in Peter's early sermon in Acts 2:17.
38. 1 Cor 13:10.
39. 1 Cor 13:12.

in faith in this world, that it triggers the hope of more to come. As Paul himself says in Romans: "we do not hope for what we already see, we wait for it with patience."[40]

Paul in Philippians articulates the very same idea in terms of "straining forward" in hope towards the goal of a more full knowledge of "Christ Jesus my Lord."[41] In faith he says he is able to reach the "grasp" or apprehension of the Raised Jesus Christ, just as Christ had already "grasped" or apprehended him.[42] This in turn is the assurance of a more intimate "face to face"[43] meeting to come, and thus provides the encouragement to "press on toward the goal for the prize of the upward call of God in Christ Jesus."[44]

It follows from all this that the eschatological hope of the first Christians was not just grounded in the propositional contention *that* Christ *had* been raised and *that* therefore Christians could hope one day to enjoy a resurrection like his. The perceived Spirit of Christ is itself the guarantee or the down payment of more to come, and the first fruits of a greater yield of an anticipated future harvest. Very importantly, something more than just a temporal distinction is being made here. The contrast is also epistemological; the difference being between a partial seeing and a hoped-for revelation of greater clarity yet to come. Among the first Christians, this Christian hope was thus connected back to their own experience of the active presence of the Spirit of Christ already at work in their lives. This means that the mentality of Paul was not past-centered, but present-centered. He thus exhorts the baptized to ". . . hold true to what we have attained."[45] A concretely experienced reality of the present, when itself interpreted in a promissory way, became the ground of hope for a greater outpouring of the Spirit in time to come. The impact of the active presence of the Spirit could be anticipated by people of Christian faith to be the fulfillment of their own transformation at the Eschaton by being raised like Christ himself, with pneumatically renewed bodies. This then was what Paul descriptively drew to their attention as "what they had already attained," and as the basis of the need to maintain appropriate standards of behavior while they awaited Christ's earthly eschatological return.

Now, it is clear from all this that Paul describes the presence of the Spirit in very concrete, experiential terms. Certainly, faith is much more than just a propositional attitude of assent to the truth of a statement asserting the occurrence of a remembered event of the past. The object of faith is no imagined or wholly abstract thing, but something palpably concrete. In epistemological terms, it is a reality known empirically by acquaintance,

---

40. Rom 8:25.
41. Phil 3:8.
42. Phil 3:12.
43. Paul's equivalent of our contemporary talk of meeting "in person."
44. Phil 3:14.
45. Phil 3:16.

rather than abstractly and purely verbally by description. This remains as true for contemporary Christian believers in the twenty-first-century as it was for those to whom Paul originally addressed his epistles. Indeed, we are able to understand the cognitive experience of faith, and what it was that the first generation of Christians described in faith as the object of their trust, by analogy with our own experience of life in the community of faith.[46] For us, as for them, faith is a commitment of trust (*fiducia*) grounded upon the knowledge (*fides*) of an object of acquaintance concretely perceived in the present—which Paul described as "the life-giving Spirit" or "the Spirit of life," and which John spoke of as "the Spirit without measure" or "abundant Spirit."

In this case, if faith is not to be reduced to a form of propositional belief, such as an assent to the truth of the proposition "*that* Jesus was raised from the dead," then it is not the role of the Spirit to bring people to a form of faith understood to be of this kind, or to give them the "gift of faith," even though many are admittedly of this view. This is essentially the understanding of faith promoted, for example, by B. L. McCormack, who contends that "Paul understands faith to be a gift of God wrought by his grace in the human heart."[47] Likewise, Robert Jewett, in his commentary on *Romans*, characterizes the "work of the spirit" among the first Christians in "faith creating" terms: "The Spirit was understood," he says, "to evoke positive responses to the gospel, making persons know in the depth of their despair and dishonor *that* together they could call God 'Abba' and live as honored 'children of God.'"[48] In this case, the object of faith becomes the good news of the Gospel itself, which, through the work of the Spirit, comes to be believed in a heart-felt way. N. T. Wright also concurs with this understanding of the "sovereign faith evoking" work of the Spirit, and so speaks of "the spirit, who through the gospel, inspires the first whisper of faith."[49] For all these New Testament theologians, the work of the Spirit is conceived in a kind of "faith generating" way focused upon the appropriation of propositional truth. Though this is a strategy often appealed to in order to explain how some come to faith and not others, it is not that faith is the "gift of the Spirit" only to those who for some inexplicable reason are so favored by God. Rather, the Spirit is itself the gift that may be perceived and received through faith by those who respond to God's call.[50] It is as itself an objectively perceived reality that the Spirit "evokes faith."

---

46. This is, quite without apology, an appeal to the historiographical "principle of analogy" of Ernst Troeltsch, somewhat cavalierly dismissed as a historiographical principle by Wright, *RSG*, 16–18.

47. McCormack, "Current Debates over Justification," 108.

48. Jewett, *Romans*, 315. My italics.

49. Wright, *Paul and the Faithfulness of God*, 954.

50. Frei sees this clearly in *The Identity of Jesus Christ*; especially "The Holy Spirit as Christ's Identity and Presence" in Part 5, "The Presence of Christ" (chapter 14): "The pattern of Christ's Presence," 187–88.

St. Paul certainly appears to have thought of faith as a response to the hearing of the Gospel. As he says in *Romans:* "Faith comes through what is heard."[51] And those who hear must first have access to a preacher.[52] Furthermore, just as he himself had been called by God to proclaim the Gospel in the first place,[53] Paul appears to have thought of those who responded to his proclamation of the Gospel as being called by God "to belong to Jesus Christ,"[54] or "called to be saints together."[55] We cannot therefore rule out the possibility that he thought of faith as an inner response to the call of God. Even so, whether he thought of faith simply as a form of assent to the call of an abstract propositional truth is problematic. The call of the Gospel may be understood, not as an exhortation to abstract belief in the truth of the Gospel itself (either with or without good reason), so much as an invitation to transformation by perceiving the objective presence and activity of the Spirit of the Raised Christ, and aligning one's own life with it. It is in this way that the Spirit evokes the response of faith. In this case, the Spirit itself may therefore be understood as the object of faith, which the Gospel celebrates and proclaims. It is the work of the Spirit of Christ not to bring people to faith in truths of a propositional kind, so much as to bring people together in faith as they discern its relationally unifying presence. This is the Spirit whose lordship they confess and by which they know in experience how it is that Jews and Gentiles together can be "children of God." This is the Spirit that actually creates the "fellowship in the Gospel" (Phil 1:5), which in turn is "the good work" which God "has begun in them," and which he will continue to enact until the day of the Messiah (v. 6). It is in this concrete way, rather than in terms of the evocation of notional beliefs in response to the Gospel, that the Spirit works to "generate faith in humans and to constitute all those who believe as the single forgiven family promised to Abraham."[56] The generation of faith and the constitution of the family promised to Abraham are, however, not two independent and sequentially arranged happenings, but two logically inter-dependent and temporally simultaneous constitutive elements of a single event.

There are, of course, other issues of an epistemological kind that must also necessarily be addressed. Just *how* is the presence of the Spirit of the Raised Christ perceived? And how is it that the claim to have perceived his Spirit is made by some and not by others? Indeed, how is the Spirit *identified* in faith *as* the Spirit of the crucified Jesus Christ? Before we tackle these important epistemological questions, however, we must first spend some time exploring the ontological question of the nature of the reality to which Paul referred as "the life giving Spirit" or the "Spirit of life in Christ Jesus," and that John spoke of as "the abundant Spirit" or "Spirit without measure."

51. Rom 10:17.
52. Rom 10:14–15.
53. Rom 1:1.
54. Rom 1:6.
55. 1 Cor 1:2.
56. These are the felicitous words of Wright, *Paul and the Faithfulness of God*, 952.

The question therefore becomes: what more can we say about the nature of the Spirit of Christ that was cognitively perceived as the object of faith, and the ground of the hope of a greater fulfillment to come, among the community of the baptized? How exactly, in other words, are we to understand the Spirit itself in more explicit ontological terms?

4

Paul and Stoicism?

To this point, it has been argued that, as important as the eschatological framework of Second Temple Judaism is for understanding the patterns of thought of the first Christians as they sought to interpret their resurrection experiences, we need also to pay attention to the hidden epistemological presuppositions of their faith claims. As Paul exhorted the communities, over which he continued to exercise a kind of pastoral interest and care, to sustain their trusting commitment to Christ and to pursue lives of moral integrity appropriate to their newfound relation with him, he necessarily assumed the trustworthiness both of God and of the one who had been Raised by God. The perception of the trustworthiness of Christ in resurrection faith logically presupposes that the first believers now claimed to know, in their continuing Christian experience, something of the one in whom they placed such trust. Indeed, it seems to be implied that they must have had some perception of why it was that they judged the one in whom they placed their trusting faith *to be* trustworthy. One does not normally place one's faith in someone who is thought to be entirely untrustworthy.[1]

A study of the unexpressed philosophical commitments that seem to have been involved in the claims to know the presence of the Raised Christ, that St. Paul and the first Christians understood to have been mediated to them through the continuing presence and activity of his Spirit, will in turn introduce us to some basic insights into the ontological status of exactly *what it was* that they perceived and claimed in faith to know. What kind of reality was being referred to when they spoke of the "life-giving Spirit," and that they specifically identified as the "Spirit of life in Christ Jesus"? We must therefore explore the nature of the philosophical presuppositions, both epistemological and ontological, which appear necessarily to have been assumed in the making of these faith claims.

---

1. The "narrative" nature of the understanding of πίστις (faith/trust) is today much discussed by New Testament scholars, who point out that "faith *in* Christ" which is logically grounded in the "faithfulness *of* Christ" often appears in narrative stories illustrating the relationship of God and Christ, and of God, Christ, and humanity. See Morgan, "Narratives of Πίστις in Paul and Deutero-Paul," and the important work of Hays on the narrative structure of Galatians 3:1–4:11 in *The Faith of Jesus Christ*.

At this point we owe an enormous debt to the Danish New Testament scholar, Troels Engberg-Pedersen.² Instead of interpreting Paul by placing him in the confined context of Second Temple Judaism's basic theological preoccupations in the manner of so many twentieth-century New Testament scholars, and therefore attempting to understand him almost exclusively from the perspective of a characteristically Jewish apocalyptic mode of eschatological belief, Engberg-Pederson rightly points to the importance for understanding Paul of the philosophical content of the contemporary intellectual culture of the wider Hellenistic world in which Paul necessarily participated. He points out that in Paul's communications to the faith communities around the Mediterranean, he was speaking into a world informed by a set of pre-existing epistemological and cosmological ideas that were clearly Stoic in character and thus were of Greek origin rather than Jewish.

This is now well-mapped territory. Over the last generation, in the world of New Testament studies a very self-conscious attempt has been made to transcend the so-called "Judaism/Hellenism" divide that so dominated (and distorted) the work of the immediately preceding generations of New Testament scholarship.³ Troels Engberg-Pedersen has in fact almost single-handedly marshaled a diverse group of scholars to explore the philosophical underpinnings of Paul's writings,⁴ and has himself argued quite specifically and impressively that the language and patterns of ethical argument of Paul betray the clear influence of the contemporary Stoicism of the age. Moreover, Engberg-Pedersen has very enthusiastically promoted the view that Stoic influences explain Paul's understanding specifically of the experience of the Spirit. Though Paul identified the Spirit as "the life-giving Spirit" of the Raised Christ,⁵ or as "the Spirit of God's Son,"⁶ what it actually *was* that was so identified, and *how* it was experienced, is to be understood therefore in terms that are essentially Stoic. At this point Troels Engberg-Pedersen's groundbreaking work, *Cosmology and Self in the Apostle Paul*

---

2. Engberg-Pedersen is now Emeritus Professor of New Testament in the Faculty of Theology at the University of Copenhagen. For a generally unsympathetic and critical assessment of Engberg-Pedersen's method of approach to the interpretation of Paul see Wright, *Paul and the Faithfulness of God*, 1386–1407.

3. Specifically, the twentieth-century movement usually referred to as the "Biblical Theology Movement," which sought to interpret the New Testament documents "from within," by focusing upon an alleged uniquely "Jewish" understanding of things, and to distance itself from the influence of "Greek" concepts and philosophical categories. Contrary to Wright (*Paul and the Faithfulness of God*, 1404), this was not a phenomenon to be confined to the nineteenth-century, for it survived well into the twentieth-century and has continued to influence even Wright's own work.

4. See the rich spectrum of work in recently published collections of essays edited by Engberg-Pedersen: *Paul in His Hellenistic Context* (1994), *Paul Beyond the Judaism/Hellenism Divide* (2001), and *From Stoicism to Platonism* (2017); and Engberg-Pedersen's own monographs, *Paul and the Stoics* (2000), *Cosmology and Self in the Apostle Paul* (2010), and *John and Philosophy*, (2017).

5. 1 Cor 15:45.

6. Gal 4:6.

(2010), is of enormous importance especially for its exploration of the ontological understanding of the Spirit.[7] As we shall see, Paul's use of "participative" language to communicate something of the quality of the experience of the Spirit "in Christ," or of living as "members of the Body of Christ" consequent to his resurrection faith, is significantly illuminated when interpreted in the light of the philosophical categories that appear to have been presupposed, even though Engberg-Pedersen himself expresses doubt as to whether Paul's talk of "participation in Christ" is a "real option" for us in the twenty-first-century. Scholars often speak of Paul's idea, he says, "as if it made immediate sense and indeed was more or less readily acceptable to us. But it is not."[8] What may constitute a "real option" for us may be a matter of some debate that each of us must pursue, but first we must explore what certainly seems to have been a very real option for Paul by pursuing the Stoic underpinning of his thought.

One of the most significant features of the cosmological background that was characteristic of Stoicism is a form of monism in which the divine and the material universe are understood as different aspects of a unified world-view. Against this background, Engberg-Pedersen argues that Paul's concept of the Spirit may be understood in association with the Stoic belief that an all-pervading intelligible *pneuma* (spirit), or "warm-breath," pervaded the entire universe. This was an indivisible combination of warmth emanating from a divine celestial fire, and air, in which the whole created order participated.

After speaking uncompromisingly of the Spirit that is perceived through faith as an objectively concrete reality, Engberg-Pedersen is, however, adventurously prepared to take things a step further. He speaks of the Pauline concept of the Spirit, not just in realistic terms as a "concrete" reality that may be objectively encountered, but as "a material and physical reality."[9] Thus, while the concept of "Spirit" is usually thought to connote a non-material reality, indeed, as the polar opposite of objects of the physical universe, Troels Engberg-Pedersen, in the cause of an uncompromising theological realism and in the light of the prevailing Stoic monism, argues that in Paul's understanding it was in ontological terms of a piece with the material and physical reality of the created order. This ontological understanding of the Spirit in Paul in turn informs a set of congruent epistemological considerations about the way in which, in Paul's understanding, the experience of the Spirit was perceived and intellectually processed. Thus, it is contended that it is congruent with Paul's view of the objective material realism of the Spirit for him to speak naturally of the Spirit

---

7. See also Engberg-Pedersen, *Paul and the Stoics*, 157–61, 342–43; and *John and Philosophy*, chapter 7 and passing references.

8. Engberg-Pedersen, *Paul and the Stoics*, 27.

9. *The Material Spirit* is in fact the fundamental theme of *Cosmology and Self in the Apostle Paul*.

as something "poured" into human hearts,[10] or that "dwells" among human people. The use of these verbs are said to confirm that the Spirit is literally a "physical and material" reality for Paul.

These propositions about the alleged Stoic underpinning of Paul's understanding of the nature of the Spirit, and of the way in which it was experienced and appropriated, clearly raise some challenging issues that we shall need to scrutinize very carefully. The first thing to be said is that, as important as the influence of the Stoicism of the popular intellectual environment of his day may be to the understanding of Paul, I incline to the view that, notwithstanding the language and patterns of *ethical* argument that appear to have been acquired from contemporary Stoicism, Paul's inherited Jewish monotheism was in fact more amenable to the accommodation of another intellectual strand of the philosophical environment of the time. For, *cosmologically* speaking, this was in fact a time of philosophical transition in which inherited Stoic ideas were being blended with a resurgent interest in ideas that originated from Plato. At least from Antiochus of Ascalon and Eudorus of Alexandria in the century immediately before Paul, Platonic and Stoic ideas had been self-consciously blended into a synthetic amalgam. By the first half of the first-century AD, Paul's contemporary, Philo, in the neighboring Jewish community in Alexandria, was actively promoting the philosophical side of Judaism in a way that clearly demonstrates the growing influence of Plato. Indeed, in many respects Philo is the paradigm example of the imminent ascendancy of Plato over Stoicism.[11]

It has, of course, to be admitted that, notwithstanding the monumentally impressive achievement of Philo in promoting this renewed interest in Plato early in the first-century, it was not really until well into the second-century AD that the philosophy of Plato had once again come into vogue in a way that made it abundantly clear that Stoicism had had its day. The period, roughly speaking, from 100 BC to AD 200 has come to be known as the period of Middle Platonism, precisely because the uniquely identifiable and growing interest in Plato was putting Stoicism into eclipse. However, even by the first half of the first-century AD, the increasing popularity of this burgeoning development was already ensuring that Platonic ideas were taken into account, even among those whose thought was still in many ways informed by Stoicism. St. Paul cannot be insulated from these developments. As we shall see, the terminology used by Paul himself moved between both the received Stoic and burgeoning Platonic styles of thought in a way that well illustrates exactly

---

10. As in Gal 4:6 and Rom 5:5.

11. Philo was born sometime between 20 and 15 BC. It is known that he went on an embassy to Rome in AD 39. His brother Alexander was, according to Josephus (*Jewish Antiquities* 20.100), the wealthiest man in Alexandria. It is a measure of the commerce that connected Alexandria with first-century Palestine that Herod Agrippa once borrowed 200,000 drachmas from him. Meanwhile, Alexander's son, Tiberius Julius Alexander, Philo's nephew, became procurator of Judaea in AD 46. These are but practical tokens of the inevitable intellectual sharing of worldview and philosophical presupposition characteristic of the era of Middle Platonism.

what was then going on quite commonly across the ancient world, which necessarily included the Jewish world at the time. As a consequence, while Stoic language and patterns of argument permeate Paul's ethical discourse, some other Pauline passages resonate very clearly with Platonic modes of thought.[12] This is particularly so in relation to issues of epistemology and ontology.

Though, in this fluid and transitional environment, there was enormous variation of thought from thinker to thinker, the general result at the time was a somewhat eclectic amalgam of loosely related Stoic and Platonic ideas. It is important to say that this was not, however, a chaotic eclecticism, but a more considered attempt to incorporate some congenial Platonic ideas, as they were received in late Platonism, into a basic Stoic matrix of thought that was considered amenable to them and vice versa. Those who might have actually thought of themselves as Platonists were able to accommodate views that were of Stoic origin. On the other hand, those whom we usually think of as Stoics often adopted ideas that had their origin in the mind of Plato. In view of this, I think that, philosophically speaking, the intellectual world of which Paul was part may have been much more "mixed" than Troels Engberg-Pedersen is inclined to allow, given the Stoic "default setting" that he tends to privilege over the re-emerging influence of Plato. In this case, we are on reasonably safe ground in concluding that the already formulated general mind-set of those to whom Paul communicated was comprised of residual Stoic ideas, but spiked with an additional input from the resurgent interest in the Platonism of the time.

Very importantly, by contrast with Stoicism's monistic cosmology, a Platonic-type distinction of a dualistic kind between the material particulars of space and time, and an orientation towards the changeless heavenly world of ideal forms, was certainly readily available in the intellectual atmosphere of the first-century. In view of this, a Platonic-type ontological dualism, within the mix of Stoic and Platonic epistemological and cosmological influences, begs to be acknowledged in the contemporary world of Middle Platonism. And this may be just as important for an understanding of Paul, and the thinking of primitive Christianity generally, as the Stoic monism favored by Engberg-Pedersen.

It is certainly true that, if prevailing philosophical categories were to be married with the apocalyptic beliefs characteristic of Second Temple Judaism, Stoicism was not going to be left out of the picture. Stoicism also worked with a specific set of images of a final eschatological conflagration that was congruent with the Stoic association of divinity with fire.[13] This may certainly explain Paul's sudden and unexpected use of the image

---

12. For example, very notably, 2 Cor 4 and 5.

13. For Engberg-Pedersen's appropriation of the Stoic doctrine of *ekpyrosis*, see *Paul and Stoicism*, 96; and Engberg-Pedersen, *Cosmology and Self in the Apostle Paul*, 35.

of fire in 1 Cor 3:12–15. Even so, a question has to be asked as to whether the dualism of a Platonic "other-worldly" orientation may have provided an even more amenable framework for the accommodation of Second Temple apocalyptic imagery than would have been allowed by the monistic framework of Stoicism. This is particularly the case with respect to notions of the ultimate revelation *in* historical time of an eternal and transcendental state of affairs, along with the earthly manifestation of timeless ideals of justice and peace in the ultimate visitation of God. Along with the divine eschatological judgment of God, primitive Christianity could also quite easily incorporate the appearance of the vindicated and glorified Christ *from heaven* into this framework. In other words, if a resurgent interest in Platonism could be embraced without necessarily obliterating remnants of the residual Stoicism of Paul's Hellenistic inheritance, it is also true that, from the very start, primitive Christianity was open to the influence of an orientation towards a transcendent or "other-worldly" cosmological mind-set of a generally dualistic or "platonic" kind as well. This could with relative ease be married both with an inherited Jewish monotheism and with ideas of a final eschatological revealing of the justice and the ultimate victory of the good purposes of God.

This means that that the growing influence of Plato, in the amalgam of ideas of the intellectual culture of which Paul was heir, has directly challenging implications with regard to the contention that Paul worked with defining categories of thought that were purely of Stoic origin and character. Indeed, the Middle Platonic synthesis of the experiential and the transcendent, the world of sense experience and the ideal world, may be quite essential to an understanding of Paul and the primitive resurrection faith and hope of early Christianity.

Among other things, an understanding of the epistemological and ontological presuppositions of this world of Middle Platonism may also be of help in resolving the long-standing division of theological opinion about the meaning of Paul's use of the phrase "in Christ," his use of the image of "the Body of Christ," and his use of "participative" language generally.[14] The theologically intuitive reader may already perceive that a Platonic dualistic cosmology may be reflected in the apparent dual reference of this characteristic Pauline language, which has to do simultaneously both with an experienced reality of this world (the visible fellowship of the baptized being "in Christ" and referred to as "the Body of Christ" as particulars of space and time) and, at the same time, with the other-worldly and eternally transcendent reality of the exalted Raised Christ himself.

However, these issues must wait to be more fully discussed when we return to consider the influence specifically of Platonism on Paul in chapter 12. For the present, it is important to focus more narrowly on Engberg-Pedersen's view of the Spirit, understood from an exclusively Stoic perspective as a "material and physical" reality. Clearly, this conclusion is reached only by assigning preferential significance to the epistemological

---

14. This apparent dual reference of Paul's "in Christ" and "Body of Christ" language was noted in chapter 1 above.

and ontological norms of a thorough-going Stoicism; if the emergent Platonism of the time is taken into account the end result may be significantly different.

At the outset we can agree that Engberg-Pedersen has certainly been able to make a very impressive case to demonstrate Paul's reliance on his Stoic intellectual inheritance. This is particularly apparent, for example, in Paul's use of characteristically Stoic language and patterns of ethical argument in the prescriptive or *parenetic* sections of his epistles. Though Paul himself is unquestionably to be understood as a Christian rather than as a Stoic, passages of his ethical writing regularly exhibit a clearly Stoic influence. Engberg-Pedersen exhaustively illustrates this in *parenetic* passages found right across the spectrum of the major Pauline epistles.[15] The epistles are also often punctuated with terms that are typically Stoic in origin, though seamlessly integrated into Paul's uncompromisingly Christian expression of faith and eschatological hope.

A fundamental difference between Paul's Christian commitment and Stoicism resides in the fact that whereas in Stoicism the ethical appeal is made to reason in determining the norms for living life well, Paul substitutes the attachment in faith to Christ. Likewise, for the Stoic, reason was the means of escape from the uncertain and threateningly disordered and challenging human predicament in the ancient world; for Paul, Christ was the agent of victory over the world's evil. He therefore viewed the trusting relation of faith in Christ as determinative of the moral precepts appropriate for the living of life well. It was Paul's view that a set of behavioral norms were to be discerned by Christian believers, almost as though these were self-evident when judged in accordance with their appropriateness or otherwise to a faith-relation to Christ that was secured through baptism and the concrete experience of his living Spirit. The resulting prescriptive norms were then to be steadfastly adhered to until his return as Judge at the Eschaton. In this way, the person of the Raised Christ replaces the Stoic appeal to reason in the discernment of behavioral norms that were then placed in the context of an essentially Jewish style of eschatological hope focused on Christ's future return.

Likewise, despite the general Stoic concern with the individual at the expense of a communitarian focus, the Stoic ideal of the discernment by reason of ethical principles of good citizenship among groups of people living together in a shared form of political and social life provides a pre-existing counterpart of Paul's unequivocal emphasis on living together in the community of faith. As he says in Philippians, "our citizenship is

---

15. Particularly in *Galatians*, *Philippians*, and *Romans*. See Engberg-Pedersen's detailed and pains-taking analysis of Paul's method of argument in these epistles in *Paul and the Stoics*. More recently, George van Kooten has also very confidently argued in similar vein for the parallels between Stoic categories and Paul's ethical discourse. See "Paul's Stoic Onto-Theology," in *Saint Paul and Philosophy*, ed., van der Heiden, et al.; especially, for example, 153–59 for the discussion of the Stoic concept of ἀδιάφορα and Paul's argumentation in 1 Cor 7.

in heaven."[16] Though once again Paul marries this with his Jewish eschatological belief, a Stoic resonance is clear. He goes on: "and from it (heaven) we await a Savior, the Lord Jesus Christ, who will transform our lowly body to be like his glorious body, by the power that enables him even to subject all things to himself."[17]

Despite these clear resonances with Stoicism in Paul's ethical passages, for present purposes it is the possible impact on Paul of Stoic *cosmological* ideas that is of more immediate interest. These are expressed, not so much in Paul's *prescriptive* ethical passages, as in those *descriptive* passages in which he reminds his addressees of the new order of being into which they had entered together by trusting faith in Christ. Even if Stoic categories and patterns of argument are reflected in Paul's treatment of ethical issues, we cannot assume that a presupposed Stoic monistic cosmology was also in play, specifically in relation to his understanding of the ontological nature of the divine Spirit. The very "mixed" nature of the thought-world of Middle Platonism means that other options of a less determinative Stoic kind have also to be considered. This is obviously of enormous significance in assessing Engberg-Pedersen's contention that the Pauline Spirit must be understood as being of a piece with, rather than other than, "material and physical" reality.

The Stoics analyzed the cosmos in terms of the four traditional elements of earth, water, fire, and air. A primordial fire in the heights of the universe, known from the observation of the Sun and other stars, was accorded an exalted divine status. By contrast with the destructive energy we often associate with fire, this was fire viewed more benignly, for it was understood to be favorable to life, or life-giving, as well also of being the source of the readily discernable intelligible order of the universe. It thus became a kind of "designing fire,"[18] or even "thinking fire"[19] that explained the ordering of material things and their conceptual differentiation. From this source, heat could be understood to penetrate the cool air so as to produce the kind of all-pervading and life-giving "warm breath" or *pneuma*, which was understood to fill the entire universe.[20] In the Stoic mind, the two constituents of fire and air are thus thoroughly blended in the elemental "warm breath" that permeates everything without interruption, and thus makes the universe as a whole a single coherent entity. For the monistic-minded Stoic, this quasi-divine all-pervading reality of "warm

---

16. Phil 3:20. Significantly, employing the characteristic Stoic term *politeuma*.
17. Phil 3:20–21.
18. *Stoicorum Veterum Fragmenta*, 2. 774.
19. As described by Plotinus, *Stoicorum Veterum Fragmenta*, 2. 443.
20. See Long and Sedley, *The Hellenistic Philosophers*, 1:289, for a discussion of the crucial importance to Stoicism of the concept of *pneuma*.

breath" or *pneuma* not only filled all things; it was what quite literally held the entire universe together and gave it life.

This "warm breath" even permeated the earth's rocks and stones as the principle of their internal coherence. All things therefore exist through its sustaining powers. But higher up the order of being from rocks and stones, sentient animal life could be differentiated from inanimate things because of an increased intensity of the presence of "warm breath" or *pneuma*, which brought with it a correspondingly increased degree of "intelligence." Because this life giving "warm breath" was also the vehicle of divine intelligence, it was therefore understood to impart a kind of intelligence to sentient animals, and supremely to the rational souls of humans. By the same token, human souls could be understood to participate in an attenuated kind of way in it as the World Soul, the intelligible all-pervading animating force of the universe.

This in turn informed a specifically Stoic permutation on the idea of the immortality of the soul. Given the knowledge that hot air rises, at death the "warm breath" of the *pneuma*/soul was understood to depart from the human body, rising in the manner of a hot air balloon to the heavens, so as to return back to the fire from which it originally drew its life, thus leaving dead bodies cold and lifeless.

From the perspective of Paul's inherited Jewish belief in the resurrection of the body, as distinct from the immortality of the soul, the impact of this Stoic idea of "warm breath" or *pneuma* is no less significant. Indeed, it is of enormous importance as the active divine agent of the transformation of the body itself into what Paul called in 1 Cor 15 a "*pneumatic* body." The raised body was here understood by Paul as a kind of transformed "heavenly body," by contrast with earthly bodies; the active agent of the transformation of earthly bodies into pneumatic bodies being, of course, an intensified infusion of *pneuma*. Certainly, what I have been speaking of as "warm breath," was an entirely unremarkable and very frequently used concept of the ordinary day-to-day Stoic world-view. It is just as unremarkable that Paul naturally utilized this concept that was part and parcel of this intellectual atmosphere in his earnest attempts to communicate to his audience, endowing it with the uniquely identifiable character of Christ.[21]

But let us not get ahead of ourselves. We must spend a little more time in coming to terms with the ontology of the Stoic conception of the "*pneuma*/warm breath" itself, which was so essential a part of the cosmology of Paul's day. It is important to note that in this monistic Stoic cosmology the "warm breath" as an indivisible fusion

---

21. As Wright pertinently observes, ". . . Paul himself, at various points in his writings, may well have done quite deliberately what he says in 1 Cor 10, that is, pick up ideas from outside the Jewish world and make them serve the gospel." *Paul and the Faithfulness of God*, 1404. However, it is also possible that this was (much less deliberately) an almost unconscious accommodation to the language and conceptual world of his time.

of heat and air is understood as a material or physical reality. It cannot have been otherwise. Insofar as it was accorded a kind of intelligible divine status the Stoic religious perspective thus approximated to a kind of all-pervading animism or, perhaps better, a panentheism in which any clear ontological distinction between divine and material things was blurred.

Now, "warm breath," as a translation of what the Greek speaking audience of St. Paul referred to as *pneuma*, in our contemporary New Testament translations from Greek into English, becomes, of course, "Spirit." It is not too difficult to appreciate that the meaning communicated by Paul's own inherited concept of the Spirit, or the *ruach* of God of the Jewish tradition, could quite easily coalesce with this technical term of Stoicism. In other words, when Paul, explaining the on-going significance of the Resurrection, spoke of the Raised Christ "becoming a life giving Spirit,"[22] or "the Spirit of life,"[23] or when he said that "the Lord is the Spirit,"[24] he was trading in the well-known linguistic currency of that ancient Stoic world of which he was part. He might well have said that the Raised Christ had become or was "a life-giving presence," "a life-giving power," or even "a life-giving love," for any of these expressions might well have been called into service for what he had to communicate. In speaking instead of "a life-giving *pneuma*," he was taking a term of the ordinary language of the Stoic world that already carried a freight of quasi-divine significance so as to put it to use to describe his own Christian experience. It is, of course, not insignificant that Paul spoke of Christ's Resurrection as having been achieved through the agency of "the Spirit of holiness,"[25] and that after he was exalted to heaven the gift that was identified as his distinctive Spirit was then distributed to those who put their trust in him. In other words, just as in ethical argument Paul replaced "reason" with a personal attachment in faith to the Raised Jesus Christ as the principal point of reference for discerning appropriate ethical norms for the living of life well, so his descriptive understanding of the new order of faith appealed to its infusion with the presence of the Raised Christ as *pneuma*. The all-pervading *pneuma* of Stoic cosmology, with its capacity for the differentiation of higher orders of being from lower, animals from rocks, and humans from animals, by distributing its presence with either decreased or increased intensity,

---

22. 1 Cor 15:45.

23. Rom 8:2.

24. 2 Cor 3:17. We may in passing note Ingo Hermann's elucidation of this verse as the key to Paul's theology regarding the relation of *Kyrios* and *pneuma* (Hermann, *Kyrios und Pneuma*, 17-58), and James Dunn's subsequent comments on this in "2 Corinthians III.17" and in *Jesus and the Spirit*, 318–26. It is Hermann's view that *pneuma* is a functionary concept (*Funktionsbegriff*) which describes the means by which Christ is present and at work in the church. To raise questions prematurely about the personal identity of the Spirit is something that would hardly have occurred to Paul. In Paul's understanding of things *pneuma* is a reality that is perceived within the experience of faith; Christ is present through the *pneuma* and as *pneuma*.: "Dieses Pneuma ist der Kyrios Christus selbst" (Hermann, *Kyrios und Pneuma*, 57. For some suggestions about the scriptural origins of trinitarian thought concerning the personal identity of the Spirit, see chapter 10, p. 240–41, footnote 50, of this book.

25. Rom 1:4.

was understood by something more than just analogy now to be the medium of the presence of the Christ of God. As a consequence of the Resurrection, the *pneuma* of Christ was at work transforming fleshly humanity into a new order of moral and spiritual value, with ontological as well as ethical implications for the ultimate transformation of all things at the Eschaton. He was thus able to communicate effectively to the world beyond the borders of cultural Judaism, which already worked with a pre-understanding of *pneuma*, but was able to transform it by endowing it with a new freight of meaning that expressed the personal identity of Jesus Christ whom he believed God had by divine power raised from the dead.

This pneumatic power of God which Paul understood to have reanimated and transformed the body of the dead Jesus, so that "the Second Adam became a life-giving *pneuma*," and made him both Lord and Christ, was thus said not only to have raised Jesus from the dead. In addition, the Raised Christ's *pneuma* could patently be seen to be already at work among those whose lives were being transformed by being aligned with him through faith. It was concretely experienced through baptism as a transforming and re-animating moral force in their lives. At Paul's hands, this technical term of Stoicism was in this way put to use to explain the Raised Christ's transformative presence, already concretely experienced and known among believers through faith, but which also assured them in hope that at the Eschaton the same Spirit would be operative to raise their bodies to be like his. Stoic resonances may be heard, for example, when he says in Romans:

> If the Spirit of him that raised up Jesus from the dead dwells in you, he that raised up Christ Jesus from the dead shall give life also to your mortal bodies through his Spirit that dwells in you.[26]

When Paul in this way drew attention to the Spirit of Christ which, clearly, could be perceived among the community of the baptized as the continuing religious Object of their new-found commitment of trusting faith and the ground of eschatological hope, his language was therefore neither unfamiliar nor strangely incomprehensible. Rather, it could be very readily appropriated by his hearers and understood by them because they had already been prepared for it, as it were, by sharing the conceptual inheritance of Stoic cosmology in which the concept of *pneuma* already held such a central place.[27]

---

26. Rom 8:11.

27. Needless to say, I am of the view that Wright's attempt to confine the impact of the Spirit to ethical and behavioral outcomes, at the expense of the ontological transformation of "spiritual bodies" as well, is mistaken. See his articulation of this view in *RSG*, 347–56. Though Wright insists that a "spiritual body" is simply a "spirit directed" body and that "spiritual" is a purely ethical term, he undermines his own argument by equally insisting that the impact of the Spirit on physical bodies is to make them (ontologically, not ethically) "incorruptible."

Also, when Paul spoke of the fellowship (*koinonia*) of the Spirit,[28] which is concretely known when the local church is constituted by the Spirit as a single inclusive community of Jews and Gentiles without distinction—a community endowed with the distinctive internal coherence and unity of *pneuma* as the defining inner texture of its life—he was likewise employing language which was readily comprehensible to his hearers. After all, they already understood the role of *pneuma*, or "warm breath," as a quasi-divine life-enabling force which, as the unitive element of the entire cosmos, gives coherence to all things. Paul's language thus resonated unmistakably with the very familiar concept of *pneuma* already in day-to-day use in the pre-existing Stoic intellectual culture, though it was now injected with a vibrant and specifically Christian content of meaning among the community of the baptized. In the deutero-Pauline epistles the Raised and glorified Christ, like God, is likewise understood to enjoy a cosmic presence that would have been readily comprehensible to a Stoic mentality insofar as he is understood to "fill all things."[29]

Troels Engberg-Pedersen also very helpfully points out that, insofar as the Stoic *pneuma* was already understood as a kind of intelligible vector connecting the human world with the heavenly, it naturally provided the basic "hardware" for the possibility of interpersonal divine/human communication. The all-pervading *pneuma* was for the Stoics the vehicle of divine intelligence. In the light of this, Paul's talk in Rom 8:26–7 of the Spirit interceding on our behalf when we do not know how to pray, takes on a specific coloring or content of meaning. Likewise, Ephesians has Paul request for prayer at all times to be offered "in the Spirit." Interestingly, once the Raised Christ's presence is understood on analogy (and perhaps more than analogy) with the Stoic way of conceiving *pneuma*, as a concretely experienced all-pervading intelligible Spirit which is perceived through faith, it seems that prayer becomes a natural accompaniment of the relationship that is thereby established with God in Christ. It seems that through the presence of the divine intelligible *pneuma*, and participation in it through baptism, prayer to God or *before* God becomes a perfectly natural activity.[30] Paul also picks up a connection between the *pneuma* that is his possession in the service of the Gospel and prayer in Rom 1:8–9.

Likewise, in the presence of the concretely experienced Spirit, Paul's prayers of thanksgiving for the faith of the Romans are also characterized as prayers to God, quite literally *through* Jesus Christ.[31] He might well have said that prayers to God were made literally "through the *pneuma* of Jesus Christ." Similarly, in 2 Cor 2:10, Paul urges that love and forgiveness be extended to a fallen Corinthian (of whom Paul had heard) *before* or in the "face" of Christ, or "in the presence of Christ." In other words, the extending of love and forgiveness, and the offering of prayers of thanksgiving, happen "in the pres-

---

28. As for example, in 2 Cor 13:14.
29. Eph 4:10.
30. 1 Thess 1:3 and 3:9.
31. Rom 1:8.

ence of Christ" or "in the Spirit" in an apparently immediate and literal sense of the word "in." Indeed, we can here discern a Stoic sense of the all-pervading presence of *pneuma* as "warm breath" informing Paul's use of the phrase "*in* Christ" or "*in* the Spirit" as something "*in which*" the baptized (quite literally) participated.[32]

Now, given the remarkable similarities that Engberg-Pedersen has drawn to our attention between this technical Stoic terminology and Paul's talk of the *pneuma*, we can understand how easy it is for him then to take the discussion a challenging step further. His contention is that Paul is to be understood to be describing the Spirit not just in terms of an epistemological realism, as an objective, concrete, and cognitively experienced reality, but, beyond this, quite explicitly also as a "material and physical" reality.[33] In other words, though Paul unequivocally identifies the *pneuma* perceived in faith as "*God's* Spirit" or "*Christ's* Spirit,"[34] Engberg-Pedersen's view is that, in the light of Stoicism's approach to *pneuma*, Paul was drawing attention not just away from something purely abstract or notionally idealistic to something concretely experienced and cognitively perceived, but, even more positively and realistically, to something as material and physical as warmth combined with air. In other words, Paul's references to the Spirit lead Engberg-Pedersen to the conclusion that, ontologically speaking, Paul actually thought of the Spirit in terms that were entirely equivalent to a Stoic understanding of things. Hence, Engberg-Pedersen's choice of the sub-title of *Cosmology and Self in the Apostle Paul*: "The Material Spirit."

Troels Engberg-Pedersen reaches this ontological conclusion as a logically associated move based upon the epistemological question of the *perception* of the Spirit. He insists that the language relating to the "pouring" out of the Spirit, and the consequent human "receiving" of the Spirit, points to a concrete experience. As a result it is said literally to "indwell" the life of the community of faith. This also then means that the Spirit must be understood as a material and physical reality. The argument is thus from the language of perception to a specific understanding of the ontological nature of the Spirit.

---

32. Engberg-Pedersen, *Cosmology and Self*, 1: "being in Christ" may be "understood in purely physical terms."

33. Engberg-Pedersen, *Cosmology and Self*, 1, where at the very outset he argues that Paul's language is "non-metaphorical and concretely physical," or "concretely physical," or even "purely physical." This contention is repeated often. For example, on page 53 there is a reference to "The (physical) pneuma they have received" (even citing Rom 8:14, where the reference is to the "Spirit of God"). On page 61, *pneuma* is said to be "a physical entity," and on page 65, ". . . this pneumatic power was a physical reality."

34. *Rom* 8 is a particularly poignant example where Paul uses these apparently inter-changeable terms almost as though it were a matter of indifference for, whatever the precise connotations of the terminology, the same reality is denoted by it.

It has to be said that some confusion is introduced into Engberg-Pedersen's discussion when he goes on to say that the seeing of the allegedly physical and material reality of the Spirit, is a "seeing with the eyes closed." If the Spirit is described, ontologically speaking, as a material and physical reality, it might be anticipated that its presence and its operation in the lives of believers would be perceived by natural sight and hearing, employing corporeal eyes and ears, if not also even by the sense of touch or feel, rather than through an apparently religious kind of seeing "with the eyes closed." I must confess that I cannot fathom this somewhat confused juxtaposition of talk of the material and physical nature of the Spirit and its perception apparently only by some kind of inner seeing.

Certainly, on repeated occasions Engberg-Pedersen stresses the material and physical nature of the Spirit as Paul allegedly conceives it.[35] "Paul's world-view—and especially his understanding of *pneuma*—was anything but 'idealistic,'" he says. "Instead, it was materialistic, concrete and tangible."[36] As a consequence, also under the influence of Stoic ways of thinking, Paul is therefore said by Engberg-Pedersen to have thought of the "pouring out" of the material Spirit by God in quite literal terms. Because Paul thought of the Spirit in a material and physical way, it was "poured out" in the same way milk is "poured" from a jug into a mug. In this way the Spirit is literally "distributed" or "supplied" by God, and "received" by believers so that it quite literally "dwells" in them.

At this point we must ask, however, if this is not just a bridge too far? We rightly appreciate Troels Engberg-Pedersen's concern to stress that Paul's understanding of the Spirit involves speaking of it in objective and realistic terms as a "concrete" reality of actual cognitive experience, rather than as an "idealistic" or imagined abstraction of thought. He is surely correct in insisting that for Paul the Spirit is something objectively known in faith *by acquaintance* and not just imagined, or known only *by verbal description*.[37] This can readily be acknowledged to be absolutely crucial for an understanding of Paul's thought about the Resurrection of Christ and the manner of the appropriation of his continuing presence through faith. We can therefore unreservedly agree that the religious Object that is received and appropriated through trusting faith is a *concrete* reality with which believers had to do and, indeed, still have to do to this day.

That said, there is unfortunately in Engberg-Pedersen's discussion of the Stoic influence in Paul's understanding of *pneuma* a tendency to slide semantically between the concepts of "concrete," on one hand, and "material" and "physical," on the other, as

---

35. Engberg-Pedersen, *Cosmology and Self*, 42: ". . . Paul conceived of the pneuma as a physical entity"; also 47: ". . . the pneuma must have been conceived all through by Paul as a physical entity."

36. Engberg-Pedersen, *Cosmology and Self*, 19.

37. Indeed, I am gratified that this confirms the account of the Spirit and its importance in the structure of faith as a commitment of trust based on a knowing by acquaintance in Carnley, *Structure of Resurrection Belief*, 259–65, and outlined again in *Resurrection in Retrospect*, chapter 7.

though these terms are not only more or less synonymous, but are all to be interpreted literally. For him all three are equally appropriate adjectives for use in descriptions of the Spirit of Christ understood as the religious Object of resurrection faith, and all three are to be understood in straightforward, matter-of-fact terms. None of them is to be understood metaphorically.[38]

However, while the realism of Paul's religious empiricism implies that the Spirit of God or of Christ that is known in faith is objective to the believer, and is therefore to be conceived as a "concretely" experienced reality rather than something entirely abstract and idealistically imagined, we are not necessarily obliged to make the next logical move, so as to conclude that a concretely objective reality of religious cognition of this kind must necessarily therefore be understood to be "material" and "physical."

Also, when we use the word "concrete" to draw a contrast with something idealistic or entirely abstract, we are obviously not using the term in a literal sense, as when the word "concrete" is used of a material substance comprised of cement powder and gravel, mixed with water and allowed to set. In other words, the term "concrete," when used in a religious context in relation to an object of religious cognition, is not necessarily synonymous with "material" and "physical." In this case, it is possible to speak of something as "concrete" rather than "abstract," and as something external to and objective to the perceiver that is cognitively perceived, but then to deny that it must necessarily therefore be "material" or "physical." These terms are not simply synonymous. In other words, my point is that we cannot assume that the use of verbs, like "pouring," and "receiving," and "dwelling," which might suggest that the perception of them involves the operation of some of the five physical senses necessarily entails that what is perceived must therefore itself be purely physical and material.

Let us pursue another example. We might say that the perception in faith of the presence of the Spirit of God or of Christ is so concrete as to be "palpable." The adjective "palpable" in its literal use refers to something that may be touched or felt, as in the statement "you could feel the palpable bump on the bridge of his nose." However, the word "palpable" when used of the Spirit of God is not necessarily used in this material and physical way. After all, the word "palpable" is also regularly and correctly used of something far from substantial, or physical and material, or touchable. Even outside a specifically theological or religious context, the word "palpable" may be used, for example, to describe a feeling, such as in the statement: "We experienced a palpable sense of loss." Or it may be used to describe the atmosphere in a room, as in the statement: "The feeling of hostility in the room was palpable." Though we may use the word "palpable" to describe a feeling, or the concretely perceived atmosphere in a room in this way, the reference is clearly not to a material or physical reality. Even though it obviously may be mediated or expressed through the reality of physical and material human bodies, it is not itself physical or material. When we say that something of this kind is "palpable," we are speaking of a feeling or atmosphere so intense as to *seem*

---

38. See Engberg-Pedersen, *Cosmology and Self*, chap. 1.

almost as though it were tangible, though in fact it is not. More precisely, we mean that the feeling or atmosphere is perceptible, detectable, and perhaps very noticeable, and thus real, but not that it is itself therefore actually touchable, substantial, or material and physical. Though there is a family likeness between the literal use of the word "palpable" in reference to a bump on the nose, and its extended use in relation to a feeling or the atmosphere in a room, we should not assume that the objects being talked about are therefore substantially or ontologically identical.

These verbal distinctions help us to appreciate that, though the Stoics certainly accepted the physical materiality of *pneuma* as a thorough blending of warmth and air, we may need to consider whether Paul's use of the same word may have been a little more subtly nuanced. In other words, while Paul's talk of the *pneuma* certainly shares a great deal of the concrete and experiential qualities of the Stoic understanding of things, in the way to which Engberg-Pedersen has so helpfully drawn our attention, Paul may not have been quite so comfortable with the literal, material and physical connotations of the "warm breath" of the Stoics.

We have to remember that Paul's God is quite categorically not synonymous with the "thinking fire" of the Stoics. This should immediately alert us to the need to exercise a little caution before assuming that the *pneuma* that Paul understood *flowed from* God, or was *distributed by* God (in a way that mediated the presence of the Raised Christ), is to be thought of as being as material and physical as the "warm breath" emanating from the divine, heavenly fire of the Stoics. The *pneuma* of God, in other words, is surely to be understood in relation to the nature of the ultimate divine source with which it is in a certain sense continuous.[39]

Engberg-Pedersen's response to this potential difficulty is to say that he cannot find anything in Paul that "connects God directly with *pneuma*."[40] This is very puzzling. He says that he regards *pneuma* as "independent"—that is to say, ontologically independent of God. By this he means that the *pneuma* is ontologically different and distinct from God. If *pneuma* is understood to be material and physical, as he would have us believe, it would certainly follow that, in ontological terms, it must be in some sense independent of or distinct from a God who is by definition ontologically infinite—non-finite and immaterial. But the physical materiality of *pneuma* is what needs to be established; it cannot simply be assumed. In fact, Paul's language frequently suggests a form of dependence or even relational continuity between God and the Spirit

---

39. The idea of Spirit being the "fluid extension of God," or God insofar as God is experienced, as distinct from God as God is in God's self, who is sublimely transcendent, ineffable and ultimately unknowable.

40. Engberg-Pedersen, *Cosmology and Self*, 59 and 61.

of God.⁴¹ In 1 Cor 2:12, the Spirit is spoken of a Spirit that is *of God* or that comes *from* God. This is in fact contrasted with what is *of the world*. We might well, therefore, speak of the experience of the Spirit of God as something palpably and concretely perceived, while insisting that the Spirit of God, *unlike* finite and visible material and physical objects, but like God, is also infinite (i.e., not finite) and invisible.

In the face of this difficulty, though Paul is said to have a clear view of the ontology of the Spirit as material and physical, Engberg-Pedersen says that Paul had no developed ontology of God. "Paul," he says, "simply understood God as an acting person without engaging in any further speculation about his ontological status."⁴² At this point we need to be aware that to contend that Paul thought of God simply as "an acting person" itself begs a number of questions. Not least, we are obliged to acknowledge that the concept of "a person" was somewhat fluid and ill-defined in the ancient world, with connotations of its meaning stretching from the idea of the mask or face (*prosōpon*) and then the role signified by it in Greek tragedy, to the more political idea of a *persona* with citizenship rights, and the right to own property including slaves, of the Roman Empire. It was not until the Cappadocian Fathers of the fourth-century superseded both these understandings of the concept of a person through their discovery of the distinction between an *individual* (conceived in isolation from others) and a *person* (conceived in relation to others), that anything like our contemporary conception of "a person" began to be clarified. This Cappadocian discovery, in the course of working out the doctrine of the Trinity of three *persons in one communion*, was an enormous step forward in the history of ideas. But we dare not read it back into the thought of earlier times. Paul inherited the personal form of addressing God derived from the Septuagint, but whether Paul entertained an idea of God as "an acting person" to the exclusion of other conceptualizations of the divine being of God is hardly transparently clear.

It has to be noted that, even if Paul does not himself engage in a speculative discussion of the ontological nature of God in his preserved epistles, we can be very clear that Paul nevertheless inherited a fundamental understanding of the divine being of God. Recent studies of Jewish monotheism in the first-century indicate that, even when Jews adopted the religious and philosophical vocabulary of Greek literature, Greek-speaking Jews nevertheless maintained their traditional views of God and expressions of his nature.⁴³ God was understood to be without rival, unique, possessing a divine glory that was not shared with any other. God was incomparable with any other purported deity, a universal sovereign monarch who created everything and rules over all, and thus was worthy of worship in a way that excluded all rivals. As Larry Hurtado has observed, the integrity of Jewish monotheism does not appear

---

41. As, for example, in Rom 8:9 and 1 Cor 2:11.

42. Engberg-Pedersen, *Cosmology and Self*, 61.

43. For example, Marcus, "Divine Names and Attributes," and Shutt, "The Concept of God in the Works of Flavius Josephus," 171–87.

to have been compromised in first-century Judaism,[44] and this we might note was even in a social and religious context heavily influenced by monistic Stoic pantheism or panentheism. Moreover, it seems clear enough from Paul's own words that Paul's God was the Jewish God;[45] and this God, while perhaps not being conceived in the refined *apophatic* categories being worked out at the time by Philo of Alexandria, or later by Albinus and subsequent classical Christian theism, was surely understood as something more than just "an acting person."[46] Given that Philo was in Paul's time remonstrating about the nature of God with his nephew, Tiberius Julius Alexander (who had been appointed Procurator of Judaea in AD46), we have concrete evidence of a direct relational connection between Palestinian and Alexandrian Judaism. At the time Tiberius Julius had become thoroughly Romanized,[47] "and did not remain true to the customs of his ancestors."[48] It is more than likely that he had succumbed to Stoic influences. Even if Philo's arguments with his skeptical nephew were private, it is unlikely that Philo's views of the divine nature were not at least to some degree already widely and publicly known. On the contrary, it is highly unlikely that Jewish circles of first-century Palestine could have been insulated from this important emergent tradition of philosophically informed theological thought about the nature of God and of God's ultimate transcendence of the created order. This aspect of the teaching of such a renowned scholar can hardly have been kept under wraps. It is therefore unlikely that the increasingly platonised theological views that are found in the treatises of Philo were somehow confined within the pages of his writing alone.

On the other hand, it is a mistake to focus narrowly on the individual contribution of Philo to theistic understanding as a kind of bubble phenomenon; it is probably more accurate to see him as a representative of a wider tradition of thought. Indeed, the ventilating breezes of negative theology were probably present in Jewish philosophy in Alexandria even before Philo, with its antecedents going back at least to Eudorus. It is true that, apart from normal descriptive epithets that are used of God, such as "eternal," "unchanging," and "immortal" or "imperishable," there are those concerning God's nature for which Philo is in fact the earliest known authority. He speaks of God

---

44. Hurtado, *How on Earth Did Jesus Become a God?* chapter 5.

45. Engberg-Pedersen, *Cosmology and Self*, 61: "Paul's God was just the Jewish God." Though I do not understand how Stoic pantheism may easily be accommodated to "the Jewish God." At this point, N. T. Wright's assessment of Paul's God in terms of "creational monotheism" in his own critique of Engberg-Pedersen's accommodation of Paul to Stoic pantheism seems correct. See chapter 14 of Wright's *Paul and the Faithfulness of God*.

46. Indeed, though Paul may not have worked with a precise concept of "a person," if we think of a person as distinct from an individual as one who is able to address another and expect a similar response (as in inter-personal give and take), then perhaps Paul thought of God as a person in this sense, as one known in his Word of address, to whom the appropriate response is worship and prayer. But who really knows if and exactly in what way, Paul thought of God as "a person"?

47. Philo actually dedicated a couple of works to him: On *Providence ii*, and *Whether Animals have Intelligence*.

48. According to Josephus, *Antiquities*, xx, 100.

as "unnamable," "unutterable," and "incomprehensible under any form."[49] John Dillon points out that none of these terms are applied to God before Philo by any surviving source.[50] Even so, there is no real evidence that those who later took theistic thought in an *apophatic* direction, such as Albinus in chapter 10 of *Didaskalikos*,[51] were directly influenced by Philo or, indeed, that they had even read Philo. This raises a question about whether Philo was responsible for introducing the notion of a surpassingly transcendent and "unknowable God" into Greek thought. It is John Dillon's considered view,[52] therefore, that earlier teachers, rather than a direct influence of Philo himself, stand behind the negative theology of Albinus.[53] Among these Eudorus of Alexandria, with his notion of the "highest God" who is "above Limit and Limitless," remains a possible candidate. This is why Dillon is of the view that Eudorus is not to be underestimated as a key seminal thinker in relation to the development of theism in first-century Palestine.[54] This means that, so far as the ontology of God is concerned, Philo is probably best understood as a representative rather than a seminal thinker: his theological mind-set was one that was more widely shared.

Thus, those who have in recent years worked on the exegetical traditions and theological insights that are preserved in Philo's treatises, and that appear to have also been used by Paul in his letters, point not to any awareness of Philo's actual work on Paul's part, so much as to a more diffused stock of tradition widely and commonly shared in Jewish synagogues by Paul's time.[55] Clearly, a considered approach to the ontology of a transcendent God can hardly have been unknown to the Jewish monotheists of the first-century world,[56] which means it is very unlikely indeed that a Stoic pantheistic monism could have somehow been uncritically accepted in Jewish circles.

The importance of this is that the clear evidence of the impact of Platonism in the philosophical mix of Middle Platonism by the first half of the first-century AD allows us to accept with a high degree of confidence that a Stoic and purely monistic cosmology would have been well and truly challenged at the time, and that Jewish monotheism was well supported and even bolstered by a clearly dualistic cosmology in which the distinction between God and the world, the Creator and the created order, finite and infinite, matter and Spirit, was clearly drawn. In this case, in Jewish circles it is very unlikely that a monistic cosmology could have remained unchallenged. It is therefore almost certainly a mistake to over-draw Paul's acquaintance with Stoicism to the point

---

49. See *Spec. Leg.* II, 176. Historically, at this point Platonism is clearly beginning to gain control over the received Stoicism in the culture of Middle Platonism.

50. Dillon, *The Middle Platonists*, 155.

51. Around AD 145.

52. Dillon, *The Middle Platonists*, 155.

53. Albinus was lecturing between AD 149 and 157 (the only available dates we have for him).

54. Dillon, *The Middle Platonists*, 128.

55. This material can be accessed via the sustained bibliographical work of Radice and especially of Runia, *Philo of Alexandria: An Annotated Bibliography*.

56. See the very helpful article by Sterling, "Hellenistic Philosophy and the New Testament."

of minimizing the possible importance of the impact of the resurgent Platonism that was also characteristic of the Middle Platonism of his day.[57]

We may agree that the *perception* of the Spirit was conceived by Paul in very realistic and concrete terms, which would have made what he had to say about it easily understood by those to whom he wrote who in general terms spoke the "same language." However, at the same time we may have clear reservations about automatically assigning additional Stoic ontological and cosmological views to Paul, without some clear evidential support for them from Paul's own writings. In other words, while acknowledging that Paul was obviously influenced by Stoicism, particularly in the patterns and concepts of ethical argument, we should not assume that Paul was bound to accept the uncompromising monism of Stoic cosmology. By the same token, if he certainly spoke of the Spirit as a concretely perceived, all-pervading, and life-giving reality that was in these respects somewhat like the life-giving Stoic *pneuma*, or "warm breath," we cannot assume that he also necessarily thought of it as a quasi-divine material and physical reality that was entirely of a piece with the material and physical fabric of the created universe. On the contrary, in accepting a more traditionally Jewish view of the divine as "wholly other" and independent of the created order, he would naturally have spoken of the divine Spirit likewise as a non-material reality. Indeed, we have to remember that Paul spoke of the Spirit fundamentally as a form of love.[58] The Spirit is real as love is real, but by contrast with the physical reality of a material thing, it is not itself a physical or material reality.

Furthermore, for Paul the Spirit was received as the gift of the Raised Christ of himself, and the Raised Christ himself was understood to be, not of this world, but heavenly and exalted "at the right hand of the Father." The experience of his Spirit was of such a nature as to point to this "other worldly" and invisible point of origin, rather than being understood as something naturally contained within the material universe. Insofar as this is so, Paul seems to have been using Stoic language while nevertheless working with a different kind of cosmology that presupposed a form of dualism of the kind reflected in the contrast between flesh and Spirit, as, for example, in Rom 8 where the "things of the Spirit" are contrasted as polar opposites of the things of the flesh (vv. 4–5), and where it is declared that those who "walk after the Spirit" cannot be separated from "the love of God that is in Christ Jesus, our Lord" (vv. 38–39). Furthermore, Eph 2:2, though it may not have come directly from Paul's own hand, draws a clear contrast, even a cosmological dichotomy, between "the spirit that now works in the children of disobedience" and that is identified with the suspiciously Stoic sounding prince of "the power of the air," and the transformation of those of faith "who are

57. While Engberg-Pedersen privileges the importance of Stoicism within Middle Platonism, and tends not to take sufficient account of the resurgent Platonism of the time (especially of kind represented by Philo), Gregory Sterling has noted that N. T. Wright is also in good company with many New Testament scholars who have also more generally ignored the tradition of Middle Platonism and its relevance for understanding Paul. See Sterling, "Wisdom or Foolishness?" 251.

58. As for example in Rom 5:5.

enlivened together with Christ" by grace (v. 5), and so are delivered from "the lusts and desires of the flesh" (v. 3). The implicit dualism here is wholly congruent with the fundamental thrust of the eclipse of Stoic monism by the resurgent Platonism of Hellenized Judaism in the world of Middle Platonism.

In all likelihood, had Paul been asked, he would have at least spoken of the divine reality of God as at once a mystery "beyond" all human understanding, and quite definitely as "holy" and "other" than the created order, even though *in part* concretely revealed to human perception and encountered *within* the created order. It does not escape our notice that the Spirit is called by Paul, not just the Spirit *of* Christ, or the Spirit *of* God, but very often the *Holy* Spirit, following an exceedingly hallowed Jewish theological tradition that is firmly secured in the Hebrew Scriptures.[59] In other words, it would be hard to argue that Paul did not work (at least tacitly) with an inherited ontological conception of God roughly in terms equivalent to the formula "transcendent *as well as* immanent." Certainly, by contrast with the theological proclivities of the Stoics, he inherited a theological tradition that was persistently resistant to human attempts to assimilate God to the material and physical natural order. Paul and Philo would surely have recognized one another as kindred spirits at this point. As Creator of all that is, the Jewish God is radically transcendent and "other" than the created order; and we can also be quite certain that the created order was not understood just as an emanation of the divine. Rather, the material order is called into being by God who in turn is revealed as the Creator of it. This means, specifically, that, in the face of the admitted possibility of the remnant survival of Stoic cosmology in the philosophical mix of Paul's day, we have to allow for the modifying influence of Paul's inherited Jewish view of the holiness of God as "other" and separate from the created order. This is the most likely and crucially significant factor in assessing Paul's own understanding of the nature of the divine Spirit. And even though the Stoics thought of *pneuma* as a life-creating force within a cosmos conceived in a monistic way, Paul could quite easily bring this into conformity with his Jewish monotheistic heritage which spoke of the "Spirit of God" as a life-creating energy exercised by God within the created order, as for example in Gen 2:7 where the *ruach* of God enlivens Adam and he becomes "a living soul," and in Job 33:4: "The Spirit of God has made me, and the breath of the Almighty gives me life."

---

59. For example, 1 Thess 1:5, 1:6, 4.8; Rom 5:5, 14:17, 15:13, 15:16; 1 Cor 6:19; and 2 Cor 6:6, 13:13. Old Testament references to the "Holy Spirit" are of course legion, particularly in the Psalms and the writings of the Prophets.

In the face of the resurgent interest in Plato that is so characteristic of Middle Platonism, Engberg-Pedersen has an obvious difficulty on his hands in sustaining a thorough-going Stoic interpretation of Paul's views. The string of definitional divine attributes, whose emergence we, to a degree, discern already in Eudorus (and certainly in Philo and later in Albinus), all of which are expressed in negative or *apophatic* terms,[60] may not feature as a logically tight-knit and inter-dependent group of concepts in Paul's theological discourse. Even so, it is not insignificant that the terms "invisible" and "eternal" certainly do.[61] We need to remember, also, that it was in large part the Jewish concept of God that gave rise to these *apophatic* conclusions of embryonic classical Christian theism concerning the attributes of God. The transcendent holiness of the Jewish God, so ably defended by the prophetic invective against all forms of idolatry, is a case in point. At the very least, we can say that this aspect of the fundamental Jewish insight into the nature of God, which stands at the genesis of the tradition of classical theism, was quite definitely shared by Paul.[62] This means, even if, as Engberg-Pedersen contends, Paul may not have spent a lot of time trying to fathom the ontological status of the divine, and did not expound this topic at any length at all, we can certainly nevertheless at least say that, as a consequence of his inherited concept of the Jewish God, Paul would have assumed a highly orthodox understanding of the nature of God. This is particularly the case insofar as he certainly shared the prophetic invective against all forms of idolatry that accommodates notions of divinity to material and physical forms.

Indeed, this is an emphasis which he appears to have picked up from his mentoring either by the author of the Wisdom of Solomon, or by a theological tradition that is also shared by and expressed in Wisdom. Paul stands in this theological tradition even to the point of following Wisdom's linkage of idolatry with all consequent immorality. In Rom 1, Paul is critical of all those whose lack of faith was manifest in their reluctance to honor God, despite what he seems to regard as a self-evident human capacity to see beyond the surface reality of material things so as to perceive the presence of the divine.[63] Thus, significantly using one of later classical theism's *apophatic* insights, Paul declares: God's "invisible attributes, namely, his eternal power and divine nature," may be "clearly perceived, ever since the creation of the world, in the things that have been made."[64] Unbelievers are therefore declared to be culpable: "they are without excuse."[65] Although they actually possessed the capacity to know God in this way, "they did

60. I.e., non-finite (or infinite), impassible, unmovable, changeless, a-temporal, immaterial, incomprehensible, and unknowable as God is in God's self.

61. In Rom 1:20, Paul speaks of the "invisible things of God" and of God's "eternal power" that may be clearly seen in created things.

62. Hence his references to the "Holy Spirit" and "the Spirit of holiness."

63. In a way this is a view also shared by the usual Stoic reasoning for the existence of an intelligible divine element "behind" or known "in and through" the created order.

64. Rom 1:20.

65. Rom 1:20.

not honor him as God or give thanks to him" but instead turned to idolatry. Though "something of God" could thus be perceived as this was revealed in and through the created order, Paul is careful to point out that God's nature as God is in God's self is invisible by contrast with those who fashioned substitute gods out of material and physical substances. Clearly, apart from pointing to the transcendence of God as the Creator of the material order, and distancing an understanding of the divine nature from all forms of idolatry, in ontological terms Paul's discourse goes well beyond simply thinking of God as "an acting person."

In this passage of Romans, Paul shows that he is well aware of the ontological distinction which needs to be drawn between the invisible God whose presence, notwithstanding its radical invisibility, may by a paradox be either inferentially or intuitively perceived, but whose presence is nevertheless in practice often ignored by being abandoned in favor of the idolatry of worshipping images of a material and physical kind.

It is clearly important, from the perspective of the Hellenized Jewish theism of which Paul was heir, to affirm that the infinite and invisible God, though revealed through his creative works in the natural order, is a transcendent mystery, always "beyond" all human conceptions of him. If the "peace of God" that flows from God and that is known in human experience, "surpasses all understanding," as St. Paul himself says,[66] then this principle of unknowability surely applies even more so to God as God is in God's self. God as God *is*, as distinct from "what of God is revealed" by way of accommodation to finite human minds through the works of creation, always remains an invisible and transcendent mystery.[67] Indeed, Paul's own words in reference to "what of God can be known,"[68] clearly imply a tacit awareness of "what of God *cannot* be humanly known." Paul's God remains transcendentally unknowable as God is in God's self. Paul may not have been a sophisticated philosophical theologian, but he at least indicates that he was aware of the distinction we would make today between the unknowable God as God is eternally in God's self, and God as God appears to us and is perceived by us in space and time. In 1 Cor 2, Paul draws an analogy with the mystery of a human being and the Being of God: "Who knows what is going on inside a human being, except the spirit of the human being who is inside them? Well, it is like that with God. Nobody knows what is going on inside God, except God's Spirit" (v. 11). But God has revealed to us [the things that God has prepared for them that love him] by his Spirit: "for the Spirit searches all things, yes, the deep things of God" (v. 10).

As in the later definitions of classical theism, for which we are indebted perhaps to Philo and to Eudorus before him, and certainly to Albinus, we have humbly to

---

66. Phil 4:7.

67. This, of course, eventually became the classic Patristic formulation of the contrast between God's *ousia* and God's *energeia*.

68. Rom 1:19.

acknowledge that God as God is in God's self is remote, sublimely ineffable, and ultimately incomprehensible to finite human mind. Paul stands in the same tradition of thought. As he himself says: "O the depth of the riches both of the wisdom and knowledge of God! How unsearchable are his judgments, and his ways past finding out! For who has known the mind of the Lord, or who has been his Counsellor."[69]

For all Paul's obvious reliance on the language of Stoicism in his communications with the communities around the Mediterranean with which he had to do, we must therefore also take account of his indigenous Hellenized Jewish monotheism, with its developing high sense of the transcendence of God, and its clear understanding that the divine is *not* to be accommodated to the created order of material and physical things. It follows also, that if the *peace of* God passes all understanding, so also do the *love of* God, and the *Spirit of* God, even when perceived, like peace itself, as a concretely experienced reality. This means that Engberg-Pedersen's contention that Paul thought ontologically of the Spirit in material and physical terms, at the very least, calls for further scrutiny.

When we look carefully at the logical steps taken by Engberg-Pedersen in coming to the conclusion that Paul followed the Stoics in thinking of the Spirit as a physical and material reality, it is clear that he places a good deal of store on what he thinks are some legitimate implications of Paul's language. The "concrete ontological underpinning of Paul's understanding of things," he says, is constituted by "having received the material pneuma."[70] But here in this very sentence we have an example of Engberg-Pedersen's tendency to move from his use of the term "concrete," as a way of drawing a contrast between the objective actuality of what is empirically known in faith (as against purely notional "abstract," "idealistic" or "imagined" and purely "inferred" realities), to the assumption that all concretely known realities must therefore be material (and physical). In other words, Engberg-Pedersen appears content to argue that the material nature of the *pneuma* is indicated by Paul's language itself. He says that the materiality of the Spirit is implied when Paul says, for example, that "one is 'clothed in' Christ, or that each believer is 'in' Christ, and 'one in' Christ (with other believers) *because* of having 'received' God's pneuma." Or again he says in reference to God that "'his son's pneuma' (Gal 4:6), or 'Christ's pneuma' (Rom 8:9), or indeed, Christ himself (Rom 8:10)" is a material reality that is received "in one's heart." As a consequence of the gift of the *pneuma* and its reception, it has come to "dwell" in believers. "This is all," he says, "very physical . . ."[71]

---

69. Rom 11:33–34.
70. Engberg-Pedersen, *Cosmology and Self*, 69.
71. Engberg-Pedersen, *Cosmology and Self*, 69.

It is true that the language of being "clothed in" or "receiving" the *pneuma* "in one's heart," and having the *pneuma* "dwell" in one, does employ physical images. But, the very use of this imagery of "clothing," "receiving," and "indwelling" does not necessarily mean that this language is being used and understood literally. Though it points to an objective reality that is concretely experienced and cognitively perceived, the language of being "clothed" with the *pneuma*, "wearing" it, "receiving" it "in one's heart," and having it "dwell" in one, is clearly metaphorical language. Likewise, when it is said that God "distributes," or "pours out" his Spirit in such a way that it is "received" by humans, or "dwells" within them, these are necessarily expressions using the irreducible metaphors of theological discourse. Though metaphors, in theological discourse of this kind they are metaphors which cannot be unpacked in literal, matter-of-fact and prosaic terms. Just how the *pneuma* is "poured out," "given," "received," and how it "dwells" in believers is an ineffable mystery. It is in a sense "beyond words." While this language points to a concretely experienced and objective reality, it, like all theological language, is not language that can be further explicated in literal or prosaic terms. This also means that it is not possible to deduce implications from it of the kind that might follow if it were language used in relation to the things of this world. Certainly, we cannot draw the implication that these metaphorical images warrant an understanding of the Spirit as a material or physical reality.

Apart from Engberg-Pedersen's appeal to the "physical" nature of the language used by Paul in reference to the Spirit—the language of the "pouring out" of the Spirit in human hearts, and of the coming of the Spirit to "dwell" among the baptized, and so on—the actual justifying reasons behind this interpretative decision are therefore not readily apparent. Particularly given the obviously metaphorical nature of these images, whether this materializing language that Paul uses in reference to the Spirit is sufficient to ground a clear ontological conclusion as to its "material and physical" nature, is clearly problematic.

Across the texts of the New Testament, it is clear that references to the Spirit indicate that primitive Christianity certainly believed that faith had to do with a concretely given reality of actual experience, but when we remember that Luke spoke of the Spirit as appearing in "divided tongues like fire," and with "a sound like the rush of a violent wind,"[72] and that John has Jesus invite Nicodemus to "listen to the wind" which is said to blow where it wills, adding that we do not know "where it comes from or where it goes,"[73] in his discussion of the life-transforming impact of the Spirit, it is clear that language descriptive of the Spirit is by nature figurative and metaphorical. Stoicism may have thought of *pneuma* literally as the combination of divine fire and air which together produce "warm breath," but Paul's commitment to the ontological transcendence of the Jewish God who, as Creator, is independent of what has been created, takes his thought about the "Spirit of God" and also the "Spirit

72. Acts 2:2.
73. John 3:8.

of Christ" in a different direction—away from a purely Stoic materialistic conception of *pneuma*. It is not insignificant that in Middle Platonic discussions of the creation of the universe, the issue of the Creator's being outside of the created order and independent of it (and indeed outside of time) was an issue that was addressed head on.[74] Meanwhile, in the tradition of Jewish monotheism there is no more reason for thinking that the Spirit must be material and physical, than for thinking that, because God is described as "the Rock of Ages," then God must therefore be thought of in material and physical terms.[75]

Moreover, when Paul does seek to describe something of the quality of the Spirit known though faith in the context of the on-going life of the Christian *koinonia*, he invariably talks of the experience of it in terms of "love." This surely cannot be thought to be a material and physical reality. Love may certainly be objectively and concretely known as it is expressed relationally in and through the finite, material, and physical bodies of human persons, but unless we are prepared to embrace a thorough-going behaviorism which reduces everything simply to observable bodily behavior itself and nothing more, love may be understood as an invisible spiritual reality that is concretely known in and through inter-personal relationships. *Like* the Stoic "warm breath," it blows where it wills, and fills the lives of human beings in a refreshing and renewing and life-transforming way, but unlike the material and physical Stoic "warm breath," it cannot be measured in calibrations centigrade or physically contained in a gas cylinder. This is particularly so when we speak of the transcendental love of God. Thus, when Paul says in Rom 5:5 that "God's love has been poured into our hearts by the Holy Spirit that has been given to us," though he is obviously describing a concretely experienced reality, he necessarily has recourse to metaphor. While God is said to "pour" love into the receptacle of human hearts in the way that milk might literally be poured from a jug into a mug, this language of "pouring" does not imply that God's love, like milk, is itself a material and physical liquid. God's love, as the gift of his Spirit, though admittedly known concretely in experience rather than purely notionally, or abstractly *known about*, is a reality belonging to a different non-physical, non-material order. It is clearly disastrous to mistake the metaphorical nature of the theological language here for literal and prosaic language, so as to assume that God's love is found in

---

74. For a brief discussion of the "timelessness" of God and of God's eternity "prior" to creation see Carnley, *Resurrection in Retrospect*, chap. 11.

75. I find it difficult to accept the view of Stanley Stowers that "Paul has no highly transcendent God" (Stowers, "The Dilemma of Paul's Physics," 245). Paul's emphasis on the invisibility of God's eternal power and divine nature in Rom 1:20, and the transcending incomprehensibility or unknowability of God which is expressed in Rom 11:33–34, have to be balanced against the unavoidable use of anthropomorphic images in reference to God emphasized by Stowers.

human hearts literally as a material and physical reality. The only liquid that is literally, materially and physically, in human hearts is blood.

Likewise, when, in 2 Cor 1:21–22, Paul says that "it is God who establishes us with you in Christ, and has anointed us, and who has also put his seal on us and given us his Spirit in our hearts as a guarantee," this talk of "anointing" and "sealing" may certainly point to something concretely experienced, but is not to be understood literally. God's anointing of those who belong to him is not to be understood, in other words, as a literal or physical anointing as though actually with oil. Likewise, Paul's talk of the imprinting of the Spirit as "a seal upon the hearts" of believers, may descriptively point to the concretely experienced spiritual reality perceived and known as the inner texture of the shared life of the community of faith in Christ. It is said to be "stamped" upon the shared life of the community of faith; but this language of "imprinting" and "stamping" as "a seal upon the heart" is obviously not to be taken literally. Clearly, this language employs an image that is drawn from the way seals are in literal terms impressed into soft wax, but it is an image used metaphorically so as to serve an other-worldly spiritual purpose.[76] As such, it cannot be unpacked literally in prosaic language. It is an irreducible metaphor, as all metaphors necessarily are when put to a theological purpose.

This means that even though in faith we might certainly claim to have to do with a divine reality that is *concretely* known as an object of experience, we may steadfastly resist any suggestion that accommodates the divine Spirit to the created order. Thus, contrary to Engberg-Pedersen, we may conclude that for Paul, the Object of the judgment specifically of resurrection faith, the life-giving presence of the Spirit of Christ, is understood as a concretely known reality of experience, by contrast with anything entirely notional, abstract, and idealistic. However, this is *not* to say that it is necessarily material and physical.

This leaves us, however, with the challenging epistemological task of explaining just how this divinely given gift is humanly perceived, and how claims to the knowledge of it in faith may be justifiably made.

---

76. See the use of the same image in Eph 1:13, and 4.30.

5

Faith and the Senses

To this point it has been argued, on the basis of the New Testament texts themselves, that Easter faith may be understood as a commitment of trust (*fiducia*) grounded in a kind of knowing of the Raised Christ *by acquaintance* (*fides*). Historically, this knowing that is appropriate to Easter faith is reflected in the reports of resurrection appearances that, from St. Paul onwards, clearly stand at the origin of this tradition. But, as we have seen,[1] the New Testament reports of appearances, whether in the summary form provided by Paul himself, or in the more graphic narrative detail of the Gospel stories, do not stand alone. This tradition of appearances is complemented by a very firmly rooted tradition of acquaintance in faith with the continuing presence of the Raised Christ as "a life-giving Spirit."[2] This invites the consideration of an approach to faith in the Easter Mystery, even for us today, as a kind of knowing not just by verbal description but by acquaintance, precisely with the presence of the Raised One who is in fact remembered to have promised to be "with" his faithful disciples until "the end of the age."[3]

In addition to its rootedness in the scriptural texts, an approach to faith of this kind brings with it the obvious advantage of avoiding the undesirable alternative of reducing religious faith to an inadequately evidenced propositional attitude, as in the case, for example, of the notional assent to the historiographical proposition "*that* Jesus Christ rose from the dead." In this latter case, a claimed knowing *about* his Resurrection would mean that the object of faith is reduced merely to something that at best is abstractly *described*. Furthermore, as a matter of belief without conclusive evidence this must ultimately be a freestanding decision of will. By contrast, the approach to resurrection faith here proposed involves more than the claim to know simply *that* it once happened in whatever manner it might be verbally described; instead, the knowing in faith upon which a trusting hope in the Raised Christ is grounded, is a knowing *of* Christ mediated through the animating presence of his Spirit. This is concretely

1. In chapter 3.
2. 1 Cor 15:45. Or "the Spirit of life in Christ Jesus" (Rom 8:2); "the abundant Spirit" (John 3:34), and "the Spirit that gives life" (John 6:63).
3. Matt 28:20.

perceived, in the first instance as an empirically observed reality that is discerned in faith to be inwardly constitutive of the corporate life of the Christian community. I say "in the first instance" because the presence of the Raised Christ, while *defined* in the experience of life in the Christian community, is not, of course, *confined* there. The Raised Christ is not a prisoner of the Church; rather, he freely allows other humans access to himself wherever he chooses. In any event, the important point at present is that those who claim such knowledge do so, not on the basis of a free-standing act of will in the face of a shortfall of evidence, but because they are constrained to do so by the perceived evidence of the experience of the Spirit itself.

Such an approach to the understanding of faith, as the knowing of a personal presence with whom believers claim to be concretely *acquainted*, might also be said to commend itself where the kind of knowing appropriate to faith has as its Object the spiritual reality of the presence of God in the world at large, as much as the presence of the Raised Christ specific to resurrection faith. In other words, in epistemological terms we may entertain the possibility that there is a continuity of pattern between religious or theistic faith generally, and its particular form in relation to the Resurrected Jesus.[4]

It also seems, at least *prima facie*, that, as a "knowing by acquaintance" rather than just by verbal description, there may also be an apparent continuity of epistemological pattern between religious perception, whether of the presence of God or of the Raised Christ, and the knowing of human persons and, for that matter, the perceptual knowing of ordinary material objects of the world, as well. Given its grounding in an acquaintance with an objectively and concretely perceived reality of cognitive experience, the kind of knowing appropriate to faith might therefore be understood to conform to the same epistemological pattern as is operative in the knowing of the quite ordinary material objects of the external world with which we are daily acquainted, even though the religious Object of faith is obviously unique.

In this case, even though it may not be "material and physical," it nevertheless follows that the more detailed epistemological structure of what may be categorized as a form of religious empiricism must now be pursued, with the aim of coming to a systematic and coherent account of the particular kind of knowing appropriate to resurrection faith.[5] Not least, we are faced with explaining not just how it might be possible to claim to be acquainted with a religiously significant personal presence or Spirit, but how believers today might be justified in claiming to identify and to know that presence *as* the continuing personal presence of Jesus of Nazareth who lived some two thousand

---

4. In relation to the endeavor of outlining an epistemology of resurrection faith, I accept the point made by Anthony Baxter in response to the argument of *The Structure of Resurrection Belief*: that "inter alia a richer treatment of human apprehension of God would have been advantageous." See, Baxter, "Historical Judgement . . . and 'Resurrection Appearances,'" 40 n. 35(ii).

5. The classical theological treatment of theistic faith in this sense is John Hick's eminently well argued *Faith and Knowledge*. See also Ian Ramsey, *Christian Empiricism*, and William P. Alston, *Perceiving God*.

years ago. After all, that is precisely what seems to be involved in the claim that Jesus rose from the dead and is living still, and in the contention that *his* continuing presence may be claimed to be known by acquaintance in faith.

The first thing that may be said is that this emphasis on an empirical knowing of a religiously significant divine Object, if it is understood to conform to the same pattern as the knowing both of human persons and the material objects of the natural world, seems to entail that it is an empirical experience based upon the deliverances of sense. This is the case regardless of whether the religious claim is to perceive the presence of God or the presence of the Spirit of the Raised Christ. More specifically, once the knowing appropriate to faith is spoken of as a kind of cognition that is similar in epistemological pattern to the knowing of material objects in the world generally, it seems that faith, like the knowing of human people and of ordinary objects, relies, in other words, upon the deliverances of one or more of the five senses.

Of course, like the deliverances of sense experience generally, what is concretely perceived necessarily requires interpretation. We identify and name material objects of sense experience in the world at large by bringing them under interpretative concepts that are furnished to us by the linguistic community to which we happen to belong. A claim to perceive and know that one is standing in front of a house, for example, requires one not only to see and perceive an object through the deliverances of sense, "with one's own eyes." In addition, one has to possess the word "house" and conceptual rules for its correct referential use. In other words, one has to possess the concept of a house before being able to identify and thus claim to know that what is being seen is "a house." In the case of the knowing of human persons, it is a matter of bringing what we perceive under a denotative proper name, rather than a conative concept (such as the concept of a house), but the same interpretative principle applies. One must possess the proper name and some kind of identifying rule for its correct use. Likewise, the religious identification of the Object of faith calls for an act of interpretation of raw experience in just the same way. It is a matter of bringing a concrete experience under the concept of "divine presence" or "Spirit." In the case of resurrection faith, it is a matter of using the proper name of "Jesus" or "Christ" in identifying claims.

Thus, in faith the deliverances of the senses have to be interpreted using the identifying concepts of the community of faith, operating as a religiously attuned linguistic community. These in turn are backed by conventionally agreed-upon rules for their correct use. Theology, as the "grammar of God," thus seeks to furnish us with the conceptual framework necessary for the religious perception of theistic faith even to be a possibility. A theist, sensitively alert to other-worldly reality, might thus claim, for example, to "*see*" or "*perceive*" the presence of "God," or to "*hear*" God's Word, just as Christian believers specifically might claim to "see" or "perceive," and thus claim to know, the objective reality of the "presence of the Raised Jesus" (in this case appealing to the proper name "Jesus," or "Christ," in lieu of an interpretative concept).

A more detailed discussion of this interpretative element in claims *to know* in faith will be left to the next chapter. In this chapter, the discussion must focus upon the concrete or raw cognitive material which gives rise to this interpretative need. For the present, it is therefore sufficient to note that it appears to follow from an empirical approach to faith as a knowing by acquaintance, that the religious cognition appropriate to faith, no less than the knowing of persons and material objects of the external world generally, is dependent upon some kind of engagement or acquaintance with a reality whose presence is initially appropriated through one or more of the receptors of the five senses—hearing, sight, taste, smell and touch. Let us explore this possibility.

There is a long tradition of theological empiricism from Scripture onwards which suggests faith's apparent reliance upon the five senses. Christians regularly speak of "*hearing*" the Word of the Lord, and it is promised in Scripture that "the pure in heart shall *see* God."[6] The foreheads of those "marked as Christ's own for ever" are baptized with the *touch* of flowing water, and often sealed with fragrantly scented anointing oil. The countenances of those in Christ are perceived to "shine," just as, Paul says, the God who said "Let light shine out of darkness, has shone in our hearts to give the light of the knowledge of the glory of God in the face of Jesus Christ."[7] This surely suggests that faith has to do with some kind of empirical perception of a religiously significant reality through the deliverances of the senses. Other religious language appeals to a sense of smell: Paul described himself and others as "a sweet *smelling* fragrance," or "the aroma of Christ to God";[8] prayers are counted as incense that rises as a "sweet smelling savor to the Lord,"[9] and the fragrance of incense fills the tabernacle of God's presence.[10] Meanwhile, countless church choirs have sung "O *taste and see* how gracious the Lord is" (Ps 34:8).[11]

This handful of randomly chosen references signaling the operation of the senses in religious perception suggests that the empirical encounter with transcendent reality may be understood to be delivered via all five physical senses, though perhaps with "seeing" and "hearing" being predominant. There is certainly an ancient tradition that suggests, *prima facie*, that the presence of God may be "seen" and "heard" by

---

6. Matt 5:8; the word used is *opsontai*.
7. 2 Cor 4:6.
8. 2 Cor 2:15.
9. Ps 141:2.
10. Exod 35:15.
11. Ps 34:8. Note also 1 Pet 2:3: "If indeed you have tasted that the Lord is good"; and Ps 119:103: "How sweet are your words to my taste."

the corporeal eye and ear. In the Book of Job, for example, the patiently suffering Job declares: "In my flesh I shall see . . . God,"[12] and "With the hearing of the ear I have heard you, but now my eye sees you."[13] In the New Testament, likewise, there are some paradigm examples where appeal is made to the senses of sight and hearing. Of these, perhaps 1 John provides the classic example: "what we have heard, what we have seen with our eyes, what we have looked at and touched with our hands, concerning the word of life—this life was revealed, and we have seen it and testify to it . . . we declare to you what we have seen and heard so that you may have fellowship with us . . ."[14]

It may be a mistake, however, to understand these apparent references to the operation of the senses literally. Perhaps the religious knowing being spoken of is actually via a parallel set of "spiritual senses," somehow metaphorically equivalent to the five physical senses. We note, for example, that in 1 Peter 2:3 what is said to be "tasted" is "goodness," and in Psalm 119 the "words of God" are said to taste sweetly. Clearly, metaphors are being used. In this case, it might justifiably be thought that references to the senses in religious language might best be understood as metaphorical or figurative pointers to some kind of inner hearing, seeing, tasting, and so on, that is appropriate to a specifically religious kind of knowing. Even in the case of Job's talk both of the "seeing" and "hearing" of the divine through what appear to be physical senses, it nevertheless has to be admitted that perhaps some kind of inner "seeing" and "hearing" is really intended as something detected *in and through* a more obvious outward improvement in Job's material circumstances, apparently at the hand of God. In other words, this is just "a manner of speaking," with references to the senses being understood merely figuratively.

Certainly, in Eph 1:17–18, by contrast with the words of 1 John quoted above, the suggestion is more clearly that God is known through some kind of inner spiritual counterpart of ocular vision: "May [God] give to you the spirit of wisdom and of revelation in the knowledge of him, having the eyes of your understanding [NRSV: "heart"] enlightened."

Whatever literal valuation we might seek to assign to this reference to the "eyes of the understanding" or "of the heart," it might be noted that in classical western theology the idea of the perception of the divine via the outward deliverances of sense has tended, especially following Aquinas, actually to be positively denied. Instead, a concentration of interest on a more inward "seeing" of God through the intellect, in disjunction from the physical senses, has tended to dominate.

---

12. Job 19:26.
13. Job 42:5.
14. 1 John 1:1–3.

Origen (c.AD185–254) is effectively the founder of this tradition of the "spiritual senses," though, of course, he finds warrant for it in Scripture .[15] In the first instance, he speaks of the "inner" and "outer" senses, the inner spiritual senses being "faculties of the heart" *by contrast* with the five physical senses.[16] Generally speaking, Origen therefore seems to have thought of a disjunction between the inner "spiritual senses," and the five actual physical senses. The language of the spiritual senses in this case becomes a metaphorical or figurative way of referring to a characteristically Platonic contemplative focus upon eternal realities via a combination of the intellect and a passionately searching desire achieved through a discipline of disengagement from the world. When detached from material reality, a kind of noetic/erotic concentration of the mind and heart therefore becomes centered upon the inner contemplative perception of the eternal Word of God.[17]

After Origen, the ensuing discussion of the spiritual senses tended to waver between talk of a single inner mystical sense of the divine perceived by the combined "divine faculties of sense," and an attempt to assign specific aspects of religious perception severally to counterparts of each of the five physical senses. Diadocus Photicus (c.AD400–c.486), for example, avoided the systematic development of five separate senses, so as to focus on "one spiritual sense" as "a single perception in contrast to the five bodily senses."[18] Even so, he sometimes nevertheless uses images of "tasting" and "savoring" to refer to religious experience. Likewise, he makes reference to the "eyes of the spirit" in the perception of the divine light. This language appears to be metaphorical. However, this primary focus of Diadocus Photicus on a single spiritual sense contrasts particularly with the later attempt of St Bonaventure (AD1221–1274) to "discover an object for every sense," though it must be admitted that he also talks (somewhat confusedly) of the spiritual senses less as senses at all, but as acts of intellect and will. Discomfort with Bonaventure's attempt to assign specific objects to each of the five senses led Karl Rahner to express serious reservations about this aspect of Bonaventure's thought. Latching on to Bonaventure's talk of the senses as acts of intellect and will, Rahner says that Bonaventure thereby renders talk of a multiplicity of senses, each

---

15. For example, Origen appeals to Proverbs 2:6: "For the Lord gives wisdom, and from his mouth are knowledge and understanding"; and to Heb 5:14: "Solid food is for the mature, for those who have their powers of discernment trained by constant practice to distinguish good from evil."

16. *De Principiis* 1. II, c. 4, n. 3 (GCS 22) 131.5. See Karl Rahner's discussion of "The 'Spiritual Senses' according to Origen," 16 and 85.

17. A contemporary use of the term "noetic sciences" was coined in 1973, when the Institute of Noetic Sciences was founded by Apollo 14 astronaut Edgar Mitchell, who two years earlier became the sixth man to walk on the moon. During the trip back home Mitchell recalls that he felt a profound sense of universal connectedness—what he later described as a samadhi experience. In Mitchell's own words, "The presence of divinity became almost palpable, and I knew that life in the universe was not just an accident based on random processes. . . .The knowledge came to me directly."

18. Rahner, "'Spiritual Senses' according to Origen," 100. See Origen, *De perfectione spirituali* 24, 25, and 29.

with a different function, superfluous: "as acts of contemplation the spiritual senses simply have God as their primary object grasped as a present reality..."[19]

It is of present interest to note that, in the writing of St Bonaventure, the primary object of divine knowledge said to be appropriated though the five spiritual senses is not only the reality of God. Rather, the Raised Christ is also spoken of as a reality that is grasped by the spiritual senses,[20] the "verbum increatum, inspiratum, incarnatum."[21] True to form, Bonaventure seeks to line up a specific object to match every sense. Spiritual hearing grasps the "*verbum increatum*," so that an inner voice is heard. Spiritual sight perceives the Word because the soul is dazzled by its light and brilliant beauty. A spiritual sense of smell is said to perceive the "*verbum inspiratum*" when the soul detects the lofty aroma of the Word. Spiritual taste savors the "*verbum increatum*" when it delights in its sweetness. The spiritual sense of touch grasps the "*verbum incarnatum*." It is actually in response to this that Rahner observes that this attempt to discover "a 'ratio' through which each of the five senses perceives the Word, is rather forced."[22] I think we might all agree. It is also of interest that, in the classical Reformed theology of John Calvin, the physical senses are passed over in favor of a more general *sensus divinitatis* as the appropriate mode of a specifically religious form of perception.[23]

Despite the lack of precision that is admittedly endemic in the theological tradition relating to the perception of the divine, we can at least recognize the existence in this long history of Christian thinking of the conviction that faith results either from a specific set of inner "spiritual senses," or perhaps from a single more generalized inner "spiritual sense." Either way, the spiritual sense(s) is/are accepted as part of the essential equipment of the religious make-up of human nature in disjunction from the five physical senses.

I do not wish to be overly derogatory of this whole approach of medieval contemplative mysticism, with its claim to a knowledge of the divine that is usually rooted back to Origen's reputed sharp Platonic disjunction between inner and outer senses. However, the possibility that religious knowledge might actually be more clearly grounded in the five *physical senses* themselves should not be too readily discounted. As it happens, this may also be sheeted back to Origen. In developing his language of engagement with the divine, Origen himself drew heavily upon the sensuously poetic words and images of the Song of Songs. As a result of Origen's influence in subsequent theology, his commentary on the Song of Songs, with all its physically affective and passionate overtones,

19. Rahner, "'Spiritual Senses' according to Origen," 114.
20. Rahner, "'Spiritual Senses' according to Origen," 114.
21. For Bonaventure on the spiritual senses, see LaNave, "Bonaventure."
22. Rahner, "'Spiritual Senses' according to Origen," 115.
23. Calvin, *Institutes of the Christian Religion*, I, iii, 1, and III, ii. 7, where Calvin says: "We shall now have a full definition of faith if we say that it is a firm and sure knowledge of the divine favour toward us, founded on the truth of a free promise of Christ, and revealed to our minds, and sealed in our hearts, by the Holy Spirit." This view of faith is exploupded by Calvin in III.ii.14–15,28– 29, 31–33.

became normative for later thought on the subject.²⁴ This theological tradition therefore regularly moved somewhat unsystematically and even promiscuously between apparently metaphorical language about the "spiritual senses" and more "earthed" and apparently literal references to the five physical senses.²⁵

The long-term influence of Origen's appeal to the Song of Songs therefore means that we are heirs to a long tradition of Christian discourse relating to the involvement of the physical senses in the perception of religiously significant reality. Even Origen's own systematic understanding of perception contains at least the seeds of a more integrated movement from things earthly to things heavenly, when he moves from reflection upon the nature of the whole of reality (*physike*), to the contemplation of moral and behavioral truth (*ethike*), and then to the more mystical knowledge of the divine (*enoptike*). The fundamental thrust of this kind of systematized progressive trajectory from material to spiritual perception was picked up by Evagrius of Pontus (AD345–399), the theoretician of the monastic asceticism of the Egyptian desert, who observed that "the perception of the spiritual organs" did not operate in utter detachment from knowledge of the external world. Rather, the spiritual senses "penetrate more deeply the reality already grasped by the bodily senses and discover much more about it than do the latter."²⁶ This is an enormously important theological insight.

It may be that we can detect here an echo of Plato's approach to the idea of the "participation" (*methexis*) of material particulars of this world in the eternal Forms, that allows the philosopher to pass from the foreground physicality of this world, perceived through the deliverances of "sight and all the senses," to the discernment of the other-worldly and eternal reality of the Forms, such as we find for example in the *Timaeus* 51a and *Phaedrus* 250a. A stereotypical reading of Plato's philosophy in which "the world of the senses was as much disjoined from noumenal reality as the world of cause and effect of Newtonian physics was closed to the divine," by contrast with a view of reality "in which spiritual and material interacted,"²⁷ is unfortunately a caricature of the actual case. Under the influence of Stoicism, the form of Platonism that became popular in the world of Middle Platonism assumed an empirical face insofar as an interest was taken in the immanence of the Ideal Forms—the way in which the universal Forms were detected as they were encountered and "remembered" in the particulars of the world of sense experience. Indeed, such encounters were understood to trigger the "mad" philosophical quest for a clearer knowledge of the Ideal Forms. The stereotypically drawn dichotomy between sense experience and Ideas was somewhat alien to the first-century reception of Platonism of the Middle

---

24. For example, and most notably, the allegorical interpretation of Gregory the Great (c. AD540–604) in his *Exposition on the Song of Songs*.

25. See Rahner, "'Spiritual Senses' according to Origen," 94.

26. Rahner, "'Spiritual Senses' according to Origen," 98. See Louth, "The Greek Tradition," 3.

27. The assessment of Plato's philosophy of James D. G. Dunn in *The Theology of Paul the Apostle*, 238–39.

Platonic "mix" of Stoicism and Platonism.[28] Likewise, in the first half of the second-century AD, Albinus was already aware of the importance of Plato's insights into the mysterious relation between sense experience and the transcendent intelligible ideas that were immanently present, "mixed" within the material and physical world. In *Didaskalikos* chapter 10, for example, he says:

> In as much as humans are filled with impressions from sensation, they do not know the intelligibles in a pure manner. Thus, whenever they propose to contemplate the intelligible, they have the sensible imagined with it and often add, for example, size, shape and colour. The gods, on the other hand, know intelligibles absolutely and in an unmixed manner apart from any sense perception.

It is possible that Origen may be understood similarly as a child of the Plato of Middle Platonism. Alternatively, and perhaps more likely, this aspect of Origen's thinking may be more characteristic of a more popular movement of assent from the physical to the spiritual, from formless matter to matter-less Form, that became so fashionable under the systematizing influence of the neo-Platonism of Origen's contemporary Plotinus. This may be a more direct influence in his thought than a more classical Platonism. Either way, Origen would have found support in the environment of the surrounding intellectual culture for working with the idea of some kind of continuity of the physical and the spiritual senses, rather than their disjunction.

Certainly, while some early thinkers used the language of the five spiritual senses in a more clearly metaphorical way to focus on "one spiritual sense" in disjunction from the physical senses in ways reminiscent of Diadocus Photicus, others such as Evagrius, and also Pseudo-Macarius (c. AD300–391) also regarded the five spiritual senses as being continuous with natural faculties. According to Pseudo-Macarius, without grace the operations of the senses can remain on a purely natural plane.[29] However, with the assistance of God's illuminating grace "spiritual eyes," previously dimmed by sin, are opened, and new ears and a new language are bestowed as new insights are gained.

Very importantly, at around the same time, Gregory of Nyssa (c. AD330–395) likewise tended towards the integration of the five natural senses with a more heavenly orientation towards things divine. Sarah Coakley, in some groundbreaking work on the contemporary relevance of the important contribution of Gregory of Nyssa to the discussion of the spiritual senses, has drawn attention, particularly, to the idea of the continuity of the deliverances of the physical senses with the spiritual senses,[30] which Gregory also developed (following Origen) on the basis of *The Song of Songs*. Coakley notes that instead of detachment from the material order of the kind that was

---

28. See a more full discussion of this in chapter 12 below.
29. Pseudo-Macarius, Homily 4 n. 7 (*Patrologia Graeca* 34, 477).
30. Gregory of Nyssa, *Commentary on the Song of Songs*, 35.

to result from the Christianized Platonism that was so much more characteristic of Origen, and particularly as it was developed in the contemplative exercises of much medieval mysticism,[31] Gregory of Nyssa perceived a kind of continuity between physical perception and the perception of spiritual realities: "the toe-hold for spiritual perception is precisely *in* the physical."[32] Coakley then explores some very suggestive comments of Ludwig Wittgenstein concerning the nature of religious commitment, which resonate with this pre-modern tradition.

This aspect of the ancient tradition of the "spiritual senses" certainly resonates with more contemporary theologies of the perception of the revelation of the divine, particularly through "hearing" and "seeing." One of the most notable recent examples of a kind of "*seeing*" of the divine, by contrast with "hearing," in western theology of the modern period, was the groundbreaking work of Rudolph Otto,[33] with his appeal to "the sense of the *numinous*" in *The Idea of the Holy*.[34] Once again, the apprehension of something "Wholly Other" than the everyday experience of knowing material reality, which Otto termed the *numinous*, was achieved not so much by way of a particular "spiritual" sixth sense in addition to the five physical senses, nor by achieving some kind of mystical detachment from the material world. Rather, for Otto the sense of the *numinous* involved the apprehension or feeling of something mysterious *within* the created order. He spoke of this as the apprehension of an "overplus of meaning"—something objectively arresting over and above the deliverances of the five senses themselves, though not detached from them. By a kind of "perfection of the senses" that refuses to allow the perceptual interest to rest content with a purely surface reading of material reality, Otto pointed to the foundational religious sense of the *numinous* as "something more" or "Wholly Other." By contrast with Schleiermacher's "feeling of absolute dependence," this was not to be mistaken for an inner subjective feeling, but involved a sense of the more objective disclosure of a given aspect of reality that Otto believed could command the attention of religiously aware and perceptive people.

Otto's analysis of the *numinous*, comprises three inter-related components, designated (famously) by the phrase: "*mysterium tremendum et fascinans*." As *mysterium*, the numinous is said to be perceived as "Wholly Other"—in other words, something entirely different from anything experienced via the senses in ordinary life. It evokes a reaction of silence. But the *numinous* is also a *mysterium tremendum*, because it presents itself as an overwhelming and inescapable power. And finally, the *numinous* presents

31. With the obvious help of the Neoplatonism of Plotinus.
32. Coakley, "The Resurrection and the 'Spiritual Senses,'" in *Powers and Submissions*, 138.
33. Otto, *Das Heilige*, 1917.
34. Otto, *Idea of the Holy*, chapters 2–4.

itself as *fascinans*, as merciful and gracious, and therefore something to be welcomed, even actively sought out. In Otto's idea of the perception of the *numinous* we thus have a more contemporary paradigm of the pre-modern sense of progression from the perception of physical things to religious faith as the sense or feeling of an ultimate spiritual reality in, through, and behind the perception of physical things.

The word "*numinous*" itself comes from the Latin root, *nuo*, to nod or wink. Following Otto, one tends today to speak of "the sense of the *numinous*" when one finds oneself attracted to, or drawn into, the observation of a scene of nature, for example, in a way that commands one's attention in a kind of arresting engagement. A sense of the fundamental and inexplicable mystery of creation, triggered by the quality of compelling attractiveness of a scene of surpassing natural beauty, which is often accompanied by the awesomely mysterious question of "why *anything* should be," is a prime example. Though Otto argued that the sense of the *numinous* is *sui generis*, and therefore distinguishable from anything else, the aesthetic sense of the beauty of a part of the natural order, which also goes beyond the mere detection of a bare assemblage of plants and animals and material things, is at least analogous. Moreover, beyond an aesthetic appreciation, Otto believed that art itself is capable of triggering a sense of the *numinous*. The experience in an art gallery, when a particular painting has the power to "stop you in your tracks" and arrest your attention, "nodding" or "winking" at you, as it were, so as in a sense to engage with you and invite you into a kind of communication with it, illustrates something of what he meant by the sense of the *numinous*.

The point here is that Otto's discussion of the essential nature of a religious sensibility though his analysis of the sense of the *numinous* illustrates the way in which an identifiable religious content may be said to be isolated from the mere outward observance of the material and physical face of reality through the deliverances of the senses. This illustrates the fact that religious perception does not only rely upon notions of detachment from the world, coupled with talk of exclusively "inner" modes of perception.

Even those who have been aggressively unsympathetic to natural theology, do not entirely disengage spiritual discernment and faith from the operation of the physical senses. In the great twentieth-century "theologies of the Word" of Karl Barth and Rudolf Bultmann, for example, access to the perception of the will of God was understood, if in different ways, through the medium of a kind of "hearing" of the Church's proclamation. For Barth, faith was a matter of discerning the Word of God *in* the physically heard words of Scripture . To his mind, an inner appropriation of meaning through a "middle-distance" reading of the words of the material texts, illumined by the grace of the Holy Spirit, allowed the Word of God to be received and appropriated. The Platonic resonances in this approach to the discernment of the eternal Word *in* the words of the scriptural text (that were self-confessed by Barth himself to be Platonic) are unmistakable. Likewise, a Platonic resonance may be detected in Barth's classic dictum concerning "the infinite qualitative distinction between time and eternity." It is not surprising that Barth, in his speech of acceptance of the Sonning Prize at Copenhagen in April 1963, acknowledged his dependence on "the great Plato."[35]

In Bultmann's case, by contrast, it was a matter of demythologizing the literal and descriptively objectifying language of Scripture, so that the hearer was enabled to "hear" it as a word of existential address in the church's proclamation. Sunday by Sunday, the hearer in the judgment of faith as a kind of renewed self-understanding is said to grasp something of his or her own creatureliness in the form of an ultimate dependence on God as Creator, so as then to respond with a decision of obedient discipleship. Thus, the Word of God's address was said to be "heard" in and through the church's proclamation of the Word. This can only be mediated through the physical senses.

Both these twentieth-century theologies of the Word, which were essentially hostile to the perception of the revelation of the divine through the natural order of classical natural theology, nevertheless effectively worked with the idea of a fundamental coincidence between an outward hearing or reading of the material texts, apparently initially appropriated through the physical senses, and an inner spiritual kind of "hearing" in which the Word of God was in different ways appropriated. In the case of both Barth and Bultmann, faith thus arises through *hearing* (Rom 10:17); in the one case it is by the perception of the eternal Word revealed in and through the words of Scripture, and in the other by hearing the church's proclamation of the Word as an address that triggers an existential grasp of one's creatureliness which, at the same time, brings with it an inner awareness of dependence upon God as Creator.

There is thus a strong tradition, from Gregory of Nyssa onwards and into the modern era, which speaks of religious perception as a "going beyond" the ordinary awareness of physical things, while at the same time maintaining continuity with the perception of physical reality though the deliverances of the five senses. In this tradition, the coming to religious knowledge in faith may be said to involve the perception of material reality through the deliverances of the five physical senses, but not interpreted in such a way as to stop at a foreground or surface reading of what is experienced merely *as* material or physical. Rather, a specifically religious perception is claimed that passes beyond a surface acquaintance with the outward and visible, so as, almost sacramentally, to discern the objective operation of "an inward and spiritual grace."

The historical discussion of the significance of the spiritual senses for faith that we can legitimately trace back to Gregory of Nyssa in the fourth-century, and even to some extent to Origen before him, thus invites us to think of the discernment of a deeper sense of spiritual reality in and through the deliverances of all the five physical senses. This transcends the disjunction between the physical senses and the development of a more purely idealistic sense of religious reality of the kind encountered in more developed form in the classical medieval mysticism of detachment from the material and physical world. As distinct from this kind of mysticism, which made so much of the metaphorical talk of the five spiritual senses in *disjunction* from the five

---

35. See Zahrnt, *The Question of God*, 27.

physical senses, this entails an approach to faith from a much more earthed, straightforwardly empirical point of view.

Before proceeding further with the exploration of an epistemology of faith understood as an empirically grounded knowing "by acquaintance" employing the deliverances of the five senses, there are two preliminary points that need to be underlined. The first is that, if we take seriously the possibility that faith simply relies upon a demystified appeal to the five actual senses themselves, a more empirically grounded approach to faith will thereby avoid the suggestion that a kind of occult endowment is involved, secretly and arbitrarily bestowed on some and not on others. A gnostic secret knowledge is thus ruled out of court. Rather, a grounding of the judgment of faith in the deliverances of the physical senses points to the possibility of a religious knowing that is, at least in principle, open to anyone who has eyes to see and ears to hear.[36]

Second, it needs to be underlined that the idea of continuity between the physical senses and a religious sensibility does not necessarily mean that claims to "see" or "perceive," as well as claims to "know by acquaintance," entail that the object of the claimed seeing, perceiving, or knowing must necessarily be understood, simply because of the use of these verbs, to be itself quite simply a finite material object. As we have already noted, this is the apparent assumption of Troels Engberg-Pedersen insofar as he argues that Pauline language in reference to the Spirit suggests a Stoic ontology that obliges us to think of the Spirit as a material and physical reality. It is also the unfortunate assumption of Stephen Davis, whose views are endorsed by N. T. Wright. This involves a false conclusion in relation to the interpretation of the New Testament tradition of the perception of the appearances of the Raised Christ.[37] Davis contended that because verbs "see," "hear," and "touch" are used in the Easter narrative traditions, they must simply map on to an unambiguously physical and material reality. The appearances of the Raised Christ are said therefore to have taken a material and physical bodily form, entirely continuous with the material and physical objects of this world, such as "a tree, a house, or another human body." Indeed, N. T. Wright takes this line of thinking a stage further: we are encouraged to think of Jesus' resurrected body, given its transformation into a material and physical body that had been made incorruptible, as even "more material than material."

However, verbs suggesting "sight" and "hearing," through the operation of the relevant physical senses, may also be employed to speak of the perception of qualities and values over and above the purely physical and material make-up of things. For example, the perception of the surpassing beauty of a scene of nature, though part

---

36. The question of how it is that some claim to "see" while others remain blind will be discussed in chapter 7 in relation to the themes of faith and freedom, ambiguity and doubt.

37. See Davis "'Seeing' the Risen Jesus," 126, and Wright, *RSG*, 376 n.4.

of the created order, likewise goes beyond the mere surface detection and perception of physical and material things to an appreciation of aesthetic value that is perceived in and through them. Similarly, the aesthetic appreciation of a work of art, such as a painting, involves the perception of values over and above the bare given-ness of the physical and material reality of the painting itself. Even though the physical senses are initially involved, an aesthetic appreciation invites a form of perception that goes beyond the mere surface detection and description of finite material things *per se*. Even an amateur admirer of a work of art, not to mention a professional art critic, may claim to see "something more" than a bare arrangement of physical patches of color on a material canvass, for example, or more than just a description of the bare subject matter of the a painting. The aesthetic appreciation of the composition of the painting, the balanced arrangement of forms and the inter-play of colors, and their subtlety of tone, which allows it to be judged as an exceptionally "good" painting, goes beyond the perception merely of a material object *qua* object and what it may represent. Indeed, comparative amateurs, and not just the experts in the field, are sometimes able to identify the original work of a specific artist by name at a glance, as in the statement "I could see immediately that it was a Cézanne." As a consequence, what is claimed to be "seen" and "known" in aesthetic appreciation is not exhausted by claims simply to see and know and describe a finite material painting and what it depicts. What is "seen" is not just a painting, but also "something more."

If we may take a leaf out of Origen's book, the same principle applies when we move from perception of physical reality to the discernment of moral value. For example, the perception of moral goodness, or of justice, in and through or "along-with" the outward observation and factual description of a piece of human behavior, may ground a claim that goes beyond the mere description of that physical behavior itself. Clearly "goodness" and "justice" are abstract nouns and do not themselves denote material and physical entities. When goodness is perceived, it is therefore for reasons above and beyond the bare factual description of the behavior itself. Specific moral reasons may be given to justify the description of a specific behavior as "good." Such a moral judgment depends upon a conventionally agreed upon understanding of the meaning of the word "good" in a linguistic community operating also as a moral community, and techniques of argument concerning what constitutes "good" behavior in a specific set of circumstances. In addition, when a person is judged to be "good" or a behavior is judged to be "right" something is thereby not only described, but also approved and commended to others as something they "ought" to pursue. We have thus moved from merely physical description to a new level of moral discourse, which is both descriptive and prescriptive at the same time. Clearly, we are no longer just existing in a physical or material context but engaging with moral values.[38]

---

38. Augustine speaks of the moral sense in similar terms: ""Yet these and all other material things have their causes hidden in nature; but they offer their forms which give loveliness [or beauty] to the structure of this visible world. It almost seems as if they long to be known, just because they cannot

Likewise, in a segment of human social behavior, people regularly claim an awareness of "something more" than the mere physical presence of material bodies, or the bare physical descriptions of their actions and inter-actions. In the course of the observation of, or involvement in, human social interaction something more is involved, in other words, than just an acquaintance with bare physical and material reality. In some kinds of circumstance, what is said to be "seen," "perceived," and "known" may be a human attitude, or a personal disposition, or an affective emotion, or a psychological or inter-personal spiritual quality. What is perceived is indicated, for example, in such statements as: "I could *see* that he was angry," or "I could *hear* by the tone of their voices that they were all very down-hearted and sad," or "The warmth of their welcome to us was palpable." Likewise, it might be said that "His generosity of spirit over-flowed to us and really *touched* us." In this kind of circumstance, the reference is not to a physical touching so much as "emotional touching," but it is no less real for that. Clearly, to speak of "seeing" and "hearing" and "being touched" does not necessarily mean that what is seen or heard, or that what touches us, must be a material object *per se*, even though it is mediated through material and physical reality, and therefore perceived through the deliverances of sense experience utilizing one or more, or even a mixture of the five physical senses

The perception of anger, warmth, sadness, and generosity of spirit, or love, as something "more than" the bare physical awareness of the presence of a person in a room is often discussed by appeal to the notion of "emotional intelligence"; the suggestion being that this capacity of discernment varies from person to person, though few are entirely lacking in it.[39] Though this "overplus of meaning" (to use Otto's phrase in relation to the perception of the *numinous*) is appropriated through the operation of the five senses, the perception of it calls for a deeper and more focused discernment than the mere surface observation of material realities and physical behaviors themselves. Certainly, it is not insignificant that these examples indicate the possibility of coming to perceptions that are said particularly to involve "seeing" and "hearing" and thus being aware of, and claiming to know, qualities in and through the material and physical texture of life that are themselves not strictly material or physical. What is in turn received by the deliverances of the five senses is therefore not fully accounted for in claims to know *purely* material bodies as they are in themselves, or even as they appear to us. Through the deliverances of the five senses we may also perceive spiritual or non-material behavioral

---

know themselves. We apprehend them by our bodily senses, but it is not by our bodily senses that we form a judgement on them. For we have another sense, far more important than any bodily sense, the sense of the inner man, by which we apprehend what is just and what is unjust, the just by means of the 'idea' which is presented to the intellect, the unjust by the absence of it. The working of this sense has nothing to do with the mechanism of eye, ear, smell, taste or touch." *City of God*, XI, 27.

39. "Emotional intelligence" can be defined as the ability to monitor one's own and other people's emotions, to discriminate between different emotions and label them appropriately, and to use emotional information to guide thinking and behavior.

qualities and dispositions so as to ground claims to know additional aspects of what there is to be perceived and known.

This means that, even though the verbs "see," "perceive," and "know" are used in relation to what is perceived within the texture of human experience, it does not follow that what is "seen," "perceived," and "known" must necessarily be itself understood to be either a material object or a purely outwardly observable event involving physical and material bodies. In this case, the same verbs are used because the same epistemological pattern applies as in claims to know material objects and observable events involving finite things and finite human bodies, even though they may now be used in relation to the perception of inter-personal attitudes and dispositions. In more personal terms, the inter-personal affective coloring of human social reality that is perceived in and through the outward and physical behaviors of material human bodies, so as to become the subject matter of claims to know, is clearly itself "something more" than just the mere materiality or physicality of an object or observed segment of human behavior.

Contrary to the contentions of Stephen Davis, in claims to Easter faith, even involving the reported appearances of the Raised Christ, exactly what is communicated as having been "seen," "perceived," and "known" may be quite unlike "a tree, a house, or another human body." These same verbs may also be correctly used in relation to the perception of something mysteriously non-material. In a way that is at least analogous to what may be perceived within human social behavior, even realities pertaining to religious faith that are perceived to be uniquely transcendent and religiously significant, may nevertheless be spoken of using the verbs "see," "perceive," and "know." The use of these verbs alone does not entail that what is "seen," "perceived," and "known" must be physical or material in nature.

Before we come to the discussion of the "seeing," "perceiving," and "knowing" that pertains to religious faith, it is important to note that the inter-personal communication that is appropriated explicitly through "seeing" as well as "hearing" in and through the behaviors of human persons may, to a very large extent, be perceived in a way that is entirely unconscious. In other words, it may be so subtle as not to draw attention to itself and thus to go unperceived. In this way it contrasts with the ordinary day to day seeing and hearing that is part and parcel of the human engagement of the senses with physical and material reality. Even so, the operation of the five physical senses is no less important.

This aspect of inter-personal human communication may be illustrated by the contemporary study of non-verbal or paralinguistic communication. We are all perfectly aware of the fact that when humans wish to communicate they naturally speak so as to be heard. We are less conscious of the fact that our verbal communications are very often accompanied by a plethora of non-verbal cues and gestures that are also enormously important in the communication of meaning. In the contemporary world, this is the paralinguistic aspect of communication that is regularly referred to as "body language." Apart from the non-verbal postures and gestures that are observable, and may thus be said to be "seen," verbal speech itself is accompanied by non-verbal paralinguistic elements that are also "heard." These include voice tone and quality, rate of speech, pitch, volume, and speaking style, as well as prosodic features such as rhythm, intonation, and stress, all of which play a part in the communication of meaning. These non-verbal deliverances of sense experience, that are discerned through physical cues and gestures in appropriate circumstances are thus often said to be "seen" or "heard," even though very often the entire phenomenon of non-verbal or paralinguistic communication operates sub-consciously. Indeed, the lack of immediate awareness of this aspect of inter-personal communication is almost certainly to be explained because so much of it takes place without drawing attention to itself. Non-verbal, paralinguistic elements in communication are nevertheless enormously important, especially in the communication of non-material or non-physical (i.e., spiritual) inter-personal qualities.

Despite the modern flowering of interest in non-verbal or paralinguistic communication, it has to be said that the study of it goes back at least to 1872, with the publication by Charles Darwin of *The Expression of the Emotions in Man and Animals*. In this book, Darwin noted that all mammals, both humans and other animals, showed emotion through facial expressions. He was intrigued by such questions as: "Why do our facial expressions of emotions take the particular forms they do?" "Why," for example, "do we wrinkle our nose when we are disgusted and bare our teeth when we are enraged?" Already, Darwin's questions imply that "disgust" and "rage" are communicated more often, not so much by verbal utterance itself, as by almost automatic and instantaneous physical cues. Darwin was interested in exploring the evolutionary development of these non-verbal modes of communication through the animal world. Since those early beginnings, the modern study of non-verbal communication has become concerned particularly with the interaction between human individuals, through bodily cues and gestures, along with the physical characteristics of communicators, and particularly the subtle behaviors, both conscious and unconscious, of communicators during a personal interaction.

All five senses are often brought into play in an inter-personal interaction: on average 83 percent sight, 11 percent hearing, 3 percent smell, 2 percent touch and 1 percent taste. Clearly, sight and hearing are the most important statistically, and, as we shall see, also theologically. Certainly, the wrong message can be communicated if the body language conveyed along with it does not match a verbal message. Conversely, non-verbal bodily communication can enhance a vocal message with the correct body language. As Darwin said, the force of language is much aided by the expressive movements of the face and body that instantaneously express meanings often of a very subtle nature.[40] For example, the "shrugging of ones shoulders" immediately expresses a kind of helplessness, "impotence or apology—something which cannot be done or cannot be avoided."[41]

One example of non-verbal communication of particular interest comes from the field of modern oculesics, which is associated with seeing and the eyes. This is the human phenomenon of gaze. When intensified and prolonged, gaze can communicate an attitude of hostility and threat, whereas aversion of gaze signals appeasement. We thus actually perceive a person's attitude towards us long before a word is uttered. We might therefore be heard to say "I knew he was angry with me by the cross way in which he looked at me." Alternatively, "I knew something was wrong because of the awkward way in which he would *not* look at me." Even before an actual verbal utterance, a person's body language may reveal a great deal about how he or she is inwardly thinking. Hence, we regularly say, for example, "I knew exactly what she was thinking from the look on her face."

There are many other examples of this: the dilation of the pupils quite unconsciously signals interest in an object or person. This is the reality behind the expression "His eyes nearly popped out of his head." It is said that salesmen in Middle Eastern markets are skilled at studying the dilation of the pupils of their customers in order to discern which articles they are really interested in before setting and revealing the prices. And there was once a time when women put a few drops of Bella Donna in their eyes in the belief that the dilation of their pupils that it effected made them look more attractive and alluring. This has now been proved scientifically actually to be the case. Michael Argyle, in his groundbreaking study *Bodily Communication* (1975), cites experiments in which subjects were shown two photographs of the same person, identical in every respect, except for the fact that in one case the pupils were shown dilated. Those to whom these photographs were shown expressed a marked preference for the one with the dilated pupils, without being told what cue it was to which they were responding.

Non-verbal communication is particularly important in the communication of an inter-personal attitude or disposition. For example, a person might say: "He was clearly very hostile." What is perceived as hostility is not only communicated by direct verbal communication, but also by sight and hearing: an angry look, a fixed and threatening gaze, a raised and angry tone of voice. However, the opposite is equally true. The reality of "being welcomed" or "made to feel welcome" may be detected not only verbally but in and through physical tokens: a smile of delight, an extended hand, the gesture ushering guests into a room, the offering of a drink. All this in behavioral terms is what

---

40. Darwin, *The Emotions in Man and Animals*, 13. Darwin's exhaustive and fascinating examination of what we would call today "body language" contains innumerable examples of movements that he notes are often "extremely slight and of fleeting nature."
41. Darwin, *The Emotions in Man and Animals*, 63.

justifies us in speaking of being "warmly welcomed," or of sensing the "generosity of spirit" and "inclusive" nature of a community gathering.

Clearly, the physical and behavioral tokens that we pick up, particularly by sight and the hearing, allow us to make judgments in which we claim to know not just that we are encountering physical and material realities and behaviors as such, but that we are perceiving non-material spiritual realities, inter-personal attitudes and dispositions, in and through such interactions.

Environmental conditions are also determinative in communication, and for this reason, the study of non-verbal communication sometimes involves the environmental circumstances within which communication takes place. When one person or group is appropriating a message communicated by another, their perceptions are conditioned by the entire environment around them. In many instances these are obvious. The statement "Hand me the line" uttered in a study where there is a telephone on the hook, means something entirely different when the same words are uttered by a fisherman in a metal dinghy on a lake. Likewise, a right hand and arm outstretched by a British bicycle rider (riding on the left carriageway) to signal an intention to turn right obviously means something different from an arm outstretched by a person directing the movement of a crowd where it means, "please move straight ahead." By this same gesture extended towards a performer an audience may be invited to express welcoming applause. In this kind of way, context is thus hugely important in the interpretation of the meaning of non-verbal gestures.

In each of these cases, a specific meaning is signaled, or an experienced and perceived disposition or attitude is mediated, through non-verbal bodily communication. In a sense, what is communicated is not itself the bare behavioral presence of a material human being so much as a non-material quality mediated through cues delivered by physical and behavioral tokens. Clearly, here something objectively real is nevertheless perceived, and known by observation, whether conscious or unconscious, which may rightly therefore be spoken of as *something* perceived, or "seen." What is perceived or "seen" in such a way as to ground claims to be aware of, or to know a state of affairs, though mediated *through* material reality, is strictly not itself a material reality. Rather, what is perceived and known is a non-material or inter-personal disposition, something revelatory of a spiritual quality pertaining to a relationship, or present in an inter-personal interaction.

Within the texture of life in the modern world, the immediate and intuitive nature of the perception of these paralinguistic features in inter-personal communication is crucial in strengthening a first impression. This is obviously so in very common situations, such as in attracting a partner or in a business interview. Indeed, such impressions are on average formed within the first four seconds of contact, thereafter strongly affecting one person's perception of another. This means that, despite the fact that it does not necessarily draw attention to itself, non-verbal or paralinguistic communication is of enormous human importance.

It is also important to note that this feature of human inter-personal communication is not something only in the minds of knowing subjects, for what is observed and known is external to a perceiving person, an objective reality or state of affairs. This is why "seeing" is a verb that may appropriately by used in relation to the apprehension of it. Hence, the regularity of such expressions as: "I could *see* that he was angry with me"; "I could *see* that she was very embarrassed and ashamed"; or "I could *see* that he was interested in it because of the way he looked at it." In each case, the epistemological pattern remains the same as for the perception of any material object or instance of human behavior, insofar as a specific inter-personal reality is perceived through the deliverances of sense and brought under an interpretative concept, such as "anger," "embarrassment," "shame," or "interest," and is thus named and identified. It is for this reason also that even non-material aspects of what is experienced are rightly the subject of claims not just to "see," but also to "know," as in the statement: "I *knew* he was interested in her" (by the way he kept looking in her direction).

Likewise, such non-material or spiritual qualities as "personal warmth," "an other-regarding care," "a welcoming generosity of spirit," or "self-giving love," that are communicated in and through the behaviors of people using their physical bodies, are perceived and known through the deliverances of the five physical senses. Even though some of the behaviors that communicate such information may be infinitesimally, or microscopically, small, as for example the dilation of the pupil of the eye, and therefore often operate to convey meaning quite unconsciously, they are indispensable to inter-personal communication.

Now, something similar to the textured quality of human inter-personal communication, both verbal and paralinguistic or non-verbal, and the perception of "something more" than the purely physical and material face of reality as it strikes us at first sight, may also be said to operate in the case of the religious perception that grounds the conviction of trusting faith. In this case, what is perceived is claimed to be, not just a reality of *human* social interaction, but also the presence of an identifiable and religiously significant transcendental reality. In other words, the operation of the five senses, particularly in the perception of non-material or spiritual aspects of experience through "seeing" and "hearing" of the kind that regularly takes place in para-linguistic interactions between human persons, may be said to be essential constitutive elements also in the judgment of faith. For, just as inter-personal warmth, forgiveness, generosity of spirit, graciously self-giving love, or a fundamental commitment to care for others, may be discerned within human behavior, and then expressed as the subject-matter of knowledge claims in relation to the engagement of human persons with one-another in ordinary every-day life, so a person of faith may claim an analogical awareness by acquaintance with the presence of "the Spirit," or the "love of God," or "the steadfast care of God." Similarly, through the subtle deliverances of sense experience, a judgment of faith may be made concerning the presence of the "life-giving Spirit" of the Raised Christ or "the Spirit of life in Christ Jesus." Such faith claims arise, not through achieving a kind of detachment from day to day commerce with physical reality, as in the tradition of much medieval spirituality, particularly as it developed through the Middle Ages under the influence of Neoplatonism. Rather, they arise as a consequence of a set of concrete cognitive experiences that are akin to the way in which the human experience of inter-personal relational qualities and dispositions may be said to be perceived and appropriated through the operation of the five physical senses, and especially through "seeing" and "hearing."

Broadly speaking, this is the empirically grounded awareness of transcendental reality that is continuous with, rather than detached from, the deliverances of the five senses, that stands in a tradition of Christian reflection on the nature of faith that goes back at least to the insights of Origen and Gregory of Nyssa. Those influenced by them distilled this kind of inter-personal insight and its religious significance, from their de-coded reading of the Song of Songs and its portrayal of the intimate relationship of the Lover and the Beloved, so as to affirm the role of the physical senses in the response of faith. By the Middle Ages, Thomas Aquinas was thus able to trace the ability of the first eyewitnesses to provide their testimony to the Resurrection to a "faith that functions through the eyes" (*oculata fide*).[42] A contemporary approach to faith as a form of religious empiricism is no less dependent upon the deliverances of the five senses.

Once we are aware of the role of the five senses in religious perception, we are able to detect it elsewhere in the scriptural tradition. Certainly, an approach to faith of the kind that values its grounding in the deliverances of sense experience appears, at least *prima facie*, to be what St. Paul had in mind, when, at the beginning of Romans he castigated those in the ancient world for being "without excuse" for abandoning an awareness of the presence of "the invisible God," though, he says, this was readily available to them through the natural order. Their fault was that instead of discerning, and living in obedience to, the presence of God, they immersed themselves in the natural order itself and thus gave themselves up to idolatry and immorality.[43]

It may be admitted that there are almost certainly Stoic resonances in this empirical approach to Paul's perception of the divine, even though, at the same time, we cannot eliminate a Platonic transcendental reference in the epistemology presupposed by Paul.[44] Insofar as St. Paul approached an understanding of the Spirit as a

42. Aquinas, *Summa Theologiae* 3a, 55.2.
43. Rom 1:19–23.
44. As will be argued in more detail in chapter 12.

concretely experienced and empirically given reality with which he was acquainted in his post-Easter faith, this appears to bear an empirical Stoic influence as something mediated through an engagement via the senses rather than in detachment from them. If he does not spell this out in as many words, this is the natural implication of all he has to say about the Spirit as a concretely experienced reality, at least in some ways akin to the Stoic conception of *pneuma* as "warm breath." Despite the fact that issue may be taken with Troels Engberg-Pedersen's view that the Spirit for Paul is itself actually a "material and physical" reality as in classical Stoicism, its apprehension even as an ultimately transcendent reality is mediated in and through the physical order. This means it remains a deliverance of the five senses. Such descriptive phrases that refer to the experience of the Spirit as something that has been "poured into" the hearts of believers or that "dwells" among them may be metaphorical, for the Spirit may not itself be "physical and material," but nevertheless, it seems unavoidable that the experience of the Spirit requires the involvement of the senses, no less than the non-verbal or paralinguistic elements within inter-personal human communication rely upon the deliverances of the senses.

Following in the tradition of Paul, St. John appears to be pointing to a transcendent reality that is likewise perceived via an apparent apprehension through the deliverances of the senses when he speaks of the Spirit which God has given to the Son "without measure"[45] and which, in the experience of believers, "blows where it wills."[46] For John, the Spirit is a reality that is objective to believers, which they perceive and know as something that surprisingly and mysteriously, even somewhat unpredictably, envelops them and "touches them" in the sense that it ventilates, refreshes, and renews their lives. The First Epistle of John in similar vein bears witness to what has been "seen," and known, and handled using language indicative of concrete engagement with, rather than detachment from, the textured experience of physical life. It may not itself be a physical and material reality, but it is something perceived and known via the deliverances of sense.

It is hard to avoid the conclusion that, in the specific case of the perception of the presence of the Spirit of the Raised Christ in resurrection faith, as both Paul and John describe it, we are dealing with a religiously apprehended phenomenon that is at least analogous to the perception via the senses of inter-personal attitudes and dispositions in and through the human behaviors of ordinary daily life. This is something that Christians continue to claim to perceive in faith in myriad ways, particularly within the experience of the specific form of community life that is characteristic of the baptized. When a scriptural text is read aloud in liturgical rehearsal, a divine communication is claimed in faith to have been "heard." A material written text is not to be turned into some kind of religious fetish, but the liturgically rehearsed words "Hear the Word of the Lord" signal a primordial Christian experience. Likewise, the perception of the

45. John 3:34.
46. John 3:8.

living presence of the Raised Christ is regularly claimed to be apprehended, and to be "seen," in the sense that it is perceived and known in the most characteristic Christian behavioral activity of gathering corporately for the four-fold liturgical action of the taking, blessing, breaking, and sharing of bread and the sharing of the cup, of which Paul originally speaks in 1 Cor 11. This necessarily "outward and visible" form of the transmission of the "inward and spiritual grace" of the sacramental life of the Christian church may be understood as the essentially non-verbal or paralinguistic communication of a transcendent reality, that is appropriated through the deliverances of the physical senses. These "visible words" of the church's most characteristic body language, its paralinguistic or non-verbal communicative activity, necessarily involve the deliverances of the five senses.

This bears upon the nature of the church's resurrection faith insofar as it is in the sacramental acts of the church that the presence of the Raised Christ may be said to be *defined*. Even though Christ's presence is not *confined* within these acts, the point is that all the while, the religious claim to know a divinely given reality in faith (whether it be the presence of God or the presence of the Raised Christ) is achieved not by detachment from the deliverances of the five senses, but by an act of interpretative discernment in and through them.

This leaves us with the task of explaining the crucial question of how some deliverances of sense perception may justifiably be interpreted in faith specifically as "the presence of the Raised Jesus of Nazareth." Before we address that challenge, however, there are yet some further issues relating to the perception of the presence of human persons generally, and the significance of this for an understanding of the specific kind of knowing that is intrinsic to faith, that must be pursued. This will in turn lead us, first into a discussion of the way in which the judgment of faith is actually arrived at on the basis of the empirically perceived deliverances of sense perception, and second, how it is that some are able to come to the judgment faith while others do not.

6

The Presence of a Person

INSOFAR AS THE NATURE of faith, whether in God or in the Raised Christ, may be unpacked by drawing an analogy with the perception of attitudes and dispositions communicated, not only through verbal practices, but through non-verbal or paralinguistic mechanisms via the deliverances of the physical senses, it is important frankly to acknowledge that the reality with which faith claims to have to do must be a reality of an essentially *personal* kind. This is already implicit in the seminal insights concerning the role of the senses in the response of faith that Origen and Gregory of Nyssa found in the passionate inter-personal relation of the Lover and the Beloved of the *Song of Songs*. Obviously, this has important implications with respect to the understanding of the precise kind of knowing that is an implicit and necessary constituent of religious faith. For faith involves an experience of knowing in which the perceiver is engaged with what is claimed to be the personal reality of God (in some sense of "personal") or, in the case specifically of resurrection faith, the personal reality of the Raised Christ (in a more straightforward sense of "personal").

It follows that the kind of knowing that is essential to faith takes the necessary form of inter-personal relationality. As Martin Buber has taught us, the knowing appropriate to faith does not just involve the perception of an inert Religious Object; it involves an I-Thou relationship.[1] This is the case irrespective of whether we are speaking generally of the theistic perception in faith of the presence of God mediated in and through the created order, or, as Christians, more specifically of the perception of the "life-giving Spirit" of the Raised Christ. What may be claimed to be discerned in faith as the animating Spirit that endows the corporate life of the Christian community with the inner texture of its distinctive identity is an essentially personal reality. In faith it is claimed to be the Spirit of the personal God, or the Spirit of the person of the Raised Jesus Christ. Either way, in drawing an analogy between the perception of aspects of inter-personal human communication through the five senses, and the knowing appropriate to faith, the implicit assumption is that the perception of transcendent reality is legitimately understood in personal terms.

---

1. Buber, *I and Thou*, (*Ich und Du*, 1923).

If the Spirit that gives the Church its characteristic identity must necessarily be conceived in essentially personal terms, it is obvious enough that the knowing appropriate specifically to resurrection faith cannot just be like the knowing of an impersonal material object, such as in the seeing or observation of "a tree or a house," or even "another human body," understood merely in an objectifying and materialist kind of way.

Admittedly, the regular tendency of those who present the Easter Event essentially as a historical event of the past suggests that it involved an apparently matter-of-fact kind of seeing of a restored material body that was quite simply and starkly "there" to be outwardly "seen." Indeed, the suggestion is perhaps even that it was a body of the kind that could have been photographed had cameras been invented at the time.

Even so, and despite this starkly materializing tendency, most accounts of the appearances do not fail also to take notice of an identifiably inter-personal element within the Easter narrative tradition: Jesus addresses those present in various ways; he assures them of his identity,[2] he talks with them[3] and questions them;[4] he commissions them for mission.[5] Very importantly, he breaks bread with them, eats fish and (in some manuscripts) honeycomb with them, and even prepares breakfast on a seashore.[6] Similarly, whether in faith we claim to know the personal divine reality of the Being of God, or the presence of the remembered historical Jesus who, as a result of his Resurrection, is understood to have been exalted and transformed so as now to be revealed as an omnipresent "life-giving Spirit," we are trading with the category not of passively inert observable objects, but of "persons." Apart from being *objects* of perception, they are *subjects* whose presence is discerned by people of faith *as they know themselves to be addressed*. Similarly, along with a response of trusting faith, believers at the same time are moved to reciprocate in response to the experience of being addressed *by addressing both God and the Raised Christ* in prayer and worship.

This element of "relationality" is in fact logically demanded by the nature of faith itself insofar as it involves not just a kind of knowing (*fides*), but also an element of trust (*fiducia*). For faith, whether in God or in the Raised Christ, is a commitment of trust of a kind that is normally placed in *persons*. It is admittedly true that it is possible to speak of placing one's trust in a material object. I might trust, for example, that the nail I have just hammered into the wall will be strong enough to hold the picture I intend to hang upon it. But the kind of trust that is integral to the response of religious faith is a trust of the more specific kind that in this world is placed in a person or persons. It is essentially persons *in whom* one places one's trust in a religious sense.

2. Luke 24:39; and John 20:20, 24–29.
3. Luke 24:17–27.
4. Luke 24:17.
5. Matt 28:18–20; John 20:19–23.
6. Luke 24:30, 41–43; John 21:12–13.

In resurrection faith, for example, we trust that Christ will be with us always, just as he promised.[7] In faith more generally understood, the believer trusts that God will be faithful to the promise of the divine covenant. It is therefore obviously important that the kind of knowledge that is intrinsic to faith involves, not just any kind of knowledge that might be delivered via the five senses; for, in addition, it must also be the kind of knowledge that makes a response of trust of a personal kind possible.

It can be cogently argued that faith as a kind of knowledge (*fides*) is always *logically* prior to faith as trust (*fiducia*). This is for the obvious reason that it would be irrational to trust the untrustworthy; a knowledge of a person precisely as trustworthy is therefore logically prior to the placing of trust in that person. In actual experience, however, *fides* and *fiducia* go hand in hand in such a way that the one is not found without the other; in other words, while *fides* is *logically* prior to *fiducia*, in *temporal* and *experiential* terms, both may be coincidental with one another, as different constituent elements of the one faith commitment.

This means that the specific kind of "seeing" and "hearing" that is appropriate to the faith of a Christian believer, informs a knowing in present experience that is not just a seeing of aspects of reality in the detached and scientific kind of way that any material object might be observed or scrutinized. Rather, what the believer claims to know by acquaintance through the deliverances of sense experience, utilizing the physical senses both in verbal and non-verbal paralinguistic communication as essential ingredients in the make-up of faith, can only be handled by appeal to the category of "a person." Resurrection faith, in other words, involves more than just "seeing" something objective to one's self.

The concept of "a person" begs an enormous number of questions, even when we are speaking in purely human terms, let alone in specifically religious terms. Indeed, a whole book could be written in relation to this topic: here we will have to be content with some sketchy and impressionistic observations that hopefully will be sufficient to secure the point that the knowing that is intrinsic to Christian faith must have to do with the knowledge of a person.

Historically, there have been some classic paradigm ways of conceiving of "a person." In Greek tragedy, for example, the concept of a person was expressed first in the form of a mask or face (*prosōpon*) and then the *role* portrayed through it. St. Paul seems to work with this inherited Greek notion insofar as he expresses his hope of meeting the Raised Christ "face to face," or "in person" as we would say today. By contrast, in the

---

7. Matt 28:20.

Roman world a more juridical concept of a *persona* denoted one who enjoyed certain legally defined rights of citizenship, such as the right to own property (including the right to own slaves), and the right to participate in civic affairs. Insofar as Paul also worked with a moral understanding influenced by Stoic norms of argument in working out the behavior appropriate to those whose "citizenship is in heaven,"[8] this Roman concept of a "person" probably also hovers in the close background.

However, the early Church Fathers of Cappadocia in the fourth-century, Gregory of Nazianzus, Gregory of Nyssa, and his brother, Basil (the Great) of Caesarea, found neither of these inherited notions of a person satisfactory as they worked out the relations of what were to become known as the "Three Persons" of the Trinity. Clearly, the Greek notion of a mask or face and the role played by it suggested a kind of modalism. It would have suggested that the one God might be understood to operate in three different masks or guises (the heresy of Sabellius). Even today, we still speak of a specific individual expressing the *persona* or "social role" of father, office boss, or teacher, in this kind of way, but that was not what the Cappadocians sought to express in their formulation of the doctrine of the Trinity. On the other hand, the Roman notion of a *persona* also had to be avoided because its use would have suggested three separate persons of equal status and dignity. In other words, three persons with equal rights. Clearly, this would have landed them in a kind of tri-theism. This was also obviously unsatisfactory for expressing what they had in mind.

Their alternative understanding of what it means to be a person was one of the really great steps forward in the history of ideas. In grappling with the inter-relatedness of the Father and the Son and the Holy Spirit, the Cappadocians effectively came to discern that there is a fundamental difference between an individual and a person. Whereas an individual is conceived in separation from others, or "over against" others in a group, a person is essentially *related to* others. Relationality, in other words, is essential to being a person, and even to the possession of a specific personal identity. The Cappadocians came to see that the Father could not be the Father without the Son, and that the one has his identity in relation to the other. Moreover, for the Father to be unchangeably the Father "from all eternity," it was entailed that the Son must have been "eternally begotten" of the Father. Likewise, the Spirit has an eternal divine identity by "proceeding" ineffably from the Father; it is the Spirit *of* the Father. Moreover, in the light of resurrection faith, it is the Spirit *of* Christ the Son that also bears witness to the Son. These are not just three separate individuals but three Persons, internally related in one indivisible Unity of Being. The tri-theism of conceiving Father, Son, and Holy Spirit as three separate individuals was not an option; instead they enjoy an essential unity as inter-dependent "persons."

It is understandable that, though the formula of "Three Persons and One Substance" was in the air at the time,[9] Basil in his *Treatise on the Holy Spirit* of c. AD375,

---

8. Phil 3:20.

9. Most notably since the Council of Nicaea of AD325, in dealing with Arius by appeal to the

shows a marked preference for the formula "Three Persons and One Communion." The Cappadocians thus arrived at the idea of three inter-related Persons, who are numerically one God because they are *relationally* one: they are of one heart and one mind; they are one by mutual self-gift. When one acts, the other two persons act together, for though identifiably distinct, all Three Persons nevertheless always move in perfect harmony of rhythm, like partners in a dance as one moving unit. Likewise, Basil says there is a "coincidence of willing" within the life of the Trinity. The Father finds his own will reflected back to himself (like an image in a mirror) by the Son, who is not under any kind of compulsion or duress, but responds freely and willingly. Such is the essential inter-relatedness in love of the Persons of the Trinity, which at the same time allows them to be known as identifiably distinct Persons by virtue of their essential and indivisible relatedness to one another.

In the West, Tertullian anticipated these Cappadocian insights, at least in some degree, by recognizing a kind of "social role" between the *personae* of Father, Son and Spirit, while thinking of the persons as ontological identities so as to avoid the pitfall of modalism.[10] But it was the Cappadocians of the fourth-century who are to be credited with working out the essential relationality of the Persons of the Trinity, with the Father as the source of the divinity of the Son and the Spirit (as against the sharing by all three in "divinity" understood as a kind of "substance"). They thus discovered the concept of "a person" as distinct from a mere individual in the process. As John Zizioulas says: "The concept of a person with its absolute and ontological content was born historically from the endeavor of the Church to give ontological expression to its faith in the Triune God."[11]

Though all this may sound as though it was worked out somewhat abstractly as a formal exercise in the logic of relations, it has to be said that the Cappadocian Fathers did their theologizing about the nature of God in the concretely experiential context of a local Eucharistic community. What they defined theologically in terms of "identifiable persons in one communion" they actually knew in concrete human experience in the inter-personal sharing of the communion of the church's life and worship. Moreover, this was not so much a Platonic "reflection" of the divine Persons-in-Communion of the Trinity, so much as a participation of the one in the other, with baptism marking the incorporation of human persons of repentance and faith not just into the life of the church, but thereby through the gift of the Spirit into the dynamics of the shared inter-personal divine life of the Trinity.

---

homoousion.

10. *Against Praxeas* 4.4; 7.9; 11.9–10; 12.9; 21–23. See Jenson, *Systematic Theology*, 1:118–19.

11. Zizioulas, *Being as Communion*, 36. Also, "On Being a Person," *Communion and Otherness*, chap. 2, 99–112.

As a consequence of this, the capacity for inter-personal give-and-take between the Persons of the Trinity is capable of an anthropological application insofar as it allows us to think of human beings as also "persons" and not just as individuals. In the Hebrew-Christian tradition, human beings are persons precisely because they may be said to have been made in "the image of God."[12] That is to say, humans are made capable of entering into a personal relationship with God, and it is this that uniquely distinguishes them from the rest of the animal world. No sooner are Adam and Eve created in the "image of God" therefore than God begins to relate to them by addressing them.[13] In a sense, it is because humans are made capable of a unique form of inter-personal relationship with God and with others in God, that they therefore understand themselves to be distinct from all other animal creatures. In other words, human beings, as distinct from all the rest of animal creation, understand themselves to have been made in the "'image of God" so as to be capable of being addressed by God and to be able to respond in a similar way *to* God in worship and prayer. Likewise, humans have their being as persons, as distinct from individuals, in relation to others rather than in separation from them, and at a social level through the experience of inter-personal give-and-take are able to grasp their own personal identity. This means that humans are created with a capacity for inter-personal communication, because there is a sense in which they too, like the Persons of the Godhead, are "persons" and not just isolated individuals. This invites the definition of a person as one who may address another and who may expect a response of similar kind. Human persons are thus unique in the animal world, not so much as "the rational animal" (following Aristotle), but as "the praying animal"—they are uniquely those who are capable of hearing the personal address of God and of responding, precisely as "persons," by addressing God in prayer and worship.[14]

It follows that, while an individual *qua* individual might be objectively observed, and said therefore to have been "seen" by others, a person is one who is both seen and known in the specific sense of being related to through the uniquely divine/human capacity to be addressed by another. Furthermore, as distinct from an individual, a person is able to respond to being addressed in a similar way. Inter-personal give-and-take means that each subject is available as object to the other as subject. It is when humans relate to others only as subjects to objects without reciprocity, that they are all personally and humanly diminished.

It follows from this understanding of what it means to be a person, that the specific kind of knowing appropriate to faith, precisely because it involves the claim to know, not just any kind of reality that happens to be objective to the believer, but an essentially *personal* knowing *of* God, or *of* the Raised Christ, must also involve a kind

---

12. Gen 1:26–27.

13. Gen 1:28: "And God said to them, be fruitful and multiply . . . etc."

14. See Jenson, "The Praying Animal," and *Systematic Theology*, II, chapter 20 titled "Human Personhood."

of "hearing" as well as "seeing." As an inter-personal relational knowing, resurrection faith must involve more than just the kind of "seeing" that is appropriate to the perception of inert material objects, for "hearing" the address of another is essential to the kind of knowing specific to *persons*. Among the deliverances of the five physical senses, "hearing" and responding by "speaking" to what is heard, as well as "seeing," are together therefore really essential to faith, for the obvious reason that, while material objects may be "seen," human *persons* are both seen *and heard*. Moreover, they are heard in the mode of address that invites a response of a similar kind. Only so are they capable of drawing a personal response from others who make themselves available to be seen and heard in similar fashion. The "seeing" appropriate to resurrection faith is therefore quite positively not to be assimilated to "the seeing of a tree, a house, and another human body," as in the theology of Stephen Davis which bears the imprimatur of N. T. Wright. Between houses and trees, and even the rest of animal creation, there is no inter-personal conversation.

Perhaps it is important to pause to point out that the howler that whales, porpoises, and even honeybees communicate with a rudimentary language fails to recognize a quite distinct feature of human language. This is the uniquely important feature of human language that it is constituted by conventionally agreed meanings being freely adopted in distinct linguistic communities. There may well be a kind of communication between whales and honeybees, but there never has been a time when a community of whales or bees has agreed on, or changed, the conventional meanings to be assigned to specific signs. By contrast with the linguistic communications of human persons, the communications of the rest of the animal world simply signal that other animals are caught in the regularities of nature.[15] This is by contrast with the freely agreed-upon conventional meanings of human linguistic communities: in human linguistic communities, the same sounds may in fact signal different conventionally agreed upon meanings, and, *vice versa*, different sounds may signal the same meanings, among different linguistic groups. This is an entirely different phenomenon from the communications between animals that are simply regularities of nature. I think we can safely hold to the conviction that human beings are uniquely created as persons in the "image of God" as "the praying animal."

An implication of the fact that faith involves engagement with "a person," whether it be God understood in personal terms, or the person of the Raised Jesus Christ, is therefore that, among the five physical senses, both "seeing" and "hearing" are essential

---

15. The so-called "dance language" of honeybees (after Karl von Frisch of Munich, *The Dance Language and Orientation of Bees*) does not qualify as a language at all, for it is not a system of conventionally agreed upon meanings. Bees in their communications are simply caught in a regularity of nature.

ingredients of the make-up of the kind of knowing appropriate to it. At the same time, if humans are made in the "image of God," and are thus "the praying animal," the response of prayer and worship addressed *to* God, or alternatively *to* the Raised Christ, is likewise a concomitant of the commitment of trusting faith. From a human point of view, both prayer and worship are a natural part of the personal response to the discernment in faith of the address both *of* God and *of* God in Christ.

On the other hand, in some recent theology of the Resurrection of Christ there has been a tendency to reduce the Easter experience to a kind of "hearing" by playing down the eyewitness quality of the first appearances. In other words, the "hearing" that is appropriate to the response of faith is privileged over "seeing," even to the point of eliminating the element of "seeing" in the interpretation of the Easter appearance narratives. Wilhelm Michaelis, for example, endeavored to assimilate the *Christophanies* to the Jewish tradition of *Theophanies* in which it is reported in faith that "the Lord appeared *and said* . . ." (as in Gen 12:7; 17:1; 26:2, 24; and 35:9).[16] Thus Michaelis argued that no particular weight should be attached to *seeing* by the original witnesses. Because the New Testament emphasis is on the revelatory nature of the Easter traditions, "No particular attention is paid in the NT to seeing as a physiological-psychological process."[17] Rather, Paul's Damascus Road experience, in which the hearing of a voice predominates, becomes the model for all the "appearances." Thus, Michaelis concludes: "in all the appearances the presence of the risen Lord is a presence in transfigured corporeality . . . It is the presence of the exalted Lord from heaven. This presence is in non-visionary reality."[18] "There can be no doubt as to the primacy of hearing . . . seeing is also a kind of hearing; that is to say, it, too, is a receiving of revelation."[19] Similarly, Pheme Perkins is also prepared to argue that the early traditions of the Resurrection are "auditory and not visionary."[20] It is difficult is see how this does justice to the tradition of "appearances" in which at least some kind of visionary element seems an essential ingredient.[21]

In any event, in response to the thesis of Michaelis, Daniel Kendall and Gerald O'Collins have pointed out the discrepancy between Easter experiences and the Old Testament prophetic tradition of the revelation of the word and the element of "hearing" that features in the Theophanic appearances.[22] They point to six instances in which resurrection appearances are reported with *no* auditory element

16. Michaelis, "ὁράω," 355–61.
Also, O'Collins, "The Appearances of the Risen Christ,"134.

17. Michaelis, "ὁράω," 346.

18. Michaelis, "ὁράω," 359.

19. Michaelis, "ὁράω," 348.

20. Pheme Perkins, *Resurrection*, 137.

21. Wright, *RSG*, 323 n. 27, says that he simply does not understand this, though he does not enter into any discussion of Perkins's reasoning.

22. Kendall and O'Collins, "The Uniqueness of the Easter Appearances," 134. Also, on the importance of "seeing," O'Collins, "The Appearances of the Risen Christ."

(the four cases of the use of ōphthē, in 1 Cor 15:5–8, and also in *Luke* 24:34 and *Acts* 13:31). It is understandable that there is an anxious desire to defend the visionary nature of the Easter appearances in this way. However, it is important not to be nervously defensive and unnecessarily apologetic, for it has to be said that of the six examples of appearances that are without mention of an auditory element listed by Kendall and O'Collins, four are in the kerygmatic summary quoted by Paul in 1 Cor 15:5–8. Apart from the questionable methodological procedure of trying to establish theological truth by citing numerical instances rather than relying upon cogent argument, it is problematic that theological significance can be read into the absence of detail from what is essentially a *summary*. Who knows if an auditory element was entirely absent from the appearance to Peter and the twelve, or James and the apostles, or to the crowd of over five hundred for that matter? Furthermore, as Michaelis point out, we certainly know of an auditory element in Luke's accounts of the appearance to Paul on the Damascus Road. On the other hand, as we have already noted, an auditory element is clearly important to the appearances tradition in order to establish an inter-personal interaction. For example, the address of the Raised Christ to a person by name as in "Saul, Saul,"[23] or "Mary,"[24] the commission to proclaim the Gospel,[25] the promise of the Raised Christ to be with his disciples to the end of the age,[26] or his promise of the gift of peace,[27] which is not just any kind of peace but explicitly "*my* peace," a personally delivered peace. This is not to mention the necessary involvement of an auditory element in the inter-personal sharing in the context of meals. At the very least, all this suggests some form of *personal* engagement as an intrinsic element of the primitive Easter experience; it was not just a bald "seeing" or impersonal "observing" of some*thing*.

Willi Marxsen has also pointed to the logical priority of the category of the personal in the Easter traditions. Given that the initial experience of faith involved the claim to have encountered the presence of *Jesus*, he argues that it was a secondary *interpretation* of this essentially personal identification by name when the first Christians then went on to employ the interpretative resources of their inherited tradition that allowed them then to speak in terms of "resurrection," rather than just the return of a resuscitated Jesus. Thus, Marxsen's thesis is that *first* they claimed to have encountered *Jesus*, and *then* as a secondary interpretation they identified him as the *Raised One*.[28] In other words, the category of the personal is initially determinative of the experience. While this two stage thesis becomes less convincing when it is remembered that, when understood as a *Christophany*, a heavenly and exalted element attached to an essentially visionary

---

23. Acts 9:4.
24. John 20:16.
25. Matt 28:19.
26. Matt 28:20.
27. John 20.
28. Marxsen, "The Resurrection of Jesus," 34.

experience from the very beginning, so as to make it *more than* just a "meeting with a person," Marxsen's point may nevertheless be taken, that the Easter encounters were claimed from the start to be encounters of a personal kind with *Jesus*.

When it comes to the faith of the church through the ages and the experience of the presence of the Spirit of Christ, a personal identification is axiomatic and unavoidable. The Spirit that is constitutive of the communion of the church, and that is perceived in faith to be "the life-giving Spirit" or the "Spirit of life in Christ Jesus," is clearly not just an anonymous presence. Far from just being a quasi-divine Stoic "warm breath," it bears the identity of the character of Christ. The fact that the church is pneumatically constituted by the Spirit as a *communion* of people reconciled to one another and to God in Christ means that the knowing of the presence of the Spirit in faith must be more than just an outward visual or observational awareness of an anonymous "something," but a knowing of a more personal kind: it is identified as the Spirit *of* the Raised Jesus. As Hans Frei was at pains to point out, presence and identity go hand in hand.[29] The presence of the Spirit is identified in faith as the love of God in Christ, the Spirit *of* Christ, or the Spirit *of* God.

This then is the specific kind of knowing that is achieved via the deliverances of the five physical senses, operating in the cause of trusting faith understood in a context of inter-personal communication. And among the five senses, it seems clear that a combination of both "seeing" and "hearing" will be important in the make-up of the experience of faith. In this way, faith may be understood as a commitment of trust based upon a knowing by acquaintance, in which an element of address of the kind that is essential to inter-personal communication in which *we* know ourselves to *be* persons, is clearly an important feature.

Now given that in faith the operation of the physical senses, and the sense of sight and hearing in particular, may be said to ground the perception of the transcendent inter-personal reality of the Being of God, and that, more specifically, the resurrection faith of Christian believers is similarly grounded in the perception of the concrete personal presence of Christ as a "life-giving Spirit," something more remains to be explained. How more exactly are we to understand the actual manner in which the deliverances of the five senses are "logically processed" by the religious believer in such a way as to ground the conviction of faith and the making of faith claims? More specifically, what is the logical process "between" the raw religious experiences that may be understood to have been delivered via the five physical senses, and actual claims to know the

---

29. Indeed, this is the fundamental thesis of Frei in *The Identity of Jesus Christ*.

personal reality of the Spirit of God or of the Raised Christ? In other words, given that perceptual experiences may be called upon to operate in a doxastic or "faith-creating" way so as to ground the judgment and commitment of faith, how are we to understand, as a matter of religious practice, the actual linkage between the deliverances of sense perception and the coming to the judgment of faith on the basis of them? What *kind* of logical processes are involved?

I have already endeavored to rule out one doxastic possibility. It has been argued that faith is not just a matter of drawing a rational conclusion of a deductive kind, so as to come to the conviction of assent to the abstract proposition *that* there is a God, or *that* Jesus actually did rise from the dead. Instead, it has been argued that faith is a response of trust (*fiducia*) based upon a knowing by acquaintance, a relational knowing (*fides*) of the personal presence *of* the Being of God. Or, in the case of Easter faith, it is a trust based upon a relational knowing *of* the person of the Raised Jesus Christ, mediated to people of faith through the active presence of his life-giving Spirit. In this way, the role of the Spirit is to bear witness to the Son. But the actual doxastic practice by which a person of faith actually arrives at a conviction of religious assent of this kind, somehow on the basis of the deliverances of the five physical senses, remains somewhat opaque.

Once again, an historical paradigm may help us towards increased clarity. In the nineteenth-century, John Henry Newman examined the logical roots of the certitude with which a human person comes to religious conviction. Newman's insights remain both intellectually impressive and practically helpful. In his *Essay in Aid of a Grammar of Assent*, Newman famously distinguished the strict logic of the formal inferences of speculative intelligence (as for example, the deductive logic employed in the traditional arguments for the existence of God), from the plethora of "informal inferences" that he believed "real persons" rely upon in the process of coming to their religious convictions. Newman's basic assumption here is that human persons are not just minds. By contrast with a more rationalistic approach, for example, to the so-called "proofs" of the existence of God through the drawing of the abstract inferences of strictly formal "paper logic" (as he disparagingly referred to it), Newman argued that real persons come to faith judgments as the result of the more subtle operation of a complex network of perceived signs and "informal inferences."[30]

By the formal inferences of "paper logic," Newman meant the kind of deductive reasoning that has traditionally been modeled on a mathematical paradigm, with its appeal to strict logical necessity. Ideally, strictly deductive reasoning aims at reaching logical conclusions which follow from the (true) premises of an argument with a logical certainty akin to that which we appreciate when we grasp the truth that 2 + 2

---

30. Newman speaks of "the cumulation of probabilities, independent of each other . . . probabilities too fine to avail separately, too subtle and circuitous to be converted into syllogisms, too numerous and various for such conversion, even were they convertible." Newman, *Grammar of Assent*, 230.

must *necessarily* equal 4. Newman contended that very few of our beliefs are actually established in his kind of strictly formal way.

Instead, he argued that the growing inner conviction of assent in faith of a whole human person is achieved through the operation of what he termed the "illative sense." By the illative sense he says he has in mind a kind of religious sensibility correlative to, and capable of discerning the basic drift within, a plethora of "informal inferences" grounded in the experience of real life. For him this was something analogous to "common sense," or a "sense of the beautiful," but brought into the arena of religion and applied to a specifically religious content. It is the capacity, he believed, that comes into play when religious believers achieve a kind of inner psychological certainty as distinct from strict logical certainty.

Though Newman believed that the "illative sense" operates with respect to belief in the religious domain, he did not confine it exclusively to religious belief. Rather, Newman contended that the operation of the illative sense is something that characterizes many other forms of belief as well. He appealed to the notion of the illative sense, therefore, to explain many day-to-day beliefs about things that are beyond the range of our own observation. For example, he noted that many of the basic beliefs by which we live our lives are ultimately somewhat abstract and even second-hand in nature, and are not based either upon strictly deductive processes of logic or even upon direct sensory experience. Apart from the rarity of coming to such beliefs on the basis of the formal deductive inferences to which he referred as "paper logic," he pointed out that most of the certainties to which we give our assent are much less formally based. He illustrated the range of day-to-day beliefs by which we conduct our lives, by citing the belief "that the earth, considered as a phenomenon, is a globe; that all of its regions see the sun by turns; that there are vast tracts on it of land and water; that there are really existing cities on definite sites, which go by the names of London, Paris, Florence and Madrid."[31] All these beliefs are based, not so much on direct observation, nor on strictly logical deductive processes, but on a mass of less formal indications and testimonies. Thus, by contrast with an approach to belief as a judgment made at the end of a perfectly cogent and logical chain of formal reasoning, reliance on the illative sense is a matter of discerning the drift of a miscellaneous mass of evidence.[32]

Now, it is important to note that this approach to religious faith does not involve a discussion of the operation of the five senses in coming to the conviction of religious assent. Indeed, Newman's focus is upon beliefs that are not based upon direct observational evidence or experience. Nor does Newman work with an understanding of the knowing that is appropriate to faith as a knowing by acquaintance. Rather, Newman's

---

31. Newman, *Grammar of Assent*, 149.

32. John Hick, in an exemplary discussion of Newman's concept of the illative sense, sums it up as "Our capacity to see large fields of evidence as a whole and divine its significance . . ." (Hick, *Faith and Knowledge*, 81).

starting point is the assumption that religious belief is fundamentally doctrinal and propositional, and that it has to do with convictions that are in fact arrived at despite the fact that they are not based upon direct observation or sensory perception of any kind. One might otherwise have imagined that what he speaks of as the "illative sense" precisely explains the way in which the complex deliverances of sense experience might, on analogy with the signs and inferences of non-verbal or paralinguistic communication, be processed so as to allow the believer to come to the conviction of faith. But this is not the case.

One reason why Newman approached religious belief on analogy with many day-to-day beliefs of a propositional kind, but took little interest in the deliverances of sense experience or an approach to faith as a form of immediate perception and acquaintance, was that Newman was from a very early time entirely alienated from the argument for the existence of God from the perception of design in the universe. His theological teachers and mentors, Richard Whately and Edward Copleston, were representatives of a post-Humean disenchantment with the design argument. Hume had engineered a trenchant demolition of the design argument though his critique of the presentation of it that he articulated through the character of Cleanthes in his *Dialogues Concerning Natural Religions*. Speaking through the opposing voices of Philo and Demea in the *Dialogues*, Hume appeared very successfully and systematically to have dealt with the argument from design. Whately and Copleston fully embraced the critique of the argument as Hume had presented it through the voices of Philo and Demea. In particular, Whately and Copleston became fully conscious of the inescapable anthropomorphism of conceiving God as a designer or architect on analogy with human designers and architects, and thus opted for Demea's contention of the sublime incomprehensibility of God as God is in God's self. For Demea, God is an unknowable mystery, always beyond the limits of religious language. Newman's approach to theology must be understood in essentially the same way.[33]

As a consequence, Newman was naturally inclined therefore to move away from any interest in perceiving the presence of God in and through the created order, and therefore away from assigning a role to the five senses in religious perception. By contrast with the design argument, he therefore found the moral argument for the existence of God far more compelling. For Newman, the experiential point of entry to the knowledge of the ultimate mystery of God was therefore through the operation of "the inner voice of conscience" understood as the moral pressure of the Divine Will. This, rather than anything perceived by the five physical senses, is thus primarily what led him to the conviction of the existence of the divine, understood as the author of the moral order of the universe.

33. If we employ the contrasting theological approaches outlined by David Hume in his *Dialogues of Natural Religion*, Newman is to be understood as a Demea theologian, with an initial commitment to the surpassing mystery of a God who is ultimately remote, sublime, and incomprehensible, as against the approach to God of Hume's Cleanthes as an exponent of the design argument. See Carnley, "Demea Tradition in Anglican Theology."

Newman's negative assessment of the design argument was thus the chief factor that led him away from any suggestion that the illative sense might be brought to bear on the myriad deliverances of the five senses in what would have been a more openly empirical approach to the understanding of the nature of faith. Unfortunately, his appeal to the illative sense therefore delivered him as hostage to a substantially propositional and doctrinal view of the ultimate content of faith. Given that religious belief tends to be understood by Newman to be of a piece precisely with day-to-day propositional beliefs, such as *that* the earth is a globe, *that* its regions see the sun by turns, *that* cities of London, Paris, Florence and Madrid exist, and so on, this is unavoidable. As a consequence, the body of specifically religious belief, as Newman conceived it, tends likewise to be understood propositionally. The content of belief is expressed in such statements as the belief *that* God exists, or *that* Christ was divine, or *that* Christ was raised from the dead. This contrasts with an empirical knowing *of* the divine or *of* the Spirit of Christ. The perception of the moral pressure of the Divine Will through the inwardly heard voice of conscience is the closest Newman comes to an understanding of faith as a knowing by acquaintance either of God or of the Raised Christ, or in terms of other forms of inter-personal communication. This inner voice, originally informed by the definitive revelation of the incarnate life and teaching of Jesus, is, for Newman, as a consequence of the Resurrection, known living still as something with which he was acquainted. He therefore spoke (famously) of conscience as the personal awareness of "the aboriginal Vicar of Christ." In this sense, "hearing" bulks large in Newman's approach to religious knowledge in a way that "seeing" does not; however, it is an inner "hearing" detached from, rather than integrated with, the deliverances of sense experience.

Even so, some of Newman's illustrations of the illative sense nevertheless come close to providing a corrective both to this nearly exclusive emphasis on the inner voice of conscience, and with it a corrective to his ultimate reliance on the propositional nature of religious beliefs. For example, apart from the operation of the illative sense in relation to beliefs that are held even in the absence of sense experience and direct observation, he (perhaps unwittingly) notes that the illative sense also operates in a more observational context: he points out that if a person's character makes a consistent impression on us over time, we tend to come to an opinion of that person. This, once again, is not so much the result of a strict procedure of deductive reasoning, but of a more inductive and intuitive assessment based upon repeated instances of encounters and informally acquired impressions. In many instances these observations and impressions are also experiences of which we are not particularly conscious. Indeed, much of Newman's talk of "informal inferences," as distinct from the strict procedures of formal logic, actually appears to be making the distinction between strictly deductive procedures in which a conclusion is reached at the end of a chain of abstract reasoning, and inductive reasoning in which an array of similar instances are appealed to in order to ground a general conclusion. In the example of the perception of a person's quality of character, it is clear that the illative sense is understood to gather and process a mass of information apparently received via the five physical senses, perhaps sometimes even functioning unconsciously as in non-verbal or paralinguistic communication.

In this case, it is important to note that the conviction of assent resulting from the drawing of "informal inferences" by the illative sense may therefore be based on actual evidence; indeed, as Newman himself says, it relies on a body of evidence so vast as often to defy the recall of separate particular items. It is the illative sense that "puts all this together," as it were, and discerns a particular significance in it. However, the sheer vastness and the subtlety and complexity of what is perceived often makes it difficult to express and verbally convey to another the actual grounds on which a particular opinion is based. The whole exercise is much more intuitive, though, if asked, at least some justifying grounds would have to be cited in order to demonstrate the ultimate rationality of a specific conclusion or conviction.[34]

The gradual accumulation of countless "informal inferences," apparently of an inductive kind, which in Newman's case were primarily triggered by the "hearing" of the inner voice of conscience, may equally be understood therefore to ground a more empirical approach to faith via the operation of the five physical senses. In this case, a concentration of interest on assent to abstract propositions or "beliefs" may be replaced by a concrete sense of the presence, let us say, *of* the love of God, or *of* the Spirit of the Raised Christ, that is accompanied by a trusting sense of well-being, along with a sense of human life being divinely directed, and of the obligation to respond in prayer and worship. Religious faith in this sense becomes a way of interpreting the experience of life, not at the end of a series of deductive steps, but by "putting together" a welter of informal inferences of a more inductive kind, so as to ground the conviction of the whole universe being divinely supported and governed, and of human life being under the obligation to respond to the moral pressure of the Divine Will.[35]

Despite reservations about the propositional nature of the beliefs that give content of Newman's theory of religious assent, what he has to say about the assent of faith through the exercise of the illative sense, rather than through reliance on more strictly formal logical inference, may therefore be judged to be well taken. At the conclusion of a searching discussion of Newman's *Grammar of Assent*, the considered assessment of the twentieth-century philosopher of religion, John Hick, is that "Newman's doctrine of the illative sense . . . is to be accepted as substantially

---

34. Just as in the case of the intuitive recognition of one's wife when one wakes next to her in the morning is intuitive in the sense that it does not rely upon the rehearsal of a list of the characteristics which warrant this judgment before coming to the conclusion: "Yes, this is my wife." However, *if asked*, the rationality of such a conclusion may be demonstrated by citing at least some of these characteristics.

35. See the epistemological discussion of various aspects of religious experience by Alston in *Perceiving God*, 1991.

correct."³⁶ However, in acknowledging the positive value of Newman's point about the operation of the illative sense as against the strictly formal inferences of "paper logic," Hick also argues that faith does not come to rest in a set of doctrines and religious propositional truths of the kind that attracted Newman. Rather, for Hick, instead of coming to a set of propositional conclusions or beliefs, faith is a matter of interpreting concrete experience in a particular way. By contrast with, and effectively as a corrective to Newman, the myriad informal inferences of the illative sense may therefore be understood to be based upon the deliverances of sense experience, understood in the widest and most inclusive way, "not only visually but through all the modes of perception functioning together."³⁷ Faith thus becomes a way in which concrete experience is interpreted, that relies upon the deliverances of all five of the physical senses, and which employs the linguistic interpretive grid of a religious community to order it and make some meaningful sense of it.

Hick's positive assessment of Newman's notion of the illative sense therefore brings us back to an appreciation of the importance of the deliverances of the five senses, and especially the senses of sight and hearing, to supply the fundamental data upon which a religious commitment is made. Religious faith, whether as a commitment of trusting allegiance to the perceived presence of God in the world at large, or specifically as a commitment of trust in the resurrected Jesus who is principally known as the life-giving Spirit of the community of the baptized, is grounded in concrete experiences of life delivered via the senses. This means that faith as a matter of trust is grounded in a kind of perceptual knowing that is achieved by focusing upon specific aspects of experience and interpreting them by employing the concepts (and proper names) of a religious linguistic tradition.

For the purposes of this discussion, let us then assume the operation of the same dynamic when believers come to the religious conviction of faith in the resurrected Jesus Christ. Following Newman, we may usefully also distinguish the strictly formal arguments of an alleged proof of the Resurrection understood as an event of the historical past, from the much less formal way in which individual believers actually come to the commitment of resurrection faith in the course of the living of their lives. Generally speaking, believers come to faith in Christ's Resurrection *without* being trained in the techniques of critical historical argument, such as those involved when Christ's Resurrection is handled in the way promoted by N. T. Wright in *The Resurrection of the Son of God*. By contrast with an exclusive reliance on the exercise of critical historical reasoning, by adopting Newman's line of argument, resurrection faith may be understood as a conviction of assent that is arrived at, not at the end of a chain of deductive

---

36. Hick, *Faith and Knowledge*, 85–86.
37. Hick, *Faith and Knowledge*, 142.

reasoning, so much as by the assessment of a complex mass of informal inferences. These are based not only on a mixture of testimony and authoritative teaching, as with Newman, but especially on a believer's own experience of life, including quite specifically the life of shared religious experience in the community of faith, that is characterized most notably by the experience of what is discerned to be "the life-giving Spirit" of the Raised Christ in "the communion of the Holy Spirit."

I suspect that most will agree that the Christian believer does not usually come to faith at the end of a strictly formal process of logical argument. We are not argued into faith. Faith in the Resurrection of Christ is certainly not normally reached as the inevitable conclusion of the formal arguments of critical-historical research. Still less is it achieved on the basis of an apologetically defensive exercise of the speculative historical imagination, which chooses to regard the evidence as "good enough" to believe "*that* it happened," despite its logical shortfall. Resurrection faith is not a mere matter of "belief" in the sense of an inadequately evidenced propositional attitude. Nor, however, is faith normally arrived at by processes that are independent of, or detached from, the deliverances of sense experience, after the fashion of much neo-Platonically influenced medieval mysticism. Rather, faith is an empirically grounded way of interpreting the concrete experience of life by discerning the presence of a religiously significant reality within the textured deliverances of the five senses. In the case specifically of resurrection faith, it is a matter of interpreting and identifying the presence of "the life-giving Spirit" of Christ, or "the Spirit of life in Christ Jesus" (Paul), or the "abundant Spirit" or "Spirit without measure" (John), that is perceived principally, though not exclusively, through the embodied and corporately shared life and worship of the Christian community, to which St. Paul very appropriately therefore referred as "the Body of Christ."

If, by contrast with the conclusions of the abstract and essentially deductive arguments of critical historical research, the resurrection faith of Christians is a conviction arrived at by actually perceiving the presence of Christ mediated through a complex of "informal inferences," then a number of entailments seem to follow. First, these "informal inferences" are principally based upon a reading of the "body language" of the community of faith itself. As Ludwig Wittgenstein once said:

> Christianity is not based on a historical truth; rather, it offers us a (historical) narrative and says: now believe! But not, believe this narrative with the belief appropriate to a historical narrative, rather: believe through thick and thin, which you can do only as the result of a life.[38]

---

38. Wittgenstein, *Culture and Value*, 32e.

Second, what is perceived as the essentially personal Spirit that is constitutive of the inner texture of inter-personal life in the communion of the church, is not something achieved by its members through their own efforts. It is essential to faith that it is not a matter of trying but of trusting; it is a grace not a work. For, from the very beginning of Christian faith and practice, the church has been conscious of receiving the Spirit of Christ as an entirely undeserved gift. We rightly speak of "the *gift* of the Spirit" which is perceived through faith. It is described, not as a human accomplishment, but as "a sudden rushing wind" which blows when and where it wills. It wells up "like a spring of living water"; it is a deeply and indeed passionately moving "flame of fire" that burns within us. All this metaphorical religious language really only makes sense as language that together possesses a certain directionality of meaning insofar as it points towards the ineffable Object that passes all understanding. Even so, it is nevertheless perceived and apprehended, even if not comprehended, through the deliverances of a religious sensibility via the physical senses as something given and received.

But how is it that some see and come to faith, while others do not? And how is it that some hear and understand, but others remain deaf? This is the question to which we shall turn in the following chapter.

7

Faith and Freedom, Ambiguity and Doubt

IN *THE PHILOSOPHICAL INVESTIGATIONS*, Ludwig Wittgenstein drew attention to the interpretive aspect in all human perception. He noted that different people "see" reality differently, and so order experience conceptually in radically different ways. In other words, within limits, they are free to bring different but equally valid interpretative concepts to the ordering of experience. Wittgenstein illustrated this point through an appeal to puzzle pictures and the way in which people "see" different things in them, interpreting them "*as*" one thing rather than another. His most famous paradigm was that of the outline drawing of a duck-rabbit, which may be identified by some as a duck and by others as a rabbit. This also offers the possibility of "flitting" from one interpretation to the other, depending upon whether one aspect of what is seen is interpreted *as* a duck's bill or *as* a rabbit's ears.[1] This inherent ambiguity led Wittgenstein to the view that visual perception is always a kind of "seeing-*as*," for the deliverances of sense experience via the visual receptors of the eyes do not come bearing their own identifying labels: they always have to be interpreted *as* one thing rather than another.

Though Wittgenstein illustrated this feature of perception by appeal to a puzzle picture, this is thus something that actually applies to perception generally. All perception requires the interpretation of what is "seen" *as something*, but different people are free to see things differently. One man's beach ball may be seen *as* large and colored red and yellow; another may see the same ball *as* "not very bouncy." In this case, one views it from the point of view of its appearance; the other sees it in more operational or functional terms. Indeed, the same person may see the same reality on different occasions and interpret it differently from one time to another.

In *The Critique of Pure Reason*, Immanuel Kant likewise noted that the deliverances of sense experience (which he termed "intuitions") are always much more rich and complex than what is actually noticed and verbally expressed in relation to them, for "every intuition contains variety."[2] This means there is always more to be said, for any intuition has a greater richness than the sum of the judgments based upon it.[3]

---

1. Wittgenstein, *Philosophical Investigations*, 205–6.
2. Kant, *Critique of Pure Reason*, A99.
3. See the exposition of this aspect of Kant's thought in Dryer, *Kant's Solution for Verification in*

John Hick picked up on Wittgenstein's fascination with puzzle pictures to develop a theory of religious perception as a kind of "seeing-*as*" in which faith is explained and defended as one legitimate way of interpreting experience. Hick used the example of an "enigmatic page covered with dots apparently scattered over it at random" which, when looked at a little more closely, suddenly dawns on the viewer as "the picture of a man standing in a grove of trees."[4] By focusing on some elements on the page rather than others, a set of enigmatic markings comes to be seen entirely differently. The famous representation of "Jesus in Snow" is another example of the kind of thing Hick had in mind: white markings suggestive of melted snow on black pavement becomes, when the focus is shifted to the center of the picture at the top, a representation of "the face of Jesus."

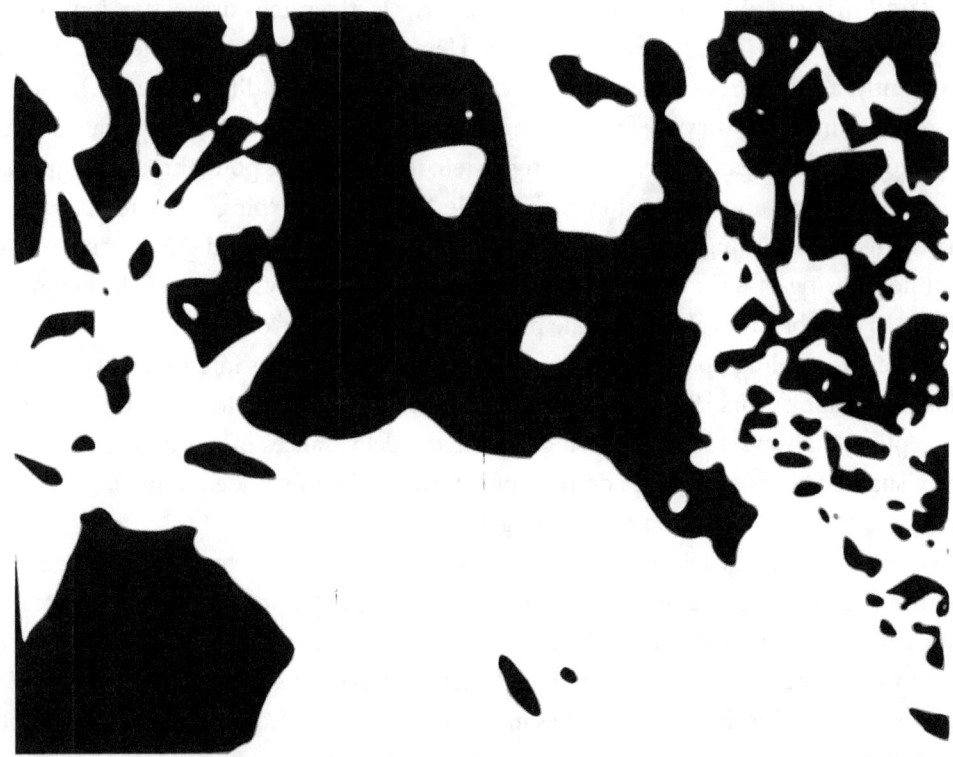

Figure 1: Jesus Christ, Face on the Snow. Used by permission of Jon Phillips of openclipart.org/. (https://openclipart.org/detail/190851/jesus-christ-face-on-the-snow)

In applying this philosophical insight about perceptual ambiguity, and the capacity to see and interpret things differently, specifically to religious perception, John Hick at the same time broadened Wittgenstein's notion of seeing-*as* to that of experiencing-*as*.[5] Hick came to see that the same interpretative principle applies to

---

Metaphysics, 66–68.

4. Hick, *Faith and Knowledge*, 142. See also, Hick, *Philosophy of Religion*, 71.

5. Hick, *Faith and Knowledge*, 142.

the deliverances of any of the five physical senses. When he spoke of experiencing-*as*, he had in mind the experience of life in its fullest sense; the many facetted personal experience of life, in other words, delivered over time by all five physical senses. Faith therefore became for Hick a commitment of trust based upon a logically prior knowing in which the experience of life as a whole is interpreted *as*, for example, "life in the presence of God," or life "*as* God-governed." From the perspective of this understanding of faith, it is easy to appreciate the reasons for Hick's positive assessment of Newman's discussion of the illative sense, and the myriad "informal inferences" upon which faith was said to rely.

Specifically in relation to his own reflections on religious commitment, Wittgenstein himself also noted the fact that different outcomes result from something more than just differences of perceptual standpoint. Indeed, in a collection of his aphoristic and somewhat enigmatic statements dating from the 1930s, which were published under the title of *Culture and Value*, it appears that Wittgenstein felt his way towards the insight that levels of religious perception not only resulted from the particular stance adopted by the beholder, but in some respects also from the inner moral and spiritual disposition of the beholder.[6]

It is important to be clear that he was not suggesting that the resulting perception of difference was just "in the eye of the beholder." In matters of religion, Wittgenstein was a realist by contrast with one committed to a non-cognitive or purely emotivist approach to religious language. Far from being an entirely subjective enterprise, wholly contained within the life of the believer, Wittgenstein suggests that the use of religious language "maps on to" something that is concretely and objectively there. However, what is there to be perceived is *interpreted* differently. Wittgenstein was apparently of the view that there were levels of perception that were accounted for by reference to corresponding levels of spiritual maturity and insight. His conclusion was that the dismantling of pride in favor of humbly seeking for truth, and levels of devoutness, lie behind the capacity of some to focus upon religious reality while others immerse themselves in what to a religious mind seem more trivial pursuits.[7]

Sarah Coakley has perceptively noted that these Wittgensteinian reflections resonate with the classic tradition of the spiritual senses going back to Gregory of Nyssa. Apart from providing for the continuity of religious perception with the deliverances of the physical senses (which was discussed in chapter 5 of this book), this tradition

---

6. This is a notion that is not foreign to the biblical tradition. For example, Jer 17:23: "Yet they did not listen or incline their ear; they stiffened their necks and would not hear or receive instruction." See also Jer 11:10, 25:4–5, 29:19, 35:16; and Psalm 28:5. We also find Paul entertaining a related notion in 2 Cor 4:3: "But if our gospel be hidden, it is hidden to them that are lost." See also, Matt 13:15; John 6:60; Rom 11:8; Heb 5:11; Acts 28:27; and 2 Tim 4:3–4.

7. Wittgenstein, *Culture and Value*, 32c.

of the spiritual senses spoke of the way in which moral and spiritual maturity allows for greater spiritual discernment.[8] The disposition of the believer, or potential believer, is determinative not of what there is to be perceived, but of what he or she perceives, given what is "there." As Coakley says ". . . when Wittgenstein talks . . . of the necessity to 'dismantle one's pride' (stressing that it is 'hard work'), or to lead a life of a *completely different* sort as a precondition of belief, or to train one's eye to look 'with practice' for the right things, one is struck by the progressive nature of the epistemological undertaking and its accompanying preparatory moral seriousness."[9] This invites the idea that possible levels of perception may be prioritized in accordance with internal perceptual dispositions, different levels of spiritual maturity, understanding, or practice. The suggestion is that, insofar as a determination to focus one's attention beyond just a surface reading of the experience of life, to the divine reality expressed in and through it, a "turn around," something akin to a conversion, may be necessary.

Coakley also notes that some of the more alluring features of the gospels' resurrection narratives are suggestive of this very thing: she cites the conscious act of "turning towards" the object of perception in Mary Magdalene's encounter with the Raised Jesus in John 20:14, for example. Before she could see anything, Mary had physically to turn herself around. Undoubtedly, this is why in the Christian tradition repentance and faith always go together. Though repentance is often understood in terms of hand-wringing and chest thumping, or even sitting in dust and ashes as in a kind of grovel, Christian repentance is essentially a turning, a conscious turning towards one thing, which is necessarily a turning away from another. The point is that, in order to perceive transcendent reality in faith, the believer may have to incline towards it, by seeking to focus on it in a spirit of attentiveness.

Wittgenstein in this way pointed to the achievement of religious perception by those perceptually attuned, while allowing others to maintain an entirely secular disinterest. In a way analogous to the aesthetic appreciation of beauty in a painting, or the moral assessment of goodness in an observable behavior, this kind of discernment involves an inclination on the part of the perceiver to focus away from the purely physical and material face of reality in order to respond to what Otto called an "overplus" of meaning and significance in relation to the discernment of the *numinous*. This, of course, is far from being a modern insight. Origen put essentially the same point when he observed that Christ "appeared after his resurrection not to all people but only to those whom he perceived to have obtained eyes which had the capacity to see the resurrection."[10]

---

8. Coakley, *Powers and Submissions*, 141–48.
9. Coakley, *Powers and Submissions*, 146.
10. Origen, *Contra Celsum*, II. 65. 116.

On the other hand, even in ordinary day-to-day perception we often look at something and do not see it. When the First Fleet of British colonists sailed through the heads of Sydney Harbor into Port Jackson on 26 January 1788, the indigenous Australian aboriginal inhabitants simply went about their business, oblivious to the arrival of those on tall ships who were soon to upturn their lives. Though the First Fleet was clearly there to be seen, it was something which was so entirely beyond their ken that, in a sense, they were not perceptually prepared for it—they were in a sense "blind" to what was happening around them. Something momentous was overlooked apparently because it was entirely outside their conceptual framework. Muskets had to be fired into the air by those on board ship to attract attention.

The significance of this is that, while there is commonly a tendency to think that the five physical senses are simply receptors, and that perception is therefore a passive enterprise, perception is actually not ever a purely passive affair. As Alva Noë has pointed out in *Action in Perception*, "Perception is not something that happens to us, or in us. It is something we do."[11] In other words, what we perceive is largely determined "by what we enact: an object looms larger in the visual field as we approach it, and its profile deforms as we move about it. A sound grows louder as we move nearer its source . . . We spontaneously crane our necks, peer, squint, reach for our glasses, or draw near to get a better look (or better to handle, sniff, lick or listen to what interests us)."[12] Also, we do not perceive everything in a visual field all at once; we gain content by looking around, and we bring ourselves by stages into contact with different aspects of reality. If we are not disposed to perceive aspects of it, we naturally ignore them and are "blind" to them, as St Mark would have said.

Those who study this feature of the philosophy of perception speak of it as "inattentional blindness."[13] Wittgenstein spoke of the same phenomenon as "aspect blindness"[14] which, in terms of religious perception, he observed was "*akin to the lack of a 'musical ear.'*" Perhaps this resonates with the teaching practice of Jesus, who is so often represented as one who invited those "with eyes to see and ears to hear" to perceive and appropriate the meaning of what he said and did; the assumption apparently being that the alternative option is simply to remain blind or deaf. Certainly, the notion of "inattentional blindness" may go some way towards explaining how it was possible for some to come to faith while others "doubted," as is found in the resurrection narrative of Matt 28:16–17, or why it was that some found it initially difficult to

11. Noë, *Action in Perception*, 1.

12. Noë, *Action in Perception*, 1–2.

13. Noë, *Action in Perception*, 52. See Mack and Rock, *Inattentional Blindness*. A classic and much celebrated example is a YouTube clip of Daniel Simons, in which viewers were asked to count how many times white-shirted players in an informal basketball game passed the ball. Fifty percent of them did not see a woman in a gorilla suit who walked right through the court in the course of play.

http://www.smithsonianmag.com/science-nature/but-did-you-see-the-gorilla-the-problem-with-inattentionalblindness17339778/#6F4sMBpkFkMcCfwb.99.

14. Wittgenstein, *Philosophical Investigations*, 214.

THE RECONSTRUCTION OF RESURRECTION BELIEF

come to faith and then later changed their perception, like Thomas in the story of John 20:24–28. Also, the concept of "inattentional blindness" may go some way towards explaining how it was that the fishermen perceived by stages in the story narrated in John 21, where Jesus was on the shore preparing breakfast but was not immediately recognized. In that story, it is only when he directed the fishermen disciples to put in their nets on the other side and they drew in a catch of fish that they looked a little more intently and declared "It is the Lord." Or again, a similar coming to sight by stages is seen particularly clearly in *Luke* 24:28–35, when the travelers on the Emmaus Road first failed to recognize the identity of the Raised Jesus, even though he is said to have walked with them, but then recognized him when he engaged in the characteristic ritual gestures of taking, blessing, breaking, and sharing. "Inattentional blindness" might certainly be preferred over some kind of deliberately perverse "obfuscation by divine intervention" in the dynamics of this story.[15]

In any event, the point is that, unless one has an inclination to attend to something, or has one's attention explicitly drawn to it, it is relatively easy simply to overlook it. Human perception is a matter of actively doing something and not just a passive matter of receiving what is there to be perceived. The human capacity for coming to the judgment of faith thus initially depends upon the interpretation of the deliverances of sense experience via the five physical senses, with the important rider that cognitive perception of this kind is not simply passive or automatic. The fact is that it is often necessary actively to attend to specific aspects of what there is to be perceived; otherwise they are quite simply, and very easily, overlooked.

In the puzzle picture below showing a young couple standing by a lake, it takes a positive visual re-adjustment to discern something more than just the couple, the water, and the over-hanging tree.

---

15. As suggested by Stephen Davis in "'Seeing' the Risen Jesus," 136: "... the two Emmaus disciples *would quite normally have recognized Jesus* had their eyes not been supernaturally kept from recognizing him" (Davis's italics). Thus Davis declares that "... their eyes were restrained or held back, and that later their eyes were opened by God."

Figure 2: Tree trunk puzzle (https://gpuzzles.com)

The outline of a baby is only seen once the viewer disengages from a focus upon the couple so as to see the picture "whole." The religious perception implicit in the commitment of faith similarly requires this kind of perceptual re-adjustment.

Likewise, what is sometimes referred to as the world's most famous illusion first appeared on a German postcard in 1888, and a later version of it was produced by William Ely Hill (1887–1962). Hill was a British cartoonist who published it in the Journal *Puck* in 1915. This was in turn re-produced by E. G. Boring, in the *American Journal of Psychology* in 1930.[16]

This image is often entitled "My wife, my Mother-in-law." It is properly speaking a "reversible image' that may be seen either as a young woman, or as a much older (not very handsome) woman. The original German version is as follows:

---

16. E. G. Boring, "A New Ambiguous Figure," 444-45.

Figure 3: My Wife, My Mother-in-Law.

The generic term "puzzle picture" is probably to be preferred to the term "illusion" to refer to this type of image, given that an "illusion" often refers to something "seen" but which is really not objectively there. In the case of "reversible images" something is there; it is just that it is over-looked or not noticed.

A similar reversible image, which complements this image with a masculine motif, was published in 1961 by Jack Botwinick (1923–2006), also in the *American Journal of Psychology*. This was entitled "Husband and Father-in Law – A Reversible Image."[17] In his brief article Botwinick cited comparative statistics relating to the numbers of males and females who first saw either the younger woman or the older woman in Hill's image, and the younger man or the older man in Botwinick's. It is of interest that some viewers could not see a second figure at all until led with the verbal suggestion that "another picture could be seen."[18]

17. Botwinick, "Husband and Father in Law—A Reversible Image," 312–13.
18. For a discussion of the psychology of "Gestalt switch" which allows a viewer to "flit" between

Figure 4: Husband and Father-in-Law.

(From *American Journal of Psychology*. Copyright 1961 by the Board of Trustees of the University of Illinois. Used with permission of the University of Illinois Press)

These, of course, are just two of thousands upon thousands of puzzle pictures that usefully illustrate the concept of "inattentional" or "aspect" blindness, and the fact that coming to perceptual sight is by active effort, rather than being something that just happens to us. Indeed, as the exercise involving these sample puzzle pictures aptly demonstrates, the seeing of "something more" in religious faith usually only occurs once the viewer is alerted to it and invited to look for it—and then in a sense "repenting" by intentionally turning towards it.

For John Hick, it was this element of "additional disclosure" of something formerly hidden in puzzle pictures that provided an analogy for understanding the kind of seeing and knowing that pertains specifically to theistic faith. The truth is that unless the believer disengages from a part of the total picture so as to see or experience

alternating images, see Fiona Macpherson, "Ambiguous Figures," though the author underestimates the role of the possession of interpretative concepts in the making of cognitive claims.

it in another way, or to see it "whole," he or she remains blind to what is there to be religiously perceived.

It is not too difficult to appreciate the relevance of all this for an understanding of resurrection faith. The difficulty of many readings of the narratives of the Easter appearances is that an over-concentration on the alleged "massive physical detail" of the stories, and on an alleged "clear and distinct" account of how the Raised Christ was perceived when he is said to have "appeared" or to have been "met," coupled with the attempt to prove historically that this occurred in a deceptively transparent kind of way, fails to appreciate some of the more subtly telling, and indeed alluring, features of those same stories. These include the focus upon the less tangible and physical inter-personal dimensions of the appearance narratives, such as Jesus' verbal address to Mary Magdalene, calling her by name, and the intriguing mention of her having to "turn" towards him. Likewise his action of taking, blessing, breaking, and sharing on the Road to Emmaus, or of directing the fishermen towards a catch in the early morning as he prepares breakfast for them on the shore. In each case, an explicit feature of this kind seems essential to the disclosure and discernment of Jesus' identity.

Apart from "inattentional blindness" of the kind just discussed, there is another form of blindness in perception that is of importance to the consideration of the nature of faith. This is a blindness that results from the perceiver's lack of an appropriate conceptual framework of the kind that, in the making of knowledge claims, is always brought to the interpretation of the data gathered by the physical senses. Our contemporary appreciation of the importance of the logically prior possession of a language that is acquired only through participation in the life of a linguistic community, which teaches us words and their conventionally agreed upon meanings, is something, of course, for which we are also enormously indebted to Ludwig Wittgenstein.

Wittgenstein's non-representational approach to meaning by appeal to the notion of "meaning as use," by which he contended that the meanings of words are conventionally agreed upon through their use in linguistic communities, along with the rules for their correct use in "language games," is these days par-for-the-course in the world of philosophical epistemology. However, long prior to Wittgenstein, Immanuel Kant made a related point. Kant demonstrated that claims to human knowledge depend upon two stems: "namely, *sensibility* and *understanding*." "Through the former," he said, "objects are given to us; through the latter, they are thought."[19] As we have already noted, Kant referred to the deliverances of sense perception as "*intuitions*."[20] By contrast with the bare deliverances of sense experience, "understanding" was said by Kant

---

19. Kant, *Critique of Pure Reason*, A15/B29.

20. Though this is not an entirely satisfactory translation of his term, *Anschauung*, a Kantian "intuition" is a kind of impression obtained only by the senses.

to rely upon "*concepts*"—the meanings signified by words with which perceptions or "intuitions" are interpreted in processes of thought and in claims to knowledge.

Kant was well aware that, without appropriate concepts, sensory perception is blind in the sense that the perceiver is prone not to notice those specific things for which he or she lacks the conceptual ability to name and identify. This renders him or her entirely unable to make claims to the knowledge of them. We cannot possibly identify a "palace" unless we possess the concept of "a palace," and this implies the rules for the correct use of the term "palace." On the other hand, the possession of concepts alone, without matching concretely experienced intuitions, which "fill" them, leaves a thinker in a rationalistic condition of perceptual and cognitive emptiness. Kant's fundamental epistemological principle is, therefore, that without appropriate concepts one is blind to what is being experienced and lacks the ability to make claims to the knowledge of it. However, the possession of bare concepts, but without matching concrete experiences that fill them, leaves those concepts themselves entirely abstract and empty. Hence Kant's famous dictum: "concepts without intuitions are empty, intuitions without concepts are blind."[21]

This means that, without the interpretative concepts, which, as Wittgenstein has taught us, are furnished by membership of a linguistic community, we would be blind to whatever it is that might offer itself as the object of a potential cognitive experience. We are blind and unable to claim to know what is delivered to us via the physical senses. In other words, we may have the sensory experience of something without the ability to claim to know it. For example, human beings had the raw experience of breathing oxygen from the day the breath of life was first breathed into them and they became living creatures. However, for century upon century they remained entirely unaware of this and of its importance. Without the concept of "oxygen" they were unable to claim to know that they breathed oxygen, and thus were blind, not only to the fact that they were breathing oxygen, but as well to the fact that it was oxygen that was keeping them alive.[22] The knowledge of the importance of oxygen to their continued existence, as distinct from their raw un-interpreted experience of actually breathing oxygen and remaining alive because of it, had to wait until oxygen was discovered by Carl Wilhelm Scheele in Uppsala in 1773,[23] and then for the actual name "oxygen" subsequently to be coined for it by Antoine Lavoisier in 1777. From then onwards, once people were put in possession of the concept "oxygen," and only from then on, was it possible for humans to claim to *know* that they breathed oxygen and that it kept

---

21. Kant: *Critique of Pure Reason*, B 75.

22. The Sumerians appear to have had no concept even of air, let alone oxygen. The physical motion of breathing was apparently attributed to the mechanical action of the ribs, thus making the rib the "principle of life." It is probably not a coincidence that in the Genesis creation story Eve was created out of Adam's rib.

23. Or perhaps a little earlier. I do not wish to question the fact that oxygen was also independently discovered by Joseph Priestley in Wiltshire, England in 1774. Priestley is often given priority over Scheele because his work was published first.

them alive. Without the concept and rules for its use they had no way of knowing what it was that they were breathing, or precisely what it was that kept them alive. Clearly, without words and the concepts they signify, including, as Wittgenstein would say, the conventionally agreed upon rules for their correct use, we are blind to the content of our raw sensory experiences; we can only make knowledge claims once we are furnished with them.

By applying these same epistemological principles in the arena of faith, it follows that religious claims, such as claims to the knowledge of God, or to the perception of the presence of a divine Spirit, or of the experience of the operation of grace, can only be made once we are furnished with such key concepts as "God," "Spirit," and "grace," along with a set of rules governing a conventionally agreed upon correct use of these terms. It is in this sense that theology is "the grammar of God," which aims to provide a coherent set of linguistic rules for the use of a specifically religious set of concepts. Only by becoming so equipped, are religious believers in principle in a position to make claims to the religious knowledge of "God," the presence of "the Spirit of God," or of the operation of divine "grace," or whatever. Without these, or some such equivalent concepts, humans are blind, and unable in faith to make claims to religious knowledge at all.

For some, a religious interpretation of reality is entirely outside the conceptual framework that they normally bring to the ordering of day-to-day experience. Those who come to faith thus may have consciously to put themselves in the way of spiritual reality by attending to it in an act of will in order to perceive and become aware of it. But first they must have heard about it at least to a degree sufficient to acquire a rudimentary conceptual framework such as is necessary to the religious interpretation of the raw deliverances of the senses.

It follows that, as a prerequisite for the making of a faith claim, one must either in some way belong to, or have some acquaintance with, a faith community, operating as a linguistic community, in order to acquire a language appropriate to the religious quest. There is no such thing as a private language. Among other things, the Christian church operates as a linguistic community in this kind of way. Those who share in its theological "language game" are furnished with a set of interpretative concepts and rules for their use. These may be quite wide-ranging: the concept of the transcendent "Wholly Other"; the idea of "the *numinous*"; the concept of a divine omnipresent Spirit; the concept of the holiness, and more specifically "the love" of a God who is by nature "faithful to his promise," as in the case of the Jewish theistic tradition. In a Christian context, "the love of God that was perceived and defined in the historical life of Jesus of Nazareth," becomes crucial, and so on. It is in this sense that theology is the grammar of God. Without it there is no knowing what one might be looking for, and the quest for faith would conceptually speaking barely even be a possibility.

In a sense, the Pauline dictum that "faith comes through hearing"[24] may therefore be understood in a way that is different from, and additional to, that outlined in the great twentieth-century theologies of the Word, notably of Barth and Bultmann, and those who labored in their theological wake.[25] It is not just that a Barthian "middle distance" reading of the words of Scripture opens the way to the hearing of the message of the "Word of God" in and through the words of the text. Nor does the proclamation and the hearing of the Word of God as "a word of address" just precipitate a kind of existential self-understanding, as in the theology of Bultmann, or generate some other alternative form of non-objectifying religious language, as in a purely emotivist evaluation of religious terms. Rather, the proclamation of the church, along with an even broader acquaintance with its linguistic tradition via its liturgical worship and teaching programs, actually equips the believer or potential believer with the necessary conceptual tools for coming to an epistemologically realist form of faith in which an objectively perceived and religiously significant reality may be identified and perceptually known, not just by description, but by acquaintance. In this way, "faith comes through hearing" in the sense that faith is impossible unless one has heard and is thus acquainted with the conceptual tools that are necessary to religious perception. The acquisition and cultivation of a religious sensibility is in the first instance therefore dependent upon the ability to use distinctively religious language of a particular kind in a specific kind of way. As St. Paul says: "How then shall they call on him in whom they have not believed? And how shall they believe in him of whom they have not heard? And how shall they hear without a preacher?"[26]

In the case of the judgment of faith, understood as a knowing by acquaintance, language is used not just abstractly and referringly, but concretely and identifyingly. That is to say, it is employed to interpret actual experience from a religious perspective or point of view, so as to isolate, and thus to facilitate a claim to know, the presence of what is understood to be the religiously significant face of reality. But this is a conceptual impossibility without some kind of contact with an appropriate religious community operating as a linguistic community capable of imparting an understanding of religious concepts and the rules for their correct use.

---

24. Rom 10:17.

25. I am thinking of Ernst Fuchs, Gerhard Ebeling, Ernst Käsemann, Günther Bornkamm, and many others.

26. Rom 10:14.

Admittedly, theological language "works" according to a set of rules of a somewhat idiosyncratic kind. Given the unique nature of the surpassing mystery and ultimate unknowability of God in descriptive terms, all religious language necessarily falls short of clear and distinct specification. Words designed to speak about what is by definition transcendent, and thus "beyond words" (as words are literally descriptive of things in this world), must therefore remain either metaphorical or analogical.[27] This is for the obvious reason that the ineffable divine transcendence of the infinite God means that, by definition, God is always "beyond" the concepts and images formulated by finite human minds. We have therefore to be aware of the descriptive limits of religious language.[28] The familiar biblical images of God, as Father, King, Judge, Shepherd, wind, rock, or fire, and so on, are clearly not to be understood in the way those words are normally used literally to refer to and identify the respective objects that they signify in this finite world. Instead they have to be "stretched" in order to refer to a reality which by definition is "beyond" the finite limits of this world.

The analogical and metaphorical use of terms is normal enough even in day-to-day discourse relative to this world. However, the logical behavior of analogy and metaphor in religious discourse about God is unique to its Object. This religious use of analogies and metaphors is idiosyncratically distinct, precisely in the sense that they are analogies and metaphors of a kind that are not capable of being unpacked and expressed in a more prosaic or literal specification. Usually the meaning of metaphors, for example, can be explained in more straightforward language. By contrast, when used in reference to God, metaphors and analogies are irreducible to any kind of matter of fact, clear, and distinct explanatory specification. This is for the obvious reason that by definition a transcendent and infinite God cannot be described in the prosaic and literally understood terms appropriate to the finite world.

---

27. We note something of the difference between the use of an essentially unrelated image to throw light upon a subject as in a metaphor, and the analogical application of a term to refer to a similarity or proportionality that holds between them. For example, the dictum that "Interest rates go up by the stairs and come down by the elevator," speaks of the manner of the rise and fall of interest rates by reference to something as different as a building's stairs and elevators. This is metaphorical language. Similarly, to speak of God as "a Rock" may be said to involve a metaphor, designed to speak of God's steadfast and unchangeable reliability. However, to speak of God as "a Father," on analogy with the fathers of this world indicates a kind of proportionality between the fatherhood of God and the experience of fatherly care among human fathers.

28. See Mansel, *The Limits of Religious Thought*, and the entire tradition of *apophatic* theology sketchily defined by Hume in his *Dialogues Concerning Natural Religion* through the utterances of the character Demea. In historical fact, the position of Demea was articulated superbly by the eighteenth century Irish bishops, William King and Peter Browne, and others. See King's Sermon before the Irish House of Lords in 1709, *The Right Method of Interpreting Scripture, in What Relates to the Nature of the Deity and His Dealings with Mankind Illustrated in a Discourse on Predestination*, and Peter Browne, *A Letter in Answer to Christianity not Mysterious* (by John Toland) published in 1697, and *Things Divine and Supernatural Conceived by Analogy with Things Natural and Human*, 1733. Hume could well have drawn on this historical articulation of the Demea position, which is only thinly presented in his *Dialogues*, but he instead chose to focus on the inadequacies of the design argument which he presented through the voice of Cleanthes.

God must always be "beyond" the words and images used of God, and thus transcendent in this sense. Otherwise it would, after all, be only too easy to fall into the idolatry of fashioning God after a humanly crafted image, for mental and verbal images can be as idolatrous as metal ones.[29] There is a sense therefore in which, even when revealed, God remains a mystery, incomprehensible and descriptively unknowable in any absolutely clear and distinct sense.[30] As Heinz Zahrnt, noted in expounding the "dialectical theology" of Karl Barth: "To us God is and remains unknown. To be known directly is the characteristic of an idol."[31] This means that, even when divinity is revealed it is disclosed *as* a transcendent mystery; it does not lose the transcendence essential to its nature in the process.

This means that, despite the way in which transcendent mystery defies all attempts to speak of it in clear and distinct literal language, theology nevertheless manages to say something. For while no one metaphorical or analogical image successfully describes God as God is in God's self in a one-to-one kind of way, the entire theological edifice at least points towards the *apprehended* mystery to which it refers, even if *comprehension* remains elusive. Like the inter-locking girders of the Eiffel Tower, the statements of theology, once ordered by its systematicians, with its images sorted into more and less refined (some being "controlling images" and others subservient to them), a certain directionality may be discerned in the whole verbal edifice. The unit of theological meaning is not just a single word, or a sentence, or a paragraph, but often a whole "story." The desired outcome of systematic theology is to discern a directionality in terms of the over-all meaning of such a kind that when the object that it seeks to talk about, and to which it points, is actually and concretely encountered and apprehended in faith the response is "Aha! This is what they were talking about!" However, as a matter of definitional principle, the surpassing mystery of God means that the language itself that points to God, and attempts to describe God, can never be absolutely clear and distinct.[32] It should not surprise us to find that attempts to

---

29. This is why the *apophatic* or "negative way" is so important in classical theism. If it is affirmed through the positive way (*via positiva*) that God is Father, this assertion must immediately be negated (using the *via negativa*) by saying "*but not* a Father in the literal sense of the word as it applies to fathers in this world."

30. Thus, when we speak of "the revelation of God," we do not clear up a puzzle. Rather, we draw attention to a mystery, for God does not abandon God's essential nature as transcendent even when revealed.

31. Zahrnt, *The Question of God*, 28.

32. My friend Dietrich Ritschl once used the kind of mobile found in children's bedrooms as a model of the way in which theological discourse operates. Just as there are over-arching wires, and subservient wires, upon which images are hung, so theology operates with over-arching themes, and lesser themes, illustrated by a variety of imagery. The theological edifice as a whole has a certain balanced directionality about it which points in a specific direction, but the hook upon which it all hangs

describe the perception of the presence of the exalted and glorified Raised Christ in resurrection faith inevitably encounter the same linguistic limitations. At best, our feeble attempts verbally to express a knowledge by acquaintance of "the Spirit of the Raised Christ" can only "point towards" the reality they seek to indicate and to which they seek to draw attention.

The language used by the first Christian believers, as they sought to express and communicate their experience of having encountered the presence of the Raised Jesus, suggests that they faced this very kind of challenge. They too were confronted by the limitations of their inherited religious language to describe something that appears to have been in many respects "beyond words." The many attempts of St. Paul to describe the impact of the "life-giving Spirit" of the Raised Christ, as this was concretely known, giving direction to the living of the life of faith, provide a good example. Likewise, his many attempts to describe how the inner texture of the community life of the baptized was experienced as a unique kind of inter-personal communion are never entirely clear and distinct. This is not to mention the attempted more graphic narrative portrayals of the appearances of the Raised Christ "from heaven," behind closed doors, or in a specific action such as the breaking and sharing of bread, or appearing unrecognizably and then being recognized and then immediately disappearing, as in the case of the Emmaus story. These are all struggling attempts to communicate something that necessarily remains transcendently elusive. Indeed, as we have seen, Mark in his wisdom is reluctant even to try to describe a resurrection appearance; it is a better strategy to point towards it and then leave it to others actually to experience it: hence the attempt verbally to describe an Easter "appearance" is abandoned in favor of the direction "He goes before you into Galilee; there you will see him."[33]

This means that, what is true of the theology of faith in a transcendent God is true of faith in the transcendent Raised and exalted Christ of heaven. In the face of having to come to terms with what is by definition a transcendent mystery that is in an important sense "beyond words," the possession of a religious language, and the unique way in which it works, remains essential. Certainly, this linguistic requirement remains logically prior to the interpretation of experience and the making of any faith claims, for it is only by using the tools of a religious language that at least some sense may be made of the experience of life by isolating conceptually manageable aspects of it and interpreting them as best it can. In other words, the same dynamic applies to the perception in faith of the presence of the Raised Christ as a "life-giving Spirit" as to the "Spirit of God." Without the appropriate conceptual tools and the rules for their correct use we unfortunately remain blind and, regrettably, but necessarily, bereft even of the possibility of coming to faith.

---

is mysteriously obscured from view. It cannot be adequately described in words but only encountered in concrete experience as that to which words of theological description point.

33. Mark 16:7.

We also have to take account of the element of freedom in perception, which is also a part of the response of faith. This is the freedom which, in ordinary day-to-day perception, allows all of us to perceive and interpret experience somewhat differently, not just by choosing a particular perceptual standpoint, but also by choosing from the array of conceptual tools that may happen to be on hand at any particular time or in any given circumstance. Given the brute fact of conceptual diversity and the possibility of interpretative variety to which Kant already pointed, there is thus, within limits, an element of freedom of choice in all perception. This is less so in the case of the perception of physical reality, for when one is confronted by a house, for example, or a horse, or a motor vehicle, what we perceive is either a house, a horse, or a motor vehicle, or it is not. Even so, a degree of freedom remains possible, for we are free to speak of "a house, a horse, or a motor vehicle" (provided there are reasons for doing so) as "as a bungalow, a nag, or a Toyota." Once again, things do not come bearing their own labels whose use is compulsory; within limits we are free to choose to identify them in different ways. But when it comes to the perception of aesthetic value or moral value, the degree of freedom rises exponentially. Life in New York might be described by some, for example, as life "in a very big and intimidating city," by others as life in "a den of iniquity," and still by others as life in "a remarkably supportive community of religious sensitivity and neighborly care, even despite its size." Thus, as it fortuitously happens, following the hallowed precedent of Gregory of Nyssa, it is possible to move with a degree of freedom from a physical description, to a moral description, to a more clearly spiritual appreciation, in coming to terms with fundamentally the same experienced reality of living in New York City. An element of freedom allows for the possibility that a sense of neighborly care may be concretely perceived and known in New York's local neighborhoods, even despite its intimidating size, and notwithstanding its complicated life of often-dubious moral diversity. Clearly, the way life in New York is experienced and interpreted conceptually will naturally vary greatly from person to person. We come to different perceptions using different conceptual tools as ways of describing essentially the same data of experience, though by focusing on different aspects of it.

Not all of us, of course, choose to exercise a religious sensibility so as to engage in a religious appreciation of what is experienced. However, when a religious quest is pursued, a successful outcome can only be achieved by drawing upon a specifically religious set of interpretative concepts. These necessarily focus upon specific aspects of experience as being of particular significance. However, within limits, a variety of possibilities is always open to us in the interpretation of experience, and we are free to interpret what we see and hear in different ways. This includes the freedom *not* to attend to some possible ways of interpreting experience so as to experience life in a purely materialist and entirely non-religious kind of way. Faith and freedom, in this sense, go hand in hand. Indeed, religious faith may be understood as a function of perceptual freedom.

In the tradition of Hebrew/Christian understanding, the knowledge of God is spoken of as "faith," rather than simply a more straightforward "knowing," precisely because the element of freedom is at a premium. In other words, the concept of "religious faith" itself arises, in a sense, *because* of this element of perceptual freedom. By this I mean that the element of freedom that pertains in all perception becomes maximal in the judgment of faith because we are *entirely* free to see or not to see in a religious kind of way. This is because of the religious and moral requirement that the divine self-disclosure that permits the religious knowledge of God in faith is, by its very nature, at the same time sufficiently hidden as not to compel assent. In other words, over and above the essential mystery of the transcendent incomprehensibility of a God, who in verbal terms is always "beyond" all words and images, God does not show God's-self in such a way as to deprive believers or potential believers of the freedom either to respond or not to respond. The same may, of course, be said of the perception of the presence of the life-giving Spirit of the Raised Christ within the texture of the work and worship of the Christian community. The element of freedom that goes hand in hand with faith ensures that faith cannot become a form of compulsory assent. This would be self-defeating for the obvious reason that a compulsory or compelled assent would not be faith.

This element of freedom in religious perception, which answers to the ambiguity and hiddenness of divine revelatory disclosure, whether of the presence of the Spirit of God or of the Spirit of the Raised Christ, may also be illustrated by appeal to puzzle pictures. The most famous example is the Peter/Paul Vase or Rubin Goblet, first publicized by Danish psychologist Edgar Rubin in 1915. Here an element of perceptual ambiguity, and the perceptual freedom that goes with it, is illustrated by the fact that what is pictured may be seen either *as* a vase-like chalice, or *as* two human faces in profile. In either case, we are entirely free to see in one-way rather than the other; the absolute ambiguity means that freedom is at a maximum:

Figure 5: The Rubin Goblet. Wikimedia Commons.
Used by permission of John Smithson 2007.

Because two different perceptions can result from the same stimulus in the case of the Rubin Goblet, twentieth-century gestalt psychologists argued that there was something going on inside the brain to determine which figure was seen. Perception involved more than just the stimuli that entered the eye, for brain processes were said to be determinative of how this was understood and interpreted. We do not need to pursue the same explanation as the original gestalt psychologists, however, in order to appreciate that we have here an example of perceptual ambiguity that allows the perceiver the freedom to see either a white chalice on a black background, or two opposing human profiles represented in black against a white background. Indeed, the absolute ambiguity of the Rubin Goblet is illustrated by the fact that it is possible to "flit" from one to the other.

If we transfer this model of perceptual ambiguity, and the maximal degree of freedom of response that it allows, to the discussion of the epistemology of faith, it is possible to suggest that the simultaneous revelation-and-hiddenness of God gives the potential believer not only the freedom to see and know in one way rather than another, but also to entertain the possibility of moving in faith from one perception to another by "flitting" from faith to un-faith, as it were, from a religious interpretation of experience back to a purely material or natural one (and vice versa).

The Kanizsa Triangle, first described by the Italian psychologist Gaetano Kanizsa in 1955, is perhaps even more instructive. Here we have a representation of three black dots or disks, each with a segment missing in the manner of a wedge cut from a pie, and with three "V" shaped chevrons between them. But this may almost simultaneously be seen as a solid white triangle superimposed upon three apparently completely circular black disks, with also the outline contour of another triangle underneath it.

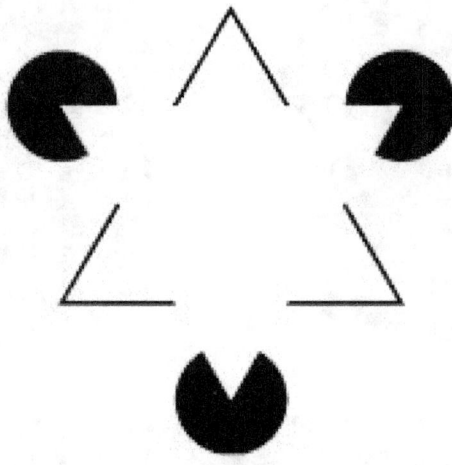

Figure 6: Kanizsa's Triangle. Created on 15 March 2007. Wikimedia Commons. Used by permission of Fibonacci under the GNU Free Documentation License, version 1.2 (https://commons.wikimedia.org/wiki/Commons: GNU_Free_Documentation_License,_version_1.2/).

Here the contour of the solid white triangle is in fact invisible, though perceived to be there, just as is the integrity of the black disks and of the triangle upon which the white triangle appears to be superimposed are perceived to be there, though in fact they are not explicitly drawn.[34] Clearly, in this case more is perceived than at first may appear to be represented.

On the other hand, the element of ambiguity and freedom-in-perception that the Kanizsa Triangle also helpfully illustrates, is enhanced by the fact that a Jewish perceiver might actually see a form of the Star of David here while others of us miss it.

---

34. This is an example of *amodal perception*—the perception of something that strictly speaking is not actually or explicitly represented. See the discussion of this in relation to Kanizsa's Triangle by Noë in *Action in Perception*, 60–1: "We experience the occluded portion of the disks . . . as *amodally* present in perception. They are *perceptually* present without being actually perceived." I think Noë can probably be interpreted to mean that "they are *perceptually* present without being unambiguously represented."

These illustrative models help to make the theological point that an essential ambiguity or "hiddenness" in the revelation of the divine puts the element of freedom in the perception of faith at a maximum. This radical freedom of the religious perceiver as the knowing subject, with an apparent capacity either "to see or not to see," that is parallel to the capacity either "to hear and not to understand," is the epistemological counter-part of the objective ambiguity of divine self-disclosure, which has traditionally been treated under the subject heading of the "hiddenness" or "incomprehensibility" of God even when God is revealed.

This element of absolute ambiguity, and the freedom of perception it enables, was expounded by John Hick by appeal to his signature theological theme of "epistemic distance." While God is understood to be immanent, and thus is perceived to be "close at hand" as an object of acquaintance, the ultimate mystery of the "hiddenness of God" means that God is set at an "epistemic distance" which allows perceivers and potential perceivers the radical freedom voluntarily to come to faith and to live religious lives, or not to come to faith, and thus to live lives in which religion has utterly no part. In other words, the object of religious faith does not compel assent.[35] This is the *deus absconditus* whose presence may just as easily be experienced as absence, for humans are always genuinely free to interpret experience religiously or not. And there is a sense in which the same freedom in faith allows the religious believer to move from one to the other, from a religious interpretation of experience to a purely materialist one. To Hick's mind this must be so if human persons are to have the capacity to mature and grow as autonomous persons who are led gradually "through their own choices" towards God's Kingdom.[36] Faith "is a correlate of freedom" for the integrity of human persons; "their individual freedom and accountability, are respected, above all by the fateful and final sphere of their confrontation by God."[37] Only by remaining "hidden" in this kind of way does God preserve the wills of humans as free, and under their own control as responsible and accountable beings: "If man is to be personal, God must be *deus absconditus*. He must, so to speak, stand back, hiding himself behind his creation, and leaving to us the freedom to recognize or fail to recognize his dealings with us."[38]

The perception of the presence of "the Spirit of life in Christ Jesus" is likewise characterized by the radical ambiguity, and corresponding perceptual freedom, that allows some to see and to respond in faith, while others remain entirely blind and

---

35. See Hick, *Faith and Knowledge*, 121: "Our knowledge of God . . . is not given to us as a compulsory perception, but is achieved as a voluntary act of interpretation."
36. Hick, *Faith and Knowledge*, 135.
37. Hick, *Faith and Knowledge*, 135.
38. Hick, *Faith and Knowledge*, 135.

unapprehending. On the other hand, the ambiguity of his residual heavenly transcendence means that full comprehension defies us all.

There is a long tradition in the thinking of classical Christian theism that has attempted an explanation of just why the perceptual freedom necessary for coming to a genuine faith, rather than a compulsory assent, might be so. Very briefly, the traditional argument suggests that if God is a God of Love, who calls forth a response of love from faithful people, and if love is essentially a matter of self-*giving*, then this is a response that *by definition* cannot be coerced. Indeed, a coerced response would not be love, but intellectual rape. Thus, in the New Testament traditions concerning the historical Jesus, for example, Jesus is said to have refused to throw himself down from the pinnacle of the temple,[39] or to turn stones into bread,[40] or to come down from the Cross,[41] in ways that would unambiguously demonstrate a divinely compelling miraculous power. This would be self-defeating, because a miraculous display of almighty power would have deprived his audience of the freedom necessary to faith, and make for what Samuel Taylor Coleridge called "a worthless because compulsory assent."[42]

Human freedom of choice is in turn essential to the exercise of genuine moral responsibility. If the being and activity of God were to be so clearly manifest as to compel assent, compliance with an entirely manifest expression of his will would in a sense be enforced. There would really be no choice about possible behaviors, and consequently there would be no real possibility of responsible human moral decision-making. It is thus, in a sense, that it is "an evil and adulterous generation [that] asks for a sign."[43]

The bare fact of the freedom that allows some to perceive and come to faith, and others not, was something that clearly captured the interest of Augustine:

> Surely this beauty should be self-evident to all who are of sound mind. Then why does it not speak to everyone in the same way? Animals both small and large see it, but they cannot put a question about it. In them reason does not sit in judgement upon the deliverances of the senses. But human beings can put a question so that "the invisible things of God are understood and seen through the things which are made" (Rom. 1: 20). Yet by love of created things they are

---

39. Matt 4:5–7; Luke 4:9–12.
40. Matt 4:3–4.
41. Mark 15:30, 32; Matt 27:40, 42.
42. Coleridge, *Biographia Literaria*, 106: God's presence "could not be intellectually more evident without becoming morally less effective; without counteracting its own end by sacrificing the life of faith to the cold mechanism of a worthless because compulsory assent."
43. Matt 12:39.

subdued by them, and being thus made subject become incapable of exercising judgement. Moreover, created things do not answer those who question them if power to judge is lost. There is no alteration in the voice which is their beauty. If one person sees while another sees and questions, it is not that they appear one way and to the first and another way to the second. It is rather that the created order speaks to all, but is understood by those who hear its outward voice and compare it with the truth within themselves.[44]

The most notable statement of the theological reasons for the radical ambiguity of the divine revelation and the human freedom that permits perceptual variety from person to person, however, comes from Hugh of St Victor (c. AD1096–1141). In the context of his sacramental theology, Hugh wrote:

> God from the beginning wished neither to be entirely manifest to human consciousness nor entirely hidden. If he were entirely hidden, faith would indeed not be aided unto knowledge, and lack of faith would be excused on the ground of ignorance.

For Hugh, it is therefore necessarily the case that:

> God should show himself, though hidden, lest he be entirely concealed and entirely unknown; and again, it was necessary that he should conceal himself, though shown and known to some degree, lest he be entirely manifest, so that there might be something which through being known would nourish the heart of man, and again which through being hidden would stimulate it.[45]

The essential hiddenness of God that is preserved by an ambiguity in revelation, of the kind that allows some to see and others not to see, was well appreciated by Blaise Pascal (AD 1623–1662) specifically in relation to the revelation of the Raised Christ:

> It was not then right that he should appear in a manner manifestly divine, and completely capable of convincing all men; but it was also not right that he should come in so hidden a manner that he could not be known by those who should sincerely seek him. He has willed to make himself quite recognizable by those; and thus willing to appear openly to those who seek him with all their heart, he so regulates the knowledge of himself that he has given signs of himself, visible to those who seek him, and not to those who seek him not. There is enough light for those who only desire to see, and enough obscurity for those who have a contrary disposition.[46]

Clearly, Pascal's argument here is that the freedom in faith to perceive or not to perceive, is the obverse side of the penny of the systematic ambiguity of the revelation of

---

44. Augustine, *Confessions*, X.vi.10. See also Sermon 159, and Sermon 150A. *The Works of Saint Augustine*, 136–37.
45. Hugh of St Victor, *On the Sacraments of the Christian Faith*, I.iii.2.
46. Pascal, *Pensées*, 430.

the presence of the Raised Christ, so as to ensure that there is sufficient evidence to warrant and justify a response of faith but insufficient to compel assent. This finds an echo in the narratives of the Easter traditions of the New Testament insofar as Jesus' purported appearances are not always presented as matter-of-fact, or unambiguously clear and distinct phenomena, but as much more mysteriously revelatory occurrences which are in fact said to have brought some to faith but to have left others to doubt. This element of perceptual freedom seems clearly present, for example, when Matthew says in his account of Jesus' appearance on the mountain top in Galilee that "when they saw him they worshipped him, but some doubted."[47] Clearly, the implication is that this somewhat enigmatic and mysterious revelatory disclosure "from heaven" was ambiguous enough for some to see and come to faith while others did not.

It may also be noted that such an apparent ambiguity in the appearances of the Raised Christ seems to be a feature of a number of other resurrection narratives. The fact that some witnesses see and come to faith, while other people did not, in this story of Matt 28:17 finds a counterpart in the story of Luke 24, where those who are portrayed walking on the Road to Emmaus at first did not identify the Raised Jesus, for "their eyes were kept from recognizing him." This speaks of the perceptual freedom not to see and recognize, until the penny dropped and "their eyes were opened, and they recognized him" in the breaking of bread.[48] On the other hand, in the doubting Thomas episode of John's Gospel, despite the compellingly physical, clear, and distinct evidential warrants that are such a feature of this story, it is intimated that this kind of experience is *not* to be regarded as normative for the more regular experience of faith. It is those who come to a free response of faith, uncompelled by such clear evidential warrants, who are declared to be "blessed."[49] Somehow, some of the most fascinating aspects of the narrative traditions of the Resurrection pull us towards the mysteriously ambiguous nature of the appearances as "revelatory disclosures," by contrast with the matter-of-factness and straightforward clarity of purported historical "meetings."[50] The hints in the Easter traditions of the freedom of perception that preserves the possibility of a voluntary un-coerced response, lingers as the experiential obverse of an apparent ambiguity in the disclosures of the Raised Christ's presence. While matter-of-fact "meetings" of an entirely clear and distinct kind might be more amenable to being handled by the methods of critical historical research, in the way championed by N. T. Wright, faith by contrast freely responds to an ambiguously disclosed reality.

47. Matt 28:17. Perhaps better "hesitated."
48. Luke 24:31.
49. John 20:29.
50. Of the kind promoted by N. T. Wright throughout his treatment of the appearance narratives in *RSG*.

It is in fact a fudge simply to pass over elements of puzzling ambiguity in the resurrection appearances as we find them presented across the Gospel narratives, in the cause of trying to handle them historically as though they conformed to any other event of the human past. J. D. G. Dunn's assessment of the nature of the appearances is far more balanced: "The bare mention of doubt in Matt. 28.17 is best seen ... as a genuine historical echo,"[51] he says. While "the strong materializing tendency of Luke and John make it difficult to get back to the original experiences,"[52] Dunn's considered assessment is that there are sufficient indications in the appearances traditions to warrant "the plausible suggestion" that "there was *a certain ambiguity* in the appearances, a lack of distinctiveness and clarity of detail, which left undisturbed the overmastering impression of the one central fact ('Jesus is risen'), but also gave scope for a degree of variety in the interpretation of the reality which had been witnessed."[53] While Paul distinguished his Damascus Road experience, as a conversion experience, with an accompanying unambiguous sense of commissioning, from all his later experiences, it was itself not unambiguous in visual terms. And, very importantly, essentially as a visionary experience, or Christophany, it was of a piece with the earlier experiences of the first witnesses as these are presented in the later Gospel narrative traditions, which appear to have been different though in important respects the same as Paul's experience. Thus, Dunn declares that *"the three most primitive characteristics of the resurrection appearances prior to Paul are a visionary seeing, an element of doubt and fear, and a sense of obligation to make the vision known."*[54] While not all three characteristics are present in all resurrection appearances, "they occur in different combinations"; this is sufficient to warrant Dunn's conviction that "a visionary and subjective element"[55] attaches to the appearances along with their perceptual ambiguity, despite the fundamental conviction *"that the conclusion to which they came was that it was Jesus himself who had encountered them."*[56]

When it comes to the perception of the Raised Christ as "a life giving Spirit" such as is found in the descriptions of the nature of faith and of the primitive *Christopaxis* in the letters of Paul, elements of ambiguity, and the concomitant perceptual freedom to see in one way rather than another, abound. Clearly, Paul himself apparently had no hesitation in exercising the perceptual and linguistic freedom to interpret the reality with which he believed he had to do in faith both *as* "the Spirit of him who raised Jesus

---

51. Dunn, *Jesus and the Spirit*, 124.
52. Dunn, *Jesus and the Spirit*, 123.
53. Dunn, *Jesus and the Spirit*, 123 (Dunn's italics).
54. Dunn, *Jesus and the Spirit*, 131.
55. Dunn, *Jesus and the Spirit*, 133.
56. Dunn, *Jesus and the Spirit*, 133. The italics in all these quotations are Dunn's.

Christ from the dead," or *as* "the Spirit of Christ" himself, and even just as "Christ" (as in Rom 8:10). Even so, Paul himself confesses that the knowing upon which these claims are based is "as though" it were "a reflection" in a polished metal mirror, for he sees "dimly," not "face to face."[57] The ambiguity, and thus the partial and incomplete nature of this "seeing" in faith, is precisely what grounds his eschatological hope for more clarity of vision in time to come: "then I will know fully, even as I have been fully known."[58] The unmistakable suggestion here is that the seeing and knowing of faith, that is the ground of hope, is necessarily somewhat ambiguous, lacking in the clear and distinct transparency of "face to face" encounter. As Paul himself says: "Now hope that is (clearly) seen is not hope. For who hopes for what is seen . . . we hope for what we do not see, we wait for it with patience."[59]

Moreover, the active presence of Christ in Paul's life through the medium of the Spirit, which we earlier discussed at some length, is always interpreted as a divine gift. As a consequence, the experience of being "put right before God"[60]—or justified as a consequence of faith, baptism, and the gift of the Spirit—is experienced and described as a "grace" by contrast with the products of human work and striving. The gift-like quality of the "Spirit of life in Christ Jesus" of his post-Easter experience means that the human behavior appropriate to life in Christ is to be interpreted *as* more than *simply* a human behavior. Though from one perspective it might be understood *as* a human behavior and the product of working sincerely at it, from the perspective of faith it is viewed rather differently *as* the outworking of the gift of the perceived presence and activity of the Spirit. In other words, while the ambiguity of its disclosure *might* allow it to be experienced *as* a human work, from St. Paul's point of view this would be a mistake. As Paul himself says, "it is no longer I who live, but it is Christ who lives in me."[61]

Despite the enormous differences of viewpoint that are so easily discerned among New Testament writers, there is a remarkable overlap between Paul and John in relation to the basic understanding of the experiential ground of faith, but also in relation to the

---

57. 1 Cor 13:12. See also 2 Cor 3:18 where "the glory of the Lord" is said by Paul to be seen "as though reflected in a mirror" as believers "are being transformed into the same image from one degree of glory to another; for this comes from the Lord, the Spirit."

58. 1 Cor 13:12.

59. Rom 8.24-25. As Maximus the Confessor might once have observed: "The past is shadow, the present ikon; the truth belongs to the things of the future." This is the temporal sequence extrapolated from the inter-relation of law/prophets/Gospel/truth in Two Hundred Texts on Theology, texts 90–93. Also Scholia on Church Hierarchy, PG 4, 137D.

60. The post-Reformation debates about whether justification means "to make righteous" or "to account righteous" I take now to be somewhat passé. See Käsemann, *Commentary on Romans*, 1980.

61. Gal 2:20.

ambiguity of its perception and the essential uncompelled freedom that is intrinsic to faith. For example, the interpersonal communion of the church celebrated by Paul, as a remarkable divinely achieved unity of Jews and Gentiles in the power of the Spirit, could possibly have been interpreted as a purely human achievement wrought by nothing more than inter-personal goodwill. Paul found it appropriate to speak of it in faith, however, as an achievement that could only be attributed to the active presence of the Spirit. In Rom 5:5, the quality of this inter-personal communion is in faith described in terms of the outpouring of a divine love: "God's love has been poured into our hearts through the Holy Spirit that has been given to us."

St. John no less than St. Paul provides us with an example of essentially the same experientially based reality. In 1 John 1:3, for example, the author's affirmation of faith is that the communion which he hoped others would come to share was not only a merely human inter-personal communion "with one another," but specifically a communion he identified in faith as a communion "with the Father and his son Jesus Christ."[62] Moreover, it is also said by John to be concretely known in faith "by the Spirit that he has given us."[63] This is in turn identified by 1 John, no less than by Paul in Rom 5:5, by appeal to a specific "kind of love" that may be concretely seen in the transformed lives of believers: "See what love the Father has given to us, that we should be called children of God; and that is what we are."[64]

John thus speaks of a Spirit that is concretely experienced in faith as the creative agent of the church's inter-personal communion. It is of such a kind that it would be a mistake to speak of it in purely human terms as a communion "only with one another." Rather, it is a communion with a transcendent face, for it is a communion "with the Father, through his Son" in which believers are called to share. In both cases, when Paul and 1 John speak of the concretely perceived experience of communion as a constitutive element of the life of the Christian community, it is in faith understood to be of more than purely human origin. Rather, it triggers the response of faith for it is always identified as an objectively given divine gift. Clearly, it is possible that the inter-personal communion across barriers of race, social class, or gender difference, of which Paul spoke,[65] that brings people of faith to declare that in Christ there is a new creation, *could* be explained as the product of human effort and goodwill. In faith, however, it is interpreted as the gift of the Holy Spirit; it is "the love of the Father" given to us, of which 1 John also speaks.

In order to allow this apparent freedom of identification so as not to compel the assent of faith, the disclosure of the reality to which faith responds must in some way therefore be ambiguous—with sufficient being revealed so as to avoid total ignorance,

---

62. 1 John 1:3.
63. 1 John 3:24.
64. 1 John 3:1.
65. Gal 3:28.

and insufficient to compel assent of the kind which would deprive faith of the freedom essential to it.

If, as I have argued, it is legitimate to assume that, epistemologically speaking, there is continuity of pattern between faith where God is its Object, and faith where the presence of the Raised Christ is its Object, then either way, faith remains a kind of basic trust (*fiducia*) that is based upon an uncompelled empirical knowing (*fides*). The humanly experienced perceptual freedom that is concomitant with the mystery and ambiguity of the divine disclosure in religious faith generally may thus also illuminate the discussion specifically of resurrection faith and the perception of what is claimed to be the living presence of the Raised Christ. Christian believers need not be coy in admitting that the fundamental assumption here is that resurrection faith may be understood in the context of an understanding of religious faith generally conceived, and not handled as a *sui generis* thing admitting of no analogical comparison.

It has to be openly acknowledged that the apparent ambiguity of divine self-disclosure, which in faith may either be experienced and recognized *as* "the communion of God," "the communion of the Holy Spirit," or *as* "the gracious divine gift of the Spirit of Christ," also permits the entirely naturalistic identification of the same experienced reality purely *as* a humanly contrived fellowship. For those who do not see with the eye of faith, it might even be described as though it were something achieved by human effort alone. The perceptual freedom that is counterpart in the judgment in faith of the necessary ambiguity of divine disclosure also entails that some may not see things in this way at all. In other words, the very epistemology which justifies the perception *in faith* of the presence and activity of God, or of the Raised Christ, also admits the possibility of an entirely *atheistic* option.

In summary: though the interpretative judgment of religious cognition is doxastically grounded in the deliverances of sense experience, the element of perceptual freedom thus always permits those not so inclined to focus their attention elsewhere and to remain blind to what others may claim to perceive in faith. Over and above what is, from the perspective of faith, an "inattentional blindness," the capacity to come to the interpretative judgment of faith also depends upon the possession by believers or potential believers of a set of interpretative concepts furnished by the church operating as a linguistic community. In this specifically religious context, this confirms Kant's dictum. Those with no access at all to the conceptual tools that are necessary to the ability to isolate and identify religiously significant reality, such as, for example, the theological concepts of "God," "Spirit," "divine love," and "grace," must remain in a sense blind. On the other hand, those actually possessing a bare set of abstract religious concepts of this kind, but without encountering anything in concrete experience on to which they map, or which "fills" them, are left with a handful of empty concepts.

Up to this point in this discussion one key epistemological question, however, has so far been begged. This is the crucial question of how it might have been possible for the first generation of Christians to recognize, and claim to know, the objective divine reality with which in faith they believed they had to do, and about which they spoke so confidently, not just *as* the active presence of the Holy Spirit, or of the Spirit of God in their lives, but *as* "the life-giving Spirit" of *Jesus Christ*. Implicit in the kind of perceiving and knowing appropriate specifically to resurrection faith is the claim to recognize and know not just "a divine presence," but the presence of the historical figure (even if now in some way radically transformed) who had lived among them and been crucified, and died, and was buried. The question is: how was this unique and specific recognition justifiably made?

The very same question has to be addressed by those who make the same faith-claim today: how is it possible for us, two thousand years later, to claim in faith to identify and know the animating Spirit of the Christian community *as* the Spirit of *Jesus Christ*? Given that we enjoy the perceptual freedom to interpret experience in a variety of different ways by employing different conceptual tools, how is the explicit interpretation of what we claim to see and know in faith *as* the Raised Jesus Christ to be explained and justified?

It is this aspect of the epistemology of resurrection faith, with its implicit interest in the continuity of the Raised Christ with the Jesus of historical time, to which we shall turn in the next chapter.

8

Faith as Remembering and Knowing

ONE OF THE QUITE essential tenets of the resurrection faith of Christians is the affirmation that it was the historical, remembered human *Jesus* whom God raised from the dead. Any gnostic or docetic tendency to suggest that Jesus did not actually live as a human being like the rest of us, or that he was not truly human but only appeared to be so, or that the church has no real interest in his unique historical life and teaching, is alien to the Christian tradition. It is fundamental to the Christian understanding of Easter and its significance that it was a genuinely human, historical person whom God raised from the dead and made "Lord and Christ." It was "this Jesus," whom his adversaries had crucified, who was believed to have returned from the grave with a proffer of forgiveness that extended even to those adversaries.[1] Only so can his Resurrection be regarded as a victory over death of the kind that faces all human beings.

The question of the continuity of the Raised Christ with the historical Jesus does not begin and end with the inspection of crucifixion wounds, of the kind we find in the doubting Thomas story, so as just to establish a continuity with "one who had been crucified." The identification appropriate to faith was much more specific than that. The Easter proclamation is not just that a crucified man had been raised from the dead, but that the crucified *Jesus* had been raised from the dead. The point is that resurrection faith is a judgment about the "aliveness" beyond death of the *particular* historical person, known as Jesus Christ, who was indeed put to death on the Cross. In resurrection faith, we are claiming to know not just a divine presence but also the presence, through the medium of the Spirit, of a quite specific human person of remembered historical time, who had actually existed and lived a human life, taught and ministered to people in an impressive variety of ways, and who was remembered to have lived his life in obedience to God in a characteristic other-serving, rather than a self-serving, manner.[2] In this way, ". . . the history of Christianity deliberately holds together the earthly identity of Jesus of Nazareth and that

---

1. Acts 2:23–4.
2. Hans Frei grasped this as long ago as 1975 in *The Identity of Jesus Christ*, 106, when he insisted on the (logical?) priority of Jesus' *identity* as a "singular unsubstitutable person" with respect to claims to know his continuing *presence*.

of the risen and ascended Christ."[3] Given that we are perceptually free to interpret experience in a variety of ways, the pressing question is how is this specific identity judgment to be rationally justified?

It is true that Christian theology through most of the twentieth-century was dominated by a concern to establish a basis for faith of a freestanding kind, independent of what was thought to be the entirely unreliable shifting sands of critical-historical research. Indeed, the so-called "Christ of faith" became so prominent in the church's understanding of its faith and proclamation that the original historical life of Jesus was allowed to slip away into the background, so as effectively to disappear from view. This development was largely a reaction to the failure of the nineteenth-century quest to reconstruct the life of the historical Jesus "behind" the dogmatically colored presentations of him in the Gospels, which notoriously ended in such a variety of competing outcomes that it inevitably began to self-destruct. At the same time, the kernel of original factual information about the historical figure of Jesus became further obscured under the influence, first of the form-critical analysis of the New Testament texts, and then later under the impact of redaction criticism's fascination with uncovering the individual theological in-put of the various Gospel writers in the course of their editing of traditional material. The conclusion became almost inevitable that the story of the Jesus of history had been so modified by christological reflection that the original eyewitness testimony was almost, if not entirely, lost. This meant that the quest to penetrate behind the traditions to reconstruct a "historical Jesus," or to find his "true identity," tended simply to be abandoned as a hopelessly futile and mistaken exercise.

Already at the beginning of the twentieth-century, Wilhelm Herrmann put the prevailing consensus about the unreliability of the conclusions of critical-historical research, and its congenital incapacity to provide a sure foundation for faith, in starkly frank terms: "It is a fatal error to attempt to establish the basis of faith by means of historical investigation. The basis of faith must be something fixed; the results of historical study are continually changing."[4] In its place, the quest for a *sturmfreies Gebiet* (storm-free area) for faith thus precipitated attempts of various kinds, right through the twentieth-century, to focus instead upon the so-called "Christ of faith." This, rather than "the Jesus of history," was thought to provide the only secure ground of faith.

This was particularly the case in the second half of the twentieth-century under the influence of Rudolf Bultmann, who was not coy in expressing his pessimistic disenchantment with the findings of critical historical research. Indeed, by this time historical skepticism had become all but axiomatic among Christian theologians:

---

3. Bockmuehl, "Resurrection," 114.

4. Herrmann, *Communion of the Christian*, 76. See Kierkegaard, *Unscientific Postscript*, 31: "an approximation is the only certainty attainable for historical knowledge."

"Historical research," Bultmann said, "can never lead to any result which could serve as a basis for faith, for all its results have only relative validity."[5] In Bultmann's theology, an aggressive and systematic attempt to shake free of any reliance on "the Jesus of history" was replaced by an equally robust and systematic exposition of an alleged existential encounter with the "living Christ" who was said in faith to be met in the "Word of address" of the Church's proclamation.

Obviously, the disjunction implicit in this characteristically twentieth-century juxtaposition of the *Jesus of history* and *Christ of faith* meant that, in epistemological terms, any attempt to identify the presence of the Raised Christ by appeal to a principle of continuity with the historical Jesus had become problematic, if not impossible. Unfortunately, this led to a somewhat arbitrary identification of what was essentially an inner and subjective religious experience of self-understanding in the present moment of existential decision *with* the presence and activity of the "Raised Christ." Bultmann thus contended (famously) that Christ had been raised not from the tomb at a point of time in the past, but "into the kerygma." Christ was said to be "present" in a manner of speaking, and "heard," not in objectifying talk *about* the Jesus of the past, but in the "Word of *address*" of the church's proclamation in an illuminative moment of revelation (most notably around 11am on Sundays). This was the time of revelation, the time when each individual believer came to grasp his or her identity as a creature under God as Creator, or as a faithful disciple owing allegiance and obedience to Christ. But just how this somewhat esoteric inner religious experience of self-understanding could justifiably be identified with, and recognized *as*, the presence of the Raised Jesus Christ remained elusively arbitrary and therefore problematic.

In more recent times, the pendulum of theological fashion has swung dramatically back towards a biographical interest in the Jesus of history. James D. G. Dunn, for example, has painstakingly worked to recover the importance of the category of "memory" as the primary motivation for the transmission of the tradition about Jesus. What we have in the New Testament gospel traditions is fundamentally a picture of Jesus *as he was remembered* by the first generation of Christians. In *Jesus Remembered* (2003), Dunn sums up his thesis in four basic points:

> (1) The only realistic objective for any 'quest of the historical Jesus' is Jesus *remembered*. (2) The Jesus tradition of the Gospels confirms *that* there was a concern within earliest Christianity to remember Jesus. (3) The Jesus tradition shows *how* Jesus was remembered; its character strongly suggests again

---

5. Bulmann, *Faith and Understanding*, 30. Also, Bultmann, *Essays: Philosophical and Theological*, 18. In *The Listener*, 1st September 1955, 329, Bultmann said: "In history there is nothing of absolute value; all values are relative. All thoughts and actions are determined by the place within history in which [man] finds himself. Where this leads is obvious: the conception of truth is dissolved."

and again a tradition given its essential shape by regular use and reuse in oral mode. (4) This suggests in turn that that essential shape was given by the original and immediate impact made by Jesus . . .[6]

The recovery of this emphasis on what was really memorable about the historical Jesus has been helpfully complemented by the work of Richard Bauckham, who mounted an attack on the foundational dogma of twentieth-century form-critical research by arguing that the original oral traditions about Jesus had not just circulated among anonymous early worshipping communities in a way that privileged community needs and interests at the expense of preserving a reliable memory of Jesus himself. Instead, he made the case for the importance of eyewitness testimony and even for the possibility that original eyewitnesses of what Jesus had said and done exercised a kind of "quality control" to ensure the authenticity of the transmitted tradition.[7] This work was in turn notably supported by Richard Burridge's questioning of the received twentieth-century view that the four Gospels were *not* "biographies" of Jesus. Burridge argued that the Gospels are properly understood within the genre of Greco-Roman biography, though they are not biographies, of course, in terms of the style of modern biography.[8]

As one would expect, the theological "U-turn" initiated by these ground-breaking studies has led to a lively new debate that may rightly be regarded as yet another "quest of the historical Jesus."[9]

However, right through the second half of the twentieth-century, and thus long before this formidable twenty-first-century recovery of interest in "the historical Jesus," the North American New Testament scholar, John Knox,[10] made a sustained

---

6. Dunn, *Jesus Remembered*, 882; also 335.

7. Bauckham, *Jesus and the Eyewitnesses* (2006). Prior to the work of Bauckham in Britain, this general interest in the importance of the oral transmission of what became the written Synoptic tradition had been pioneered characteristically by Scandinavian scholars. See for example, the seminal works of Birger Gerhardsson: *Memory and Manuscript*; *Oral Tradition and Written Transmission in Rabbinic Judaism and Early Christianity*; *The Gospel Tradition*; and *The Reliability of the Gospel Tradition*. See also Samuel Byrskog, *Story as History—History as Story: The Gospel Tradition in the Context of Ancient Oral History*; and Werner Kelber and Samuel Byrskog, eds., *Jesus in Memory: Traditions in Oral and Scribal Perspectives*.

8. Richard Burridge, *What Are the Gospels? A Comparison with Graeco-Roman Biography*, and *Four Gospels One Jesus*? See also, Rafael Rodriguez, *Structuring Early Christian Memory*.

9. For a collection of related articles, see Robert B. Stewart and Gary R. Habermas, eds., *Memories of Jesus: A Critical Appraisal of James Dunn's Jesus Remembered*. For earlier responses to Dunn's proposals, see Bengt Holmberg, "Questions of Method in James Dunn's *Jesus Remembered*," and Samuel Byrskog, "A New Perspective on the Jesus Tradition: Reflections on James D. G. Dunn's *Jesus Remembered*," along with Dunn's reply to both, "On History, Memory and Eyewitnesses: In Response to Bengt Holmberg and Samuel Bryskog."

10. John Knox originally taught at the University of Chicago Divinity School (1939 to 1943) and was Baldwin Professor of Sacred Literature at Union Theological Seminary in Manhattan from 1943 to 1966. He then became professor of the New Testament at the Episcopal Theological Seminary of the Southwest in Austin, Texas, until 1971.

and spirited attempt to provide an alternative to the proposals of Bultmann. Knox wrote and published right through the second half of the twentieth-century, at a time when the Word theology of Rudolf Bultmann was in the ascendant in the world of New Testament studies. While sharing the pessimism of twentieth-century theology about the possibility of coming to any settled historical conclusions in relation to the historical Jesus using the methods of critical historical research, Knox already saw the clear difficulty of the prevailing theological disconnect from the historical life of Jesus, particularly in relation to any account of faith in *his* resurrection from the dead. He thus came up with an alternative solution. By contrast with Bultmann's aggressively overt and systematic avoidance of any interest in the "Jesus of history," Knox insisted, in a succession of books, that the corporate or shared memory of the historical Jesus was integral both to the self-identity of the church itself and to the understanding of its faith. A Bultmannian-type abandonment of any interest in the so-called "Jesus of history" in favor of a concentration on "the heavenly Raised Christ" of the church's post-Easter faith just did not seem to Knox to do justice to the Gospel's focus on the remembered historical person whose life and death stood at the center of the Easter proclamation.

Knox was therefore of the view that it is important to say, in any discussion of the church's Easter faith, that the resurrected Christ is also (in some sense of "is also") the remembered historical Jesus. The essence of the church's continuing Easter faith is that the one whose presence we now claim in faith to recognize and *know* as the living Christ and Lord of the Christian community is precisely the one whom we also *remember* to have lived and died in Palestine in the first-century. This means that Easter faith is essentially a matter of both *remembering* and *knowing*, and indeed of remembering *in order* to know, for, in epistemological terms, we can only be said to recognize those whom we in some way remember. A claim to identify someone implies that we can recall at least something of an identifying nature. Thus, it seemed to follow that the one whose living presence is claimed to be known in Easter faith may be recognized and identified *as* the Raised *Jesus* only because of a logically prior remembrance of *him*.[11] The continuity of the Raised Christ of faith with the identity of the historical Jesus was thus said to have been secured by appeal to this key notion of the church's corporately shared "memory."

---

11. At this crucial point his position contrasts with Frei's tendency to argue that Jesus' identity and his presence somehow coincide in a single self-authenticating experience: "His identity and his presence are given together in indissoluble unity" (*The Identity of Jesus Christ*, 182). At this point Knox's epistemological insight is that a reasoned account can be given to justify claims to know and identify the presence specifically of the Raised Christ by appeal to the concept of a logically prior "memory of him."

It is something of a puzzle that John Knox rates only a single passing reference in James D. G. Dunn's monumental *Jesus Remembered*. Given Knox's groundbreaking and sustained work on the very same theme right through the second half of the twentieth-century, one might expect to find a plethora of references to Knox in the index to Dunn's book. It comes as something of a surprise to find just a single footnote reference.[12]

Dunn shares with Knox the fundamental contention that "what is now the synoptic tradition" was originally, as Dunn himself puts it, "the memories of the first disciples—not Jesus himself, but the remembered Jesus."[13] Though Knox differs from Dunn insofar as he does not make this distinction between "Jesus himself" (i.e., Jesus as he actually was in historical time) and "the remembered Jesus," he, like Dunn after him, was well aware that the Jesus of the documents of the Christian tradition is a Jesus who was remembered from a highly specific perspective, given the particular impact that he obviously had on those who in the first-century had to do with him. This was the perspective of those who came to faith. In Knox's view nobody remembers Jesus in the way the church remembers him. Others may have remembered him in other ways. No doubt the soldiers who crucified Jesus remembered him, if they remembered him at all, as a petty troublemaker; but the first Christians remembered him for the highly distinctive and impressive impact he made upon their lives, which they sought to describe and communicate in a variety of very distinctive ways.

Despite what appears to be an obvious similarity of interest in approaching an understanding of Jesus through the category of a distinctive form of "remembrance," Dunn's passing reference to Knox is dismissive. Even while he acknowledges that Knox's *remembered* Jesus gives him the leitmotif for his own work,[14] he says that Knox treats the theme of the remembered Jesus in "too broad and ill-defined a manner to be helpful."

Alas, I am mortified to say that the reason Dunn cites for this abrupt dismissal is attributed to me! Readers are simply referred by Dunn to "the critique of P. Carnley, *The Structure of Resurrection Belief*, . . . pp. 268–75 and 280–94." I hasten to say, however, that while I think Knox's work must certainly be carefully and critically evaluated, I am far from thinking of Knox's contribution to the theme of the

---

12. Dunn, *Jesus Remembered*, 131 n. 111.

13. Dunn, *Jesus Remembered*, 130–31. When Dunn says "not Jesus himself," what he means (if I can presume to sharpen his expression) is "not the actual Jesus of past historical time," but "Jesus *as* the disciples remembered him." As we shall see, to Knox's mind Jesus actually *was* as he *was remembered*. Dunn's disjunction between "Jesus as he actually was," and "Jesus as he was remembered" is the source of considerable comment if not confusion. I empathize with the comment of Markus Bockmuehl, in "Whose Memory? Whose Orality?," 42, when he says: "Dunn's repeated and emphatic prioritization of Jesus' 'impact' as opposed to 'Jesus himself' will inevitably leave some readers wondering to what extent 'the historical Jesus' remains a viable object of inquiry at all." See also, A. F. Gregory, "An Oral and Written Gospel?" 7–12, and contributions of Stephen T. Davis and Gary R. Habermas in Stewart and Habermas, *Memories of Jesus*, chaps. 12 and 13.

14. Dunn, *Jesus Remembered*, 131.

"Church's shared memory of Jesus" in terms that might be so easily dismissed. We have a lot to learn from him, particularly with regard to the epistemological question of the means of identifying the presence of the Raised Christ by reference to his remembered identity.

Interestingly enough, both Knox and Dunn work with a fundamental distinction between bare facts *about* Jesus and a more essential memory of Jesus *himself*. For example, Knox tried (though I think ultimately unsuccessfully) to distinguish the memory of Jesus *himself*, interpreted from the perspective of faith and communicated through the living voice of the church's tradition, from the memory of facts *about* Jesus that might be established by critical historical research. Dunn likewise distinguishes "facts about Jesus," which might be established by critical historical research (which, following Martin Kähler, he calls *Historie*), from the historic Jesus of the church's faith (which he calls *Geschichte*), and which he also thinks is found in the New Testament documents. This latter is "the significant Jesus, the Jesus who made the impact that he did" (on the disciples).[15] This is the Jesus at the "stable core" of the Gospel traditions.

However, there is a clear difference between Knox and Dunn insofar as Knox contends that what Dunn refers to as the "stable core" of the church's memory of Jesus, the memory of "Jesus *himself*," is something of which the believer may be certain (by contrast with the insecurity of the historian's attempts to establish "facts *about* Jesus"). Dunn, on the other hand, is of the view that even the outline shape of the "remembered Jesus" (the stable core of the tradition) is established by critical historical research, and that, unfortunately, certainty evades both the historian and the believer alike, given that all historical judgments are plagued by an alleged permanent and unavoidable insecurity.[16] Indeed, for Dunn, faith arises because of the shortfall in the historian's ability to establish the truth about Jesus with certainty. By contrast, for Knox, the confidently entertained memory of Jesus *himself* (Dunn's stable core of the tradition, as distinct from detailed factual information about him) not only furnishes the believer with certainty but also provides the epistemic ability to recognize the presence of the raised Christ in faith in the present.

This means that Dunn is content to focus upon the "Jesus remembered" who provides the central subject matter of the New Testament texts, and is almost exclusively interested in the processes of oral transmission of what was remembered of Jesus *prior* to the formation of the written synoptic tradition. However, Knox's "memory of Jesus" is something that is constantly being received and formed in the life of the church so

---

15. Dunn's crisp clarification of this distinction may be found in his response to Stephen Davis in Stewart and Habermas, *Memories of Jesus*, "A Grateful Response," 319.

16. For a refutation of this form of historical skepticism, see the companion volume to this, *Resurrection in Retrospect*, chapter 7, where the focus is on N. T. Wright's acceptance of the same ultimate skepticism.

as to enable the recognition of the Raised Christ even in the present. In a sense, Knox is primarily interested in the church's "living memory" in the life of the Christian community *this* side of texts, and its epistemic importance for faith today. Dunn, by contrast, is primarily interested in the "stable core" of the memory of Jesus on the *far side* of the texts, or *behind* the texts, that is now found embodied in them. So, despite the fundamental common ground that they share in relation to the "stable core" of the historical "memory of Jesus," that is to be distinguished from the memory of detailed facts *about* him, there are nevertheless significant differences between the handling of the notion respectively by Knox and Dunn.

We shall attempt to unscramble something of this as we proceed in this chapter. For the present I simply need to affirm that, despite criticisms I shall make, I am still of the view that Knox's use of the category of "the Church's shared memory" is not only of importance as the point of departure for understanding the material now found in the synoptic tradition, but also for an understanding both of the continuing nature of faith itself, and also for ecclesiology, for one of Knox's key themes involves the idea that the church has its own continuing identity even today precisely as the community that "remembers Jesus" in a particular kind of way.

Certainly, Knox's writing on this theme was of enormous historical importance insofar as he valiantly sought to sustain the connection of the church's faith with the identity of "the historical Jesus" right through the period of the Bultmannian onslaught on the propriety of placing any theological interest in the findings of historiography. Indeed, this theme of the church's memory of Jesus was almost certainly the most characteristic theme of Knox's prodigious theological output. Beyond its place in that original context, his work remains of importance still today, even despite the fact that it may be admitted that it contains some logical flaws. Far from being "too broad and ill-defined" for us to find it helpful, with a little "tweaking" a sympathetic reading of Knox's reflections on the concept of the church's "memory of Jesus" remains of enormous importance to an understanding both of resurrection faith itself, and of the nature and identity of the community of faith.

John Knox wrote with enthusiasm on the theme of "the Church and her memory" of Jesus because he was convinced that, despite the difficulty of penetrating the theologically and dogmatically pregnant christological interpretations to which the first generations of Christians resorted in expressing their newfound faith, it was a mistake to abandon all interest in the identity of the historical human person at their center.

Knox was inclined, simply through the weight of the then prevailing scholarly consensus, to accept the conclusions of the form-critical approach to the New Testament texts. The view that the oral transmission of stories in the context of the preaching and worship of early faith communities meant that the original kernel of historical fact about Jesus was overlaid with community interests and concerns was difficult to avoid in that era. While thus conceding much of the ground claimed by form-critical scholasticism, which insisted therefore that detailed information about the historical figure of Jesus was almost entirely camouflaged and obscured by the over-lay of theological interpretation that had been put on the tradition about him, Knox nevertheless contended that what remains crucial to the church's understanding of Jesus, so far as faith is concerned, is nevertheless its "memory of *him*."

In this way, the church's memory *of him* was contrasted with facts *about him* of the kind that critical historical research found so difficult to establish and pin down. Knox was convinced that, though some of the details of what Jesus is said to have done, and what he may have taught, may have been lost in the process of transmission of the early traditions about him, the actual man, the human person, and the identity of the distinctive self that he was remembered to have been, remains at the center of the tradition of the church's memory of *him*. Indeed, so integral to the church's own self-understanding was the corporate or shared memory of the historical person of Jesus said to be, that Knox argued that the church could not *be* the church apart from its "memory of Jesus." The internal thread of the church's living memory of Jesus is, in other words, constitutive of its own self-identity and self-understanding. Thus, speaking of the certitude that he alleged attaches to the church's memory of Jesus as the center of the Christ-Event, he said "it is of the very nature of the community to remember the event and the person around whom it occurred; and one simply cannot doubt the existence of what one remembers."[17]

Effectively, Knox was in this way endeavoring to provide his own distinctive version of a kind of *sturmfreies Gebiet* for faith that was independent of the findings of critical historical research.[18] It was the church's corporately shared memory, rather than historical research, that was said to put the contemporary believer in touch with the historical Jesus via its own "living and sustained voice" (to use a term of Papias of Hierapolis, much favored by Knox). This "living and sustained voice" was said to equip the church with the capacity in faith to recognize the contemporary living presence of the one remembered.[19]

17. Knox, *The Early Church*, 78.

18. In other words, appeal to the notion of the church's corporately shared memory of Jesus is an attempt to settle questions of faith and history. It is an attempt to show how "faith in Christ can be essentially related to historical fact and yet be as sure as faith must be." *The Church and the Reality of Christ*, 10.

19. Knox would have welcomed and the more recent work of Richard Bauckham on the importance of eyewitness testimony of the kind much valued by Papias. See Bauckham, *Jesus and the Eyewitnesses*, especially chapter 2: "Papias on the Eyewitnesses." However, Knox's own interest came to focus more on the continuing cross-generational transmission of the church's memory of Jesus than on the importance of the oral history of eyewitnesses in the production of the synoptic traditions that is of such concern to Bauckham.

Not a few found Knox's talk of "the Church and her memory" somewhat enigmatic and puzzling. To many, talk of the church's corporate or shared memory of Jesus sounded as though it were self-authenticating. In other words, it sounded almost like a definitional or analytic truth rather than a contingent one—as though the shared memory of Jesus was as logically necessary for the church to be the church, as it is in ordinary language for a bachelor to be unmarried. "This memory of Jesus himself," he said, "was a central element in the life of primitive Christianity and still belongs to the very being of the church."[20] This led some critics, such as E. L. Mascall, to write off the notion of "the Church and her memory" as nothing more than "ecclesiastical psychology," and to accuse Knox of being a reductionist theologian by embracing a kind of idealism.[21] This was a complete misinterpretation of Knox, who was in fact intent upon articulating an unequivocal theological realism. The church's memory was not self-contained; rather, it provided the necessary reference point for recognizing and identifying the objective presence of the Raised Christ that he unequivocally believed was external to believers. His was an unquestionably realist position.

This is not to say, however, that Knox's idea of "the Church and her memory of Jesus" is without difficulty; and there are certainly indications that he was himself responsible in some degree for the confused reaction triggered by it, because his presentation of this theme is not always entirely consistent. On the face of it, talk of the "corporate memory" of the church appears to be essentially metaphorical or, better, analogical; something similar to, but at the same time different from, an individual person's memory.[22] On the other hand, sometimes he spoke as though there are in fact no differences between the logic of the literal predication of the notion of "memory" in relation to an individual person, and its logic when predicated, apparently metaphorically or analogically, of the church. He often suggests, for example, that because the church "remembers Jesus" it cannot regard its impression of Jesus as illusory, for "*one* simply cannot doubt the existence of what *one* remembers."[23] The suggestion is that the logical behavior of the word "remember," when predicated of the church, and its behavior when predicated literally of an individual human person, is identical.[24]

20. Knox, *The Church and the Reality of Christ*, 54.

21. Mascall, *The Secularisation of Christianity*, 255. See also Mascall's *Theology and the Future*, 106, where Knox's thought is said to be "somewhat Pickwickian."

22. If an analogy may be contrasted with an entirely different and unrelated image that is brought to refer to something else, as in the case of a metaphor, then the church's memory was understood on analogy with the memory of a human individual. It is not strictly speaking a metaphor.

23. Knox, *The Early Church*, 78. My italics. In one sense, Knox's logic here is correct. One cannot assert "I remember that p" and at the same time doubt "that p," since the assertion "I remember that p" entails "that p," and to deny "that p" would be to fall into a self-contradiction. The logic of the word "remember" thus runs parallel to the logic of the word "know." One cannot claim to know something and at the same time doubt it. However, whether the word "remember" operates according to the same logic in relation to the church is of course the crucial question.

24. See Knox, *The Church and the Reality of Christ*, 56, where it is implied that because the church "remembers Jesus" it cannot regard its impression of Jesus as illusory.

Indeed, at one place he speaks of his own memory of his father and then goes on to say, "So Jesus was remembered."[25]

On other occasions Knox is somewhat more cautious. "I hope no one will suppose," he says, "that I am arguing that I can remember Jesus in the way Peter or John or Mary did"—thereby indicating that his use of the term is not to be understood in a straight-forward literal way.[26] In his more mature reflection on the subject in *The Humanity and Divinity of Christ*, moreover, he sometimes used the term "memory" in quotation marks to warn his readers that it is predicated of the church in some unusual sense.[27] In this case, it is important to come to some understanding of the specific respects in which it might be said to be similar to personal memory, literally understood, and those respects in which it is understood to be different. Unfortunately we are not actually in a position to do this, because we have yet to pin down exactly what it is we are reading about when Knox writes of "the Church and her memory" of Jesus.

Knox's insistence that the content of the church's memory does not consist of *facts about Jesus* of the kind with which critical historians deal, but was rather a memory of Jesus *himself*, also raises a raft of questions. For Knox, this distinction between a memory of facts *about* Jesus and the memory of Jesus *himself* was quite fundamental. He contrasts "authentic primitive memories,"[28] or "earliest shared memories,"[29] with "the memory *of* Jesus," or "the Church's corporate memory of Jesus." It is clear that the earliest authentic memories *about* Jesus are the memories of the first Christians, which the historian now tries to separate from the over-lay of theological interpretation with which from the start they were clothed, and in which they are still embedded in the New Testament texts. But when Knox speaks of the church's memory *of* Jesus, what he has in mind is not a memory possessed by the first Christians only,[30] but a memory transmitted within the life of the church through the ages. It is not the historian's task to discover the true content of this memory because it is a memory of Jesus that is already possessed by contemporary believers. Immediately, one must ask if the contemporary church's memory of Jesus is not formed by acquaintance with the New Testament texts, and whether such a contrast between the memory *of facts about Jesus* and the church's memory *of him* can actually be sustained.

25. Knox, *Christ the Lord*, 56.
26. Knox, *Christ the Lord*, 39.
27. Knox, *The Humanity and Divinity of Christ*, 77.
28. Knox, *The Death of Christ*, 29.
29. Knox, *The Church and the Reality of Christ*, 53.
30. Such as is now found in the documents of the synoptic tradition, which is the chief focus of James Dunn's interest.

FAITH AS REMEMBERING AND KNOWING

However, for the moment we should note that implicit in what Knox has to say in his reflections about the content of the church's memory of Jesus, are some indications of his thinking about the actual nature of the human faculty of memory itself. In making the distinction between the memory of facts about Jesus and the memory of Jesus himself in *The Church and the Reality of Christ* (1962), he states his position in very explicit terms: "When I say," he says, "that the Church remembers Jesus, I do not mean that it remembers *facts about him*. Indeed, it is doubtful that we can ever properly be said to *remember* a fact about anything. Facts about things are abstractions; only the things themselves can in the strict sense be remembered."[31]

Putting aside, for the moment, the claim that the church's memory is not constituted by facts *about* Jesus, it is important to examine what Knox says here about the nature of memory generally. Certainly, if the concept of the church's memory of Jesus is to be called upon to justify claims to perceive, recognize, and thus know his living presence in faith, it will obviously be necessary to have a reasonably clear picture of exactly what this memory is. If its function is to allow the interpretative identification of what is perceived *as* the presence of the Raised Jesus, then this is crucial. Its key importance for securing the continuity of what is known in faith *as* the presence of the Raised Christ with the historical Jesus, calls for its more clear definition.

To begin, we may well ask if Knox is right when he says that it is doubtful that we can ever properly be said to remember a fact but that "only things themselves" can in the strict sense be remembered.[32] This is an understandable point of view. Bertrand Russell and Henri Bergson held similar views. Both held that an individual person's perceptual memory of things, as distinct from habit memory or factual memory, is the true or real kind of memory.[33]

However, at this point I think Knox, no less than Russell and Bergson, is quite mistaken. The verb "remember" enters into a variety of grammatical constructions, all with a family resemblance, and it is wrong to think it is properly used in only one of them. Professor Norman Malcolm, for example, in some ground-breaking

---

31. Knox, *The Church and the Reality of Christ*, 51–52. See *The Church and the Reality of Christ*, 35 and 54, esp. n. 3. Also, *Criticism and Faith*, 49. It is because the memory of the Church does not contain facts about Jesus, over and above those found in the New Testament, nor doctrinal formulations, that Knox says he prefers his term "memory" to "tradition." For an account of what has been conceived as "tradition" in the history of the church see Congar, *Tradition and Traditions*, especially chapter 2. Even so, Knox admits that what he calls "memory" is related to what the church has called "Tradition" (as distinct from "traditions"). For the use of this distinction see also Campenhausen, *Tradition and Life in the Early Church*, especially chapter 1: "Tradition and Spirit in Early Christianity," and Ebeling, *The Word of God and Tradition*.

32. Material on the pages that follow is taken from Carnley (1993), *The Structure of Resurrection Belief*, 275–87. Used by permission of Oxford University Press.

33. Russell, *The Analysis of Mind*, 167 and 175–76; Bergson, *Matter and Memory*, 86.

philosophical reflection on the nature of memory, once distinguished three different forms of memory, each of which is expressed by employing the verb "remember" in a different, but perfectly correct or "strict" sense.[34] There may well be more than these three forms of memory, but a consideration of Malcolm's categories will help us analyze Knox's position.

Malcolm called the three forms of memory *perceptual* memory, *factual* memory, and *personal* memory. The meaning of *perceptual* memory, as Malcolm defined it, is roughly equivalent to a definition of C. D. Broad, who said that "perceptual memory" is "the memory of particular events, places, persons, or things."[35] Perceptual memory is the memory *of* some past object rather than a memory *about* a past object; it is the memory of a past event itself, or of a person him or herself. For example, perceptual memory is expressed in such assertions as "I remember it raining last week" or "I remember the launching of the Queen Elizabeth II," or "I remember him, though I do not remember his age." Perceptual memory is roughly what Gilbert Ryle called a person's occurrent recollecting of something, a "recalling, reviving, or dwelling on some episode" of a person's "own past."[36] This is in distinction from habit memories or memories of how to perform certain tasks, such as remembering the way to church, or how to tie one's shoelace.

Malcolm's definition of perceptual memory differs from Broad's in that he requires that the memory of persons, places, events or things always involves mental imagery: "It belongs to the concept of perceptual memory, that it requires mental imagery," he says, noting that Bertrand Russell seems to be conceiving of this kind of memory when he says that the "process of remembering will consist of calling up images . . ."[37] Perceptual memory as Malcolm defines it involves seeing a person, place, event, or thing "before the mind's eye."

Malcolm's second form of memory, *factual* memory, is quite different. It is not the memory of a person, place, event, or thing, but is a memory of facts *about* persons, places, events, or things. To Malcolm's mind, it is distinguishable from perceptual memory because it does not involve mental imagery. Rather, factual memory denotes a use of the word "remember," "in which this verb is followed by a clause of the form 'that p' where for 'p' there may be substituted any sentence expressing a proposition."[38] Broad's parallel to Malcolm's factual memory is referred to as "propositional memory," but Malcolm prefers "factual memory" because when the subordinate "that" clause expresses a true proposition, it expresses a fact. By con-

---

34. Malcolm, "Three Forms of Memory," 205.
35. Broad, *The Mind and its Place in Nature*, 222.
36. Ryle, *The Concept of Mind*, 258.
37. Malcolm, "Three Forms of Memory," 208. See Russell, *The Analysis of Mind*, 175 (quoted by Malcolm on 210).
38. Malcolm, "Three Forms of Memory," 203–4. See also Malcolm, "A Definition of Factual Memory."

trast with perceptual memory, factual memory may be quite abstract. For example, the statements, "I remember *that* 2 + 2 = 4," or "I remember *that* Jones is 31 years of age," are examples of factual memory.[39]

The difference between factual memory and perceptual memory becomes clear if somebody were to claim to remember "*that* the Queen Elizabeth II was launched in 1968," but then add, "however, I do not remember the actual launching *itself*." Malcolm goes on to say that the distinction he is making between factual memory and perceptual memory could be stated as the distinction between "memory by description" and "memory by acquaintance." Perhaps a better way of putting this distinction would be to say that factual memory is "memory by description" and perceptual memory is "acquaintance by memory."[40]

Another important distinction between these two forms of memory is that, while in examples of perceptual memory the referent is always past, a factual memory may be about the past, present or future. Thus all the following examples of factual memory are valid: "I remember *that* Napoleon lost the Battle of Waterloo"; "I remember *that* the mayor is opening the flower show"; and "I remember *that* there will be an election next weekend."[41] But perceptual memory must always be of a person, place, event, or thing of the past. One cannot intelligently claim to have a memory *of* the mayor opening the flower show at the present moment, nor to remember, recall, or have a memory *of* next week's election.

Something must now be said about the third of Malcolm's three forms of memory, *personal* memory. Malcolm defines personal memory as the memory of persons, places, events, or things, that one has oneself previously perceived or experienced *in one's own lifetime*. It is represented in statements of the kind: "I *personally* remember *p*." The examples that have already been used to illustrate perceptual memory are also examples of personal memory. One could say, "I personally remember it raining last week"; "I personally remember the launching of Queen Elizabeth II"; or "I personally remember *him*, though I do not remember his age." Indeed, all personal memory is perceptual memory since one cannot claim a previous acquaintance with persons, places, events, or things that lies beyond one's own personal experience. That is to say, one cannot have perceptual memory of objects or events that lie temporally or geographically outside the bounds of one's own past experience. One obviously cannot have perceptual memory *of* events that occurred before one was born, or of persons who died before one was born, or of places and things that lie geographically outside of the field of one's past experience. It would clearly be absurd if I, a person living in the twenty-first-century, were to say "I personally remember Napoleon losing the Battle of Waterloo," or, if I have never been to Antarctica, that "I personally remember

---

39. Thus Broad says "The propositions which I remember . . . *may* be about past events, but they need not be." *The Mind and its Place in Nature*, 272.

40. A phrase of Bertrand Russell, *The Problems of Philosophy*, 76.

41. See Ryle, *The Concept of Mind*, 257–58.

Antarctica." As Gilbert Ryle put it, "these are not the sorts of things that can be recalled, in the same sense of the verb in which what I recall must be something that I have myself witnessed, done or experienced."[42]

However, while perceptual memory is always also personal memory, personal memory is not always perceptual memory, for personal memory does not always involve seeing images "before one's mind's eye." Personal memory *may* be expressed as factual memory. One may say, "I personally remember p" (an example of perceptual memory), or "I personally remember *that* p" (an example of factual memory). On the other hand, while all perceptual memory is personal memory, and while personal memory may be either perceptual or factual, not all factual memory is personal memory, for what is said to be remembered in instances of factual memory need not necessarily be about a person, place, event or thing previously witnessed or experienced in one's own lifetime. To say "I remember *that* Napoleon lost the Battle of Waterloo" is neither personal nor perceptual. It is simply a factual memory.

Many philosophers have thought that all memory must be of the personal/perceptual or personal/factual type. That is to say, many have thought that the only permissible form of memory is memory of persons, places, events, or things that one previously witnessed or experienced oneself. W. von Leyden, for example, says: "Everyone would agree that what we can remember is not always just any past event or fact, but a certain kind of past events or facts, namely those that form part of one's own previous experience."[43] We have to dissent from this, however, for a number of reasons. First of all, we are inclined to claim to remember events which were not actually previously witnessed or experienced, but which we otherwise come to know about around the time of their occurrence. Even if one has no experience of the Second World War at firsthand, one is nevertheless inclined to claim to remember it if one was alive at the time it was occurring and if one knew *that* it was going on at the time. Many of us, similarly, are inclined to say "I personally remember the assassination of President John F. Kennedy" or "the tragic death of Diana, Princess of Wales," though we did not actually witness these events, but came to know about them at the time of their occurrence through the media. However, even if these are allowed as legitimate memory-claims, this still limits memory to events or facts that have occurred within one's own lifetime. Malcolm correctly insists that even this limitation is invalid. Factual memory need not be of facts falling within one's previous experience, or even occurring within one's own lifetime. It is perfectly correct to say, "I remember *that* Napoleon lost the Battle of Waterloo." That is to say, not all factual memory is personal memory.

It is clearly true that nobody today personally remembers "William the Conqueror winning the Battle of Hastings in 1066."[44] We obviously cannot have a perceptual

---

42. Ryle, *The Concept of Mind*, 258–59.
43. Leyden, *Remembering*, 60.
44. An example of Moore, *Philosophical Papers*, 215.

or personal memory *of* William the Conqueror winning the Battle of Hastings. It is hardly possible to claim to have an image of William winning the battle "before one's mind's eye." If we do we are imagining not remembering. However, it is nevertheless perfectly correct for anyone today to claim to remember "*that* William the Conqueror won the Battle of Hastings."[45]

In summary, the basic relations between the three forms of memory as Malcolm defines them may be expressed as follows:

a. All perceptual memory is also personal memory.

b. Not all personal memory is perceptual memory since personal memory may be factual or perceptual.

c. Not all factual memory is personal memory, since remembered facts may be very remote ones, lying outside one's own personal experience.

Now, let us bring these distinctions to the clarification of John Knox's statements concerning the church's "corporate memory" of Jesus. The first thing to be said is that when Knox makes the distinction between remembering his own father, but not remembering facts *about* him, he is saying something of importance. He is effectively working with Malcolm's distinction between perceptual/personal memory and factual memory. Though Knox does not explicitly say that his (personal/perceptual) memory of his father involves a mental image of his father, perhaps as much is implied. He says he remembers his father *himself*, and this is to be contrasted with his inability to remember facts *about* him. However, when Knox claims that "in the strict sense" we can only be said to remember "things themselves," he apparently means that only what Malcolm calls "personal/perceptual memory" can strictly be called memory. This is certainly similar to the views of Bertrand Russell and Henri Bergson who both held that what Malcolm calls "personal/perceptual memory," as distinct from other forms of memory, is the paradigm of memory. It is not possible to say, however, that we can never properly be said to remember facts about things, and when Knox says "one does not 'remember' ideas or concepts or generalizations or formal definitions, however true they may be; one remembers only persons and things and happenings,"[46] he is clearly mistaken. It is perfectly correct to say "I remember *that* 2 + 2 = 4," or "*that* Napoleon lost the Battle of Waterloo," or even, providing these propositions are true, "*that* there was once a man called Jesus," "*that* he died a terrible death on a cross," or even "*that* he displayed a particular quality of character." Factual memory, indeed, is

---

45. Broad concurs: "I certainly do remember that Caesar crossed the Rubicon," he says, "and I certainly do not remember the event which is described as 'Caesar crossing the Rubicon.'" *The Mind and Its Place in Nature*, 272.

46. Knox, *The Church and the Reality of Christ*, 46.

the only form of memory that allows references to persons, places, events, or things *that lie outside of one's own personal experience*. It would be as absurd to say "I personally remember Jesus dying on the Cross," or "I personally remember Jesus," or "I personally remember Jesus *himself*" as it would be to say "I personally remember William the Conqueror winning the Battle of Hastings," or "I personally remember Napoleon losing the Battle of Waterloo." However, one can remember "*that* there was a Jesus" and "*that* he died on a cross" as properly as one can claim to remember "*that* William the Conqueror won the Battle of Hastings," or "*that* there was a Napoleon and *that* he lost the Battle of Waterloo."

Unfortunately, however, factual memory seems exactly the kind of memory that Knox will not allow. He claims that he remembers his father, but that he does not remember facts *about* him. Similarly, he claims that the church's memory of Jesus is not comprised of factual memories *about* Jesus, but that the church remembers *him*. The church remembers Jesus *himself*. This seems to suggest that the church has a perceptual memory *of* Jesus. But this is exactly the kind of memory the church cannot have because perceptual memory is always also personal memory; it is the recalling *of* persons, places, events, or things, previously experienced *in one's own lifetime*.

That said, there is a sense in which factual memory is the most logically primitive form of memory. If I were to claim a personal/perceptual memory of my father, it follows that I should be able to cite at least *some* factual memories *about* him. To claim a personal memory of my father but be unable to articulate any factual memories about him at all would suggest that I do not really have a personal or perceptual memory of him after all. Knox's suggestion that the church claims to remember Jesus *himself*, but cannot articulate any factual information about him, seriously raises a doubt about whether the church actually remembers him in any sense at all.

We may therefore well ask that, if the historian experiences difficulty in separating the earliest memories from the over-lay of theological interpretation put on them and with which they are now clothed and found in the New Testament texts, and if the historian can therefore not be really certain about individual words and deeds of Jesus, what exactly is the content of the church's memory of Jesus of which Knox says the Christian may be certain?

At this point Knox is actually better than his word: he says that while we cannot "regard every item in the Gospels as belonging to this authentic and abiding memory,"[47] there is "a certain small but essential minimum of historical truth of which the Christian believer is. . . sure."[48] The church's memory is said to assure the believer not just "of the historicity of Jesus," but of something relating to the distinctive quality of his

---

47. Knox, *On the Meaning of Christ*, 38.
48. Knox, *Criticism and Faith*. 36.

character. This seems to mean that the church's memory contains at least the fact *that* there was a Jesus, and the fact *that* he exhibited a certain quality of character. What are these if they are not statements of fact *about* Jesus? However, Knox continues to assert firmly, even if somewhat equivocally, that when he speaks of what is remembered of Jesus he is referring "not to any fact *about* Jesus but to the person himself as remembered in the Church."[49] It is at this point that Knox was laboring to make a distinction that is also of importance to James Dunn insofar as he seeks to distinguish "facts about Jesus" from the memory of Jesus *himself*. In Dunn's terminology this is "the significant Jesus," the "Jesus who made an impact."[50]

Curiously, however, the logical primitiveness of factual memories to which Norman Malcolm has drawn attention, is actually demonstrated in relation to the church's memory of Jesus *himself* by Knox himself in his own writing. Indeed, this notion remains somewhat shadowy and vague until Knox himself gives it precise content by resorting to certain facts. Even in his early work, *The Man Christ Jesus* (1941), Knox argued that the church remembers Jesus as a person "supremely great and good." What is this but the memory of the fact *that* Jesus was supremely great and good? On the other hand, in his much later work, *The Humanity and Divinity of Christ* (1967), Knox emphasizes that the church remembers Jesus as an actual human being: what the church "remembers" is a man—"a man 'full of grace and truth', but nevertheless a man . . ."[51] Jesus was remembered as "a truly human person."[52] Thus, the church's memory of Jesus is at least the purported factual memory *that* he was a truly human person who lived a life "full of grace and truth."

Beyond this, in the church's remembering of Jesus the man, Knox goes on to say that he was remembered as a particular and uniquely individual character. This is also described in a number of statements of fact. In *The Death of Christ*, Knox argued that "the moral personality of Jesus and the character of his life"[53] are remembered. This memory is constituted not only by "the fact of the historical life but also the quality of it as a life in which . . . *agapē* . . . began to be revealed."[54] "It belongs to the very nature of the Church," he says, "to know not only that Jesus lived but that *Jesus* lived. I mean that it is of the nature of the Church to remember a man who in word and act expressed that *agapē* which later became the breath, the spirit, of the Church's life and which even then began to evoke a characteristic response."[55] James Dunn expresses a similar

---

49. Knox, *Criticism and Faith*, 37. This is reaffirmed often in Knox's writings. E.g., in *The Early Church*, 54, he says: "the memory we are considering was a memory of Jesus himself, not of any fact about him or of any word he spoke."

50. Dunn, "A Grateful Response," 319.

51. Knox, *The Humanity and Divinity of Christ*, 78.

52. Knox, *The Humanity and Divinity of Christ*, 76; see also 78–79.

53. Knox, *The Death of Christ*, 110.

54. Knox, *The Death of Christ*, 111.

55. Knox, *The Death of Christ*, 11.

insight when he says: "We can recognize the character of the one who made the impact that he did from the impression left by that impact."[56]

Again, in *The Church and the Reality of Christ*, Knox affirms that *agapē* is "remembered as the essential and distinctive quality of Jesus' own life."[57] His character is remembered as the character of the "full integrity and utter abundance of love."[58] In other words, it is clear that content is given to the notion of the church's memory of Jesus by Knox himself in a series of factual statements—*that* Jesus was a human person, *that* he possessed a distinctive moral character, and *that* the quality of this distinctive character may be expressed as *agapē*.

Moreover, Knox continually stresses the importance of the fact of Jesus' death in the church's memory of him. "To remember Jesus," he says, "is to remember his cross."[59] Indeed, the memory of the Cross enjoys a certain priority: ". . . thence forth to remember Jesus is to remember first of all his cross."[60] Jesus was "poignantly remembered to have suffered a terrible death."[61] Indeed, Knox argues that for the early Christians, "the remembrance of Jesus himself would have been associated in their minds with the remembrance of his death,"[62] and that, because the Cross was for the first Christians, "*the* center of their memory of Jesus, and since our memory of him is theirs conveyed to us, it is the center of ours too."[63] Thus the Cross "has a place of special significance in the event to which we find ourselves looking back in memory and faith."[64] In this way, the Cross therefore assumes a key place as "the focus of the community's memory."[65]

Clearly, though Knox says that no facts are transmitted in the church's memory of Jesus, when he comes to give content to what would otherwise be a very shadowy notion, he is obliged to resort to statements of fact. It does actually contain some facts after all—*that* Jesus was a man, *that* he lived in Palestine in the first-century, and even *that* he exhibited an impressive character of a kind that attracted others to follow him. Not least among them is the fact *that* Jesus died on the Cross, and *that* this death on the Cross is a central element in the church's memory. In this way, Knox's own statements demonstrate the logical primitiveness of factual memory, specifically in relation to the church's shared or corporate memory of Jesus, and to which

---

56. Dunn, "In Grateful Dialogue," 319.
57. Knox, *The Church and the Reality of Christ*, 56.
58. Knox, *The Humanity and Divinity of Christ*, 45.
59. Knox, *Christ the Lord*, 56.
60. Knox, *The Death of Christ*, 114; see also Knox, *The Early Church*, 61: Jesus was "the man and Master whose death was remembered."
61. Knox, *The Death of Christ*, 36.
62. *Knox, The Death of Christ*, 113 and 117.
63. Knox, *The Church and the Reality of Christ*, 39.
64. Knox, *The Church and the Reality of Christ*, 38.
65. Knox, *The Early Church*, 53. See also Knox, *Life in Christ Jesus*, 34.

in general philosophical terms Norman Malcolm pointed. It is of interest that though James Dunn, like Knox, says that what was remembered by the first believers was not "facts about Jesus" but "Jesus remembered," those who have responded to Dunn have immediately also insisted that surely the fact "that he died on the Cross" is part of the early remembrance of him.[66]

I think we must conclude that when Knox says that the church remembers Jesus *himself*, but not facts *about* Jesus, he is somewhat confused. The reality is that he tends to treat the construction "the Church remembers Jesus *himself*" as an ellipsis, in the grammarians' sense, the meaning of which is given in a series of putatively factual statements.

Nevertheless, Knox clearly believed that in making the distinction between the memory of Jesus *himself* and the memory of facts *about* Jesus he was making a distinction of importance, and so he was. Implicit in a great deal of what Knox had to say in relation to this theme is the distinction between dispositional and episodic statements. A sympathetic reader will quickly perceive that when Knox says that the church does not remember facts *about* Jesus, what he really means is that the church does not necessarily remember factual statements narrating particular incidents of Jesus' career of an episodic or occurrent nature. For example, he says "Jesus is remembered... and therefore his existence cannot be doubted by the Christian. But no mere incident or circumstance in Jesus' career belongs to this memory."[67] It seems fairly clear that, when Knox says there are no facts in the church's memory of Jesus, he means there are no factual statements reporting specific incidents or episodes in Jesus' career.[68]

On the other hand, when he says that the church remembers Jesus *himself*, what he actually seems to mean is that the bare fact of Jesus' existence may be given content in statements reporting certain dispositional truths relating to the *kind* of person the historical Jesus was remembered to have been. Indeed, more important than statements reporting episodes or incidents in Jesus career, are statements that report certain dispositions relating to Jesus himself *as* the person he was remembered to have been.[69]

66. This question is asked both by Stephen T. Davis and Gary R. Habermas in their responses to Dunn in Stewart and Habermas, *Memories of Jesus*, chapters 12 and 13 respectively. In reply, Dunn concedes that the memory of the Cross is certainly integral to the synoptic tradition, but he nevertheless emphasizes the importance of the "stable core" memory of the "significant Jesus, the Jesus who made an impact" (*Memories of Jesus*, 319).

67. Knox, *Criticism and Faith*, 48–49.

68. Knox, *Criticism and Faith*, 51: "I am not suggesting that it (the memory) contains a single specific datum concerning the circumstances or incidents of Jesus' career or a single sentence from his lips..."

69. In James Dunn's understanding of things, this is the historic (*Geschichte*) Jesus, the "significant Jesus," whose memory is constituted by his character as "what it was that made an impact" on

Gilbert Ryle has pointed out that dispositional statements do not report "observed or observable states of affairs... They narrate no incidents."[70] "When a cow is said to be a ruminant, or a man is said to be a cigarette-smoker, it is not being said that the cow is ruminating now or that the man is smoking a cigarette now. To be a ruminant is to tend to ruminate from time to time, and to be a cigarette-smoker is to be in the habit of smoking cigarettes."[71] A dispositional statement, as distinct from a categorical statement of fact, does not report any particular incident or occurrence; rather, it has a tendency-stating or capacity-stating function. To say that a glass is brittle means that *if* it is hit with a hammer, *then* it will shatter and fly into splinters, not that it is now shattering and flying into splinters. To say that sugar is soluble is to say that *whenever* sugar is put in water it will dissolve, not that it is even now dissolving.

Now, statements describing qualities of character are dispositional statements and, despite the fact that they refer to specific persons, are capable of expression in the way I have just expressed them: as statements of universal conditional form.[72] To say that Bill is an angry person is not to say that he is even now exhibiting anger, or that he is always and at every moment exhibiting anger, but that *if* he is crossed, *then* he will tend to show anger rather than forbearance. To say that Tom is compassionate is to say that *whenever* Tom is in certain kinds of situation, *then* Tom will tend to exhibit the quality of compassion, not that he is always or at every moment exhibiting compassion. Sometimes Tom goes to sleep, at other times he reads books, and is engrossed in his work. To say that he is compassionate is to say that he is *liable* to exhibit compassion in specific circumstances.

Now, when Knox says that the Jesus whom the church remembers was a truly human person and that he exhibited a specific quality of character called "*agape*" this does not report any particular incident or occurrence. Nor does it mean that in every instant of his career Jesus was exhibiting this particular quality of character. Rather, it means that in certain kinds of circumstance, Jesus is remembered to have tended to act in such a way as to exhibit what came to be called "*agape*."[73] The same may be said of the remembrance of him as one who in word and deed served others in lowly

---

the disciples, rather than specific individual bare facts *about* him. The distinction being made here between episodic and dispositional memories, with respect to John Knox, may help unscramble some of the confusion commentators have encountered in interpreting James Dunn's distinction between "Jesus remembered" and bare factual statements *about* him.

70. Ryle, *The Concept of Mind*, 120.

71. Ryle, *The Concept of Mind*, 113.

72. The logical behavior of dispositional statements has much in common with general laws or open hypotheticals which do not themselves assert particular states of affairs, but precisely because they are general or "open" statements, may be "filled" by *particular* instances of states of affairs. Like general laws, they are statements of universal conditional form of the "if p then q" variety: to say that a sheep is a grass-eating animal is to say "*if* a sheep is put into a field, *then* it will tend to eat grass."

73. This disposition can be cast in universal conditional form as a kind of law: "Whenever Jesus was in circumstances of kind k, then he tended to exhibit the character of kind l."

humility rather than demanded obedience and service from them. This is the way the church remembered *him* and remembers him still.

I suspect that the same distinction between dispositions and episodes may help to clarify what James Dunn is getting at when he speaks of "Jesus remembered" and of the "impact" Jesus made on the first disciples which was what warranted their memory of him. What it was about "Jesus remembered" and the specific "impact" he made may be expressed in dispositional terms which may in turn be illustrated by recounting specific incidents and episodes, but is not simply reducible to them.

Consequently, the claim that the church remembers Jesus *himself* and that this involves, not just the bare fact of Jesus' past existence, but something of the distinctive quality of his personal character and the tenor of his teaching, means that we may justifiably say that the content of this memory may be given, not in categorical statements reporting particular incidents, but in dispositional statements. In addition, we are able to say that these statements may be expressed in hypothetical form. If Jesus is remembered as a person who exhibited *agape*, this is to say that he was a person who exhibited a liability or regular tendency to act in a certain kind of way. It is to say that *whenever* or *if* Jesus was found in a situation of kind k, then he is remembered to have tended to act in way l. In this way, content may be given to the notion of the church's memory of Jesus *himself* in a number of descriptive assertions relating to the uniquely remembered nature of his dispositional quality of character. This is what impacted upon the lives of his disciples and drew from them the first flicker of trusting faith and commitment to him.

To say that the church remembers Jesus *himself*, and that this is to remember a disposition not an episode, means that the church in this view of things does not necessarily remember any specific words or deeds of Jesus. Rather, the church remembers Jesus *himself*, in much the same way that we remember our own fathers and mothers, and people who have been mentors to us, without necessarily remembering specific episodes or events in which they were involved. And if we cannot be sure that Jesus spoke particular words, or did particular things, he is nevertheless remembered as the kind of person who *could* have spoken them, or who could well have done them.

Even so, it might be objected, the statement *that* Jesus died upon the Cross is surely an episodic statement. It reports an occurrence. What is remembered when the Cross of Jesus is remembered is a specific purported event of history. So, despite Knox's contention that the church's memory of Jesus himself contains no facts, insofar as he speaks of the Cross, not only as part of this memory but as a central element of it, we have to note that this certainly reports a fact *about* Jesus of an episodic kind. That said, the memory of Jesus' death on the Cross does not *just* report a bare incident or episode. The indubitable witness of almost the entire New Testament is that Jesus' death on the Cross is an episode which took on supreme symbolic significance, precisely as a particular instantiation of the kind of love or self-giving that Jesus had exhibited in his words and works throughout his life. In other words, the Cross stands as a symbol of the self-giving of the remembered Jesus. Thus, in remembering the Cross even as an episode, the early Christians actually tended to interpret its significance in dispositional terms. He was remembered as one who "having loved his own who were in the world, he loved them to the end."[74] In this way, the Cross became more than just an incident or episode, for it took on meaning as a controlling instantiation of a remembered judgment of a dispositional kind. The Cross, perhaps more than anything Jesus said or did, acquired its capacity to express the characteristically steadfast self-giving in obedience to his calling that was, and still is, remembered as the essential defining quality of Jesus' historical life.

Apart from the remembrance of the Cross, the Gospels purport to communicate innumerable remembrances of incidents in which Jesus taught and acted, and re-acted to others, all of which help to communicate something of his dispositional quality of character, a kind of remembered identifying description of him. The task of New Testament scholarship on the historical Jesus is to try to sift purported statements of historical fact concerning Jesus as he actually appears to have been, from subsequent embroidering of the traditions about him. Either way, however, even purported incidental instantiations of dispositional truths *about* him may serve the same purpose of communicating the church's remembrance of *him*.

In this event, the "memory of Jesus himself" which is embodied in the texts of the New Testament, and transmitted and shared within the life of the church, and which Knox says is essential to its self-understanding and its faith, may be understood as a basic set of identity criteria largely of a dispositional kind for the object "Jesus." As we will see, this set of criteria also functions as the generally or conventionally accepted "rules for the use" of the proper name "Jesus" when used referringly, and also identifyingly, in claims to recognize and know his living presence.

Before moving immediately to the further discussion of the logic of proper names, it is important to pause to note that we are now in a position to address some implications that arise from Eric Mascall's contention that Knox engaged in a kind of "ecclesiastical psychology." Following Mascall, it might be thought that, though Knox sought to articulate a positively realist account of resurrection faith, when he spoke of the church's memory what he had in mind was some kind of shared psychological mental particular. This might be assumed to be the case, either as an epistemic requirement of claims to recognize the objective presence of the Raised Jesus, or of claims to identify,

---

74. John 13:1. This is explicitly a reference to his act of foot washing as servant of his own disciples at the beginning of his Passion.

and know persons and things generally. In other words, it might be envisaged that what is involved in recognizing and identifying an object, is that the knowing subject conjures up an image "before the mind's eye" with which to compare it. In this way, an object might be identified as "yellow" by consulting a kind of remembered mental image of a patch of "yellow" with which it matches up.

Certainly, some of Knox's statements about the church's memory of Jesus might be interpreted to mean that what he had in mind was a kind of identifying impression or image of Jesus. It might be supposed that this is what he envisaged being conjured up before "the mind's eye" of the church, as it were, in order to recognize and identify, and thus claim to know, the presence of the Raised *Jesus*. In other words, in epistemological terms it might be thought that what Knox thought necessary to warrant this kind of identity judgment was something like an image called up before the mind's eye of believers, as in what Malcolm called personal/perceptual memory.

We can categorically say, however, that whatever Knox actually had in mind, it is not only possible to avoid thinking of the church's memory as an introspectible mental particular of this kind, but that it is positively advisable to do so. What appears to be involved epistemologically when claims are made to identify things generally, and specifically when the church makes claims in faith to identify the presence of "Jesus," is not a particular psychological episode in which a mental image is introspected and somehow compared with a given reality of concrete experience, which is then judged to be identical with it. Under the influence of British empiricism from Hume through to the Logical Positivists who thought of "sense data" or "sense impressions" in this representational kind of way, one might be tempted to fall into that kind of disastrous cul-de-sac.[75] However, what is required is more simply the communal possession of certain identity criteria of a factual nature for correctly using the identifying concept or proper name. In the case of a claim to identify the presence of the "Spirit of Jesus," what it needed is a memory of Jesus in the form of certain factual identity criteria for correctly using the proper name "Jesus." In other words, we should think of the church's "memory of Jesus," not in terms of a psychological or mental particular, but quite positively in terms of certain publicly shared criteria of a conceptual nature that permit the meaningful and justifiable use of the proper name "Jesus." This is what warrants the church's claim to be able to use that name meaningfully, and in particular to use it identifyingly to interpret and recognize the presence of the life-giving Spirit of "Jesus."

Consequently, when, in the life of the church certain claims are made in faith concerning the *recognition* of the living presence of "*Jesus*," or the "life-giving Spirit" of Jesus, what is in fact presupposed is the possession of certain identity criteria of a

---

75. The identification of a yellow object is no longer to be thought of as an exercise in which an inner remembered "patch of yellow" is summoned before the mind's eye, consulted, and then compared with an object being seen visually so as to allow the judgment: "Oh, yes that is yellow." This simply raises the question of how it is known that the alleged "introspected patch" is to be identified as "yellow."

conceptual nature for using the proper name. This is what is referred to as the church's "memory of Jesus." It has nothing to do with psychology.

Finally, it is important to note that the very use of a proper name, either referringly or identifyingly, always seems to presuppose some kind of identifying description that warrants it. It is true that proper names denote but normally do not connote meaning. In this way the interpretation of experience by calling upon a proper name differs somewhat from the interpretative function of the conventionally agreed-upon concepts that are endowed with meaning by a linguistic community, of which we spoke earlier in relation to Wittgenstein (and Kant).

John R. Searle has drawn attention to the fact that proper names *refer* but do not normally have *meaning* or *sense*.[76] If they happen to have an explicit meaning, as a small number of proper names do,[77] that meaning is incidental to their normal denotative function. That said, Searle argues that to use "a proper name referringly is to *presuppose* the truth of certain uniquely referring descriptive statements."[78] Though it is not ordinarily to assert these statements, or even to indicate which of an unspecified number of possible descriptive statements are presupposed, some must be presupposed as a precondition for using the proper name. Proper names must therefore have sense "in a loose sort of way."

In other words, we would not be able to use the name "Napoleon" referringly unless we knew, for example, *that* he was a French General, the husband of Josephine, and *that* he lost the Battle of Waterloo. Some of the descriptive statements, which are presupposed when we use the proper name "Napoleon" may turn out to be false, but a sub-set of the possible descriptive statements about Napoleon must nevertheless be true. If all of these were found to be false there would be no valid criteria for using the proper name at all.

Similarly, we would not be able to use the proper name "Jesus" referringly unless we knew, for example, some such things about him, as *that* Jesus lived, and died upon a Cross, *that* he taught such and such a kind of thing, or exhibited a certain kind of character, and even *that* his former followers claimed to encounter him alive after his

---

76. Searle, "Proper Names." See Searle, "Proper Names and Descriptions"; Mill, *A System of Logic*, Book 1, chapter 2, esp., Sec. 5; and Wittgenstein, *Philosophical Investigations*, paras. 4–79.

77. For example, we know that *Petros* means "rock," and "Christ" means "anointed." Given initial identification of Jesus as *the* Christ, it was not long before the article was dropped and the term "Christ" effectively became a proper name that was used to refer to or denote the person named "Jesus Christ." Whether it continued also to carry an allusion to its original meaning is a matter of some discussion, but its original conative meaning was superseded by its denotative use, as in the claim to know the "Spirit of life in Christ Jesus."

78. Searle, "Proper Names," 94.

death and burial. Some bare facts of this kind are needed if we are meaningfully to use the proper name "Jesus" at all.

If the use of the proper name, even referringly, thus presupposes the knowledge of certain uniquely referring descriptive characteristics about him, then the same goes for the use of the proper name "Jesus" identifyingly—as in claims to recognize and in faith identify an ostensively given and concretely experienced religious Object *as* "the presence of *Jesus*," or the "life giving Spirit of *Jesus*," or "the Spirit of life in Christ *Jesus*." In order to use the proper name in this way, it is necessary to know certain uniquely referring descriptive characteristics of Jesus by virtue of which the object of acquaintance may be identified using the proper name "Jesus," "Christ Jesus," or "Jesus Christ."

Now, the perceptive reader will have noticed the appearance of the phrase "uniquely referring" in that last sentence. I will return to the requirement that these descriptive characteristics of Jesus need be "uniquely referring" if they are to serve this specific identifying purpose in a future chapter. For the moment it is sufficient to note that the very use of the proper name "Jesus" entails that we must be able to cite at least *some* information of a putatively factual kind that allows us meaningfully to use it so. Thus, "the Church's memory of Jesus" may be understood as a set of descriptive statements about Jesus as he was in the days of his flesh—a verbal picture of the Jesus of history of a largely dispositional kind that is shared by members of the Christian community and which warrants the use of his proper name both referringly and (in faith) identifyingly.

In this way, some kind of memory of Jesus, expressed in a number of putatively factual dispositional statements is, as Knox insistently endeavored to contend, an essential ingredient of the life of the church. Simply as the community that uses the name "Jesus" in a particular way, it must possess this kind of memory of *him*. Likewise, in terms of the epistemology of faith, what is necessarily presupposed in the judgment of faith is the possession of a set of statements, which express a sufficient but unspecified number of demonstrative characteristics by virtue of which we are able to use the name "Jesus."

This means that the "memory of Jesus" may be understood in terms of a set of descriptive factual statements of a largely dispositional kind, that were formulated on the basis of empirical encounter and observation by the first Christians, and transmitted in the life of the early church, and then from generation to generation. These same descriptively factual statements that purport to embody the church's memory of Jesus, now provide the descriptive backing for the name "Jesus," and thus the criteria for applying this name in demonstrative assertions or judgments of faith. As James Dunn has observed in his account of the way in which the memory of Jesus was given its essential shape: "by regular use and reuse in oral mode," that "essential shape" was set by "the original and immediate impact made by Jesus."[79]

Despite the critical points that have here been raised with regard to Knox's articulation of the notion of "the Church's memory of Jesus," it has to be acknowledged that he made a most significant and enduring contribution to Christian theology. Insofar as he focused attention on the church's memory of Jesus, his distinctive contribution through the second half of the twentieth-century was to recognize the epistemological importance of the memory of Jesus *himself*, as distinct from the memory of episodic facts *about* Jesus, precisely as an element in the make up of faith, whether in the first-century or now. In doing so, he has provided an enormously important service to systematic and dogmatic theology. At a time when it was not theologically fashionable to focus on the "Jesus of history," he saw that the church's "memory of Jesus" is essential to the understanding of faith as a response of trust in the person of Jesus. The truth is that *something* must be known about Jesus to warrant the use of the proper name, let alone to the placing of trusting faith in him. The church's memory of Jesus delivers the knowledge in faith therefore that is in epistemological terms essential to trusting faith.

On the other hand, the "memory of Jesus" is essential to the make up specifically of *resurrection faith* as a recognition of the presence of the Crucified *Jesus*. This is for the obvious reason that some identifying criteria must be known about him to permit such a claim to recognition, for we recognize and identify only those whom we *in some way* remember. The presence of the Raised Jesus can only be known in faith on the basis of some kind of remembrance of him. For this reason, claims to recognize and know him in faith were only made by those who first remembered him. The same applies with respect to those who claim in faith to perceive his living presence today. The epistemological importance of Knox's insights to the systematic and dogmatic theology of resurrection faith is enormous.

---

79. Dunn, *Jesus Remembered*, 882. Also 132: "Jesus can be perceived only through the impact he made on his first disciples (that is, their faith) which is the key to a historical recognition (and assessment) of that impact."

9

A Veridical Memory?

ONE MIGHT BE FORGIVEN for thinking that the returning interest in "the Jesus of history" among twenty-first-century New Testament scholars might by now have confirmed the basic insights of the theme of "the Church and her memory of Jesus" that John Knox pioneered in the 1940s, 50s, and 60s. Alas, unfortunately this is not the case. In part this is owing to the fact that the current focus has largely been upon the processes of the oral transmission of the tradition in the thirty-to-fifty-year period between the life and death of Jesus and the time when it was given written form in the gospels. Unfortunately, an oral and essentially hidden process necessarily entails that judgments made about it are unavoidably speculative in nature, and to a degree tentative, and therefore incapable of winning widespread assent. This means that contemporary New Testament studies invite the image of a dog chasing its tail: it never quite gets to its desired end.[1]

In addition, and perhaps of much more serious concern, the methodological historical skepticism that exercised a noxious controlling influence in Christian theology right through the twentieth-century, continues to undermine confidence in the ability of critical historical research *ever* to produce any fixed and secure results at all. In a sense, the ghost of Ernst Troeltsch continues to spook New Testament studies to the point of inhibiting the drawing of any fixed and certain conclusions. This means that there is a sense in which the contemporary study of Christian origins invites the image of a group of entrepreneurial people ship-wrecked on a desert island, who all take in one another's washing to keep one another in business. Systematic theology faces the challenge of breaking free from this kind of circularity.

---

1. James Dunn identifies about forty scholars around the world who currently share this interest, which had an identifiable origin in Scandinavia at the hands of Birger Gerhardsson, and has more recently been pursued by Samuel Byrskog. The work of some of the prominent contemporary "questers" apart from Dunn himself may be found in Stewart and Habermas, *Memories of Jesus*. Richard Bauckham's *Jesus and the Eyewitnesses* is also another importantly influential contribution to this discussion.

Many contemporary New Testament scholars who have become involved in the post-Bultmannian renewal of interest in "the historical Jesus" have themselves been at pains to focus, not just on identifying the nature and content of the original memories of Jesus as these are said to have been preserved in the testimony of the first witnesses, but particularly on the mechanisms of the oral transmission of that testimony, apparently in the hope of generating a sense of its over-all trustworthiness. Generally speaking, there is today an inclination to credit those mechanisms with securing the basic integrity of the tradition as against the form critics' assumption that the original Jesus all but disappeared under an over-lay of christological accretions that were placed upon it.[2] Hence, the contemporary focus on the tradition's passage through time, prior to the work of Mark, Matthew, John, and Luke in giving it permanent expression in literary form. Given a loss of confidence in the form critics' belief that the tradition was seriously corrupted in the course of its transmission during the first fifty or so years, a somewhat mysterious "gap" between Jesus himself and the writing of the gospels cries out to be filled in. For James Dunn, the "remembered Jesus who impacted upon the lives of the first Christians" fills this bill: the usefulness of "Jesus as he was remembered" is that this Jesus is said to provide "a bridge" between the actual Jesus of historical time and the written texts which we now have in the New Testament.[3] At the same time, the rehabilitation of the concept of "remembrance" itself, already goes some way towards countering notions of the unwitting free-wheeling manipulation of the tradition by worshipping communities in the process of adapting it to meet their own immediate needs and concerns. In this context, Richard Bauckham's plea for the category of "eyewitness testimony" to be taken seriously bulks large as a potential stimulus to the generation of a more optimistic way of looking at the Jesus tradition.

In the nature of the case, the task of filling in the picture between "Jesus himself as he actually was in historical time," and the writing of the first gospel, has therefore resulted in what is unavoidably a somewhat speculative discussion of a range of possible mechanical processes imagined to have been involved in the transmission of the tradition. As with form-critical research itself, telltale clues have to be found in the written tradition of the gospels that may be said to disclose something of the specific form of its previous oral existence. Argument about the precise nature of these imagined oral communicative processes tends to focus upon such questions as whether the memory of Jesus' words and actions was transmitted from week-to-week and year-to-year through the involvement of very intentional rabbinic-type procedures (including

---

2. In Germany, Hermann Gunkel, Martin Noth, Gerhard von Rad, and other scholars originally developed form criticism in relation to Old Testament studies; they used it to supplement the documentary hypothesis concerning the origin of the Pentateuch, so as to seek to uncover the original forms of the oral tradition. Karl Ludwig Schmidt, Martin Dibelius, and Rudolf Bultmann later applied form criticism to the oral foundations of the gospels.

3. Thus, in response to Scot McKnight, in Stewart and Habermas, *Memories of Jesus*, 295, Dunn argues that the Remembered Jesus "bridges the gap between Jesus' . . . mission in the late 20s and the narrative Jesus of the 70s and 80s."

learning by memorization),[4] or, alternatively, through essentially group procedures of oral rehearsal analogous to those found in other ancient or even contemporary non-literate communities,[5] and whether these processes were formal or informal, controlled or hardly controlled at all (as was alleged to have been the case by the form critics). Precisely because this was a time of oral exchange prior to written records, possibilities abound.[6] But then, even the evangelists may also have had access to *some* already written bits and pieces (the hypothetical document Q, and the connected Passion narrative, perhaps being the chief contenders). All the while, one senses in these discussions a nervous concern to secure the basic trustworthiness of the tradition about the historical Jesus by appealing to some degree of involvement of eyewitnesses, not just at the beginning, but even perhaps right through the shared community procedures of these crucial fifty or so years.

There is a sense in which all of this would have been of secondary, even of antiquarian interest to Knox, though his own primary inclination would certainly have been to stress the corporate and shared nature of the imagined processes of oral transmission rather than to elevate the role of individual eyewitnesses. His own primary theological education at the Chicago Divinity School, which proudly promoted what was then called "the Socio-historical method,"[7] meant that he was naturally persuaded to the view that the tradition about Jesus was a social or community possession. This blended with the purported new discoveries of German form-critical research of the time, which inclined Knox to accept the view that the first generation of Christian believers exercised a creative role in scattered communities by bending the traditions, at least to some degree, to serve their own needs and interests. However, despite the obvious appeal of this way of explaining the diversity and disparity now found in the New Testament texts, Knox was persuaded that, in and through it all, an authentic "memory of Jesus himself" was nevertheless clearly and intentionally preserved.

Almost certainly, the most important factor in bringing him to this conclusion was that he could see that, in affirming their resurrection faith, the first generation believers could not have claimed to recognize and know the living presence of *Jesus* without some logically prior "memory of him." Despite the corrupting influences

---

4. The view originally championed by Birger Gerhardsson in *Memory and Manuscript* (1961), and more recently re-stated in *The Reliability of the Gospel Tradition*, 9–10.

5. A view promoted with the help of the work of Kenneth Bailey, "Informal Controlled Oral Tradition and the Synoptic Gospels," and "Middle Eastern Oral Tradition and the Synoptic Gospels."

6. In Dunn's case, "informal, controlled oral tradition," defined by Bailey on the basis of the anecdotal observations of contemporary village life in the Middle East in which anyone in the village, though usually the elders, assumed the story-telling role at community gatherings, provides the model for the practices of primitive Christian communities.

7. Promoted by Shailer Mathews and Shirley Jackson Case.

alleged to have unavoidably been at work in the passing on of the tradition that the form critics tended to obsess about, the continuing identity of the church itself, as the community which professed *resurrection* faith in the Raised One who had lived among them and been crucified, was living witness also to the preservation of his memory. Indeed, as was pointed out in the previous chapter, just to use the proper name "Jesus," even referringly, is to presuppose some remembered information to warrant the reference. But, if faith is a form of trust (*fiducia*) that is necessarily grounded in a claimed relational knowledge (*fides*) of the Raised Christ (who must necessarily be trustworthy), then that claim to knowledge can in turn only be logically enabled or made possible by the sharing of the church's memory of Jesus as he *was* in historical time. Moreover, this must be more than just the memory of the bare fact of his existence; it must necessarily be a memory of him containing information at least sufficient both for creating the capacity to recognize *his* living presence, and for judging his trustworthiness. Faith as a response of trust, grounded in a knowledge of the presence of the Raised Christ through the medium of *his* life-giving Spirit, can therefore be discerned and acquired only by those who are privileged to share the remembrance of *him*, for only so can claims be made to recognize and identify the Raised One using the proper name "*Jesus*."

This meant that, though Knox was not so concerned to identify the actual mechanisms of the "living voice" of the church by which its memory of Jesus was transmitted and received, he perceived and emphasized the role of the "memory of Jesus" because of its quite essential epistemological importance in the make-up of the response of faith. By contrast with the current interest in the mechanisms of the transmission of the tradition up to the point of its triumphal emergence in the written form of "gospel," he thus grasped the crucial importance of "the memory of Jesus himself" to the very possibility of faith itself. It was an essential element in the kind of knowing by acquaintance of the living presence of the Raised Christ that in turn underpins and warrants the Christian commitment of faith as a form of inter-personal trust. In this respect, there is a sense in which Knox's interests naturally migrated from the arena of New Testament studies into that of systematic and dogmatic theology.

The "memory of Jesus" was thus not just a "bridge" between the Jesus of historical time and the verbal expression of that memory in written form in the gospels, but an essential epistemic ingredient in the make-up of faith itself, not only the faith of the first generation of Christian believers, but faith in Christ's Resurrection entertained in every day and age. Even after the emergence of the written gospels from the inchoate shadows of the time of oral exchange, the "memory of him" lives on to play this epistemic role, now with the rehearsal of the written texts themselves to guarantee its integrity and ensure its transmission through time primarily in (formal, highly controlled!) liturgical contexts.

In its day, Knox's objectively cognitive and realist approach to faith contrasted with the non-cognitive assimilation of faith to existential self-understanding of the kind popularized by Rudolf Bultmann, and which was vigorously promoted through the second half of the twentieth-century by an influential cohort of scholars either directly taught or influenced by Bultmann. But Knox's uncompromisingly cognitive approach to faith also contrasts with contemporary approaches to the understanding of faith found among those dedicated to the pursuit of the historical Jesus in the current world of New Testament scholarship.

For example, James Dunn confesses that in writing *Jesus Remembered*, he set out to articulate "a realistic historical appreciation of the impact Jesus made on his first disciples."[8] Given that Jesus is historically significant "because he made an impact," the present endeavor is "to grasp as far as possible the character and force of that impact (perhaps even, in a real sense, to experience something of that impact as the Jesus tradition is read and reflected on today)."[9] Dunn's interest thus comes to rest in "Jesus remembered," not as an aid to a concrete recognitional knowledge of the Raised Jesus Christ, but as *itself* the essential object of faith.

In *Jesus Remembered*, Dunn does not devote a great deal of time to the subject of "faith"[10] apart from pursuing his over-riding concern to ensure that a dichotomy is not drawn up between the "Jesus of history" and the "Christ of faith," as was regularly done in the wake of the failure of the nineteenth-century "Jesus of history" movement. He is concerned to emphasize that Christian faith is not just a post-Easter phenomenon. Dunn correctly contends that, prior to his crucifixion, the historical Jesus made an impact of the kind that already triggered the first flickering of faith. The impact he made as he lived his historical life itself produced an interpretation of his significance from the perspective of faith.[11] This faith was then confirmed and expanded by the belief that he had been raised from the dead by God and exalted "to the right hand of the Father." This means, however, that there is a sense in which Jesus is found, not "raised into the kerygma," where he is met in a critical moment of self-understanding as the one who addresses the believer through the proclamation of his Word (famously, the view of Bultmann); rather, the "remembered Jesus" is now found embodied in the written form of the scriptural texts, where something of the impact he made is to be discerned, and where in a manner of speaking he "comes to life" for those who "read and reflect upon" it. By "encountering the Jesus tradition today,"[12] Jesus is known through sharing in the impact he made. In this way, "Jesus remembered" continues to make his mark to this day, for we are able to share in his continuing "impact." The

---

8. Dunn, "In Grateful Dialogue," 293.
9. Dunn, "In Grateful Dialogue," 292–3.
10. A glimpse at the Index of Subjects indicates only a handful of entries.
11. That is, from the perspective of the inclination to trust and follow Jesus as his disciples.
12. Dunn, "In Grateful Dialogue," 293.

"remembered Jesus" who made this impact, rather than the actual Jesus of historical time, thus becomes the object of faith.

This is a remarkably idealist articulation of faith. For the initial impact that Jesus made is fundamentally a *verbal* picture of Jesus now found in the pages of the New Testament.[13] Hence the importance of the New Testament scholar's work of discerning the outline shape of "Jesus Remembered." We have access to him/it via critical historical research, which calls for an element of belief in us, because (for Dunn at least), historiography itself can never reach secure results with any certainty, but must always remain a matter of possibilities and probabilities. Thus, for Dunn, the faith that we share with the first disciples is a kind of interpretation, which was evoked by the words and acts of the historical Jesus. By hearing "the initial impact itself"[14] that Jesus made, which survives within the written text of the New Testament, and reflecting upon it, we are able today in faith to experience and share in something of that same impact. Dunn can therefore say that the "remembered Jesus" is the object of Christian interest and reflection and is known by "encountering the Jesus tradition today."[15]

We have here an echo reminiscent of the idealism of R. G. Collingwood, for whom historiography was not a science but an art, which involved "re-thinking the thoughts" of people who lived in the past.[16] Likewise, for Dunn the cognitive element of faith in Jesus is the knowing, or re-experiencing, of something of the impact or impression first made on the disciples of "Jesus remembered."[17] The Easter experience is not just a "right understanding" of the remembered Jesus prior to his crucifixion (as proposed by Willi Marxsen),[18] but a totally new and objective post-crucifixion experience. It is also said to have made its own specific "impact." Despite the fact that we have difficulty in pinning down exactly what made that impact in finite words, and must necessarily refer to it

---

13. Thus in *Jesus Remembered* we have Dunn's "substantive depiction of the remembered Jesus" (309); this is his "attempt to join the debate about what and how much can be said today regarding the beginnings of the history of Jesus" (287).

14. Dunn, *Jesus Remembered*, 293.

15. Dunn, *Jesus Remembered*, 293.

16. Collingwood's idealism of 'thinking the thoughts" of the past contrasts with scientific historiography that employs the same explanatory models as natural science. When science explains "that x happened *because* of y," a general law is presupposed in the form of a statement of universal conditional form: "Whenever y, then x" or "If y, then x." Thus, the historian's explanation that "Tom fell into a coma *because* he ate a pound of sugar" presupposes the general law (specific to Tom) that *whenever*, or *if*, Tom (being diabetic) eats a pound of sugar, *then* he will fall into a coma. Scientific historiography, like science generally, explains occurrences by appeal to general laws of this kind.

17. It is Dunn's hope that someone who recognizes and experiences the impact of Jesus through encountering the Jesus tradition today "will be encouraged to follow out the further trial of that impact."

18. Marxsen, *The Resurrection of Jesus of Nazareth*. For Marxsen, Easter faith is an unverifiable response to the Jesus who is "present in the word of proclamation" (142). Faith becomes a "right" understanding of the pre-Easter Jesus, for "today the crucified Jesus is calling us to believe" (128). The miracle of the Resurrection thus becomes the coming to faith itself: "*the miracle is the birth of faith*" (128; Marxsen's italics).

metaphorically using the concept "resurrection," we can also share in the impact that it made as we read the resurrection traditions.[19] All the while, both the historical Jesus as he actually was in historical time (i.e., the one whose impact triggered the emergence of the oral tradition of "Jesus as he was remembered"), and the Easter Jesus who has gone from history to the timeless eternity of God, remain tantalizingly elusive. We have to be content to share in the past-and-continuing "impact," which the historical Jesus and the Raised Jesus Christ respectively made.

Clearly, Dunn's idealism contrasts with the uncompromising realism of John Knox. Dunn's Jesus is not concretely encountered as "the life-giving and abundant Spirit" who is confidently recognized and known by acquaintance among the baptized, and identified within the Christian community by reference to the shared memory of him. It is not, in other words, that the church's shared memory of Jesus from the perspective of faith is brought to the identification of a living reality of concrete experience who is *known* precisely *as* the presence of "the remembered Jesus." Rather than being an epistemic aid to faith, the shared memory of Jesus and the impact he made itself becomes the object of faith. Instead of being a living Jesus who is known by acquaintance and recognized by reference to the memory of him, the object of faith for Dunn is a Jesus known by description. As such, he is even said *not* to be the actual Jesus of historical time, for that Jesus is somehow always beyond cognitive grasp. Likewise, the post-Easter Jesus, is in turn an equally elusive figure, who is actually also beyond our cognitive grasp insofar as he is now exalted in heaven and believed to be "at the right hand of the Father," where he can only be *imagined* or *believed* still to be alive.

Thus, today we can believe *that* there *was* a Jesus (in Palestine around AD 28–30), and *that* there *is* a Raised Christ (at the right hand of the Father), but we cannot *know* either of these propositions to be true. In the first instance, this is because of the congenital defects of all historical judgments, which always fall short of knowledge. In the second instance, it is due to the post-Easter reality that Jesus is understood to have gone to a wholly transcendental life that is beyond history and beyond words. All we are left with is the metaphorical use of the concept of "resurrection" to refer to whatever it was that had the post-Easter impact on the first disciples and that continues to confront us in the Easter traditions of the New Testament.

The essentially non-cognitive nature of Dunn's approach to faith has been found troublesome to many of his interpreters, insofar as faith is said to be a kind of interpretation of Jesus from the point of view of the impact that he made, but which is clearly and resolutely said *not* to be "Jesus himself," or Jesus *as he actually was* in

---

19. Thus, Dunn says that Christians "need have no qualms about affirming their faith in 'Jesus as risen'" on the basis of "the first Christian interpretation" of their experience ("In Grateful Dialogue," 322).

historical time.[20] It is clearly puzzling why Dunn is prepared, with a high degree of confidence to affirm that "the remembered Jesus remained a stable element"[21] in the transmitted oral tradition of Jesus, but is not prepared to draw the inference from "Jesus remembered" to the judgment that Jesus actually *was* as he was remembered to have been. Indeed, Dunn becomes somewhat coy and equivocal at this point. He says: "I do remain confident that the record of the actual impact made by Jesus enables us to get as clear a picture of the one who made that impact as is both possible and necessary."[22] Or again, in relation to what can be known of Jesus and his mission, he says: "we can actually discern the character of the person who made the impact and the character of the mission."[23] Even so, he denies the apparently implied logical conclusion of these statements, "that Jesus's character actually *was* as it is remembered to have been," or "that his mission actually *was* as the evidence relative to it suggests." Instead, all we have is the remembered character of Jesus and his mission as this was entertained by the first Christians because of the impact made by it *on them*. The actual person, the historical Jesus "behind" the memory, or behind the impact he made, continues to evade our grasp.

At this point, both Knox and Dunn agree that we cannot be convinced about every remembered detail of the tradition, and both insist that basic facts *about* Jesus of a detailed kind are to be distinguished from the discernment of the "impact" made by him, or the memory he left in his wake. Dunn says, for example, that facts about Jesus that are the subject matter of critical historical research are established with mixed results. Under pressure of cross-examination by his critics, he concedes that while some facts are disputed, we can easily access others of them (for example, that Jesus was from Galilee and that he died on the Cross). Beyond some such basic facts, there are few that can be entertained with undisputed confidence. This deficit is made good, however, for while we cannot speak with confidence about many specific things Jesus said and did, "we can recognize the character of the one who made the impact that he did from the impression left by that impact."[24] This was the "significant Jesus" who made an impact, the Jesus who had meaning and significance for the disciples who interpreted his life and mission from a specific perspective. This is "Jesus remembered."

---

20. Bockmuehl pertinently observes that "Dunn's repeated and emphatic prioritization of Jesus' 'impact' as opposed to 'Jesus himself' will inevitably leave some readers wondering to what extent 'the historical Jesus' remains a viable object of enquiry at all" ("Whose memory? Whose Orality," 42).
21. Dunn, "In Grateful Dialogue," in *Memories of Jesus*, 296.
22. Dunn, "In Grateful Dialogue," in *Memories of Jesus*, 319.
23. Dunn, "In Grateful Dialogue," in *Memories of Jesus*, 295.
24. Dunn, "In Grateful Dialogue," 319.

John Knox also spoke of the memory of facts *about* Jesus as distinct from of the church's memory of Jesus himself, the former being the often-disputed subject matter of critical historical research on the New Testament texts, the latter being the church's continuing memory of Jesus himself which is integral to the judgment of faith. Clearly, there is a broad agreement between Knox and Dunn in relation to the making of this basic distinction between the memory of bare facts *about* Jesus, and the memory of Jesus himself, or "Jesus remembered." However, even though Dunn speaks with confidence of the "stability" of the element of the tradition constituted by "Jesus remembered," we still cannot be certain of it. Even so, there is (somewhat paradoxically) one thing we can be certain about: we *certainly* must not equate "Jesus Remembered" with the historical Jesus as he actually was.

By contrast, Knox views "the memory of Jesus *himself*" as something that can be entertained with confidence and certainty, and thus as something which permits the claim that Jesus *was* as he is remembered to have been. Dunn, however, steadfastly refuses to draw this inference. The "remembered Jesus" is *not* necessarily Jesus as he actually was in the time of his historical existence. That Jesus lies beyond our ken. Thus, in response to Stephen Davis, Dunn declares that even if some bare facts can be established about Jesus, these do not "give us access to Jesus himself."[25]

Dunn offers two basic reasons for this conclusion. The first is his fundamental methodological contention that no historical judgment can ever be entertained with certainty because of the ever-present possibility that a newly discovered document or a new interpretation of the available evidence will over-turn even the best attested facts of the past. In this, he uncritically accepts the historical skepticism characteristic of late-nineteenth and twentieth-century theology, which, at least in its most tightly argued philosophical expression, is to be attributed to Ernst Troeltsch. However, as I have consistently argued elsewhere,[26] the systematic flight of much twentieth-century theology from the nineteenth-century attempt to base faith on the findings of critical historical research, on the ground that historians can *never*, as a matter of principle, reach fixed and secure results, was founded on a logical mistake.

Even so, Dunn unfortunately remains firmly wedded to an uncompromising historiographical skepticism. In what is in fact a contemporary re-statement of the Troeltschian argument,[27] Dunn, (quite appropriately) compares the procedures of courts of criminal law and the work of scientific critical historians, insofar as both seek to

---

25. Dunn, "In Grateful Dialogue," 318.

26. See Carnley, "The Poverty of Historical Scepticism" (1972), and the rehearsal of the same argument (including a response to N. T. Wright's acceptance of the same position originally articulated by Troeltsch) in chapter 7 of *Resurrection in Retrospect*.

27. Dunn's argument for his methodological commitment to "historical skepticism" is set out in *Jesus Remembered*, sec. 6.3.

establish the facts of a case by evaluating concrete evidence. He then goes on to cite the sequence of successful appeals against "several notorious sentences in British courts over the last fifteen years on the basis of revised scientific evaluation of the evidence," apparently with a view to demonstrating the analogous vulnerability of all historical judgments to similar possible future discoveries and evaluations of evidence.[28] Since the discovery of DNA, and its usefulness for the scientific identification of criminals, the acquittal of the innocent has certainly been a recent experience in many countries. A number of those previously convicted of crimes, not just in Britain, have been found to be innocent because their DNA does not match samples taken from crime scenes. However, this does not mean that every finding of "Guilty" in the British legal system over the centuries must now be deemed to have been "unsafe," or that criminal courts of law can *never* ascertain the truth of a matter by evaluating the available evidence because of the *thinkable* possibility that at some future time somebody might discover something that could be used to prove a conviction mistaken. Clearly, the logical or thinkable possibility that somebody might make a new discovery in thirty years' time, that might prove the innocence of some wrongly convicted person, does not mean that every convicted person should therefore be released from prison on the ground that we cannot ever be sure of their guilt! Likewise, the *thinkable* possibility that the future discovery of a document might cause a historian to re-think his or her position does not mean that *every* historical judgment is therefore somehow flawed, and that historiography must *always* inevitably only deal in possibilities and at best probabilities. The legal parallel would be that the procedures of a criminal court of law could only ever deal in possibilities and probabilities because it is thinkable or logically possible that further evidence might some day come to hand to prove a conviction unsafe. In fact, if a historian possesses perfectly good and compelling evidence with which to demonstrate that a specific event did in fact occur, and if there is no actual evidence whatever to suggest that it might not have occurred, the historian is perfectly justified in claiming to know that the event occurred and is also justified in claiming to be certain in this knowledge. If the evidence is good enough, then the thinkable possibility that there could be evidence that might one day call such a judgment in question can in fact be discounted. That is what "being certain" means: logically possible or purely thinkable possibilities of error do not entail actual possibilities or error. It is, for example, quite certain that there was a war in Europe between 1914 and 1918, and that a horrendous pogrom was perpetrated against the Jews in Nazi Germany during the Second World War. These are not mere possibilities or probabilities. The purely notional idea that there might be documents yet to be found to disprove either of these judgments is quite absurd.

Once it is accepted that logical or thinkable possibilities of error do not entail actual possibilities of error, and that evidence of the kind that is judged to secure the certainty of a purported statement of historical fact means precisely that "thinkable" or

---

28. Dunn, *Jesus Remembered*, 103 n. 9.

purely logical possibilities of the future that might cause one to revise one's judgments can be discounted, then this troublesome ghost of Ernst Troeltsch may be dismissed. I honestly think it is time to consign this kind of methodological "historical skepticism" to oblivion. The determination of the historicity or otherwise of a judgment about the past is purely a matter to be decided on the basis of the available evidence. Sometimes the evidence will be fragmentary and insecure; on other occasions it will be sufficiently good to deliver a conclusion with certainty.

Clearly, the drawing of the inference that Jesus *was* as he was remembered to have been by those upon whom he made a very memorable impact is not inhibited in the way Dunn imagines it to be, simply because of the mistaken belief that no historical judgment is ever secure or that historical knowledge is *never* possible.[29] We are no longer involved therefore in a systematic retreat from any interest in the historical Jesus, on the grounds that historiography as such is incapable of achieving fixed and certain results, so as then to focus attention exclusively on the "Christ of faith." This makes the notion that faith may be understood in a freestanding way, entirely detached from the historical Jesus Christ (as most notably in the theology of Rudolf Bultmann), entirely problematic. But it also means that if Dunn has sufficient evidence to secure the "stable core" of the Jesus tradition, as to demonstrate with confidence how Jesus was remembered to have been by his disciples, then he does not in the next breath have apologetically to add "but of course we can never be assured of historical judgments, so we are prevented from saying that Jesus *was* as he is remembered to have been."

Dunn's second reason for not drawing the inference from "Jesus as he was remembered to have been" to "Jesus as he actually was," is that the specific memory of Jesus from the point of view of the impact he made on the first disciples was only *one* way of responding to him and of interpreting his meaning and significance. We simply do not have "portrayals of Jesus as seen through the eyes of the high priests or the Roman authorities or the people of the land." All we have is the Jesus who was remembered from the particular perspective of the disciples. Dunn appears to be troubled by the view that we do not have a "neutral" portrayal of Jesus: "All we have in the NT Gospels is Jesus seen with the eye of faith."[30] Dunn seems to be of the view that while ever there is the possibility of other alternative interpretations, we can never be certain about the objective reliability of *this* particular interpretation. But this too is surely a pseudo problem.

---

29. Thus, in principle, we need no longer subscribe to the view of Wilhelm Herrmann, that it is a fatal error to attempt to establish the basis for faith by historical investigation because historical truth is *always* relative (*The Communion of the Christian with God*, 77).

30. Dunn, *Jesus Remembered*, 127.

The logic of descriptions allows us to admit many different but equally true descriptions of the same object. Often this issue is confused by the use of the word "objective," when it is said that a description of an "aspect" or a description from a particular (subjective) "point of view" is said not to be objective. The words "objective" and "subjective" are very deceitful ones, their uses various and liable to mislead. That history is written from a specific point of view does not mean that it is viciously subjective in the sense that it does not report what is the case, or that it is incapable of achieving fixed and certain results.[31] Alan Richardson mistakenly equated "objectivity" with "omniscience" by suggesting that a historian cannot produce an objective account of the past simply because he or she is not God.[32] Maurice Mandelbaum held a similar secularized view, insofar as he held that objectivity is achieved only when all aspects or points of view are held together: objectivity is a kind of encyclopediasm.[33] However, just because one does not tell the "whole truth," this does not mean that one does not have sufficient justifying grounds to warrant *what one does assert*. Objectivity is not achieved when everything that could be said is said. For example, the assertion may be objectively true that a ball is red and not green if it has been checked that it is in fact the case that it is red and not green. Whether it is round or oval shaped, or not very bouncy, is quite irrelevant to the truth of this judgment. That mere difference is not itself vicious with respect to claims to objectivity is demonstrated by the fact that the same ball may be described differently, as "big, red, and not very bouncy." In other words, difference does not automatically entail incompatibility. It is only when someone asserts that the same ball is "big, *green*, and not very bouncy" that we have a problem constituted by obvious logical competition. Clearly, it is not necessary to know everything; rather, one must simply have sufficient justifying grounds for what one does claim to know.

In this case, though others may have remembered Jesus differently from the way he was remembered by his disciples, the fact of difference is not in itself logically vicious. This would only be a problem if a purported different memory of Jesus were to be patently in logical competition with the way the first Christians remembered him.

---

31. Alan Richardson in *History, Sacred and Profane*, 192, even goes so far as to say that the subjective point of view of a historian entails that the "historian cannot see the historical reality but only the images in his own mind." Likewise, Carl Becker, "Detachment and the Writing of History," 528, says: "The reality of history has forever disappeared, and the 'facts' of history, whatever they once were, are only mental images or pictures which the historian makes in order to comprehend it."

32. Richardson, *Christian Apologetics*, 107; and Richardson, *History, Sacred and Profane*, 191–92. R. G. Collingwood also said that the historian is not God: *The Idea of History*, 108–9 and 262–63. However, while arguing that the historian always writes from within the historical process, and from a point of view, Collingwood did not argue from relativism to skepticism by drawing the conclusion that one must always doubt one's judgments about the past.

33. Mandelbaum, "Objectivism in History," 43–56.

Despite the fact that the logic of descriptions admits of various portrayals of the one object, all of which may be equally true, provided they are not in logical competition with one another, it is often assumed in theological writing that there can only be one objectively true history of the past, and that this must be an account formulated from a neutral point of view. For example, we are often told that the account of the past which the historian gives us is to be compared with a portrait rather than a photograph. Talk of the "picture" of Jesus communicated through the gospel traditions, or the "impression" of Jesus that was entertained in faith by his disciples might suggest something akin to a portrait by contrast with a photograph. Unfortunately this all too easily suggests that a photograph gives an objective representation whereas a portrait is the product of an artist's intentions and interests or "point of view." On analogy it is argued that, because of the distorting factor of the historian's "point of view" the account of the past he or she gives cannot really represent what really happened or was the case. Once again, Alan Richardson provides us with a clear statement of this kind of argument. Quoting Walter Hofer, he says: "Naïve historical realism, according to which something like recognition of an historical object 'in itself' (*an sich*) is possible has long since been overcome." I think this is a highly questionable contention. In any event Richardson goes on:

> The picture which we form of the past must not be compared to a photograph but to a painting. And, just as we can see a landscape only from a given place, similarly all historical vision is determined by that place from which we view it. It means seeing in *perspective*. Broadly conceived, an historical problem, therefore, is always a question by the present to the past. Hence, in point of fact the questioner's interest and principle of selection and in the final analysis his value system and his ideology, are decisive factors in the definition of the question."[34]

However, even Benedetto Croce, the doyen of idealist philosophers of history, saw the weakness in this kind of argument.[35] For a photograph is the product of a photographer who arranges his camera, sets the lens and shutter speed, arranges the lighting and composes the picture in order to capture just such-and-such an effect. Indeed, even the most fumbling amateur points his or her camera at an object from a "point of view." And how often do we hear that a photograph is "nothing like" the person photographed! Even a camera is capable of distorting and misrepresenting. On the other hand, is it not a fact that we sometimes say that a portrait really and truly represents a particular aspect of a person's character with an accuracy that is astonishing? The difference between a photograph and a portrait is perhaps better made by

---

34. Richardson, *History, Sacred and Profane*, 183, quoting Hofer, "Towards a Revision of the German Concept of History," 188.

35. Croce, *Aesthetic*, 17: "if photography have in it anything artistic, it will be to the extent that it transmits the intuition of the photographer, his point of view, the pose and grouping which he has striven to attain."

saying, not that one is objective and the other subjective, but that the photograph represents what is the case from the point of view of a 1/250th of a second glimpse, whereas the portrait embodies the product of continued observation and social intercourse and can therefore capture the character of a person whose portrait is being painted in ways that the photograph cannot. Both, however, may truly and objectively represent different aspects of a person.

In the case of the gospels, the selection of purported episodes and incidents in Jesus' life is obviously made from a specific "point of view" and with the specific intention of communicating a particular impression both of Jesus' character and of the nature of his teaching. That does not necessarily mean, however, that the transmission of a specific set of traditions about him of itself therefore renders the more dispositional impression or picture of him that is communicated somehow invalid.

Once again, the variety produced by different "points of view" is not as such an issue when attempts are made objectively to describe what is the case. Variety of interpretation can be accepted, accommodated, and even embraced as an enrichment, without it (necessarily) leading to insecurity and doubt about the accuracy or otherwise of one's own interpretative descriptions. What would be needed to prevent us from concluding that Jesus *was* as he was remembered to have been from the perspective or "point of view" of his disciples would be an alternative and *logically competing* interpretation that is judged to be far more accurate and trustworthy. Indeed, it would need to possess the capacity to render the disciples' perspective on Jesus entirely untenable. Even though others might well have responded to the very same Jesus differently, using an alternative and perhaps equally justifiable set of linguistic concepts from their point of view, the first disciples may well have been perfectly justified in entertaining the specific view of him that they came to in faith which, ironically, is exactly what Dunn impressively outlines as "Jesus remembered." In order to bring such a view of him into question, a historian would have to have evidence to suggest that the first witnesses were deluded in their estimate of him, or were deliberately seeking to mislead. If there is in fact sufficient evidence to support the veracity of Dunn's presentation of "Jesus remembered," then the purely logical or thinkable possibility that others may have remembered him differently becomes irrelevant.

I therefore suggest we may justifiably conclude that, in the absence of good reasons to think otherwise, we may place a good deal of confidence in the "stable core" of the tradition about the kind of person Jesus was remembered to have been, even despite the admitted fact that this was an assessment of Jesus that was formed from a specific point of view. Dunn's assurance that we can recognize the character of the one who made the impact (and that we can actually discern not only the character of the person who made the impact but the character of his mission), and his further assurance that he remains confident that the record of the actual impact made by Jesus enables us to get as clear a picture of the one who made that impact as is both possible and necessary, surely indicates that Dunn is personally inclined to discount any purely "possible" or "thinkable" logically competing alternative account of Jesus and his character that might indicate that Jesus *was not* as he was remembered to have been.

Clearly, the fact that we know Jesus in the way he was remembered to have been by the disciples, does not mean that we must stall on the evidence of that memory itself, and refuse, like reluctant pack-donkeys, to go a step further. The discernment of the impact Jesus made, as "the most stable element" in what is otherwise the plastic and sometimes conflicting tradition about Jesus' words and works surely implies *that* the impact he made was perfectly justified. Indeed, in *Jesus Remembered*, Dunn has so persuasively argued his case for the account of the one who caused the impact that we could say that he would be justified in affirming his conclusions with certainty. One suspects that the only reason for his refusal to do this is his *a priori* methodological belief that such certainty is *always* impossible of achievement for historians!

Unfortunately, his methodological historical skepticism unwittingly leads Dunn into a cul-de-sac where what he gives with his right hand in *Jesus Remembered*, he withdraws with the left. On one hand, he says that we can all be confident and feel assured, and that no Christian need be concerned, for "Jesus remembered" is as close as it is possible or necessary to get. Yet, even so, nobody can claim to be certain, and therefore nobody can really claim to *know* these things. They are, like all historical judgments must be, just probabilities and possibilities. In reply to Stephen Davis (in his response to his interlocutors in *Memories of Jesus*), Dunn even questions the use of the word "accurate" in relation to historical judgments, on the ground that all historical judgments may be entertained only as probabilities. How, he asks, can a mere probability be regarded as "accurate"? Indeed, Dunn says these historical judgments are essentially a matter of faith: "The language of faith uses words like 'confidence' and 'assurance' rather than 'certainty.'"[36] We are not only discouraged from being certain of every narrated detail concerning Jesus (like fundamentalists), but we cannot even be certain that the "Jesus remembered" that is established by critical historical research can be entertained with any certainty. Rather, he says, we should be prepared to live by faith with ambiguity and doubt. But alas, we can only really proceed with confidence and assurance if we have good reasons to claim at least that the person in whom we place our confidence and trust is actually worthy of it. We can hardly have faith in Jesus, or place our trust in "the remembered Jesus," with confidence and assurance and commit our lives to him as his disciples, and at the same time admit that we really are unsure about whether he actually was as he was remembered by his first disciples to have been. If "Jesus remembered" is not to be equated with Jesus as he actually was in historical time, as Dunn would have us believe, then his actual character may have been entirely different from that which reportedly impressed his disciples and impacted on them.

36. Dunn, *Jesus Remembered*, 104.

Indeed, perhaps we must even doubt that Jesus really did exist, for this is also, after all, a historical judgment. Fortunately, Dunn himself saves us from this predicament: "That there was a Jesus who *did* inspire the faith which in due course found expression in the Gospels is not in question." Yet, in the next breath he is anxious to affirm that it is fanciful to hope "to strip out the theological impact which he actually made on his disciples, to uncover a different Jesus (the real Jesus!)."[37]

Unfortunately, Dunn's articulation of "Jesus remembered," and how this relates to Jesus as he actually was, is somewhat confusing and confused. And this seems primarily due to the fact that he is anxious positively to affirm something with confidence in the kind of judgment that he has already declared to be at best a probability, or even just a possibility.

Once this mistaken methodological commitment is abandoned, however, the judgment that the Jesus whom the disciples remembered *was* in fact the real Jesus is not automatically inhibited. All such judgments are made on the basis of the available evidence. If the evidence is found to be sufficient to warrant a set of judgments concerning the "stable core" of the memory of Jesus, then Dunn may have much more confidence in the "stable core" of the Jesus tradition than he is prepared to venture in *Jesus Remembered*.

While Dunn is led into this unfortunate cul-de-sac through his uncritical acceptance of the Troeltschian historiographical principle that no historical judgment can ever be known and entertained with certainty, John Knox, on the other hand, is clearly equally mistaken in contending that unlike specific facts *about* him, the church's memory of "Jesus *himself*" is something of which it is certain simply *because* it "*remembers* him." Like Dunn, Knox accepts that the judgments of New Testament scholars, in matters of detail, are often open to confirmation or otherwise by employing the techniques of critical historical research. However, he also suggests that it is almost an analytic truth (as necessarily true as the truth that all bachelors are unmarried), that the church is the community that "remembers Jesus," and that this is something which it entertains with confidence and certainty for it would cease to be the church if it failed to remember him.

It is true that there is something logically odd about saying "The church remembers Jesus, but is not certain that he ever lived," or "The church remembers Jesus but is not certain that he was as he was remembered to have been." This is because the word "remember" usually operates in the same way as the word "know" in claims "to know." It is not possible to claim to know something, then to add "but I am not certain of it." However, despite the fact that Knox believes that it is of the nature of something "remembered," that it did actually once occur, for unless it did

---

37. Dunn, *Jesus Remembered*, 126.

occur it cannot be "remembered," we have nevertheless to take account of the fact that sometimes our memories are mistaken. Even our own personal "memories" sometimes turn out to be defective. If we are ever justified in saying, "If I remember correctly...," then this means in principle that purported memories have sometimes to be independently verified. Despite Knox's conviction that the church cannot fail but remember Jesus, we therefore have to contend with the fact that there are ostensible and veridical memories, and it may be prudent to check the church's memory of Jesus against the available evidence.

We dare not assume that all memories are veridical and self-authenticating simply because they present themselves as "memories." While it may be hard to imagine the scenario where there is some hesitation among Christians in affirming that the actual Jesus of historical time was, at least in general terms, *as* he is remembered to have been by his disciples, it remains *in principle* true that the church *could* be mistaken about its received memory of him. This, after all, is a contingent matter. It is the kind of judgment that may be verified by appeal to the relevant evidence. Indeed, that is why the painstaking work of James Dunn and scholars working in the same field to discern the outline shape of "Jesus remembered" is so important. It seems clear enough that not just details of particular episodes, but the general picture of Jesus *himself* (or in Dunn's words, the "stable core" of the tradition constituted by the impact of "Jesus remembered"), must be open to confirmation or otherwise by critical historical research. It has to be accepted, therefore, that, even if memories are dispositional rather than episodic, the validity of the church's memory of "Jesus himself" is still in principle subject to the judgments of critical historical research. In this respect, Knox's belief that the church's memory of Jesus *himself* was something of which it could be certain in the face of the admitted insecurity of historical judgments *about* facts about Jesus, was, at least in part, illusory. Insofar as he relied upon the memory of Jesus *himself* to function as a kind of *sturmfreies Gebiet* for faith, entirely independent of critical historical research, this was something of a false hope. Confidence in the "stable core" of the memory of Jesus himself may in principle, however, be established and confirmed precisely by critical historical research.

Now, at the end of the last chapter I made the point that while Knox sought to distinguish "memories *about* Jesus" from the memory of "Jesus *himself*," he was mistaken in saying that the memory of Jesus himself contained no factual memories, or no statements of fact. Indeed, it was shown that Knox himself gives content to a concept that would otherwise be very elusive and baffling, by filling it out with a series of statements of fact: the memory of Jesus *himself* includes the memory of the facts *that* he was a man, *that* he lived at a particular point in time, *that* he was remembered to have been "supremely great and good," *that* he died upon the Cross, *that* in living and dying he exhibited a specific quality of character that was congruent with his own teaching, and *that* he was remembered as one who came among others in lowly manner as their servant, rather than as one lauding it over them and insisting upon being served by them. The memory of Jesus *himself* included the fact *that* he forsook worldly power of popular acclaim, and the fact *that* this quality of character was described as a particularly impressive kind of love, and so on. Clearly, Knox himself demonstrated by his own words that the memory of Jesus *himself* does contain some statements of fact.[38]

I then went on suggest, however, that in trying to distinguish "the memory of facts *about* Jesus" and the memory of "Jesus *himself*," Knox was actually nevertheless making a distinction of importance. This is the distinction between episodic and dispositional statements. In speaking of the memory of "Jesus *himself*," Knox was apparently referring to a memory content that may be expressed in dispositional statements rather than statements describing specific episodes. The same may be said of Dunn's references to the remembered "stable element" of the "impact" Jesus is said to have made, and of the meaning and significance of the character of the person he was remembered to have been, as distinct from bare facts *about* him. In speaking of the remembered impact of Jesus (or of the character of the one who made the impact that he did), we are not pointing to specific incidents and episodes, so much as to dispositional truths about him. A dispositional statement reports a proneness to act in a certain kind of way, not that a person is always or even now acting in that way. It is this "proneness" that gives content to the remembered character of Jesus as this was exhibited through his life even unto death.

Now, it is important to appreciate that, in giving content to the concept of the church's "corporately shared memory of Jesus" by appealing to statements reporting dispositions rather than to statements of an episodic kind, this is not to say that dispositional statements are not, or cannot be, putatively factual. Even dispositional statements do state facts. It is a fact that sheep are grass-eating animals, that glass is brittle, that sugar is soluble in water, or it may be a fact that a certain person is a cigarette-smoker. It may also be a fact, if it is true, that Jesus exhibited a certain quality of character that was described as a self-giving love, or was the kind of character who produced a particular kind of impact. Likewise, it may be a fact, if it is true, that Jesus was remembered as one who came among others as one who was dedicated to being of service to them, rather than as one to be waited upon by them. In other words, the dispositional statements of what Dunn calls the "stable core" of the tradition of the remembered Jesus, despite the fact that they are not episodic statements, nevertheless still state putative facts.

This means that dispositional statements of this kind are no less capable of being shown to be true or false than episodic statements, even though "they do not state truths

---

38. The same may be said of James Dunn's descriptions of the impact made by Jesus and "the character of the person who made that impact": this will be given concrete content by appeal to a similar set of statements of purported fact.

or falsehoods of the same type as those asserted by the statements of fact to which they apply."[39] In this case, despite the fact that the Christian normally becomes aware of the past existence of Jesus, and also of something of his life and character, through acquaintance with the "living memory" of the church, rather than as a consequence of an acquaintance with the methods and techniques of scientific historiography, it would be unwise to recoil from the work of critical historical research as it seeks to verify the purported facts relating to this dispositional memory.

Furthermore, the factual and contingent nature of remembered dispositions has to be brought to Knox's contention that, while not every word said to have been uttered by Jesus in the gospels, and every incident in which he is said to have been involved, is necessarily a veridical part of the church's memory of him, this insecurity does *not* apply to the church's memory of Jesus *himself*. If this is taken to mean that the church's memory of Jesus himself is somehow exempt from critical examination, and somehow above the processes of verification of critical historical research, then this is clearly mistaken. Even if this is something of which the church is said to be certain, we have to own, however, that even basic dispositional statements of fact concerning the general tenor of Jesus' teaching and the quality of his remembered character may, at least in principle, be judged to be either true or false by appeal to the relevant historical evidence, and it is in fact the confirmatory nature of the evidence that establishes the church's certainty.

This means, however, that we therefore have to contend with the view, specifically of the form critics, that even the general quality of the teaching and character of the historical Jesus was in fact camouflaged by the church's post-Easter christological reflection to the point where the "real" facts about him were so obscured by the "Christ of faith" that even an authentic dispositional memory of him has been lost. In other words, it is important to respond to the widely held pessimistic view of the form critics, that it is impossible to penetrate the over-lay of early christological interpretation to which form-critical research drew such sustained attention in relation to the traditions about Jesus.

It has already been noted that the general reliability and trustworthiness of the Jesus tradition, particularly at its "stable core" (by contrast with the very pessimistic basic assumptions of twentieth-century form-critical research), has recently been championed by Richard Bauckham by pointing to the importance of the category of original "eyewitness testimony" to bolster confidence in the general historical reliability of the New Testament traditions.[40] In one sense, it is obvious that these traditions found

---

39. Ryle, *The Concept of Mind*, 116–17.
40. Bauckham in *Jesus and the Eyewitnesses*. See above, 173, 198.

their way into the gospels through processes of transmission from original eyewitnesses.[41] However, Bauckham's contention is that the importance of the role of eyewitnesses is not confined just to the beginning of this process. Rather, he speculates that eyewitnesses could have exercised a role right through the fifty or so year period of the transmission of the tradition to the point when it received written form.[42] Even in the face of limited life-expectancy in the ancient world, and the generally accepted time-line of the production of the gospels late into the first-century, Bauckham argues that there would still have been sufficient eyewitnesses around to exercise a kind of "quality control" on the free and unfettered, or maverick, development of the tradition. He acknowledges the role of communities in relation to the preservation and transmission of their collective memories, but argues that this does not rule out the possibility that individual eyewitness testimony also operated within early faith communities as a check on the free development of their traditions, particularly in the first generations of the Christian era. His thesis is, therefore, that theologians have tended to over-estimate the degree to which the original traditions about Jesus passed through the filter of a set of anonymous Christian communities in such a way as to obscure from view the outline of the actual historical person behind them.

Bauckham acknowledges that there was undoubtedly a collective tradition or shared community memory, rather than a single pipe-line sharing of information from one person to the next, for it is understandable that much of the tradition about Jesus would have been shared sporadically at community gatherings of one kind or another.[43] His point is, however, that "a collective memory produced by frequent recitation of traditions in a communal context does not at all exclude the role of particular individuals who are especially competent to perform (the transmission of) the tradition."[44] The collective nature of the transmission of memory does not therefore necessarily exclude or take the place of individual informants or, importantly, individual guarantors of the veracity of the tradition, at least at a time when eyewitnesses and those who had known them were still living.

We are talking here about the couple of generations immediately following the death and Resurrection of Jesus, including the years towards the last four decades

---

41. Even a cautious skeptic like Dennis Nineham acknowledged that a combination of personal testimony and modifications by community use is to be found in the gospel traditions. See "Eyewitness Testimony and the Gospel Tradition." Also Taylor, *The Formation of the Gospel Tradition*, 42; and Hengel, *The Four Gospels*, 142–44.

42. A position embraced in the heavily apologetic work of Christopher Bryan, *The Resurrection of the Messiah*; especially "Additional Note B: On Whether the New Testament Narratives are Useful Sources of Information about Anything that May Actually Have Happened."

43. See Vansina, *Oral Tradition as History*, 149: "The corpus is more than what a single person remembers because the information is a memory, that is it does not go only from one person to another. Performances are held for audiences, not for single auditors, and historical gossip gets around as any other gossip does. So in practice the corpus becomes what is known to a community or to a society in the same way that culture is so defined."

44. Bauckham, *Jesus and the Eyewitness*, 33.

of the first-century when the gospels were actually being put together. It is understandable that there would have been a tendency to modify and change the tradition about Jesus in the process of making it relevant to particular changing situations of the kind that form criticism made much of, but this would not have been an entirely open process, free of any constraints imposed by the presence and testimony of those still living who had been eyewitnesses. Indeed, even in the next generation it seems to have been the case that the testimony of those who had actually been eyewitnesses was enormously valued and sought after. The historical evidence of Papias of Hierapolis, for example, suggests that the eyewitness testimony of the original disciples, and subsequent elders who transmitted it, was valued *even over written sources* as a means of getting at the truth about Jesus and his message and what had transpired concerning him. Eyewitness testimony thus may be more valuable, particularly for preserving the unique amalgam of historical tradition about Jesus, and the theological significance that was originally attached to it, than much contemporary theology has been prepared to accept.

For Richard Bauckham, by contrast with James Dunn, it is not the "impact" of Jesus in the testimony that is all we have. Rather, in the end, the testimony itself "is all we have."[45] He is therefore committed to championing the trustworthiness of eyewitness testimony. He exhorts us to trust the testimony in a way that is analogous to the trust we place in the word of another human person, of the kind that is "spontaneous and essential in everyday life,"[46] unless we have good reason to distrust it. This means that "the testimony can be checked in appropriate ways but nevertheless has to be trusted."[47] At the end of the day, for Bauckham, Christian faith is the belief *that* the testimony of Jesus "discloses God's definitive action for human salvation."[48] Alternatively, faith is a kind of inchoate propositional assent to a Jesus who is met within the text of the synoptic tradition itself: "the Gospels are to be believed."

However, it is surely a big ask to assume that eyewitness testimony was on hand to check the veracity of every reported incident in which Jesus was alleged to have said or done something, or every episode in which he is said to have been involved. The array of eyewitness quality controllers needed across the ancient world to make sure that every reported word attributed to Jesus, or incident in which Jesus was said to be involved, actually passed muster in terms of its authenticity would have had to have been so extensive as not to seem at all plausible. While it would be possible for an eyewitness

---

45. Bauckham, *Jesus and the Eyewitness*, 490.
46. Bauckham, *Jesus and the Eyewitness*, 489.
47. Bauckham, *Jesus and the Eyewitness*, 502.
48. Bauckham, *Jesus and the Eyewitness*, 499.

to affirm the historicity of a statement or deed of Jesus by stating "I was there," it is hardly possible that an eyewitness could have been "there" all of the time.

So the question is, could they have actually been present on sufficient occasions in the life of the historical Jesus so as to adjudicate on the veracity of the myriad specific episodes in which Jesus was said to have been involved? To have eyewitnesses still alive who were present at every moment of Jesus' life so as to guarantee the authenticity of every specific saying of Jesus, or episode in which he is alleged to have been involved, seems exceedingly unlikely. After all, how could eyewitnesses vouch for the fact that a particular statement was definitely uttered by Jesus or not uttered by him, without having shadowed him on every conceivable moment of his earthly existence? In the face of various purported statements or deeds of Jesus, even Bauckham's notional "eyewitness quality controllers" might simply have had to say "If Jesus said or did x or y, I was not there at every moment of Jesus' historical existence, and so I am afraid I cannot verify it."

Furthermore, Bauckham also relies on the *theoretical and speculative* possibility that eyewitnesses *could* have still been alive into the final decades of the first-century to perform this function. While the activity of eyewitness quality controllers is theoretically possible (or thinkable without self-contradiction), it has to be owned that we unfortunately do not have actual evidential reports of the work of such eyewitnesses to back this theoretical and speculative possibility.

Richard Bauckham contends that the purpose of communication generally is to convey information; we are therefore justified in presuming the reliability of what is being communicated, *unless* there are good reasons to doubt it. Bauckham illustrates this by appeal to the psychology of "trusting testimony" in communication.[49] However, it seems clearer to demonstrate this as a logical point, for the very concept of inter-personal human communication assumes that it is intended precisely for the purpose of communicating truth. Communication could not function otherwise than on this basis. If it were to be assumed that communication was always designed to mislead, the very possibility of human communication would be undermined. We are therefore normally justified in assuming that this is so, *unless we have good reasons* to think otherwise.

Unfortunately, however, if it is true that in normal inter-personal communication we generally accept the testimony of others (for this is the purpose of communication), unless there are good reasons to doubt it, then this is the Achilles heel of Bauckham's general argument that the scriptural testimony is to be trusted. Given the theoretically possible operation of eyewitnesses right through the period of its transmission prior to being given written form in the gospels, it is nevertheless actually

---

49. Bauckham, *Jesus and the Eyewitnesses*, chapter 18.

the case that the gospels themselves throw up a troublesome array of "good reasons" that might cause us to doubt their unquestioned historicity. In other words, in the case of the gospel traditions there are good reasons to doubt that it simply reports eyewitness testimony. Indeed, the all-too-apparent differences and contradictions that are patently to be found in the tradition was the trigger of the form critics' attempts to demonstrate that they were not simply dealing with straight-forward eyewitness testimony. If eyewitnesses were on hand to guarantee its authentic transmission from generation to generation, they were often clearly asleep on the job. For example, even in defending his contention that there was a process of "informal, controlled transmission" with some original eyewitness input, James Dunn points to the difficulty posed by the three different accounts of Paul's conversion on the Damascus Road in *Acts*. Here the variety between accounts of who actually saw and heard, and what it was that was seen and heard, differs in such a way as to suggest to Dunn precisely the kind of thing that might be expected from a process of "informal, controlled transmission." However, N. T. Wright accounts for the very same differences between the three versions of Paul's story as Luke's own attempt to create literary interests by introducing variety of detail![50] Clearly, there is a lot of guesswork going on here.

Moreover, if we are to rely on eyewitness testimony to guarantee the trustworthiness of the tradition, we actually know who the eyewitnesses were in this case: Paul and those travelling with him. However, despite this, discrepancies persist, and the point is that the persistence of diversity and, in fact, logically competing difference, means that not all can be historically accurate. In this case, we may have to conclude that these differences resulted from confusion at the time. Paul himself may not have been entirely clear about exactly what happened, and about what was seen and heard and by whom. Clearly, eyewitness testimony as such does not speak of historical trustworthiness when there are discrepancies in the resulting traditions.

For the same reasons, the three accounts of Jesus' prediction of the passion in Mark's Gospel[51] contain sufficient "good reasons" to cause us to pause before judging them all to be historically accurate eyewitness testimony. Whether Jesus actually predicted his passion more than once is obviously possible. Whether he did so on the each of the three specific occasions narrated by Mark, or whether this is largely a literary creation of Mark, is an open question. I myself incline to the view that this is largely the product of the redactional inventiveness of Mark, effectively working as a systematic theologian rather than as a disinterested chronicler of events wedded to the transmission of eyewitness testimony. Moreover, there are "good reasons" for suggesting that hindsight may well have been involved in the transmission of the tradition of these passion predictions, given that details are provided relating to precisely who was responsible for the persecution and mistreatment of Jesus. These details are also at variance across these three texts. In Mark 8:31, the responsible

50. Wright, *RSG*, 388–93.
51. Mark 8:31; 9:31; 10:32–34.

parties are explicitly identified as "the elders, the chief priests, and the scribes." By contrast, Mark 9:31 has Jesus predicting more generally that he will fall into "human hands." In Mark 10:33, these men are identified as the "chief priests and the scribes," with no mention of elders. The suggestion is easily made that these details have entered the tradition through hindsight, given what actually transpired. And this is not to mention that these explicit identifications (attributed to Jesus before the event) of who would be responsible for his suffering, are followed by predictions of his rising again. It is hard to avoid the implication that this material may have been conditioned in the light of the Resurrection by what actually was understood to have occurred. These sayings of Jesus thus appear to bear the mark of embroidery in matters of such detail. It is hard to accept the historicity of this three-fold tradition by appeal to the alleged controlling role of eyewitnesses. We may not be convinced that form-critical scholasticism and over-confidence got it exactly right by accounting for differences in the tradition by appeal to the almost unrestrained creative role of anonymous worshipping communities in bending the tradition to meet their own pragmatic needs. But the reliance on the theoretical possibility of eyewitness quality control almost certainly claims too much for the alleged trustworthiness and historicity of the tradition. This is particularly so in the face of the many discrepancies in the tradition, particularly in relation to the details of specific instances and episodes in which Jesus is said to have been involved.

However, that said, provided it is acknowledged that we are working with theoretical possibilities, what is much more likely is that a kind of eyewitness quality control *could* have operated in relation to the general *kind of thing* that Jesus was remembered to have said and done. In other words, this kind of control could have operated in the case of remembered dispositional truths about Jesus in a way that would not necessarily have been the case in relation to purported incidents and episodes. In this case, various purported incidents and episodes in which Jesus was alleged to have been involved might conceivably have been judged to be congruent or not congruent with "what was remembered of him"—that is to say, congruent with the general tenor of his teaching or the abiding dispositional memory of the quality of his character.

Even in courts of law today, character witnesses are prone to say, for example, that "such and such a specific behavior" is not in accordance with the regular behavior of the person "as I know him," or not congruent with his character "as I remember him, based on my previous acquaintance with him." A specific behavior may be judged to be either "in character," or "out of character," without it being necessary to determine whether it is itself veridical or not as an actual incident or occurrence. While it is far less likely that an eyewitness could claim to have been present on every occasion when Jesus uttered a teaching, or on every occasion when he either acted or reacted, eyewitnesses may well have been in a position to vouch for the general tenor, or the "drift," of Jesus' teaching, or for the kind of dispositional behavioral qualities he was remembered to have exhibited.

The distinction made both by John Knox and James Dunn, in slightly differing ways, between statements of historical fact *about* particular episodes in which Jesus taught, and incidents in his life, (which usually form the chief concern of critical historical research), and the statements of a dispositional kind that might be called upon to unpack the content of the church's memory of Jesus *himself*, may thus still be legitimately maintained. If the more general *kind of thing* that Jesus taught, and the general way in which he acted, and reacted to others, was what eyewitness testimony could have secured, then specific instances or exemplifications of those more general dispositional truths might still, of course, have been embroidered and otherwise altered in the telling. Indeed, even if somewhat legendary and even mythical stories about Jesus did develop in the course of the transmission of the original tradition about him, this does not mean that this kind of material has no capacity to communicate truths about him of a more dispositional kind. Unless there is evidence to the contrary, the presumption must be that the originative purpose of christological reflection on the significance of Jesus was not intended to camouflage and obscure, but precisely to illuminate and communicate by bearing testimony to essential insights concerning him and his significance.

Certainly, if eyewitness testimony exercised a kind of quality control on the development of the tradition, as Bauckham would have us believe, this is much more likely to have been the case in relation to the *kind* of thing Jesus was remembered to have taught, and the *kind* of qualities and general traits of character he exhibited in his life, rather than for the specific incidents and episodes that might be said to illustrate them. If we are to doubt the veracity of this "memory of Jesus himself," then we would need some very "good reasons" for doing so.

In summary, I think we are able to say that, while there will obviously be continuing disagreements among New Testament scholars about the historicity or otherwise of particular reported incidents and episodes in the life of Jesus, this will not be nearly so much of a problem in relation to the remembered kind of thing that Jesus taught, or the kind of person he was remembered to have been. Even so, this is a contingent matter that relies upon a careful consideration of the available evidence. It is not a consideration to be abandoned because of the alleged view that historical judgments are always congenitally defective and can only ever be asserted with a degree of probability and never with certainty. Despite the unnecessary hesitations and equivocations of James Dunn, unless there are some very good evidential reasons for doubting the veracity of the church's memory of Jesus himself, or of the "stable core" of the tradition about him, we may be justified in contending that, in general dispositional terms, Jesus *was* as he is remembered to have been.

Whether this is specific enough to constitute a "uniquely referring" description of Jesus as he was remembered to have been, and of such a kind of warrant the identification of his presence in faith through the medium of his gift of his "life-giving Spirit," is the question to which we shall now turn.

10

A Uniquely Referring Memory?

DESPITE THE IMPORTANT DISTINCTION that John Knox made between the memory of facts *about* Jesus and the memory of Jesus *himself*, which has been resolved into a distinction between memories expressed in episodic statements and memories expressed in dispositional statements, it has to be acknowledged that the difference between the two cannot be drawn into a kind of polar opposition. Insofar as Knox was inclined to emphasize the fact that the church remembers Jesus himself *and not* facts about him, he tended to overlook an important interrelation between the two. Even if the content of the church's memory of Jesus is expressed in more general dispositional terms rather than in episodic statements, it remains true that, in order to appreciate something of its distinctive quality, a remembered disposition has to be *illustrated by* the rehearsal of the myriad incidents and episodes in which Jesus was said to have been involved. The episodes and instances in which he is reported to have spoken, and acted, and re-acted to people, are what reveal the dispositional quality of his remembered character.

In general terms this is actually something to which Martin Kähler appears to have been seeking to draw attention early in the twentieth-century. In making his point about "the Biblical Historic Christ," in distinction from attempts to discover "the Jesus of history," Kähler stressed that his aim was to explain "how inadvisable and indeed impossible it is to reach a Christian understanding of Jesus when one deviates from the *total* biblical proclamation about him—his life as well as its significance."[1]

This is also something of which Hans Frei became acutely aware as he explored the theme of the unique identity of Jesus. In championing the crucial significance of Jesus' "inalienable identity" for pointing us to his "inescapable presence,"[2] Frei stressed the fundamental importance of the category of "story" for the definition and communication of Jesus' identity. Indeed, if anything, he was suspicious of any tendency to dwell upon a dispositional presentation of Jesus' identity in abstract terms that he believed might tend to detach it from its more detailed presentation through the nar-

---

1. Kahler, *The So-Called Historical Jesus*, 68.
2. Frei, *The Identity of Jesus Christ*, 145.

ration of the episodes of Jesus' life and work in story form. He saw clearly, for example, that "we grasp the identity of Jesus within his story";[3] "his identity is grasped only by means of the story told about him."[4] In a sense, the communication of a dispositional memory of Jesus *himself* is necessarily dependent upon the rehearsal of incidents and episodes in which he is said to have been involved.

This insight led Frei to question whether it is even possible to excerpt features (or, in other words, dispositions) relating Jesus' qualities of character from the episodes of the biblical narrative. Indeed, Frei was even prompted to counsel that we should positively resist doing so because of the dangerous possibility of bias creeping in with regard to the subjective choice of identifiable more general features of Jesus character, but especially because of the dangerous possibility that "speculative inference" may lead to a kind of "story behind the story" that may actually distort the story itself.[5] In this case, incidents of the story may be used to illustrate a pre-conceived character, to the detriment of the possibility that the character is actually "shaped" by those very incidents themselves. Hence, Frei became committed to the importance of telling the actual story of a person's life for the grasping of that person's identity, rather than seeking to define a kind of "depth dimension" behind it. In general terms, this was essentially the same concern that Kähler expressed when he questioned the possibility of isolating "the historical Jesus" *behind* the "historic Biblical Christ" of the narrative traditions of the New Testament.

Even so, Frei himself went on, perhaps somewhat inconsistently, to speak in more dispositional terms of the identity of Jesus as one who was remembered for his "steadfast obedience to the will of God even unto death,"[6] citing, for example, Rom 5:19, Phil 2:8, and Heb 5:8.[7] Nevertheless, we take his point that the highly distinctive dispositional characteristics of Jesus' "unsubstitutable identity" was gained "in unsubstitutable circumstances," and so can only really be communicated through the telling of the Jesus' story. This necessarily means recounting the numerous specific purported episodes and incidents in which Jesus is portrayed as teaching, and acting and reacting. In other words, a presentation of the distinctive dispositional qualities of character for which Jesus is remembered cannot be divorced from the story comprised of the incidents and episodes of his historical life that illustrate them. In this respect, Frei valued the insightful observation of Henry James: "What is character but the determination of incident? What is incident but the illustration of character?"[8]

3. Frei, *The Identity of Jesus Christ*, 133.
4. Frei, *The Identity of Jesus Christ*, 133.
5. Frei, *The Identity of Jesus Christ*, 135.
6. Frei, *The Identity of Jesus Christ*, Part 4: "The New Testament Depiction of Jesus Christ," chapter 9: "Identity Description and Jesus Christ."
7. Frei, *The Identity of Jesus Christ*, 146.
8. Frei, *The Identity of Jesus Christ*, 133–34, quoting Henry James, "The Art of Fiction," in Besant and James, *The Art of Fiction*, 69. What is true of fiction is, of course, also true of historical and biographical narrative in this respect.

The purported episodic instantiations illustrative of the set of dispositions concerning the *kind* of person Jesus was remembered to have been, or concerning the specific character to which the original disciples claimed to have responded, cannot therefore be entirely replaced by statements of a dispositional kind. Moreover, even if most believers will find it difficult to disbelieve their inherited picture of the kind of person Jesus is remembered to have been, insofar as the church's dispositional memory of Jesus *himself* is communicated by rehearsing the stories of the words and works of his historical life, these must in principle be open to the scrutiny of critical historical research. Because this is a contingent matter that can only be settled by appeal to actual evidence, the church's assessment of the significance of Jesus must therefore continue in principle to be the subject matter of historical scrutiny. It has to be accepted, therefore, that, whether memories are dispositional or episodic, the validity of the church's memory of "Jesus himself" is still in principle subject to the judgments of critical historical research. As we have already noted, in this respect, Knox's belief that the church's memory of Jesus *himself* was something of which it could be certain in the face of the admitted insecurity of historical judgments about facts *about* Jesus, was, at least in part, illusory. Insofar as he relied upon the memory of Jesus *himself* to function as a kind of *sturmfreies Gebiet* for faith, entirely independent of critical historical research, this was something of a false hope.

It is obvious enough that not every purported historical statement of the gospels can be accepted as certainly true. For a start, even at a very superficial reading, discrepancies and contradictions in the tradition abound.[9] As James Dunn correctly says, "the varied memories prevent us from 'certainty' as to the accuracy of particular details in the Jesus tradition."[10] Notwithstanding Richard Bauckham's plea for the category of eyewitness testimony to be taken seriously, and for the New Testament witness to be received as being more rather than less reliable, the obvious discrepancies across the gospel accounts render it impossible that all of their episodic details may simply be accounted accurate.

There can therefore clearly be a debate among those involved in critical historical research about the veracity or otherwise of detailed incidents in which Jesus is said to have been involved, or about specific statements that he is alleged to have made.[11]

---

9. Did Jesus enter Jerusalem on a donkey a week or so before his trial and crucifixion (as in Mark), or much closer to the beginning of his ministry (as in John)? Was the Last Supper a Passover meal, or did Jesus die upon the Cross at around the time of the sacrifice of Passover lambs *before* the scheduled time of the Passover meal? Was Jesus' mission intended initially for the Jews in his lifetime and only universalized after his Resurrection (as in Matthew), or did it carry a universalist dimension from the start (as in Mark)? And so on.

10. Dunn, "In Grateful Dialogue," 319.

11. Witness the attempts to reach fixed conclusions among members of the Jesus Seminar, a group of about one hundred and fifty scholars, founded in 1985 under the auspices of the Westar

However, that said, while critical historical research might find it difficult to pass judgment on particular words of Jesus, or particular incidents in which he was said to have been involved, there are a number of reasons for thinking that it may reach more confident conclusions in its assessment of the general *kind* of thing that Jesus was said to have taught, and the more general dispositional quality of his character as it was remembered to have been by the first community of believers.

For example, as we have already noted, in the Gospel of Mark, Jesus is said to have predicted his passion, death, and Resurrection on three separate occasions;[12] on each occasion there is textual similarity but also some differences between them. However, the general dispositional truth *that* Jesus rejected suggestions that he was the awaited Messiah of military authority and power, by predicting his own ultimate mistreatment at the hands of that very kind of earthly power, is surely much more secure. The same may be said of his call to discipleship, insofar as he is said, following these predictions of his passion, to have taught the value of being the self-giving servant of others.[13] We may question the historicity of the exact detail in relation to the explicit manner of discipleship of "taking up the Cross and following in the same way," for this kind of detail is likely to have been specified only subsequent to his actual dying upon the Cross. On the other hand, if death by crucifixion was commonplace, it is not inconceivable that Jesus may have sensed that this would also be his fate. However, even if the threefold nature of the repetition of his call to lowly service might appear to result from Mark's theological and literary creativity, the very occurrence of this three-fold repetition emphasizes the fact that this was important to the way in which he was remembered. That the first believers apparently perceived this dispositional truth, both as a feature of Jesus' teaching and of his own exemplary life (that was definitively exemplified also in the manner of his dying), so that his call to the discipleship of serving others came to be a call to "take up your Cross and follow in the same way," simply confirms the point.

On the other hand, it is important to note that the dispositional memory of Jesus as one who called his disciples to a life of serving others, such as is contained in this sustained dispositional tradition of Jesus' "open" or "plain" teaching in the second half of St Mark's Gospel, is confirmed by its much earlier appearance in the Christ hymn preserved by Paul in Phil 2:5–11. There it is made clear that "the mind" that was remembered to have been "in Christ Jesus" was that he "emptied himself, taking the form of a slave."[14] Moreover, this is also the very same dispositional character that

---

Institute, including most notably Robert Funk, Marcus Borg, and John Dominic Crossan. This group (famously) worked with the method of democratic voting by placing colored beads in a box to establish an event's historicity or otherwise. Though the reports of its results are not without interest, unfortunately democratic procedures do not replace sound argument in establishing truth. Even majorities are sometimes mistaken.

12. Mark 8:31; 9:31; and 10:33–34.
13. Mark 8:34; 9:35; and 10:42–45.
14. Phil 2:7.

St. John transmits in the classic episode of the washing of the disciples' feet in John 13:3–17. Indeed, for John this episodic act of the service of others is actually said to have demonstrated the dispositional quality of *agape* that was remembered to have informed the life of Jesus from beginning to end: "having loved his own who were in the world, he loved them to the end,"[15] and so "poured water into a basin and began to wash the disciples' feet."[16] Moreover, John, like Mark, does not resile from seeing this as a paradigm of Jesus' teaching *about* the nature of discipleship and of his characteristic call *to* discipleship.[17] It is difficult to avoid the conclusion that the dispositional memory of Jesus, "the servant of others," that was preserved and expressed in entirely different ways by Paul, Mark, and John are nevertheless of a piece. Despite verbal and episodic differences in communicating it, the substance of what is remembered is essentially the same. As James Dunn would say, this "core element" of the account of the impact that Jesus made on the disciples is remarkably "stable."

At the end of the day, while it is admittedly difficult to pin down and separate original factual information from the over-lay of statements expressing the meaning and significance that was seen in it, not to mention ultimately the theological interpretation with which from an early time it was clothed, this may therefore not be as epistemologically troublesome as at first it might appear.

Paul is witness to the fact that the remembered humanly impressive disposition of the distinctive self-giving of Jesus was from an early time spoken of theologically as "God's love"; the activity of the Spirit of God in and through his life. This is clearly a theological or christological interpretation that was put upon the factual experience of encounter with Jesus. But even this does not obscure so much as facilitate the communication of something of the uniquely and transcendentally impressive dispositional memory of *him*, and the nature of the impact he made. In other words, even if it is difficult to unscramble purported statements of historical fact from the layers of early theological and christological interpretation put on them, this may not be noxious with regard to the capacity of the resulting amalgam of putative statements of fact, *plus* theologically pregnant interpretative statements, to function effectively together in the transmission of the set of dispositional truths that encapsulated and expressed the disciples memory of *him*.

Even specific stories that have become exaggerated in the telling, or stretched so as to become partly legendary, or that have acquired specific detail in hindsight, or even if they have acquired a "mythical" over-lay by the addition of other-worldly transcendental references, may nevertheless illustrate the dispositional insights about Jesus *as he actually was*, and for which he was remembered. To talk of his remembered self-giving love not just as "steadfast" to the end, but as "God's love," an ultimately eternal and unchangeable reality, incarnate in him, may actually say something of enormous

---

15. John 13:1.
16. John 13:5.
17. John 13:14–15.

importance about the verbally transcending distinctiveness of its remembered quality. Without having to make a judgment as to whether it was necessarily the case that the love of Jesus was (in some sense of "was") God's love, we can appreciate the role of this kind of language in communicating something of the historical distinctiveness of the quality of Jesus' remembered self-giving. Ultimately, this will essentially involve a judgment of faith that will be made by some but not by others. However, we should not automatically jump to the conclusion that, because a statement falls into the category of a theological or christological reflection or interpretation of Jesus' significance, it must therefore obscure rather than have a capacity to illuminate something of a dispositional kind that was factually memorable about him.

It was par for the course in the nineteenth-century simply to assume that the overlay of theological interpretation, the "glorious dogmatic apparel" with which Jesus had been clothed by the faith of the church, automatically obscured the historical Jesus, who therefore had somehow to be recovered beneath it. However, the idea that christology arises deductively on the basis of the historical fact of the Resurrection abstractly conceived as an event of the past, first interpreted in the form of the insight *that* Jesus was "the Christ," then the vindicated "Son of Man" perhaps by association with the images of Daniel, then the heavenly "Lord," then "Son of God" (located with the help of Psalm 110 "at the right hand of the Father"), as though this represented at each stage an inexorable evolution *away* from historical reality is entirely unwarranted.[18] Christological reflection on Jesus' significance is not just an exercise of deductive logic of this kind that can easily become detached from the initial set of perceptions that triggered these thought processes in the first place. Eventually, in the light of the Easter experience, the distinctive character of the human self-giving of Jesus was spoken of theologically as "God's love" in him. Its *development* from a concretely experienced beginning, as progressively things originally implicit were made more explicit, and their implications drawn out with the help of interpretative categories drawn from the traditions of the Hebrew Scripture s, is not automatically to be mistaken for an inexorable, deductively driven, *evolution* away from its point of origin.[19] Rather, if I am correct (as I have argued in *Resurrection in Retrospect* in criticism of N. T. Wright's commitment to a purely deductive model)[20] this kind of christological and theological language arose *inductively* out of a continuing concrete post-Easter experience. Moreover, if its dispositional judgments and conclusions are to be perceived

---

18. See the discussion of the alleged deductive nature of the process of christological development (though not necessarily evolution *away* from its point of origin) in relation to the theology of N. T. Wright, in Carnley, *Resurrection in Retrospect*, chapter 8.

19. As C. F. D. Moule pointed out long ago in relation to christological "development of an initial perception" as against "evolution away from it" (Moule, *The Origin of Christology*, 135–41).

20. Carnley, *Resurrection in Retrospect*, chapter 8.

in a way akin to the exercise of the illative sense described by Newman,[21] then it may be understood to convey a freight of *descriptive* meaning. Christological reflection was, indeed, integral to the particular way in which the church claimed to know the remembered Jesus through its continuing acquaintance with his "life-giving Spirit." Thus, while much critical historical research has been committed to the separation of statements of "historical fact" in the form both of episodic and dispositional facts *about* Jesus from the over-lay of early christological interpretation put on them, the transmission of the memory of Jesus *himself*, may actually depend on maintaining the integrity of statements of fact and interpretation *together*.[22] Paul Minear once perceptively observed that, in order to discover the facts about the circumstances of Jesus' death, "the historian must accomplish the *fission* of history and interpretation," showing perhaps how far were the original facts from the subsequent Christian understanding of them in sacrificial terms. But in order to understand the *meaning* of the death for the early church of the kind that informed its continuing memory of Jesus, what is necessary is "the *fusion* of history and interpretation."[23] If this is so in relation to the death of Jesus, the same applies more generally to his historical life as a whole: the unit of meaning for the communication of the memory of Jesus is an amalgam of different kinds of statement.

In the post-Easter period, some of the first disciples of Jesus certainly went on to express what was impressive about him, and to celebrate his alleged impact in their lives, by using explicitly theological categories. Not least, their theological reflection was aided by employing the inherited titles of Messiah, Savior, Son of God, and so on. Others, while being impressed by the remembered impact of his person and teaching, might not have been so quick to resort to that kind of specifically theological language. There could well have been diversity of opinion in relation to such matters, given that they touch directly on the issue of faith, doubt, and perceptual freedom. But who is prepared to say that the disciples were entirely mistaken or unjustified in their assessment of the human character of the historical Jesus? After all, there is no concrete evidence to suggest that the first disciples were manipulated or duped, or unwittingly deluded, or simply mistaken when they reported the outline shape of the impact Jesus made upon them. There is no convincing evidence to suggest that they deliberately sought to mislead anyone who would listen to them when they reported what it was about Jesus that they found so memorable. At this point, Richard Bauckham is surely right in pointing us in the direction of the possible role of eyewitnesses. Despite the varied nature of the

---

21. As I have argued in chapters 5 and 6 of this book.

22. This appears to have been Kähler's point about the total proclamation of biblical historic Christ that was noted at the beginning of this chapter (Kähler, *The So-Called Historical Jesus*, 68).

23. Minear, in his review of Knox's *The Death of Christ*, *Religion in Life*, 610–11.

memories of individual episodes that "prevent us from any 'certainty' as to the accuracy of particular details of the Jesus tradition,"[24] there is no evidence that suggests that Jesus himself was not as he was remembered to have been in terms of the character he displayed in his words and works, or the impressively memorable kind of person he was.[25] In this case we may need to be open to the possibility that something of the uniqueness of this memory was also actually expressed even through the over-lay of theological and christological reflection with which it was clothed, so that this communicated and revealed rather than camouflaged and obscured the truth that the disciples discerned in him. In other words, christological reflection is not automatically to be regarded as unhelpfully speculative, but plays a role, along with the narration of historical incident, in expressing and communicating something of Jesus' remembered uniquely referring character. After all, to speak of Jesus' self-giving love as "God's love" revealed in him, may actually say something of importance about the perception of its unique quality. If there is no actual evidence so much as to suggest that it was not the case that Jesus *was* as the disciples remembered him, then we might also conclude that resort to theological and christological language amongst the first generation of Christians may well represent a valid attempt to wrestle down and express something of the perceived uniqueness of the particular human self that Jesus was remembered to have been.

Now, let us bring these possibilities to bear upon the epistemic function of the church's memory of Jesus himself in the make up of faith. Provided the church's "memory of Jesus himself" is understood as a set of putatively factual statements reporting (for the most part) a dispositional memory of the kind of things Jesus said and did, and the kind of person therefore he was remembered to have been, John Knox's fundamental insight in his writing on this theme is well taken: a claim to recognize the presence of the Raised Jesus Christ in faith presupposes some kind of logically prior memory of him. Or as Hans Frei has so vehemently insisted, Jesus' *identity* must be treated before his *presence*, for it enjoys a logical priority. In epistemological terms this is certainly the case: normally, we recognize someone by reference to some kind of previously experienced, and now remembered, acquaintance with them. The fundamental conviction implicit in Easter faith is, therefore, that on both sides of the Cross what was remembered to have informed the historical life and character of Jesus himself, and the Spirit that was known as it informed the life of the post-Easter community, was perceived as being, in identifiable qualitative terms, identical. It was the very same reality to which people responded in faith, whether perceived in Jesus' historical life,

---

24. Dunn, "In Grateful Dialogue," 319.

25. I am gratified to find that, even in the face of his rationalist critique of both Judaism and Christianity, the "failed" Jew Baruch/Benedict Spinoza concluded that Jesus was to be acclaimed for "giving by His life and death a matchless example of holiness" (see Spinoza's Letter XXIII to Oldenburg, in *On the Improvement of the Understanding*, 304).

or as an identified presence in the life of the church after his crucifixion and Resurrection. Either way, it was an index to the *same* Jesus, whether before or after his crucifixion. And here, it is important to say that the word "same" is used not just in a comparative sense, but in a numerical sense. What was claimed to be perceived and known in Easter faith was recognized to be the life-giving Spirit *of* the remembered and Raised *Jesus*. In this way, the dispositional character of Jesus, as revealed in the episodic words and works of his historical ministry, becomes the defining index that enables the judgment of Easter faith, in which claims are made to recognize Jesus' living presence, now as the animating Spirit of the Christian community. The tantalizing question, however, remains: is what is remembered a "uniquely referring" memory of Jesus, such that appeal may be made to it to justify claims to identify and know *him*? Is it capable of warranting the use of Jesus' name in such identifying claims?

We have already noted John R. Searle's point that, though proper names do not strictly speaking have meaning or sense, certain descriptive statements are *presupposed* when proper names are used. In addition we should now note that, if a proper name is used *to identify* a human individual, it is essential that what is presupposed in the use of the proper name is specific enough to apply to a particular person.

In other words, the set of descriptive characteristics presupposed when it is used identifyingly, must be *uniquely referring*. Gottlob Frege, held that proper names do in fact have sense as well as reference,[26] and that the sense of a proper name contains the "mode of presentation" which identifies its referent.[27] If a proper name is used to identify a particular person, it is essential that the presupposed sense of the proper name should be specific enough to indicate a "mode of presentation." Clearly, the descriptive statements that allow for the proper name "Jesus" to be used, both to refer to and to identify his living presence, must be specific enough to apply uniquely to him.

This means that if the contemporary church claims in faith to recognize the presence of the Raised Jesus Christ now, as the animating Spirit of its continuing community life and mission, it must have some "memory of him" in the form of some *uniquely referring* factual statements to which appeal may be made to justify such a claim. If, as we noted at the beginning of this chapter, resurrection faith is essentially a matter of interpreting a concretely experienced reality in faith *as* the presence of "*Jesus*," and if a memory of Jesus is a logically necessary prerequisite for being able to make such an identity judgment, the crucial question therefore becomes: are the putative statements of fact, that have so far been drawn upon to give content to the idea of "the Church

---

26. In other words, they connote as well as denote.

27. As distinct from Searle's contention that the sense of the proper name is "presupposed." For the purposes of the argument here, this distinction is immaterial. See Frege, "On Sense and Reference," in *Translations from the Philosophical Writings of Gottlob Frege*, 57.

and her memory of Jesus," of such a caliber as would apply *only* to the historical Jesus, and thus possess the capacity to warrant the recognition and identification in faith of *his* living presence in the life of the community of believers today?

Clearly, the statement that Jesus was remembered to be a man, and perhaps even a man who was "supremely great and good," or a man who was remembered to have exhibited "a distinctive quality of character," would not be sufficient. These statements might be necessary, but they would not be sufficient to this identifying purpose.

When we come to unpack something of that distinctive character in terms of the lowly, other-regarding humanity of the one who was remembered to have taken "the *form* of a slave,"[28] or to have washed his disciples feet,[29] or in terms of steadfast self-giving such as was displayed not only in the words and works of Jesus' historical life, but in the way that was sustained through the specter of his death on the Cross, we begin to edge towards something more telling. After all, it was the Cross, and the way in which Jesus was remembered to have embraced it, which thus became the center and symbol of the remembered quality of his life. It is this distinctive dispositional quality of character of self-giving that was defined on the Cross that was instantiated in the many incidents and episodes attributed to Jesus in the narrative traditions of the synoptic gospels. Though it was communicated with less interest in its narrative expression by St. Paul, and others, in the epistles of the New Testament (for whom this was still essentially a live oral tradition), it was clearly no less celebrated, cherished, and remembered. As Paul says: "May I never boast of anything except the cross of our Lord Jesus Christ."[30] In a sense, the Cross encapsulated and said it all.

It is certainly thinkable that a distinctive quality of character *could* qualify as an identifying token of a specific person. It might be said, for example, that "You will recognize Tom because he is the most boisterous boy in the class." The disposition of boisterousness, in other words, might certainly operate as an identifying description of Tom in certain circumstances. Or it might be said that "Jane is the member of the group who is prone to talk endlessly, while the rest are measured and restrained, even to the point of not expressing an opinion at all." Clearly, the identification of Jane by reference to a specific dispositional quality is not beyond possibility. This means that the question before us becomes: is there anything in the church's memory of *Jesus* that could qualify as a uniquely identifying description of him? Does the church actually possess an adequate "mode of presentation" to back the identifying use of the proper name "Jesus"?

---

28. Phil 2:7.
29. John 13:5.
30. Gal 6:14.

It will not come as a surprise that the answer to this question is "Yes, I think it does." It has already been noted, in unpacking John Knox's account of the content of the church's memory of Jesus, that Knox often spoke of the distinctive quality of the self-giving and other-regarding love that informed his life and death as the identifying quality of his distinctive character. This was the love that the first generation of Christians spoke of as "*agape*," as the love of God that was in Christ Jesus. In the choice of the term *agape* for this specific purpose, they were utilizing a somewhat out-of-fashion and under-used pre-biblical Greek word in the process.[31] However, the choice of the term was not haphazard or unintentional. It was clearly chosen to communicate a highly specific freight of meaning.

Unfortunately, those writing under the influence of the Biblical Theology Movement, such as Ethelbert Stauffer and Gottfried Quell (and many others of that time),[32] tended to be content to draw a contrast between so-called Greek and more distinctly Christian understandings of love. They thus focused on *agape* as a general form of love, over against *eros*, *philia*, and *storgē*. This failed to take sufficient account of the fact that, as defined in the life and death of Jesus, *agape* was a highly specific love, and not of a general variety. Among the first generation of Christians, this form of self-giving was remembered, not *as* one of four different general kinds of loving, in the way that C. S. Lewis has unhelpfully led us to believe,[33] but precisely *as* the kind of loving that was remembered to have come to definitive expression in the life and death of *Jesus*.

In its early Christian use, *agape* was not used, in other words, as though it belonged in an abstract philosophical analysis of four aspects or species of the genus "love," but always with *an explicit historical reference*. It is at this point that Frei's contention that the attempt to distill a general quality of character from the specifics of the Jesus story has to be taken to heart. *Agape* is, indeed, in the first instance, the self-giving *of* the remembered *Jesus*. It is his life that was remembered for having given definitive expression to it. Far from being one of four species of the genus "love," it was remembered as the impressively distinctive and highly specific quality that was remembered to have been characteristic of Jesus' words and works and "lifted up in awful beauty on the Cross."[34] In order to communicate its meaning-content it is necessary to rehearse something, if not the whole, of the narrative story of Jesus' words and works through to his death on the Cross. In this way, the concept of *agape* was drawn upon to encapsulate something of the distinctive disposition of

---

31. See Stauffer, "Words for Love in Pre-Biblical Greek," in the entry for "ἀγαπάω, ἀγάπη, ἀγαπητός," by Quell and Stauffer, 35–38.

32. For example, Moffatt, *Love in the New Testament*, 35–40; and Richardson, "Love: Greek and Christian."

33. Lewis, *The Four Loves*. Generally speaking, Stauffer, Moffatt, Richardson, as well as Lewis, were all content to focus on *agapē* as a distinctively Christian (alleged) species of love, by contrast with Greek conceptions of love.

34. John Knox's felicitous phrase.

self-giving, faithful, and steadfast to the end, of the incidents and episodes of the story of the remembered Jesus.

Of course, in the process of remembering and celebrating something of the distinctiveness of *agape*, as it was remembered to have characterized the life of Jesus, analogies were dawn. 1 John speaks of it as a particular "quality of love,"[35] and then, going on to try to unpack something more of its distinctive character, draws on the analogy of a father's love for his children. The love of Christian experience was, for 1 John, a love which brought with it a sense of acceptance, reconciliation, and belonging of the kind that assures children not just of the fact that they are valued and loved by their fathers as persons in the present, but that also grounded the hope that they will share in an inheritance of the kind that fathers prepare for their children.[36] This, of course, once again follows in the tradition of St. Paul, who likewise drew on the same analogy. In speaking of the relation of the baptized Galatians to God in Christ that was created by the gift of the Spirit that bound them together in love, Paul affirms that they enjoyed the status of sons with God as Father: "God has sent the Spirit of his Son into our hearts crying 'Abba! Father!'"[37]

In describing the distinctive nature of the *agape* of Jesus, John also wrote that "no one has greater love than this":[38] there is "no greater love" than that exhibited in the laying down of life for one's friends. The self-sacrifice of the Cross is the definitive instantiation of the love remembered to have been defined in the person of Jesus: "We know love by this, that he laid down his life for us."[39] St. Paul, in Rom 5:5–8, had already taken it a step further. The love poured out into the hearts of Christian believers by the gift of the Holy Spirit, (v. 5) and concretely known, is "God's love." This is demonstrated not just in Christ's willingness to die for his friends, but in his willingness to die even for the ungodly: "God proves his love for us in that while we still were sinners Christ died for us" (v. 8). Jesus' death was not just for the close circle of his friends, but also for his enemies. Henceforward, any love expressing courageous self-sacrifice would be spoken of as "Christ-like." This is why the Cross features so centrally in the communication of the distinctive quality of the *agape* that was remembered to have been defined in the life of Jesus.

At the end of the day, however, as Frei correctly says, it is necessary to tell the whole Jesus story in order to communicate something of the distinctiveness of the quality of character that Jesus exhibited as his disciples remembered him. Indeed, if love is *self*-abnegating, *self*-sacrificing, *self*-giving, there are not just four kinds of

---

35. 1 John 3:1. Which we could translate: "See what quality of love the Father has given us . . ." The Greek word used is *agapēn*—the nominative singular form of *agapē*.

36. 1 John 3:2: "Beloved, we are God's children now; what we will be has not yet been revealed. What we do know is this: when he is revealed, we will be like him, for we will see him as he is."

37. Gal 4:6 and Rom 8:15–17; see also Mark 14:36.

38. John 15:13. Perhaps even with St. Anselm "a love than which none greater can be conceived"?

39. 1 John 3:16.

love, but as many different loves as there are *selves* to love and be loved, for every human self is unique. As Knox says, "love is not one of the attributes of the person; it is the person himself, going out to, and giving himself to, another."[40] Our self-giving is as unique as we are. As Søren Kierkegaard put it: "Spirit is the self. But what is the self? The self is a relation which relates itself to its own self."[41]

We now know it to be so that we are all unique human selves—both in genetic terms, and in terms of nurture, through the distinctive thread of a specific historical life, each self is unique; it is as unique human selves that we all give our*selves* uniquely. In so far as love is self-*giving*, it is a relation of the self with others that is only achieved through the self-determining self-gift of an individual self to another. This means that if *agape* is treated as a class name, it denotes a *unit class*; in its distinctive Christian use, it is the love that was remembered to have been definitively known in the historical life and death of a single, unique individual self: Jesus.

Perhaps, it is possible to tighten up the presentation of these insights, and clinch their veracity, by unpacking some additional aspects of the logical behavior of dispositional statements A useful distinction may be made between single-track or specific dispositions, and highly generic dispositions. Single-track dispositions are dispositions in which the verbs reporting occurrences that actualize and thus illustrate the disposition are determinate, and correspond closely to the words that express the disposition itself. For example, to describe a man as a cigarette smoker, implies that there will be particular occasions when he will be found smoking cigarettes. To describe a man as a baker means that there will be particular times when he will be found to be baking. By contrast, generic dispositions are expressed in disposition-concepts whose actualization cannot be described by employing only one verb, because they take a wide variety of shapes. Their actualizations are not determinate but, rather, are determinable. To describe a man as a grocer does not mean that on particular occasions he will be found to be "grocing," but that on particular occasions he will be found to be doing a great variety of things—in a former age, selling sugar, weighing butter, wrapping tea; today, stacking a shelf with pre-packaged items, or overseeing the check-out. Similarly, to describe a man as a solicitor does not mean that on particular occasions he will be found "solicitoring," still less "soliciting." Rather, on particular occasions he will be found to be drafting wills, drawing up tenancy agreements, or representing clients in court.

Now, as Gilbert Ryle has observed, the higher grade dispositions of people, particularly those describing qualities of character that are unique to a specific person,

---

40. Knox, *Life in Christ Jesus*, 10.
41. Kierkegaard, *Sickness unto Death*, 17.

are in general not single-track dispositions, but highly generic and determinable.[42] Their actualizations are, in other words, heterogeneous. For example, when Jane Austen sought to show the specific pride that characterized the heroine of *Pride and Prejudice*, she had to portray her words and deeds, her actions and reactions, in many, many different situations. This is because the disposition of pride is a generic or determinable one, which is actualized in an enormous variety of different situations and occurrences. There is no one standard word, action, or reaction that will adequately communicate the specific quality of the disposition concerned.

Now, love, as the self-giving of a specific person, is also a highly generic and determinable disposition. A wide range of actions and reactions are predictable from the description of a person as "supremely" or "uniquely" loving. These might include deeds, utterances, perhaps some characteristic body language, such as glances of a certain kind, reactions expressive of respect, steadfast loyalty, concern for others, and so on. Clearly, if *agape* is remembered as the specific self-giving of the human *Jesus*, it will signal not just a proneness to do a single thing, but things of many kinds. Thus, the total range of purported episodes and occurrences of the story of Jesus' life will be called upon to express something of the concrete quality of his remembered self-giving. This is why, in order to communicate something of what was remembered in relation to the church's memory of Jesus *himself*, resort has to be made to the rehearsal of the rich narrative tradition of Gospel stories about him, along with something of the way in which those close to him responded to him, so as to produce the composite of Jesus-and-his-significance found in the biblical texts. At the end of the day, the distinctively specific love that was remembered to have been expressed in the life of the remembered Jesus can *only* be communicated by rehearsing the accounts of purported episodes and incidents of the narrative traditions of the Gospel story, as instantiations of it.

In order to unpack the distinctive quality of it, the church therefore has systematically to rehearse all the purported incidents and episodes remembered to have been associated with Jesus. The normative role both of the gospels and epistles of the New Testament must together be taken into account in transmitting the remembered tradition about him for, both his purported words and actions, and the theological and christological significance these were originally understood to reveal, play a part in the transmission of the church's memory of *him*. The fact of the church's continuing memory of Jesus in general dispositional terms can only be expressed through a variety of incident and episode may help to account for the fact that the church has deemed all these documents to be authoritative.[43] Rather than going behind them to try to reconstruct a purely factual historical estimate of the human Jesus, free of theological and christological reflection relating to his significance (still less instead of

---

42. Ryle, *The Concept of Mind*, 44 and 114.

43. Rather than simply rely of considerations of date, apostolic claims to authorship, and general assessments of the "quality," both in literary terms and in relation to matters of content.

abandoning all interest in the historical person of Jesus altogether in favor of a "Christ of faith" encountered in the church's preaching or whatever), we may rest content to focus upon the collective or shared memory of Jesus-as-he-was-originally-interpreted from the perspective of his perceived theological significance. This composite of purported fact and its significance indeed communicates something of the uniquely distinctive way in which the church originally remembered *him*. This is the case even if details of the incidents illustrative of aspects of his teaching and character are open to dispute, and even if some of the stories are legendary. What is communicated through the composite Jesus-and-his-theological-significance is what is now found in the textual records as the authoritative means of expression of the uniqueness of the church's continuing corporately shared memory of Jesus.[44]

At the end of the day, the self-giving love of Jesus' *agape*, is a love of such kind that recourse to many words therefore became necessary even in order to come just a little way towards capturing the specific and highly distinctive quality of it. In one respect, this inability to capture it in mere words is due precisely to its specificity. It is like trying to describe the highly distinctive flavor of lychees or the way in which wine buffs notoriously resort to many words, images, and metaphors in their struggle to communicate something of the unique flavors of their wine-tasting—for example, the bouquet and rich depth of flavor of a Vasse Felix Margaret River shiraz. In the end, however, the difficulty of expressing the specific quality of Jesus' self-giving in mere words is not just because it was remembered specifically *as* the love or self-giving of the uniquely human self who was *Jesus*, but also because it was perceived in faith *as God's love* revealed in and through his uniquely remembered life, a transcendentally ineffable love, and thus a love that was *by definition* "beyond words."

The theological edifice can never expect to encapsulate the divine mystery in a few well-chosen, clear, and distinct formulations literally understood. What is asked of a theology of faith is to provide a sufficiently coherent indication about the nature of divine reality as to warrant claims to interpret and identify God's presence when it is actually empirically encountered. When the penny drops, the response of faith conforms to the model: "Aha, this is what they were trying to talk about!"

The same applies with regard specifically to resurrection faith, where the interpretation of experience is found in claims to recognize and know Jesus' living presence by employing such interpretative concepts as "the Spirit of life in Christ Jesus," "life-giving Spirit," and also the identifying use of the proper name "Jesus" as in references to the recognition in faith simply of the presence "of Jesus."

---

44. As I understand it, this is roughly equivalent to what James Dunn has in mind when he speaks of "Jesus remembered," though without Dunn's misplaced felt need to deny that "Jesus remembered" is "Jesus as he actually was."

However, the remembered picture we have of Jesus, and something of the distinctive quality of his character in the form of self-giving *agape*, does not have to be established as something which is linguistically clear and distinct, nor need it be secured with absolute historical certainty. Rather, what is said to have been uniquely remembered about Jesus simply needs to be sufficient to make it possible to use the proper name both referringly and identifyingly. The verbal expressions of this linguistic tradition may in fact be somewhat disorganized and vague, even fragmentary. However, even if it remains in some respects unclear and ambiguous, so long as it is sufficient to *point towards* the unique reality it seeks to describe, it will fulfill its epistemic function. In other words, as long as it at least points towards the specific person Jesus was remembered to have been, with sufficient clarity to allow for the recognition of the very same reality of his self-giving love or "life-giving Spirit" in the life and worship of the church, it will be adequate to the job it has to do. Once again, when the penny drops, the response is "Aha, this (concretely given reality with which I am now acquainted) is what they were talking about!" "This is no other than the life-giving Spirit of Jesus whom I now claim to know!" Ordinarily just a rough outline description when remembered is usually sufficient to enable an identification to be made. This is why it is possible to say, for example, "I knew it was Veronica Lake because of the lock of hair I remember her to have falling over one eye." Or, "I knew it was a Mercedes because of the distinctive three pointed star in a circle of its logo." Sometimes a single key-identifying characteristic may be sufficient to serve an identifying purpose and to allow a claim to knowledge. Clearly, the identification of a uniquely specific quality of character will call upon a much more complex set of indicators. While they do not have to be exhaustive, they need to be uniquely referring and thus sufficient to inspire confidence among those of faith who use them to warrant the claim to identify and recognize "the presence of the Raised Jesus."

This, then, is the essence of the continuing resurrection faith of Christians. If *agape* is remembered specifically as the distinctive self-giving of *Jesus*, this empirically perceived reality, that is known by acquaintance as the animating Spirit of the community of the baptized, is identified in faith *as* none other than Jesus himself, for to know the *self-giving* of Jesus is to know Jesus *himself, giving*. In this way, in resurrection faith we remember him whom we now know, and we know him whom we remember.

Finally, it is often the case that the actual experience of recognizing a person or place, so as to ground the claim of having met before or of being there before, brings the memory to the surface. Thus, while the possession of a memory is logically prior to the experience of recognizing and knowing, in the actual experience itself both remembering and knowing may, in temporal as distinct from logical terms, be coincidental. Recognition is often not a matter of first conjuring up a memory, and then running through a checklist of identifying characteristics, or comparing an image that is "before the mind's eye" with what is actually presenting itself. It is rather that we more intuitively recognize persons and places as persons and places that we *thereby* instantaneously remember. This puts us in the position to justify our identity claims by citing the remembered characteristics that warrant the claim. But in the actual experience itself, the actual encounter with some person or place triggers the instantaneous memory of it.

If the church's corporate or shared memory of Jesus is logically prior to claims to see and perceive and thus to know the presence of his "life-giving Spirit" now as the constitutive animating principle of its life, then a remembered identifying criterion is a logically prior requirement which can then be cited in justifying the claim. However, by the same token, the experience of encounter with the presence of the Raised Christ in faith in this way, in its turn may act to clarify the memory of him. Just as we identify people by reference to our memory of them, even though it may be a bit indistinct and "fuzzy," so the experience of actually meeting them again sometimes reactivates and sharpens the memory. Thus, in resurrection faith Christians justifiably claim to remember the Jesus whom they now in faith claim to know; but in so doing they remember him whom they now know, and what it was about him that was so memorable, a little more clearly. Faith is thus a response of remembering and therefore knowing, but with an element of reciprocity also between the knowing and therefore remembering.

It is not insignificant that in the scriptural tradition, the role of the actual experience of the Holy Spirit is therefore to bear witness to the Son[45] or to "declare what is of the Son."[46] Thus, while the memory of the historical person and the dispositional characteristics unique to his identification together facilitate the recognition of his living Spirit in Easter faith *as* the Spirit of the Raised Christ, the recognition of his living Spirit in faith in turn bears witness to the Son as he is remembered to have been. The current concrete experience of what is identified in faith as "the Spirit of the Raised Christ" clarifies what it was about him that was so memorable. Also, at the same time, the presence of Christ as a life-giving Spirit is experienced in such a way as to bear witness, or point, to his timelessly eternal status and role, theologically imagined as the one who, having offered for all time a single sacrifice for sins, now sits "at the right hand of God," eternally interceding in our behalf.[47] Thus, the experience of the Spirit almost automatically triggers a thrust towards the transcendental and heavenly. This is implicit in the earthly experience of the Spirit insofar as it triggered an awareness of its heavenly origin. If the Spirit that was perceived in faith was understood as the medium of Christ's continuing presence, it was also (in some sense of "was also") the medium of the presence of God.

---

45. Heb 10:15. Just as in Acts 5:32 Luke makes it clear that it is not just the apostolic band that 'bears witness" to Jesus' death and Resurrection, for the Holy Spirit itself "bears witness to these things."

46. John 16:14: "He will glorify me: for he will take what is mine, and declare it to you."

47. Heb 10:11–15.

As James Dunn aptly says, ". . . if the character of Christ had now defined the character of the Spirit, it was the Spirit *of God* which was so defined."[48]

In Paul's understanding of things, as a consequence of the resurrection, "God was now to be known definitively by reference to Christ."[49] This was because God was understood to have acted in such a way as to reveal himself and his character "most fully in terms of Christ." For Paul, the empirically encountered Spirit that was perceived in faith to be the Spirit of the Raised Christ is identical (in some sense of "identical") with the Spirit of God at work in him. Thus, if in the remembered Jesus we perceive a uniquely specific or, as Hans Frei put it, an "unsubstitutable" dispositional quality of character, which in turn enables the identification of the continuing presence of the Spirit of the Raised Christ by reference to that very same quality of character, then from henceforth, that same quality of character points us to the character of the eternal God.[50]

48. Dunn, *The Theology of Paul the Apostle*, 717 (my italics).

49. Dunn, *The Theology of Paul the Apostle*, 723; *Jesus and the Spirit*, 325: "In Paul . . . *the distinctive mark of the Spirit becomes his Christness. The charismatic Spirit is brought to the test of the Christ event*" (Dunn's italics). It is probably advisable to speak of the perception of the Spirit by reference to the "character" of Christ, rather than to speak of Christ as "the personality of the Spirit" (as Dunn unfortunately did in *Jesus and the Spirit*, 324–25). Out of deference to the church's later reflection on the personal identify of the Spirit, it may likewise to wise to avoid speaking of the "dual relationship—to God as Father, and to Jesus as Lord" and of the Spirit as making the first believers "conscious of this dual relationship" (*Jesus and the Spirit,* 326). Though Dunn is wary of the "speculative metaphysics" that allegedly "elaborated the experience of sonship into the doctrine of the Trinity" so that, in his view, "the net result has been more to retard the gospel than to advance it," an (Augustinian?) binitarian understanding of things is just as much a mater of "speculative metaphysics." As may be seen in the footnote immediately below, the doctrine of the Trinity may in fact pick up and positively advance aspects of the scriptural tradition relating to the identity and action of the Spirit that have tended to be overlooked.

50. It has to be said that the scriptural tradition that the Spirit bears witness to the Son, or "declares what is" of the Son (John 16.14) has not featured at all in the church's trinitarian theology of personal diversity within the essential singularity of God. This has unfortunately been to its detriment. Against a potentially noxious and troublesome binitarian understanding of things, which identifies the Spirit as the fellowship or love *between* the Father and the Son (as in Augustine), the Spirit has its own standing ground as a divine identity in the Spirit's own right. This is a basic reason why the Spirit is not just the Spirit *of* the Son, or the Spirit *of* the Father for that matter. But this has been difficult to secure theologically.

Thomas Aquinas correctly noted that some kind of "relation of opposition" was needed to distinguish the independent identity of the Spirit (*Summa Theologiae*, I.q.36.a2). Historically, trinitarian theology has found it incapable of getting beyond "relations of origin" (the Son being begotten of the Father, and the Spirit proceeding ineffably from the Father) as the only "relations of opposition." In the belief that "there cannot be any other opposed relations in God other than relations of origin," Aquinas therefore unfortunately proposed the *filioque*: the Spirit was said to proceed not only from the Father but also from the Son! (Though admittedly the divine Spirit's supposed origin in the Son served his purpose of securing the full divinity of the Son).

However, "relations of origin" are not the only thinkable "relations of opposition" within the Trinity. In the economy of salvation the divine self-giving Spirit has not just a protological character but an eschatological character: the Spirit "glorifies" and "fulfills," and otherwise accomplishes the good purposes of God—as is made clear, for example, in the ministry of Jesus (Matt 12:28) and in accomplishing his resurrection from the dead (Rom 1:4). Not least, the self-gifting role of the Spirit is seen

However, that said, if Christian faith in the Resurrection of Christ is a matter of knowing and identifying the continuing presence of Christ in the medium of his "life-giving Spirit" by reference to church's distinctive memory of him, what has become of the traditional belief in the "Resurrection of the Body?" It is clear enough in the New Testament tradition that the Raised Christ was not recognized by physical tokens of any kind. Indeed, while the New Testament traditions of the historical Jesus are concentrated exclusively on his uniquely remembered dispositional quality of character as this was exhibited in his manner of living, teaching, and relating to people, and especially in the manner of his dying, they show no interest at all in his physical appearance or bodily form. Likewise, the resurrection narrative traditions in particular, with the exception perhaps of the crucifixion wounds in the doubting Thomas story, contain no interest in accounting for his recognition by physical or bodily tokens—his bodily height, the color of his hair, and the shape of his nose are entirely irrelevant to Easter faith. It is almost as though physical make-up has no epistemic significance in securing faith in the Resurrection of Jesus, yet the Christian creedal conviction is nevertheless focused upon "the Resurrection of the Body." To this aspect of resurrection belief we shall now turn.

---

in relating the Raised Christ to his brothers and sisters in the eschatological community of faith and transforming their lives, as the down payment or guarantee of the Kingdom. In this way, the Spirit by being the Spirit, has an identifiable identity and role opposed to (or "over against") the other two triune identifies.

It is not possible here to pursue the details of a trinitarian theology of relations, but the scriptural insight concerning the Spirit's role in declaring what is of the Son (not only in John 16:14 but in Heb 10:11-15), invites the thought that the Spirit eternally shows the available and lovable Son to the Father, and the Father to the Son, not just as source or origin, but precisely *as* the available and lovable Father. Hence Robert Jenson, is able to say concerning the Spirit: "The Father and the Son love each other with a love that is identical with (the Spirit's) gift of himself to each of them" (*Systematic Theology*, I, 158). Jenson's whole discussion of these issues is refreshingly helpful, even if some of us entertain reservations with regard to his view of the temporality of God implicit in his notion of the Spirit as the "goal" or "fulfillment" of God. The alternative would be to think of the fulfilling role of the Spirit in the ultimate consummation of its "pouring out on all flesh" as the revealing (*apokalypsis*) in time of the ultimate sovereignty and good purposes of God from the essential timelessness of God's eternity.

11

The Resurrection of the Body

THE QUESTIONABLE METHODOLOGICAL DISTINCTION that was drawn in the second half of the twentieth-century by the theologians of the Biblical Theology Movement between what were alleged to be purely Greek modes of thought, on one hand, and authentically biblical ways of thinking, on the other, played out quite specifically in the drawing of an aggressively radical contrast between the ideas of the "immortality of the soul" and the "resurrection of the body."[1]

Behind this difference of viewpoint in relation to the ultimate fate of the dead, the theologians of the Biblical Theology Movement presupposed an equally clear opposition between Greek and Hebrew-Christian anthropological thought. Whereas the Greeks were said to have worked with a dichotomy between the respective notions of "body" and "soul" as identifiable constituent parts of human nature, the more "clearly biblical" understanding of things was said to have studiously avoided any hint of this kind of body/soul dualism, so as to think instead simply of "the total person" as a psychosomatic unity.

We now appreciate that this was clearly a mistake. Apart from the fact that Matthew presents Jesus himself as one who worked with a body/soul dualism (in Matt 10:28),[2] the difficulties facing those hell-bent on drawing a radical dichotomy between Greek and so-called biblical ways of thinking may also be illustrated by St. Paul, who was not averse to speaking of the whole human make-up in terms of "spirit and soul and body."[3] All three of these elements are to be preserved blameless "unto the coming of the Lord Jesus Christ" at the parousia. Certainly, Paul works with a body/soul dualism explicitly in relation to his understanding of the Resurrection. In his attempt to reduce the mystery of new life beyond death to manageable conceptual proportions, Paul worked with ideas that are in many ways remarkably resonant with a more characteristically Greek and clearly dualistic manner of speaking. Indeed, at

---

1. In the generation prior to N. T. Wright, this is most notable in the theology of Oscar Cullmann and Krister Stendahl.

2. "Do not fear those who kill the body but cannot kill the soul; rather fear him who can destroy both soul and body in hell."

3. 1 Thess 5:23.

this point Paul himself provides evidence of a kind of complementarity of thought, a typical example of the pervasive hybridization of Jewish/Hellenistic culture of his time, insofar as he had to face the challenge of incorporating popular notions of Greek origin into his inherited apocalyptic eschatology.

In 2 Cor 5, Paul speaks of the unavoidable "destruction" of the body at death,[4] and, in the face of it, affirms his Christian hope of being re-clothed with a new body by resurrection from the dead. In the course of this discussion, he speaks metaphorically of the body as an earthly "tent," perhaps drawing an image from his own tent-making profession,[5] but, almost certainly, in a way also suggested to him in contemporary linguistic conventions, not least those that are found in the Wisdom of Solomon with which he was apparently acquainted. Wisdom 9:15 reads: "a perishable body weighs down the soul, and this earthly tent burdens the thoughtful mind."[6] Even without this possible influence from Wisdom, there is already implicit in Paul's own words a distinction between an inner self and its outward "housing" in the body understood as a "tent."[7] Moreover, though we should not push the tent metaphor so as to wring more from it than it may have been intended to bear, it is certainly intimated that the earthly tent is understood not only as "temporary,"[8] but that at death it is to be replaced with a "heavenly" dwelling that is apparently much less temporary, if not the very opposite of temporary. Indeed, this new clothing is said to be "eternal in the heavens," being a body not made by human agency but miraculously provided by God. Clearly, for Paul we are not just body-soul unities, we are "clothed" with our bodies; we "inhabit" them. Ultimately, before the judgment seat of the returning Christ we will be judged according to what *we* have done *in* our earthly bodies.[9] Moreover, it was even possible for Paul to envisage the unwelcome fear of being left bereft of a new replacement (heavenly) body in lieu of the one destroyed by death. He expresses the anxiety of being

---

4. He speaks of it as a "dissolution" or, literally, "down-loosing" (2 Cor 5:1).

5. Acts 18:3. However, the convention of referring to the body as a "tent" was well established in the Hellenistic world as a way of emphasizing its temporary and insubstantial nature. Wisdom 9:15 is itself dependent upon Plato (*Phaedo* 81c; see also 88b). Philo, *Questions and Answers on Genesis* 1:28 actually says "the human or corporeal tabernacle (*skēnē*) is the combination of bones, and flesh, and entrails, and veins, and nerves, and ligaments, and blood-vessels, and breathing tubes, and blood."

See Aune, "Anthropological Duality," 225.

6. There are very close verbal parallels with 2 Cor 5:1–10. Alfred Plummer noted the verbal parallels with Plato's text in *Phaedo*. See Plummer, *Second Epistle of St Paul to the Corinthians*, 142.

7. In 2 Cor 4:16 Paul draws an antithesis between the "outer man" and the "inner man," the "outer man" being a way of referring to the physical body which is subject to disease, aging, and death, while the "inner man" seems fairly clearly a reference to the soul, though in *Rom* 7:22 it is used to refer to *nous*/mind. This is an equation common in Philo, who apparently obtained the concept of outer appearance and the inner constitution from Plato (*Republic* 9.588a–589b). Exactly how Paul acquired the phrase "inner man" is unknown, but it may well have been simply that he was influenced by popular forms of Platonism which thought in terms of an inner person and an outer person as a matter of course.

8. As in a booth or tabernacle.

9. 2 Cor 5:10. This is the one echo of apocalyptic thought in this passage.

found unclothed and, indeed, of being left naked should he perhaps fail to be provided with a new body. In the Hellenistic world, the concept of nakedness was regularly used precisely to speak of the soul when divested of the body.[10]

Clearly, there are traces of a dualistic understanding of human anthropology in this passage, and even an attempt to express belief in the resurrection of the body in a way that, perhaps unconsciously, resonates in at least some important respects with the idea of the immortality of the soul and its ultimate eternal destiny. C. F. D. Moule, possibly following an earlier discussion signaled by Michael Ramsey,[11] even went so far as to suggest that between 1 Cor 15 and 2 Cor 5 Paul changed his mind by abandoning the idea of "putting on" immortality—over the top of the mortal body, as it were—in favor of the even more dualistic view of "*exchanging*" the one for the other, the mortal for the immortal.[12]

I think it has to be admitted that a self-conscious "change of mind" may perhaps be claiming a little too much here.[13] If we allow that, in all this, Paul is engaging in speculative thought as he seeks to penetrate what he himself says is the "mystery" of life beyond the grave, then we should not expect a neat and systematic understanding of things. A fluid variety of expression is a more likely result. From Paul's point of view, in speaking of the resurrection body, he may have been resorting to various images and ways of expressing his point without too much regard for the logical tensions that modern analytic minds find in them. In any event, the point is sufficiently taken that in 2 Corinthians, Paul's language actually resonates with the characteristically Platonic, and thus originally Greek, idea of immortality of the kind that the Biblical Theology Movement mistakenly had us believe was entirely at odds with a biblical understanding of things.

Despite these Platonic resonances in 2 Corinthians it is clear that, in affirming their resurrection belief, Paul and the first generation of Christians were clearly not signing up to a belief in a permanently disembodied future state of a thoroughgoing Platonic kind. An alternative to thinking in fully-fledged Platonic terms of a "permanently disembodied future state" might actually have been to think of a form of resurrection belief understood as a re-clothing of the soul (or "inner self") with a new and much more radically transformed body. If we take Paul's emphasis on *different kinds* of bodies in 1 Cor 15 with seriousness, this would be an (obviously imagined) body of a kind

---

10. Even N. T. Wright himself acknowledges this. See Wright, *RSG*, 367. The idea of nakedness of the soul is found in Plato in *Gorgias* 524d; and *Cratylus* 403b; and also in the writing of Paul's contemporary Philo in nearby Alexandria in *On the Virtues*, 76; and *Allegorical Interpretation* 2:57 and 59.

11. See Ramsey, *The Resurrection of Christ*, 108.

12. Moule, "St Paul and Dualism: The Pauline Conception of Resurrection."

13. Ramsey concluded that "the argument for variations in Paul's belief has been unwarrantedly exaggerated" (*The Resurrection of Christ*, 108).

appropriate to an eternal heavenly existence with God, by contrast with a continued material existence of a physical kind in this world.[14] When Paul struggles in 1 Cor 15 to communicate some understanding of the nature of the resurrection body, he resorts to the analogy of a seed planted in the ground, which in a sense is dead and is buried, and then springs to new life. He declares loud and clear that what is sown a "physical" body is raised a "spiritual" body.[15] This, at the very least, suggests that the resurrected body is different from our present bodies, and that between the body of this "earthly tent," and the body of "eternal heavenly dwelling," a radical and transformative change has occurred. Once again, the logical implications of a metaphorical image cannot, of course, be pushed too far, but Paul's image of a seed is not really amenable to the idea that what is produced from it after its burial in the ground is just its own restoration still as a seed, though now made "incorruptible." It is not somehow just made harder and stronger and more resistant to disease and decay than before. Rather, the flourishing new life produced from the seed is a radically different form of new botanical life. Clearly, in seeking to penetrate the mystery of resurrected life in Christ, Paul is grappling with concepts of continuity through change, but with a heavy emphasis on change and transformation.

In announcing the Gospel of Jesus Christ, at the beginning of the Epistle to the Romans, Paul identifies Jesus as one who was "descended from David according to the flesh and was declared to be Son of God with power according to the spirit of holiness by resurrection from the dead."[16] We note the juxtaposition of "flesh" and "spirit" in this passage, as tokens of natural life on one side of the Cross, and what characterizes the new resurrected life of the Raised Christ on the other. Also noteworthy is the very important suggestion that the Spirit was operative in the raising of Jesus from the dead. Elsewhere it is also made clear that the same "life-giving Spirit," or "Spirit of life in Christ Jesus," that was known in faith as a transformative power in the lives of the baptised, was day-by-day preparing them for their own ultimate resurrection as well.[17]

In 2 Cor 4–5, Paul therefore envisages that the power of God in this life is to prepare believers for the ultimate transformation of their bodies beyond death. In this case, one might be forgiven for assuming that the bodily transformation wrought by the Spirit is

---

14. As in the detailed eschatology of N. T. Wright in *RSG*, which expresses his preference for the physical and material incorruptibility of the Raised Jesus restored to *this* world, as against the eternal immortality of the Raised Christ exalted to heaven. See the detailed critique of this in Carnley, *Resurrection in Retrospect*, chapter 10.

15. 1 Cor 15:44.

16. Rom 1:3–4.

17. 2 Cor 4:16. Just as the *ruach* of God is the agent of creation in Gen 1, and is the operative power in the restoration sequence of the valley of dry bones in Ezek 37.

to be understood in the first instance in ethical and spiritual terms so that, by working in their earthly lives, the Spirit might help them conform more nearly to the pattern of Christ in a way appropriate to the future life of sharing with him in the immortality of God. In other words, the gift of the Spirit may be intended both to prepare the baptized in moral and spiritual terms for life in a world beyond this one, and ultimately for the ontological transformation of their physical bodies into something appropriate to that heavenly existence. Hence, the final outcome would be a radically transformed "spiritual body" that enjoys continuity with the "natural" or "physical body" of this earthly life, but is nevertheless radically different from it.

This is an understanding of things that is congruent with what Paul said in his famous statement in 1 Cor 15:44: "It is sown a physical body; it is raised a spiritual body." For many, this seems to suggest a form of resurrection belief not dissimilar to belief in the immortality of the soul at least insofar as the righteous dead may be said to enjoy an eternal heavenly life of immortality with God, but in which they are not stripped of a body (as in classical Platonic schemas) but are reclothed with a new *pneumatically* transformed body appropriate to heavenly life.

From N. T. Wright's perspective, however, the contrary is the case: it is a mistake to think that the role of the Spirit is to transform the earthly body of flesh and blood into a "spiritual body" understood as the non-material antithesis of a "physical" or natural body. If, at face value, Paul's statement in 1 Cor 15:44 seems to suggest the "putting on" of a heavenly body over a physical body (or in 2 Cor 5, the replacement by exchange of a physical body for a new spiritual body), this meaning appears to be reiterated when, a few verses later, Paul also says that "flesh and blood cannot inherit the kingdom of God."[18] However, the interpretation of this text is not at all clear. As we shall see, if we follow N. T. Wright's reading of it, what appears to be the case at face value may not be the only way to understand it.

Wright is certainly anxious to read 1 Cor 15:44 differently. He points out that, when Paul talks of a "spiritual body" he is not referring to the substance of which the body is composed; nor should we say that he is suggesting *a lack* of material substance, and its replacement with something "spiritual." It is a mistake, in other words, to think of what is described as "spiritual" as something non-material or heavenly. In making this point, Wright insists that the adjective *pneumatikon* is used to describe "not what something *is composed of*, but what it is *animated by*,"[19] and further that Greek words ending in "*-ikos/-ikon*" generally "have ethical or functional meanings rather than referring to the material or substance of which something is composed."[20] For Wright, a "spiritual

---

18. 1 Cor 15:50.
19. *RSG*, 352; Wright's italics.
20. *RSG*, 351.

body" is therefore not composed of something called "spirit"; it is *animated by* the Spirit. Likewise, a natural or "physical" (*psychikon*) body is not composed of physical earthly matter, but is a body animated by or directed by the *psyche* (soul).

Moreover, Wright proffers the contention that when Paul declares a few verses later that "flesh and blood cannot inherit the kingdom of Heaven,"[21] he is not speaking in ontological terms, so much as in historical terms. He is aware that the eschatological End could come before his own death, even while he, and those whom he addresses, are still living. Paul's point is that it is thus not just the dead, but still living "flesh and blood" who will necessarily therefore be transformed and caught up with Christ at the Eschaton.[22] Even the living cannot enter the Kingdom of God, in other words, without the impact of transformative change. But, despite the language of "being caught up," Wright's point is that change is not a change from physical to a non-physical or heavenly form. It is not, in other words, that they will leave "flesh and blood" behind. Rather, the transformation of perishable, corruptible physicality is a transition to "the future world of non-corruptible physicality."[23]

In order to reach this conclusion, N. T. Wright correctly observes that when Paul speaks of a "spiritual body," as distinct from a "physical body,"[24] what is primarily meant is a "spirit directed" body, rather than just a "soul directed" body. Just as the natural body is directed by the inner soul (*psyche*), so the raised body will be directed by the Spirit (*pneuma*). It is at this point that Paul draws upon the Adam/Christ typology. Just as "the first man, Adam, became a living soul (*psyche*); [so] the last Adam has become a life-giving Spirit (*pneuma*)."[25] Indeed, Paul's understanding was that this transformative process had already begun for those who had died with Christ in baptism, and who had received the gift of the Spirit. Even in the course of their earthly existence, the Spirit was at work in their material lives, day-by-day changing them in a way that was promissory of an ultimate fulfilment in the form of continued transformation beyond death. Wright is anxious to say, therefore, that a "Spirit directed" or a "Spirit informed" body is not a body made of some kind of vaporous spiritual substance. The misleading translation of *sōma psychikon* as a "physical body" by contrast with a "spiritual body" (*sōma pneumatikon*) should therefore be avoided in favour of more ethical categories.

The same point is made by Richard Hays, who notes that "the phrase *psychikon soma* is notoriously difficult to translate into English, and that the NRSV translation ('physical body') is especially unfortunate," given that ". . . *psychikon* certainly does not mean 'physical.'"[26] Rather, Paul's point is that "our mortal bodies embody

---

21. 1 Cor 15:50.
22. *RSG*, 359: "The referent of the phrase is not the presently dead but the presently living . . ."
23. *RSG*, 359.
24. 1 Cor 15:44.
25. 1 Cor 15:45.
26. Hays, *First Corinthians*, 272.

the *psyche* ('soul'). This is the animating force of our present existence, but the resurrection body will embody the divinely given *pneuma* ('spirit')."[27] Thus, the *sōma pneumatikon* is not a body made of spirit, so much as a body determined by, or directed by, the Spirit. Hays is therefore anxious to say that the Pauline contrast between *psychikon* and *pneumatikon* is not to be understood to reinstate the dualistic dichotomy between physical and spiritual.

However, whereas Hays nevertheless says that the effect of "Spirit directedness" is that the body associated with the Raised Christ "will be immortal and stamped with the image of 'the man of heaven,'"[28] Wright insists that the animating and transformative work of the Spirit, which is already known in its preparatory activity in this world, does not make the body more "god-like," in the sense of "spiritual" or "heavenly," and thus immortal. Instead, the Spirit makes the body even more substantial, and thus "incorruptible."[29] This means, however, that it is not *just* that the Spirit animates the body, or directs it in an ethical and moral sense, for it does impact upon what it is *composed of* after all!

In other words, Wright argues, somewhat surprisingly, that the effect of the life-transforming Spirit is to make the resurrected body "more substantial, more solid, more what a human being was made to be, as a result of the preparatory work that is already being accomplished through the Spirit."[30] The transformative work of the Spirit is to make the resurrected body more material, in the sense of transforming it into material that is resistant to, or not susceptible to, corruption. It is the role of the life-giving Spirit to ensure that the resurrected bodies of the dead are ultimately composed of material that is incorruptible in the sense of imperishable. Unfortunately, this puts paid to Wright's thesis that "*-ikos/-ikon*" words have an ethical and moral sense rather than an ontological one.

There is clearly a good deal of confusion in all this. If anything, one would have thought that the gift of the Spirit would prepare people, morally and spiritually, not in some transformed material or physical sense for a continuing life in this world, but by making them more loving, more just, more morally wholesome, more graciously open and welcoming to others, and thus (morally and spiritually speaking) more heavenly or "God-like" as a preparation for eternal life "with the immortal God."

Moreover, it is clearly a mistake to think that the impact of the Spirit is *purely* ethical or moral in Paul's thought. The ancient world did not compliantly conform to the departmental demarcations that distinguish the study of ethics from biology in a modern university. It is also clear, even to us today, that ethical and moral decisions

27. Hays, *First Corinthians*, 272.
28. Citing 1 Cor 15:48–49.
29. *RSG*, 355: "The whole argument runs in the opposite direction not only to Philo but to all kinds of Platonism ancient an modern. The point is not to escape from earth and find oneself at last in heaven. But to let the present 'heavenly' life change the present earthly reality."
30. *RSG*, 367.

do have a physical impact on the body: a dissolute life is liable to become a life cut short in physical terms; the sin of gluttony has a cardiovascular impact on the body of a negative kind; excessive consumption of alcohol has a propensity to destroy the liver and to addle the brain, and so on. Certainly, it appears to have been clear to Paul that the impact of the Spirit in a "spirit-directed life" has a transformative bodily impact of an ontological kind *for good*. Indeed, it is exactly at this point in Paul's discourse, as he speaks of the ultimate heavenly outcome of the impact of the Spirit on human life, that Paul declares that "flesh and blood" alone "cannot inherit the kingdom of God." One can imagine the preparatory work of the Spirit being known through empirically experienced ethical and spiritual gains; it is hard to imagine preparatory experiences that are said to be "on the way" simply to a more robust and ultimately incorruptible physicality. Even so, in Wright's understanding of things, a body raised to new life and indwelt by the animating Spirit of God becomes physically and materially "more solid and substantial" as a result.

When Paul declared that "flesh and blood" cannot inherit the Kingdom of God, it is true that he was well aware that the day of resurrection and final judgment might come in his own lifetime and, at that point, it was not just the dead but those still living as well who would undergo bodily transformation. At that time, "we will *all* be changed." However, just *how* the body was to be transformed remained for Paul as it is for us, an unexplained mystery. That is why the best he can do is draw upon analogies from nature, most notably on the metaphor of a seed, and the new life of a plant that is continuous with, but quite different in form from, the seed itself. When he goes further to speak of different *kinds* of bodies, he speaks of animal bodies, celestial bodies, and bodies that, like the stars, shine with glory. He does not appear just to be thinking of the old body refurbished and restored like a piece of antique furniture, and returned to its original sitting room. Even so, Paul is clearly at a loss for words to express the mystery of the body's ultimate transformation by the "life-giving Spirit" of Christ.

Two things are quite clear. First, Paul is unequivocally certain of the impact of the Spirit as the agent of change and bodily transformation. Second, a pneumatically transformed body will be a body appropriate to its new heavenly status:

> The first man was from the earth, a man of dust; the second man is from heaven. As was the man of dust, so are those who are of the dust; and as is the man of heaven, so are those who are of heaven. Just as we have borne the image of the man of dust, we will also bear the image of the man of heaven.[31]

---

31. 1 Cor 15:47–49.

If we free ourselves from attachment to the concept of material and physical "incorruptibility" as the outcome of a purely material or physical transformation, then the alternate suggestion would be that the Spirit's role is to prepare the body both ethically and spiritually (and ultimately ontologically) for immortality with God. It is the animation and direction of the body by the Spirit, which starts in this world with baptism into Christ, which prepares believers to be "inheritors of the kingdom of God" with him. However, from N. T. Wright's point of view, this more heavenly, "spiritual" alternative, would, lamentably, be too close for comfort to an unwelcome Platonic outcome, involving a leaving of this world for an eternal life with God. To Wright's mind, the resurrected life of Christ, and the eschatological life of all the righteous (including both those still living along with all the departed), must be conceived as a life physically restored to *this* world in a very concrete material sense. Thus, the final outcome is that the resurrected body is to be diametrically opposed to the idea of an immediate resurrection of individuals at death to a timelessly eternal immortal life in the eternity of God.

In arguing that Jesus' earthly physical body was reconstituted at the resurrection and made "incorruptible," Wright resorts, as to a kind of repeated mantra, to declare that Jesus' body was "*transformed*, not abandoned."[32] Likewise, in making his point about the alleged "incorruptibility" of Jesus' resurrected body, Wright also insists that the whole of Jesus' body was involved in this transformative process, leaving the tomb entirely empty—for the body was not abandoned but transformed. Once again, Wright is allowing a Platonic ogre to inhabit the sub-text here. In his use of the slogan "transformed, not abandoned," Wright almost certainly has in mind the idea of the abandonment of the body by the soul, as in the full blown Platonic way of thinking in which, at death, the body is actually left behind in this world as the soul "escapes" to immortality. We have already noted, in Wright's alternative interpretation of 1 Cor 15 and 2 Cor 5, the transformative processes which are alleged to have made Jesus' body "incorruptible" are being contrasted not just with the idea of the "immortality of the soul," but also with an alternative understanding of the resurrection body as of a non-material or heavenly kind. Even so, Wright believes that any notion of the transformation of the body in the direction of making it more "heavenly," rather than "earthly," and more material (such as might be suggested, for example, by saying that the exalted body of the Resurrected Christ was "exchanged" for his earthly body) is unacceptable. Even Paul's language of "exchange" in 2 Cor 5 might inevitably lead us to think of the "abandonment" of the mortal in order to take on immortality. However, for Wright, resurrection is not a matter of the exchange of the mortal for the immortal. In no way might it suggest the "abandonment" of the mortal body.

---

32. See, for example, *RSG*, 230.

Rather, a "transphysical" restoration means that the physical and historical body is itself reconstituted to become resistant to decay, thereby being rendered incorruptible and capable of everlasting life in this continuing world, never to die again. Nothing is abandoned. The transformation of resurrection is "without remainder."

What are we to make of this denial of "abandonment" in favor of the affirmation of the physical transformation of the body, as though these terms were polar opposites? First, we may, of course, wish to avoid the full-blown Platonic idea of the "immortality of the soul" with its suggestion that the body is simply "written off" as of no worth. But, on the other hand, if we dare to think of the resurrection of all the faithful at the Eschaton (which Jesus' Resurrection was understood to have anticipated) as a re-clothing by the provision of essentially new, glorified, and exalted bodies, in some ineffable way more suited to the conditions of eternal life with God, it would be possible also to think of some physical remains being left behind in graves. Clearly, the logic of this kind of transformation, as distinct from simply making their restored material bodies "incorruptible," does not need to insist that the entire process is achieved "without remainder." This is particularly so if we pick up Paul's language of *exchanging* the old for the new in 2 Cor 5 for, in this case, the mortal body that is "destroyed" at death could possibly be understood to return to dust at the time of the exchange. However, this would necessarily fall under condemnation by Wright as a kind of "abandonment."

We have to assume that it would have been as clear to Paul as it is to us today, that dead bodies do normally corrupt and return to the dust, just as we do mean what we say at funerals today when bodies are committed to the earth with the words "ashes to ashes; dust to dust." The common practice in the ancient world of gathering remaining bones for safe-keeping in ossuaries indicates that it must have been well-known that any "re-clothing" of the righteous dead must take account of this apparent "abandonment" of those bodily remains that return to the dust.[33] If we are prepared to think of life beyond death as a resurrection of a body that is in some way exalted and glorified, and *exchanged* for the body of "flesh and blood" that clearly normally decays in the grave, we would be logically obliged to say that what remains of the mortal body has in a sense been "abandoned." The residual physical remains in the grave would themselves be indicators of such "abandonment." The other side of the penny, once resurrection belief is conceived in terms of heavenly transformation of the body by exchange and re-clothing, is that some kind of "abandonment" is hard to avoid.

Indeed, if the residual remains of the righteous dead can be found and identified, while we continue to entertain the resurrection hope that they will be re-clothed with some kind of heavenly and immortal body in the eternity of God, then a kind of abandonment seems not only congruent with this, but logically inevitable. Yet this does not inhibit resurrection belief among contemporary Christians. It should be

---

33. Anthony Harvey usefully discusses the significance of bones in "They discussed among themselves what this 'rising from the dead' might mean."

emphasized that, whilst talk of a "glorification" and "exaltation" of the body, and of its going to immortality "with God," suggests this understanding of things, such ideas are clearly different from original Greek notions of the "immortality of the soul" in the sense that the soul is said to enjoy an entirely disembodied existence. Once again, however, this nevertheless falls under Wright's condemnation of "abandonment" and is for him no great advance on the Platonic idea of the immortality of the soul. Thus, even if a nuanced attempt is made to imagine the resurrection of the body as a new creation, rather than the old creation refurbished, it is open to being condemned as an "abandonment, not a transformation." Thus, while many contemporary Christians would want to speak of their resurrection belief in terms both an "abandonment *and* a transformation," this is for Wright strictly an either/or.

We have to question, however, why we should necessarily think of "abandonment" in such an entirely negative way, and why "abandonment" must always be diametrically opposed to "transformation," in the way that Wright's mantra "transformed, not abandoned" suggests. Let us first address the pejorative and negative connotations of Wright's use of the language of "abandonment."

Even as we live our lives in this world, we necessarily *do* abandon elements of our bodies constantly as we grow and mature. Every time we visit a barber we abandon some part of what was formerly integral to our physical constitution. This kind of abandonment is usually understood as an enhancement. Likewise, when fingernails are cut, parts of our physical bodies are consciously abandoned and consigned to the dustbin. But these very obvious minor and entirely humdrum illustrations of "physical abandonment" are simply day-by-day tokens of the more radical abandonment of quite significant parts of our bodies as we grow and develop: wisdom teeth, tonsils, appendix, parts of organs affected by cancerous growths, gall bladders, kidneys, often thyroids, and even limbs and other body parts sometimes have to be abandoned in the course of a human life in the interests of a person's earthly survival—if survival only for a time.

Moreover, at a microscopic level, from day-to-day abandoned somatic cells are regularly replaced through the active agency of stem cells, so that we might continue to live. In every second of the life of a living body, blood cells are reproduced in their millions, precisely to replace cells that are just as rapidly abandoned to the elements and lost. Likewise, a principle of regular abandonment cannot be avoided when it is known that eyebrows renew themselves every sixty-four days, or that the surface of the cornea is covered in a thin layer of cells that is continually renewed, with a complete turnover every seven to ten days, and this is not to mention the replacement of ten percent of bodily fat each year. Even an organ such as the brain, which was formerly thought not to contain stem cells, is today understood to be far more plastic than was imagined even a decade ago.[34] In more recent times, it has been discovered that even bones are "turned over" in terms of their composition—this despite the ancient world's respect for bones as the most enduring bodily structure. It is sometimes said, though this may be something of an exaggeration, that every seven years almost our entire cellular structure is replaced through the regular abandonment of somatic cells and their replacement.

That the shedding of somatic cells is a constant process in the course of life is also plain to many of us who are only too aware of the wrinkly outcome of aging. Stem cells attend to their replenishment, for a time at least, but eventually the body has to admit defeat. Indeed, the aging process can be understood as the gradual failure of the body to keep up with the reproduction of a cellular structure that is in an inexorable process of systematic abandonment. Hence the contemporary quest to seek to reduce serum myostatin levels that in recent years has apparently become a focus of interest of the medical research community with respect to the process of aging. Wright's insistence that the resurrected physical body will become no longer subject to corruption, and will therefore never die, may perhaps be thought to embody the ultimate physical answer to this modern medical problem.

In any event, all this means that we should probably think of the physical body in much more fluid and less static and substantial ways than we are normally prone to do. Given our fundamental subjective awareness of bodily continuity through time, we tend to over-look the hard truth that the body is in fact much more plastic than we are regularly prepared even to imagine. So, the point for the moment is that the physical body, even in life, is much more subject to processes of change and replacement than might ordinarily enter our consciousness. Change, and to some degree decay, involving the abandonment of elements of our physical makeup, is a regular part of the life processes of living organisms. In order to have life we must, as Jesus said, be prepared to "lose it"—or, dare we say, abandon it? It therefore cannot simply be assumed that the word "abandonment" must always be interpreted in the pejorative way that N. T. Wright employs it, simply by associating it with negative Platonic overtones of "escape" from the body. Still less are we obliged to think of the abandonment of much of our bodily make-up as a kind of Gnostic devaluing of the body.

In purely logical terms, this means we are not obliged to accept Wright's use of the concept of "abandonment" as the simple polar opposite of "transformation." As we live our lives, our bodily transformation for good or ill relies upon the abandonment of much of what we have formerly been. In the midst of life we are in death, in the sense that daily components of our bodies are literally dying; indeed, we have to die to what we once were, by surrendering much of our physical make up in routine abandonment, in order to live.

---

34. See Doidge, *The Brain that Changes Itself*.

It follows that the transformation of a body may indeed involve some element of abandonment at death, no less than it does in the course of living. In the course of life the physical body changes, and the changes to which the body is subject in the course of a human being's existence involve both abandonment *and* transformation. Clearly, this is not the either/or that Wright assumes. The fact that the physical remains of human bodies are patently abandoned in graves does not necessarily mean that resurrection belief is no longer possible; nor does it mean that it is not possible imaginatively to conceive a post-mortem bodily transformation at the creative hand of God in a way that involves our re-clothing with a new and different kind of body appropriate to an immortal, heavenly existence—the *exchange* of the mortal for the immortal.

Some kind of abandonment seems implicit in the language used by Paul himself in the important passage 2 Cor 4:16—5:10. In 2 Cor 5:1, he seems to accept the destruction of the body as an item of uncontested knowledge that he shared with those to whom he wrote, for the body that is destroyed at death is compared with the destruction of a house.[35] Now, it is significant that in referring to the body in this context Paul does not employ the word *sōma*, but simply relies upon the image of a house. However, though elsewhere *sōma* tends to be used specifically with reference to the resurrection body,[36] in this passage of 2 Corinthians he goes on to use *sōma* for the body of earthly mortal existence. In 2 Cor 4:10, he speaks positively that "the life of Jesus may also be made visible in our bodies (*sōmati*)," even while being aware of the disadvantage that the body imposes, for by being "at home in the body (*sōma*)" he was "away from the Lord."[37] In the one eschatological allusion in this passage,[38] it is declared that at the ultimate judgment actions done in the body (*sōma*) will be taken to account. The suggestion here is that, in the course of the historical earthly existence of the body, there is some tension between soul and body, but this is not the radical antagonism found in Platonism.

However, when Paul comes to speak of the death of the body, *soma* is displaced by an alternative. This is the image of the temporary and insubstantial tent—*skēnē*[39]—that has a pathetic sense of the ephemeral and transient nature of the physical body that is not normally part of the meaning of *sōma*. This is the body that is destroyed at death. When this happens, the original inhabitant of the body has to vacate, as when a house is destroyed, so as to occupy a new, in this case heavenly, abode. The sense of Paul's

---

35. The same verb (*katalusō*) used by Paul to refer to the destruction of the body was commonly used of the demolition of buildings. See also *Mark* 13:2 and 14:58.

36. As, for example, in 1 Cor 15:50–57 and Phil 3:20–21.

37. 2 Cor 5:6 and 8.

38. 2 Cor 5:10.

39. Or *skēnos*.

protasis/apodosis is that *when* death happens, *then* something much more acceptable immediately follows.[40] This passage holds no joy for those wedded to the idea of an intermediate state. Paul's sense is that the transition from earthly tent to heavenly abode is immediate. On the other hand, Paul does not seem to have been over-concerned about suggesting that when this happens, one body (tent), with its sense of the ephemeral and transient, is abandoned or left behind in order to take possession of another, which Paul elsewhere spoke of the resurrected body (*sōma*), as in 1 Cor 15:50–57 and Phil 3:20–21. For Paul, the idea was that the house, the physical body, would be destroyed at death, not just that it would be renovated or re-furbished.

The very same language may be found in 2 Peter 1:13–14, where the author is conscious of being in the earthly "body" (*skēnōmati*). He actually says that the "abandonment" or "putting off" of his body (*skēnōmatos*) in death will be imminent "as indeed our Lord Jesus Christ has made clear to me." These cognates of *skēnē* carry its same transient and ephemeral connotations. It seems clear that resurrection faith may legitimately think in terms of both abandonment of the body *and* its transformative replacement.

Interestingly enough, St. Paul stands at the beginning of a long tradition of thinking about the nature of the resurrection of the body that distinguishes it from the mere restoration of physical flesh and bones, whether made incorruptible or otherwise. This theological tradition thinks of the fate of the dead in terms both of abandonment *and* transformation.

We must therefore return to Paul's forthright declaration that "flesh and blood cannot inherit the kingdom of God, nor does the perishable inherit the imperishable."[41] It has already been noted that N. T. Wright interprets this parallelism to mean that those who were still present and living in corruptible "flesh and blood" at the time of the arrival of the Eschaton, possibly including Paul himself, would also be transformed, along with those who had already died.[42] The sense is that the present-day living "flesh and blood" of Paul's own time cannot inherit the kingdom of heaven without also being changed. Wright's point therefore is that it is not a categorical statement that contrasts physical or natural, earthly humanity with a transformed heavenly humanity by suggesting that "flesh and blood" would be left behind and

---

40. See the very compelling exposition of this by David E. Aune, "Anthropological Duality," 223: "The formulation of the protasis leaves no room for the possible occurrence of the parousia." Paul's sense is that physical death awaits everyone, but for the believer at death, the inhabitant vacates one dwelling to take up residence in another. Also, see the earlier observations of Windisch, *Der Zweite Korintherbrief*, 159.

41. 1 Cor 15:50.

42. A point originally made by A. M. Ramsey, though with regard to 2 Cor 5 rather than 1 Cor 15, in Ramsey, *The Resurrection of Christ*, 108.

replaced by an *altogether different* kind of body. Nor is it that the corruptible flesh and blood of those still living would inherit the kingdom of heaven untransformed. Rather, Wright's point is that those still living would have their corruptible "flesh and blood" transformed into incorruptible flesh and blood. One kind of physicality would thus be exchanged for another kind of physicality. In this case, "flesh and blood" will no longer be subject to "the infirmities of the flesh."

However, it has to be remembered that Paul's declaration that "flesh and blood cannot inherit the kingdom of God" is found in the general context of his spirited attempt to express something of the transformative impact of resurrection on the body in 1 Cor 15, in which he stresses the *difference* between earthly and heavenly bodies. Rather than contrasting the physical flesh and blood of living humanity, which is subject to degeneration and death, with a "new type of physicality,"[43] belonging to the future time of the inheritance of the kingdom of God in this earthly realm, an alternate reading of 1 Cor 15:50 is therefore nevertheless possible, and I think, in fact, preferable. In making this declaration about the ultimate fate of "flesh and blood," Paul may in fact be drawing an ontological contrast precisely between the "resurrection of the body" and the perishable flesh and blood that is in fact "destroyed" or "dissolved" at death, as he so clearly says in 2 Cor 5:1.[44] In other words, a valid contrast may be being drawn between the corruptible "flesh and blood" that does not inherit the kingdom of God, and the "transformed body" that does.

Now, it is pertinent to note that the Hebrew Old Testament has no equivalent word for "body" as a living reality. It speaks of the dead corpse, and of the living *flesh (and blood)*, but not of the living "body." The absence of a clear view of the afterlife, except in terms of the hope of living on in one's descendants, is to some degree explained by the fact that the ancient Hebrews knew as well as we do that the flesh returns to the dust from which it was made. The living flesh and blood of descendants bearing the familial likeness that we today ascribe to genetic inheritance was all there was. Likewise, when Ezekiel in Exile delivered his prophecy about the restoration of Israel, it is not insignificant that he had to resort to the imagery of the dry *bones*.[45] The persistent respect accorded to the bones of the deceased, the preservation of bones in small stone ossuaries, and the care taken not to break them, probably speaks of the importance of bones in the developing hope that God might reverse the brute fact of physical corruption and decay. But, by contrast with the persisting bones, flesh and blood quite simply disappeared into the dust.

Given the absence of the concept of the "body," the belief in the resurrection "of the body" was necessarily slow to develop, and even then, in Maccabean times, the first resurrection hopes, grounded in a firm conviction of the justice of God, were often expressed in terms of the restoration of the physical remains, literally in terms

---

43. *RSG*, 357–8.
44. Where the word is *kataluthē*, literally "down loosed" or demolished.
45. Ezek 37. Only the bones of the dead remained after the flesh and blood had long since gone.

of flesh and blood, as in the story of Razis.[46] An echo of this kind of belief may be found in Acts 2:27, quoting Psalm 16: "*My flesh* also will dwell in hope. For you will not abandon my soul to Hades, or let your Holy One see corruption."

It is enormously significant that these emerging ideas of resurrection are coincident with the Hellenization of Jewish culture. At the same time, it is fairly clear that the use of the Greek concept "*sōma*/body" is itself a new import that filled the void in early Hebrew language and culture. That it was freely imported into the LXX translation of the Old Testament where there is no Hebrew equivalent can be very clearly demonstrated.[47] This is particularly so with respect to the LXX translation of Job, where the translators pepper the text with the use of *sōma* even in cases where there is no Hebrew word to translate. Apart from this, *sōma* appears sparingly in the Old Testament books until the apocryphal books of the Hellenistic period, such as Wisdom, where its use begins to flourish. Curiously, the Biblical Theology Movement, in its attempt to distance so-called Greek ways of thinking from Hebrew-Christian ways of thinking, recoiled from the allegedly alien concepts both of "immortality" and of the "soul," but did not realize that the concept of the "body," as the other side of the body/soul dualism, was equally a characteristically Greek concept! Paul is a direct heir of the Hellenistic origin of the concept of *sōma* in his articulation of belief in the "resurrection of the body."

From this perspective, 1 Cor 15:50 is not to be used to suggest that Paul did not believe in the resurrection of the *body*, but rather to suggest that the resurrection of the body is to be understood as distinct from the resurrection of *flesh and blood*. It is not a surprise that he says "flesh and blood" cannot inherit the kingdom of God, for Paul believes in "the resurrection of the *body*." If "flesh and blood" refers to the present living humanity of Paul's own time, that is precisely the old humanity whose life is characterized by corruptible physicality, contrasted not with an alleged non-corruptible physicality in a new phase of historical time to come, but rather with humanity made immortal in the eternity of God.

In promoting the idea of the "resurrection of the body," the first Christians were in fact drawing upon a concept distinct from the characteristic Hebrew reliance on the concept of the flesh. Wright often speaks of Paul's ability to retain his authentically Jewish intellectual identity, even in the face of the highly Hellenized environment which badgered him on all sides. However, Wright fails to acknowledge that in fact Paul's appeal to the idea of the resurrection of the *body* (as distinct from the "flesh and blood" of which perishable bodies are composed) could only have been made because he was in fact heir to this very Hellenistic influence. In declaring that "flesh and blood cannot inherit the kingdom of God" and "nor does the perishable inherit the imperishable," Paul actually stands apart from his inherited Old Testament tradition. Instead, he identifies himself as a product of the Hellenized culture of his day.

46. In 2 Macc 14:37–46.
47. James Barr forcefully makes this point; see Barr, *The Garden of Eden*, 112–3.

The hard fact that Paul nowhere finds it necessary, or even helpful, anywhere in his epistles to refer to the empty tomb in relation to Jesus's Resurrection from the dead may not be entirely irrelevant with respect to this particular issue. The cross-fertilization of the originally independent idea of the immortality of the soul with the idea of the resurrection of the *body* becomes an entirely relevant datum at this point. Indeed, Paul's apparent capacity to think of the re-clothing of the resurrected *body* in terms that resonated with the more Hellenistic views of immortality in 2 Cor 5, by contrast with the restoration of the flesh such as we find in the Maccabean literature, may mean that the question of whether the tomb was left empty was not really as live or troublesome an issue for him as it has become for later Christian theology. Certainly, it does not bulk large enough for him to trouble to mention it (if he knew of it), even when he is explicitly defending or expounding resurrection belief. The more absorbing issue for Paul was the ultimate destination of the Raised Jesus in his *pneumatically* transformed *body*, at the Father's right hand, enjoying heavenly immortality with God. And then, congruent with that heavenly focus, Paul's next concern was how he himself and others of faith had received the gift of the "life-giving Spirit," which he understood was bestowed on the baptized by the Raised Christ from that exalted place. It was the concrete experience of the gift of the Spirit, rather than a memory of the empty tomb or even reports of appearances, that justified his forward-looking hope.[48]

While the primary thought relating to the Resurrection of the Raised Jesus is that he is now exalted and vindicated in heaven, "at the right hand of the Father," this does not, of course, invalidate the eschatological hope of a final day of visitation when the justice of God will be fully revealed, and when Jesus' vindication by God will be made transparently manifest, with his "enemies under his feet." Given this hope, the baptized continue to live within the tension of the "now" and the "not yet" of the Eschaton. The ultimate triumphant revealing of the victory of God over sin and death, and the transcendental consummation of all things in the good purposes of God at the Last Day, was certainly of enormous interest to Paul. However, the return of the righteous in restored physical bodies of "flesh and blood" to this material world, even if made incorruptible, appears not to have been an item of pressing interest to him. Undoubtedly there were some Jews, including at least some Pharisees, who thought of resurrection in terms of the restoration of physical remains, but for Paul "flesh and blood cannot inherit the kingdom of God"; the resurrection of the *body* and its glorification in exaltation to the immortality of heaven was for him quite another matter.

---

48. His hope being grounded upon the "down payment" or "first-fruits" of the experience of the Spirit perceived in faith.

It is, of course, undeniable that in the ancient church, some clearly thought of the resurrection in terms of the reconstitution of the body of flesh and blood (and bones) in much the same way as N. T. Wright has championed in our own day. Tertullian, for example, said that no part of the constituents of the body will be lost in the resurrection, "not even a hair, as neither an eye nor a tooth," for, he argued, when Christ affirms "that all the hairs of our head are numbered he at once promises their salvation."[49] Likewise, Thomas Aquinas thought in similar terms of the restoration of flesh and bones. No part is to be abandoned.[50]

However, a concentration on "the resurrection of the body" as distinct from a restoration of material flesh and bones, actually initiated by Paul's insistence that "flesh and blood cannot inherit the kingdom of God," has also had a sustained life in the history of the church, despite the prevalence and popularity of matter-of-fact literal portrayals of physical restoration. In other words, by contrast with the tradition represented so clearly by Tertullian and Aquinas, which affirms that nothing will be lost in the bodily transformation that coincides with the transition from death to resurrection, historically there has always been an alternative strain of thought, more true to Paul's original insights. This is certainly not a modern phenomenon. Even in the ancient church some obviously thought it theologically useful to make a distinction between the terms "flesh" and "body"; the "flesh" being taken to mean the component parts *of* the body. This led to the idea that the term "resurrection of the body" may not necessarily mean the one-to-one restoration of the fleshly members of the physical body. Instead, it could mean something closer to the continuing form of the body, a kind of organizing principle that, in this world, ensures that it maintains its spacio-temporal continuity and location as "the same body," despite obvious growth to maturity and dramatic changes in the component parts of its physical make-up.

In Christian speculation about the after-life this is certainly no new thought. For example, Origen in the third-century observed that the matter by which bodies exist is characterized by constant mutation. Just as wood is changed into fire, fire into smoke, smoke into air, so, as bodies mature and grow old, the matter of which they are composed is always changing.[51] Origen was suspicious of "disciples of the mere letter"[52] who imagined that resurrection simply meant the restoration of the physical body. He knew

---

49. Tertullian, *The Resurrection of the Flesh* 35, quoting Matt 10:30/Luke 12:1.

50. See Aquinas, *Summa Theologiae*, III, Q 54.1, on the qualities of the risen Christ: ". . . it was necessary for a true resurrection of Christ that the same body be once more united to the same soul . . . and was of the same nature as before."

51. We note that Origen's analogy of the transformation of wood, by fire, to smoke and air, suggests an orientation from material to less material. We may conjecture whether he intended to mean, by the drift of the analogy, bodily change from the solidly material to less material through death, but this probably pushes the analogy too far.

52. Origen, *On First Principles* 2.11.2.

well that Paul had said that "flesh and blood cannot inherit the kingdom of God,"[53] and took seriously Paul's image of the inert seed planted in the ground, from which a new and glorious ear of grain emerged. Thus, a body appropriate "for occupying a material locality to which the body must be adapted"[54] was to be replaced by "the body assigned by God."[55] This enjoyed continuity with a person's "own body" but was a new spiritual body "suited to the purer ethereal regions of heaven."[56]

Origen also sustains a distinction between a body and the material parts of which it is composed by comparing the body to a river: just as the constituent drops of water flow by and depart from sight, but the river itself remains, so the member particles composing the body depart, but the body itself is said to remain. This idea of Origen's is open to a little further development. We might say that just as the constituent liquid make-up of a river flows along and passes by, while the river itself remains identifiably before our eyes, so in the human body the fluidity of its constituent parts means they are always in fact changing despite the illusion of the apparent solidity of flesh and blood, bone structure, sinews, and skeletal muscle. In other words, despite obvious change, in another sense the "same" body remains. It enjoys an identifiable spacio-temporal continuity despite the obvious material changes in its composition that take place over time. Likewise, the Christian belief in resurrection focuses not on the passing component particles of the flesh and blood, but on the *body* of which the fleshly particles are constituent members. Thus, for Origen the body is maintained as the same body through time not by material continuity, so much as by the permanence of that which provides the law or the principle of its constitution.[57] At a time when genetic inheritance was still many centuries away, Origen seems to have discerned that bodies can be identified through the passage of time, even despite the obvious physical changes to which they are naturally subject in the process of aging. Origen recognized that there was something which defines and organizes the constituent members of physical constitution, and holds them together as a single identifiable bodily unit through time.

Origen's theory of the resurrection of the body was bitterly attacked by Jerome and others. However, it never entirely died out. Among his most ardent adherents were St. John Chrysostom in his commentaries, and St Gregory of Nyssa, particularly in his work *On the Soul and the Resurrection*.[58] The abiding question with which they

53. Origen, *Contra Celsum* V.19.
54. Origen, *Contra Celsum* VII.33.
55. Origen, *Contra Celsum* V.19.
56. Origen, *Contra Celsum* VII.32.

57. In maintaining that the body that is raised in resurrection is continuous with the physical body in principle but different in substance, Origen believed he was being true to St. Paul's teaching about the "spiritual body." See Origen, *On First Principles*, 2.11.2.

58. Gregory repeats the fluid imagery of a river: "It is the peculiarity of the natural body to be always moving on a stream, to be always altering from its state for the moment and changing into something else . . . ," (Gregory of Nyssa, *Soul and Resurrection*, 466).

grappled was whether, in speaking of the "resurrection of the body," they were necessarily obliged to think in terms of the restoration of every component particle of "flesh and blood." The tradition of Origen and Gregory of Nyssa forthrightly rejects this in the interests of following what was accepted as Paul's unequivocal teaching that "flesh and blood cannot inherit the kingdom of God," and that the resurrection involved a re-clothing with a new spiritual body "assigned by God."

This unresolved issue appears to have been found troublesome in the process of the formulation of the church's creedal statements of resurrection belief. In the second-century, in response to negative Gnostic views about the evil nature of the body, the developing Western baptismal creeds, including the Apostles' Creed, almost without exception followed Tertullian's lead in professing a belief in "the resurrection of the flesh," and this expression also appeared in some Eastern creeds. For example, the Creed of Jerusalem, witnessed to by St Cyril of Jerusalem,[59] is a case in point, though Cyril himself held a less realistic view. However, from the middle of the fourth-century, the prevailing form in the East became the resurrection not "of the flesh" but, more neutrally, "of the dead." This was the form that found its way into the Nicene Creed.

In the Anglican liturgical tradition at the time of the Reformation, the words "I look for the resurrection of the dead" were retained in the Nicene Creed, but the Apostles' Creed was changed by Cranmer from "the resurrection of the flesh" to the "resurrection of the body."[60] Once again, the purpose of changing the word "flesh" to "body" was probably an acknowledgement of the empirically known reality that the flesh decays and returns to the dust. Cranmer thus sought to affirm the resurrection hope in the "resurrection of the body."

The decision in the West to follow the Eastern phrase "resurrection of the dead," or "resurrection of the body," appears to have been motivated by a desire to use more neutral terms than "flesh" conceived in starkly material or purely biological ways. In 1945, A. M. Ramsey noted that there are echoes of Origen's ideas in the thought of the nineteenth-century biblical theologian B. F. Westcott, who appreciated Origen's view that the body of the resurrection is the same as the body laid in the grave, but not so much in terms of its material continuity, as in the permanence of "that which provides the organizational law of its constitution." Westcott noted that Origen believed that in this he was being true to the teaching of St. Paul.[61]

---

59. Robert Morgan in "Flesh is Precious: The Significance of Luke 24:36–43" in Barton and Stanton, *Resurrection*, 13, rightly points to the influence of Luke's very physical presentation of the appearance of the Raised Christ on "Orthodox second-century writers," who went even further than Luke "along the line of flesh-and-bones resurrection . . ."

60. At least in the form of the Apostles' Creed used at Anglican Morning and Evening Prayer. In the Baptismal rite, the phrase "resurrection of the flesh" persisted.

61. Ramsey, *The Resurrection of Christ*, 112.

Michael Ramsey is himself even more forthright. He categorized an over-concentration on the resurrection of the component particles of the earthly or fleshly body as "crude," and a belief that "Paul deliberately avoided."[62] Furthermore, Ramsey, acknowledging the seminal influence of Origen, went on to observe the modern ring in Origen's words, insofar as modern science tends to regard physical objects as the "organization of energy in particular forms."[63] One aspect of contemporary science that Ramsay may have had in mind is the view within quantum physics that invites us to think of all material objects, not just human bodies, in extraordinarily fluid and indeterminate subatomic terms. This suggests the notion that the persistence of "a body" lies not in the immutability of its physical constituent members understood as static substances, but in the continued organization of myriad cellular and molecular entities in accordance with the broader, governing principles of the body's self-identity. When we speak of the "resurrection of the body," we may not be obliged to think in "crudely" materialist terms, as the simple restoration to this world of the same constituent particles that happened to make up the human body at one particular point of time in its historical existence.

Despite the fact that physical bodies may be understood in a more fluid or plastic way than in a substantial or biologically static way, it can nevertheless be acknowledged that humans often become pre-occupied, even obsessed, with their biological composition and make-up. Despite Paul's use of the analogy of the many members of which one body is made up, we should not automatically allow ourselves to think that when Paul spoke of the "body of Christ" he had just come out of a modern university lecture theatre after hearing a presentation in "Biology 101." Even if "the body" that has continuity through time may be differentiated from the component members of which it is composed, we may also understand "the body" in a functional or instrumental sense. By contrast with a purely material or biological sense, this may be much closer to the way St. Paul thought of the physical bodies of this world than we imagine.

The body may be understood functionally, as that which gives a human person not only continuity of identity, but also location in the world of space and time. Then, in turn, the importance of a person's bodily location in space and time is that this is what permits others access to that person, just as removal to another location denies inter-personal access. This "functional" understanding of the body clearly contrasts with a purely "biological" understanding of the actual composition of the body.

Eduard Schweizer once helpfully pointed out that the term "body" may be seen as being restricted to itself or self-contained, in the sense that "we can measure it and define from where to where it expands" (extends?). But he also observed that a "body"

---

62. Ramsey, *The Resurrection of Christ*, 109.
63. Ramsey, *The Resurrection of Christ*, 112.

may also be viewed functionally, as "having eyes to see the neighbour, feet to visit him, hands to help him or to receive help from him, ears to hear him," etc. Schweizer argued that, despite Paul's more biological sounding talk of "the body of Christ and its constituent members,"[64] it is often in this second sense that he understands the "body."[65] In other words, the idea of the body, as distinct from its composition of fleshly component parts, could be conceived by Paul in relational and functional terms, rather than in purely biological or material terms. On this point, I think James Dunn has clearly and correctly grasped this Pauline insight. In responding to Stephen Davis' contention that the concept of the body "entails physicality," Dunn says, "I simply have to disagree. In my view, 'body' for Paul denoted the embodiment that makes relationship and communication possible—in a physical context, of course, a physical body—but in a different context? And of course Paul believed in a *bodily* resurrection (1 Cor 15), but it does not follow that he believed the resurrection body to be 'physical.'"[66] Whatever Paul understood by "the spiritual body," his fundamental insight has to do with an "embodiment that makes relationship and communication possible."

This is the sense in which Paul refers to the body in 2 Cor 4–5. When he says that "while we are at home in the body we are away from the Lord,"[67] he refers to the limitations of his personal bodily location, along with that of his addressees. In this earthly life, being necessarily at an epistemic distance, they are "away" from the Raised and glorified Christ whom Paul located in the radical hiddenness of heaven. Paul expresses essentially the same sentiment in Phil 1:23, where he says he has a desire to depart this world to be with Christ "that is far better." If Christ's resurrected and glorified body was understood to have been re-located "at the right hand of God,"[68] it is entailed that Paul no longer had direct or immediate access to him. While, in faith he perceived and claimed to know the Raised Christ through the medium of the "life-giving Spirit" in a concretely experiential way, this was acknowledged to be a knowing in a partial sense. However, in departing this world and "being with Christ," it is clear that Paul envisages that the Raised Christ would be "fully known" and recognized, no longer in faith, but by clarity of "sight." He thus speaks of his hope of knowing Christ in a more ultimate sense "face to face," or "in person," as we would say today. This relational "being with Christ" is what Paul counts as "far better" than life in the physical body of flesh and blood in this world. Because of Christ's heavenly location, Paul knows Christ in faith through his presence as the life-giving Spirit in the church, as a "gift from heaven" that permitted a kind of indirect access, but could

---

64. As in Rom 12.

65. Schweizer, "Resurrection—Fact or Illusion?" 150.

66. Dunn, "In Grateful Dialogue," 320. Dunn, *The Theology of Paul the Apostle*, Sec. 3.2, 56: For Paul, "*soma* is a relational concept. It denotes the person embodied in a particular environment." It enables individuals to "interact with each other . . ." Stephen Davis' original remark is found in Stewart and Habermas, *Memories of Jesus*, chapter 12, 263.

67. 2 Cor 5:6.

68. Rom 8:34.

not allow Paul to claim to enjoy direct or immediate access to him. What he knew in faith was therefore promissory of what was to come. In this sense, while ever he is in his earthly body, he understands himself to be in a degree of separation from the Lord. Clearly, in all this Paul is thinking of the body in a functional and instrumental sense rather than in purely biological terms.

This Pauline appeal to the concept of "the body" in functional and relational terms invites us to the view that physical bodies function not just to give human persons identity through time, but also to allow others to identify and relate to them. Our bodies are instruments of relationality through which we are able to commune with one another, and enjoy inter-personal engagement with one another. Our bodies thus give us location, and in the first instance it is because of the location of our bodies that others either have or are denied intimate access to us.

It is of interest that, in actual fact, though Paul located Christ "at the right hand of the Father," he does not actually speak of the Raised and exalted *Body* of Christ being "in heaven." Rather, seeing him "face to face" or "in person" is as close as we get to this kind of thought. In relation to this functional understanding of the idea of the body, with its importance in relation to issues of *location* and inter-personal *access* in mind, we could then ask Paul the question: "Where then *is* the resurrected *Body* of Christ now?" Where are we to think of it as being located, and where do we have access to Christ? If the question were simply to ask where the raised Christ is, he would presumably have given the answer "in heaven," and we naturally assume that his *pneumatically* transformed Body would be located there also. It is remarkable, however, that while he would undoubtedly in the first instance say that Christ is "in heaven, at the right hand of God," Paul nowhere actually says that the "*Body* of Christ" is in heaven.

When Paul himself speaks of the resurrected "Body of Christ," it is clear that his focus is not on the exalted and vindicated one in heaven precisely because he thinks of "the body" in functional terms. It is because he thinks of "the body" in such functional terms, rather than in purely biological and physical terms, that it becomes more natural that the Body of Christ be located more proximately and "at hand" so that Christ might be functionally available to be known.

As a consequence, when Paul speaks *explicitly* of the "Body of Christ" it is not located in heaven, in a way that causes Paul himself to be conscious "in his body" of being "away from the Lord";[69] rather, the Body of Christ is located in the time and space of this world, where indeed he *does* have access to him through the medium of his embodied Spirit. Thus he locates the "Body of Christ" precisely where Christ becomes functionally available, on the table of the Lord and in the community which comes to be in time and space around it: "The bread that we break, is it not the sharing

---

69. As he says in 2 Cor 5:6–8.

in the body of Christ."[70] In other words, the sharing of the bread of the Eucharist is the place, functionally speaking, where Christ is understood to be located and where the baptized have access to him. This is thus "the Body of Christ."

If the bread which is broken in remembrance of Jesus in Eucharistic sharing is Christ's Body, as Paul indicates in 1 Cor 11:24, then, likewise, the community which comes concretely into being *as* the Eucharistic community is the place where, functionally speaking, the Body of Christ is located and where humans have access to him. For Paul, the church is "the Body of Christ," particularly when it visibly assembles to be constituted Eucharistically in the taking, blessing, breaking, and sharing of bread, and the sharing of the cup. This is where the Raised and exalted Christ who is "with God in heaven" becomes available and accessible in time and space.

It is the Eucharistic sharing that in this way *makes* the church one body: "we being many are one body, for we all partake of the one bread."[71] It is noteworthy that Paul publicly rehearses these basic truths to the Corinthians, whose perceived error is that they are not "discerning the body,"[72] for they are guilty of fracturing the unity of the communion of the church by selfish behavior, possibly outside the Eucharist itself, by not exhibiting the dispositional attitude of service to others. It is by over-eating on the part of some, while others have insufficient to eat, and by not really welcoming others as guests, thereby fostering human disunity and fracturing the unity and peace which should be a note of the communion of the eschatological community, that constitutes this all too obvious failure of discernment.

Elsewhere, Paul therefore speaks of the inter-personal communion of the church as "the communion of the Holy Spirit."[73] It is the gift of the Spirit of Christ that constitutes the human unity in the one communion and fellowship of the Body of Christ, the inclusive community in which human divisions based on race, social status, or gender difference are overcome.[74] It is clear that the inappropriate behavior of the Corinthians, by failing to "discern the Lord's body" at what should have been a community defining moment of sharing, is compounded by the fact that it fails at the very point where Christ's achievement of human reconciliation and peace through his death and Resurrection should have been most clearly manifest and proclaimed. It thus fails to be an *anamnetic* proclamation of the self-sacrificial death of Christ's Cross "until he comes."

---

70. 1 Cor 10:16.
71. 1 Cor 10:17.
72. 1 Cor 11:29.
73. 2 Cor 13:13.
74. Gal 3:28.

In Eph 2, where the Pauline vision of the inclusive community in which Jews and Gentiles are reconciled together "to God in one body by the cross,"[75] the image of the Body gives way to the image of the re-constituted Temple. The Gentiles who were outside of "the commonwealth of Israel" are now reconciled, together with Jews, to God. This occurs in the New Israel instituted by Christ which is, once again, constituted by the gift of his Spirit: "for through him both of us have access in one Spirit to the Father."[76] In the building of the new Temple, "Christ Jesus himself" is the chief cornerstone, in whom "the whole structure is joined together and grows into a holy temple in the Lord."[77] The author of the epistle can therefore confidently assure the Ephesians that, in Christ, "you also are built together spiritually into a dwelling-place for God."[78]

All the while, whether the image used is that of the Body or of the Temple, it is the concrete experience of the Spirit, that is claimed to be concretely known in faith, which gives rise to these interpretative images. In this way, the Pauline vision of the Body of Christ is extended and developed by the author of Ephesians (it is of course immaterial if it was not Paul himself). The gift of the life-giving Spirit to the church, which constitutes it as an inclusive and humanly reconciled community in love and peace, endows the church with its distinctive form and its identity as the Body of Christ. If we continue to think in functional terms, rather than biological and material terms, the gathered community of the church (particularly when it assembles for its characteristic outward and visible activity of breaking and sharing of bread and the sharing of the cup) is where the Body of Christ is found, and where access to him becomes a most poignant possibility. The living body of the church itself is the place where in space and time Christ is located and where the baptized have access to him, and through him to God the Father in the Spirit.

This means that Paul would say that, as a consequence of the Resurrection, Christ is no longer just located in Palestine as he was in the first-century, for we no longer now know him *according to the flesh*. He is now known as "Jesus Christ our Lord," who has been "declared to be the Son of God with power according to the spirit of holiness by resurrection from the dead."[79] As John makes clear, it is because he has gone to the timeless eternity of the immortal God, that access to him is now "according to the Spirit," and this means he may in principle now be known across time and in all places.[80] For we know that God is not located in any particular place, at least not in a place

---

75. Eph 2:16.
76. Eph 2:18.
77. Eph 2:21.
78. Eph 2:22.
79. Rom 1:3–4.
80. John 7:39.

related to other places, but in principle in every place. If the Raised Christ is with God in heaven, then he too is equally proximate to every physical place, and makes himself available in the event of Eucharistic sharing which creates the Eucharistic community. This is the local manifestation of the Body of Christ.

This means that Christ is located in a way that makes access to him available to others in the inclusive Eucharistic community of every local church. This was a point made very forcefully by Westcott, who noted the absence of the definite article in 1 Cor 12:27, despite the unhelpful creative activity of translators who so regularly conjure up the article. Thus, Westcott notes, St. Paul says to the church at Corinth, "You are a body (*not* the body) of Christ, and members in particular."[81] Every local community is "a Body of Christ," complete in itself. Thus says Westcott in reference to Paul: "The definite article destroys the force of his argument." The Corinthian community is not just a part of the Body of Christ, but a local manifestation *of* the Body of Christ. Similarly, Westcott notes, in 1 Cor 11:2, that Paul says explicitly that he espoused the Corinthian Church—the congregation to which he is writing—to one husband to "present you as a chaste virgin to Christ." It seems that the local church is not a part of the Body of Christ, as a part of a greater whole. Rather, the universal church is the sum of local churches, all having "a completeness in themselves."[82] Each is a local manifestation of the Body of Christ, the place where his presence is to be located and found and where people therefore have access in faith to *him*.

If we then press the question, where is the Body of Christ, meaning where is Christ located and where do we have access to him, Paul's uncompromisingly clear answer has a dual reference. On one hand, the Raised Christ is located in heaven, "at the right hand of God." We have access to him through the medium of the gift of his reconciling Spirit. But on the other hand, if we think functionally of his Body as that which gives him location and the possibility of human access to him in terms of time and space in the Spirit, Paul's answer is "Christ's Body is on the table of the Lord and in the community that comes to be gathered around it." Paul is uncompromisingly clear about this. When he thinks of Christ, he thinks of the *Totus Christus*, Christ-with-his-own. The visible local church is the "Body of Christ," and the broken and shared Eucharistic bread that constitutes the church in time and space is also the "Body of Christ," the primary means of access to him. It is in and through the gathering of the baptized for the outward and visible Eucharistic action of the taking, blessing, breaking, and sharing of bread, and the sharing of the cup, that the church is pneumatically *constituted* inwardly, spiritually, and ontologically, *as* the eschatological community in the manner apparently envisaged and *instituted* by Jesus himself.[83]

---

81. Westcott, *The Gospel of the Resurrection*, 181.

82. Westcott, *The Gospel of the Resurrection*, 182.

83. By early in the second-century, Paul's eschatological vision of the inclusive community in which divisions based on ethnic identity, social status, or differences of gender are transcended, is characterized by Ignatius of Antioch as the local Eucharistic community inclusive also of all orders of

Just how Paul was able to get his head around the dual reference involved in thinking, with apparent ease, of the Raised Christ being both exalted in heaven (at the "right hand of God"), and at the same time being present and available in space and time at various particular locations (and known through the gift of the Spirit as the church was constituted as the Body of Christ), requires us to return to some basic epistemological insights that were already available in the world of Middle Platonism of which Paul was part. It will be no surprise to find that this means that we must revisit some basic insights of Plato or, if not insights of Plato himself, at least insights of Plato as Plato was received in the world of Middle Platonism. To this we shall turn in the next chapter.

---

ministry—laity, deacons and presbyters—under the visible shepherding of the local bishop. Hence the dictum for which Ignatius is famous: "Where the Bishop is, there is the Church." The local church, as the local manifestation of the Body of Christ, is thus the church of the city to which Paul addresses his letters—Corinth, Thessalonica, Rome, or wherever.

12

A Little More Platonic Light

THE FULL RE-EMERGENCE OF Plato as an intellectual force in an already thoroughly Hellenized Judaism had a long gestation. The first known Jewish philosopher of religion, Aristobulus of Alexandria,[1] set the direction of this trend around 160 BC.[2] While an interest in the ethical traditions of ancient Greek philosophy made for common ground with the Jewish moral tradition, there are some clear indications that mutual sympathies with regard to more clearly theological issues were also exploited. The fragmentary remains of the writings of Aristobulus indicate that he believed Pythagoras, Socrates, and Plato had in fact learned an ethical monotheism from Moses, and even specifically that Plato knew what was then thought to be Moses' account of Creation in Genesis. He drew attention, for example, to the similarities between the Greek translation of Prov 8:22–31 and Plato's *Timaeus*, noting particularly Plato's view of the original "formlessness of matter" which appeared to echo Gen 1:2.[3]

In Jewish and Alexandrian philosophy from the second-century BC onwards, the increasing interaction of philosophical elements of Platonic and Stoic origin may be discerned without too much difficulty.[4] Antiochus of Ascalon, who was born in Palestine around 125 BC, was responsible for making considerable gains in consolidating the turning in this new direction; indeed, the incorporation of Stoic elements into a form of platonism became his trademark. Having fled from Athens to Rome in 88 BC in the wake of the Mithridatic wars, he is known to have been lecturing on Plato in Rome. Fortuitously, this also brought him into direct interaction with Stoic ideas, and Cicero in fact credits him with the identification of Platonic Ideas and Stoic notions/conceptions (*ennoiai*).[5] It is significant that Antiochus used the Stoic term *poiotês* to

---

1. An Aristobulus is referred to in 2 Macc 1:10.

2. See Hengel, *Judaism and Hellenism*, 169: "in Aristobulus Jewish/Palestinian and Pythagorean-Platonic and Stoic conceptions are intermingled."

3. *Timaeus* 51a, also 30a; and *Statesman* 273b, where the Composer of the Universe is referred to as the "Creator and Father" who brings order to disordered chaos.

4. Dillon, *The Middle Platonists*, remains a standard work on the influence of Plato in the Hellenistic period. See also Hadas, "Plato in Hellenistic Fusion"; and Hadas, *Hellenistic Cultures*, 72.

5. Among other claims to fame, Antiochus was the teacher of Cicero. See Plutarch, *Cicero* 4, 1: "On coming to Athens he attended the lectures of Antiochus of Ascalon, and was charmed by his

describe the Platonic Forms in their material embodiment in particulars of space and time.⁶ This initiated a practice that was to become a regular feature among Middle Platonists, though Platonists and Stoics parted company over opposing approaches as to the way in which cognitive intellectual capacities were acquired. Platonists remained true to their namesake by opting for an uncompromising pre-natal acquaintance with transcendental Forms/Ideas which was thought to be reactivated in experience by "recollection," while the Stoics held out for an empirical acquisition of conceptions/preconceptions by repeated inductive processes of a more natural kind.

Then, subsequent to Antiochus, the further development of beliefs in the transcendence and immateriality of God, and the existence of immaterial substance generally, signaled a rapidly increasing interest in Plato. At the same time, a Stoic focus upon the chief good as a kind of ethical life lived according to the natural moral law that was thought also to be implicit in the regularities of nature, and accessible by the exercise of reason, began to give way to a more Platonic interest in "becoming like God."⁷

The growing interest in Plato was moved even further in a more overtly theological direction when Eudorus of Alexandria⁸ introduced an additional Neopythagorean transcendentalist emphasis⁹ into his reception of Plato in the first-century BC. In very broad terms, the addition of this transcendentalist element that was drawn from Neopythagorean sources to the blend of Stoic and Platonic thought, meant that the three basic ingredients of the amalgam of ideas that has become known as Middle Platonism were now in place.¹⁰ By the first-century AD, the inherited Stoicism of the age was therefore already well on the way to being transformed and, indeed, we now know it was actually in process of being eclipsed, for this new infusion of interest in the thought of Plato was destined to triumph. Philo, Paul's contemporary in neighboring Alexandria,¹¹ is the paradigm representative of the growing success of this transition to what was by this time clearly becoming the unmistakable, unapologetic, and confidently dominant form of platonism that was eventually to become known as Neoplatonism at the hands of Plotinus in the third-century AD.

---

fluency and grace of diction, although he disapproved of his innovations in doctrine."

6. See the account of this Dillon, *The Middle Platonists*, 82–83. The basic Stoic categories are substance (ὑποκείμενον), the primary matter or formless substance (οὐσία) that things are made of, and quality (ποιόν), the way matter is organized, all held together by the intelligible divine warm breath (λογος–πνευμα).

7. Plato's *Theaetetus* occupied an important place in this development.

8. His dates are unknown, but he was a little ahead of Strabo (64 BC—AD 19).

9 Based on a fascination with the apparent autonomy of abstract numerical truths independent of whether or not there were material things in the physical world to be counted: i.e. the truth of 2 + 2 = 4, whether or not there are actual two countable sets of two things.

10. Sometimes "Middle Platonism" is referred to as "Imperial Platonism."

11. Philo was born between 20 and 15 BC, and it is known that he led a Jewish embassy to Caligula in AD 39 (Josephus, *Antiquities*, xviii, 257–60).

It is important to reiterate that this philosophical transition was not so much characterized by an eclecticism of an insouciant or even chaotic "pick and mix kind,"[12] as by a more considered appreciation of specific selected aspects of one tradition of thought that were thought amenable to being accommodated and received into the traditions of the other.[13] The identification of Platonic Ideas/Forms with Stoic *ennoiai/prolepseis* (conceptions and preconceptions), despite disagreements as to the method of their acquisition, is a case in point. On the other hand, sometimes terms were co-opted from the language of opponents in disputes of a more polemic nature, without necessarily being used in a transparently univocal way. Indeed, in recent years there has been a sustained discussion of whether the interaction between Stoicism and Platonism between 100 BC and AD 200 should be described by the word "eclectic" at all,[14] given its suggestion of unsystematic and intellectually chaotic outcomes. Some have spoken instead of a kind of "harmonization," a "merging," or an "appropriation" of ideas, or the "assimilation" of elements drawn from these alternative original sources, and of their "integration," one with the other, in an amalgam of a more or less harmonious kind.

On the other hand, after the enforced closure of the philosophical schools in Athens in 86 BC, and in the absence of a single dominant and authoritative teacher capable of initiating and sustaining a "school" of philosophical thought with a capacity to maintain its own internal integrity, the philosophy of the period tends to be characterized by a more fluid diversity of viewpoint. This lack of a single authoritative system, and the unresolved persistence of inconsistencies and differences of opinion from thinker to thinker, probably means that the search for an appropriate over-all term to describe the interactions of the philosophies of the age will remain elusive. Provided the term is not used as though it were univocal and transparently clear, and so long as it is not understood pejoratively, I am not averse to speaking of a kind of "eclecticism" to indicate a kind of amalgam of ideas of diverse origin.

Insofar as this bears upon the interpretation of early Christian writers, the challenge is to try to determine whether the bare use of either Platonic or Stoic *language* also signals a predisposition towards an assumed epistemological similarity that in turn points to a particular ontological and cosmological understanding of things as well. What we may be certain of with some confidence is that Stoicism and Platonism were interacting in this period in such a way that it is possible to detect

---

12. "Pick and mix" is Troels Engberg-Pedersen's term (following Christopher Gill) in his introductory essay in Engberg-Pederson, *From Stoicism to Platonism*, 5.

13. Some speak of the "harmonization" of elements in a kind of dialogue between Stoicism and Platonism.

14. Thus, Mauro Bonazzi says, "The period was not an epoch of eclecticism, if eclecticism is regarded as the passive adoption of terms and doctrines that neglects the question of the compatibility of those terms and doctrines—these philosophers were well aware of what they were doing and their strategies of appropriation are often interesting" (Bonazzi, "The Platonist Appropriation of Stoic Epistemology," 141).

elements that are capable of being labeled either as having a "Platonic" or a more clearly "Stoic" character.

Already in the Wisdom of Solomon,[15] for example (which as we have noted, appears to have been directly influential on Paul),[16] we see early evidence of the modification of Jewish ideas through their commerce both with Stoic modes of thought and also with the re-emergent Platonism of the age, without any sense of awkward dissonance. The influence of Plato may obviously be discerned in relation particularly to belief in the immortality of the soul, which Wisdom teaches without any clear references to the resurrection of the body. Even more important for this present discussion, unmistakably Stoic resonances may be discerned when Wisdom specifically associates the concept of *pneuma* with wisdom. Insofar as within wisdom there is said to be a *pneuma* that, among other attributes, is described as "intelligent, holy, unique,"[17] we hear a clear Stoic voice. Moreover, the spirit of wisdom is spoken of as a "breath of the power of God, and a pure emanation of the glory of the Almighty."[18] While these insights appear to exhibit the coloring of Stoic categories, in the very next verse we find more characteristically Platonic images when wisdom is described as "a reflection of eternal light," a "spotless mirror" of the working of God, and "an image" of God's goodness.[19] In this way, Wisdom unapologetically uses language that is reminiscent of both Stoicism and Platonism at the same time.[20]

Given the peculiar mixture of Stoic and Platonic ideas that were already in the intellectual atmosphere in the south-eastern Mediterranean world, such as we see here in the Wisdom of Solomon, we therefore have to take account at least of the possibility that Paul was influenced both by Stoicism and also by the developing intellectual interest, of his time, in the philosophical categories of Plato. Despite the remarkable similarities between much of Paul's language and the Stoic ethical discourse of his day,[21] it is clearly important therefore also to consider the possible modifying influence of Platonic ideas in Paul's reception of Stoicism. Indeed, as was argued in

---

15. Probably late in the first-century BC.

16. As indicated by comparing parallel texts: Rom 1:18–32 with Wis 13:1–19 and 14:8–31; Rom 2:4 with Wis 12:10; Rom 9:14–23 with Wis 12:12–22; Rom 9:20 with Wis 15:7; and Rom 13:1–7 with Wis 6:3.

17. Wis 7:22.

18. Wis 7:25.

19. Wis 7:26.

20. For a much closer analysis of these Stoic and Platonic elements in Wisdom, see Sterling, "The Love of Wisdom."

21. To which Troels Engberg-Pedersen has drawn attention with such enthusiasm in a succession of publications: *Paul in His Hellenistic* (1994); *Paul Beyond the Judaism/Hellenism Divide* (2001); and *From Stoicism to Platonism* (2017).

chapter 4, it is hard to discount the presumptive sense in which Paul's foundational Jewish theism would have found the popular dualistic philosophy of Plato much more amenable than a Stoic monism. This is why Paul's conception of the Spirit appears not have been quite as closely assimilated to the material and physical "warm breath" of Stoicism, and thus ontologically independent of the transcendent God, as Troels Engberg-Pederson is inclined to believe.

We do not, of course, know a great deal about the exact epistemological presuppositions that were operative in Palestine of the first-century. We have no crowd-sourced picture of the prevailing popular philosophical orientations of the time, and have no knowledge of the degree to which philosophical categories had permeated, and become domiciled in, day-to-day discourse. Though it is obvious that Paul was well educated, we have no knowledge of the specifics of his education.

Just to read Paul's various epistles indicates, however, that Paul was obviously much further removed from the burgeoning Platonic philosophical developments of the time than his Alexandrian Jewish contemporary, Philo; we do not have anything like Philo's unashamedly open and self-conscious embrace of Plato. But, nevertheless, to read Paul's epistles is to be alerted to the readily apparent contribution of both Stoic and Platonic influences. In both cases these are influences of the kind that are likely to have become available to him as elements of the popular intellectual environment without his being necessarily conscious of the fact. This has at least to be taken into account, for example, in coming to terms with the epistemology that is presupposed and expressed, even if unwittingly, in Paul's descriptions of faith and the life of the Spirit. Clearly, given Paul's acquaintance with the Wisdom of Solomon, he could himself well have thought of *pneuma* in Stoic terms as the "breath of the power of God, and a pure emanation of the glory of the Almighty,"[22] but also, more platonically, of the knowledge of the Spirit in faith as an "image" or "reflection" of the invisible God, as in a mirror.

Certainly, even if Paul may not have had direct first-hand acquaintance with any of Plato's actual texts, at significant points his language appears to have been conditioned by a diffused popular platonism of the kind that had long since become part of the intellectual atmosphere. Not least, among the passages where this may be discerned is 2 Cor 4:16—5:10 where, speaking of his resurrection hope, even though Paul does not abandon resurrection belief in favor of the immortality of the soul, he refers in Platonic fashion to the *dissolution* of the flesh at death, and contrasts the "outer nature," which is "wasting away," with the "inner nature," which is "being renewed day by day." That this reference to the "inner nature" is not just a passing verbal oddity of no real significance is confirmed by the appearance of essentially the same concept in Rom 7 where Paul's "true self" is somewhat dualistically contrasted with his morally rebellious body, which is referred to negatively as "this body of death."[23] And then, as

22. Wis 7:25.
23. Rom 7:24.

was noted in the last chapter, in 2 Cor 5:1–4 in apparently Platonic fashion he contrasts the body as a temporary "earthly tent" with a hoped-for "building from God, a house not made with hands, eternal in the heavens." As Engberg-Pedersen himself in fact acknowledges, "All of this looks rather Platonic."[24]

Even so, when Engberg-Pedersen actually discusses 2 Cor 4–5, in association with Phil 3:2 and Rom 8, to explain Paul's understanding of the alleged "physical *pneuma*" as the agent of the transformation of the body, not only at the final resurrection but already in the life of the baptized in their earthly lives,[25] he is nevertheless inclined to minimize the importance of these Platonic elements. Instead, the transformation of the body by the action of the *pneuma* is said once again to entail that the *pneuma* must itself be understood in simply Stoic "material and physical" terms. Just how this bypassing of Plato is reached is not really clear. In fact, Troels Engberg-Pedersen actually notes the integration of Platonic and Stoic-like language in the discussion in 2 Cor 4–5, and comments on Paul's versatility in being able to move between the two: "the virtuosity with which Paul handles these different types of philosophical input," he says, "is quite impressive."[26] However, despite these concessions to the influence of Plato in Paul's *language*, at the end of the day Engberg-Pedersen nevertheless opts for his more purely Stoic reading of Paul in relation to his understanding of *pneuma* and the presupposed ontological status to be accorded to it. His conclusion is that "a concrete, physicalist understanding of the operation of the pneuma . . . is very strongly present."[27] The end result is that Engberg-Pedersen preferentially emphasizes the Stoic input in Paul's writing at the expense of minimizing the possible influence of Platonic patterns of thought.

As we noted in chapter 4, it is very doubtful that the use of apparently metaphorical images of God "pouring" the Spirit into human hearts and of the Spirit "dwelling" among the baptized can justifiably warrant Troels Engberg-Pedersen's conclusion about the physical materiality of the Spirit. We are on more secure ground when we remember that, as in all theological language of the Judeo-Christian theistic tradition, the divine is beyond all humanly crafted images and metaphors, and conforms to none. As a consequence, Engberg-Pedersen's characterization of the Pauline understanding of the Spirit as a "physical" and "material" reality, which is therefore necessarily "ontologically independent" of God, cannot be embraced on the linguistic grounds upon which he relies without the exercise of considerable caution.[28]

24. Engberg-Pedersen, *Cosmology and Self*, 49.
25. Engberg-Pedersen, *Cosmology and Self*, 49; see the extended discussion, 49–55.
26. Engberg-Pedersen, *Cosmology and Self*, 50.
27. Engberg-Pedersen, *Cosmology and Self*, 51.
28. We may profitably heed the warning of Richard Hooker: "Dangerous it were for the feeble

However, over and above this linguistic difficulty, the major problem with Troels Engberg-Pedersen's contention about the "materiality of the Spirit" is that it can be attributed to his enthusiasm for drawing parallels between Paul and Stoicism in a way that tends to be exclusive of any real influence from Plato. In this process, he certainly tends to minimize and undervalue the Platonic influences. For example, apart from his reliance on an apparently literal reading of Paul's (metaphorical) language, his conclusion about the materiality of the Spirit is almost certainly embraced because, while he is impressed by the linguistic virtuosity of Paul, he gives the overall impression that Stoicism is to be regarded as the polar opposite of the idealistic emphasis on immateriality in Plato's philosophy. He thus works with a natural inclination to keep them apart.

Unfortunately, however, insofar as he tends to characterize Plato's thought as exclusively "idealistic" and "immaterial," and the very opposite of the empiricism of Stoicism,[29] he works with a somewhat stereotypical view of Platonism. As a consequence, the Platonic element in the Stoic/Platonic amalgam of thought, of the kind for which Middle Platonism is famous, tends to be overlooked in favor of Stoicism as the more dominant controlling partner rather than vice versa.

For example, as we have already seen, by contrast with the materializing tendencies of Stoicism, which means that the Stoic *pneuma* is understood as a "warm breath" that infuses the whole created order, a more transcendental thrust of the kind that is fundamental to a Platonic orientation of thought might think of the Spirit as essentially immaterial. The problem with this, from Engberg-Pedersen's point of view, is that it keeps God separate from the world: "In the Platonizing case, it is the attempt to keep the divine aloof, that is free of any direct and tangible contact with the world."[30] This echoes the stereotypical reading of Plato, which emphasizes the juxtaposition of the ideal and the material. The effect of this assumed Platonic separation of God and the world is that in each case where Engberg-Pedersen has to judge whether Paul is to be placed either on the Stoic (and material) or the Platonic (and transcendently idealistic) side of the fence, he naturally opts for the Stoic. In other words, Stoicism is his "default position" in his handling of Paul. Hence, Paul's understanding of the Spirit is accommodated to the material and physical views of Stoicism, with the result that the possible corrective influence of Plato is kept at bay:

---

brain of man to wade far into the doings of the Most High; whom although to know be life, and joy to make mention of His name; yet our soundest knowledge is to know that we know Him not as indeed He is; neither can know Him: and our safest eloquence concerning Him is our silence, when we confess without confession that His glory is inexplicable, His greatness above our capacity and reach. He is above, and we upon earth; therefore it behoveth our words to be wary and few" (Hooker, *Laws of Ecclesiastical Polity*, I, ii, 2). See also, Calvin, *Institutes* II.15.5, where Christ the Mediator is understood as "descending from the bosom and *incomprehensible* glory of the Father."

29. See Engberg-Pedersen, *Cosmology and Self*, 16: An emphasis on Platonism leads to "an understanding that saw pneuma as an immaterial entity issuing from the immaterial God." It is not clear why this should necessarily be viewed a bad thing.

30. Engberg-Pedersen, *Cosmology and Self*, 18.

the "fundamental corporeality of Stoicism," he says, "was to a large degree an articulation of a more popular ontology in the ancient world. By contrast a Platonist reading of pneuma is excluded."[31] In this way, Engberg-Pederson unfortunately tends, as a matter of his regular preference, to privilege Stoicism over Platonism as an influence on Paul, but this is achieved only by treating Stoicism and Platonism virtually as polar opposites, which, as we shall see, may be a mistake.

This same dynamic may be seen in Engberg-Pedersen's recent very impressive study of *John and Philosophy*. In expounding John, no less than Paul, also in terms of unmistakable Stoic influences, he is at pains to say that it is mistaken to interpret John through a Platonic lens. This is said to be particularly so, for example, when John's use of the concept of the "Word," or "*Logos*," of God is brought into association with Philo's Platonism, as has been popular over the decades among Johannine scholars. His reasoning is clear: "Platonism, certainly as developed by Philo, is a form of ontological dualism that distinguishes sharply between the world of the senses and the world of ideas. By contrast Stoicism is a form of ontological monism."[32] "In Platonism, the relationship between the world of the senses and the world of ideas is one that can only be expressed in terms of an 'image' (*eikôn*) vis-à-vis its 'model' or 'paradigm'. There is no physical connection between the immaterial (*a-sômatos*) world of ideas and the material world of the senses."[33]

This effectively means that the regular suggestion that Philo is the source of John's use of the notion of the Word (or *Logos*) is ruled out because Philo's Platonic commitments would really make the idea of "the incarnation of the Word" impossible. As Engberg-Pedersen clearly states it: "If, then, Christ is divine *logos* in that (Platonic) sense, how can he also be a human being of flesh and blood?" A Platonic view of the Word is said to make it so remote from the world as to make an "incarnation of the Word" impossible. By contrast "a Stoic-like, material *pneuma* is thought to operate in a monistically conceived world: it comes down on Jesus, thereby making him literally one with God (who is himself *pneuma*) . . ."[34] Whatever we make of this Stoic approach to the divine Word or *logos-pneuma* in relation to Jesus, it is obvious that Engberg-Pedersen has a clear view of Platonism and Stoicism effectively as polar opposites. As a consequence, even if both Paul and John sometimes use platonic-sounding language, a consistent Stoicism is said to underlie their thinking.

31. Engberg-Pedersen, *Cosmology and Self*, 19.
32. Engberg-Pedersen, *John and Philosophy*, 33.
33. Engberg-Pedersen, *John and Philosophy*, 33.
34. Engberg-Pedersen, *John and Philosophy*, 34.

There is, however, another way of looking at Plato, particularly in the light of the way in which Plato was received in the world of Middle Platonism of Paul's time. The usual (somewhat stereotypical) view of Platonism, almost exclusively as an other-worldly, immaterial, or purely "idealistic" philosophy by contrast with the materialistic empiricism of Stoicism, certainly overlooks an important aspect of the particular reading of Plato entertained by the Middle Platonists. For, as Plato's idealism passed through the prism of their minds, it was not so much the eternal and ideal qualities of the Platonic Forms or Ideas that claimed attention, so much as the way in which those Forms were perceived as they were embodied in the particulars of the created order.[35] Ironically, this is a reading of Plato that was facilitated precisely by the influence of its prevailing commerce at the time with a residual Stoic empiricism. In other words, there are some respects in which the Middle Platonists read Plato through a lens conditioned by Stoic interests.

Indeed, the usual ultra-idealistic reading of Plato may even misrepresent Plato himself. For we can now appreciate that there is a sense in which Plato's so-called theory of Ideal Forms is not really a single systematically worked out theory at all, but something which is itself less than systematized, and which he returned to a number of times during his writing career, with no really definitive result.[36] Commentators regularly make much of Plato's idealism by concentrating on the absolute transcendence of the Ideal Forms and the manner in which pre-existent souls are said to have originally acquired the pre-natal knowledge of them. This, along with a heavy reliance on the myth of the cave, and its shadowy representation of material reality in the *Republic*, chapter 7, and the general Platonic suspicion of the unreliability of the deliverances of sense experience, accounts for the popular interpretation of Plato's philosophy in almost exclusively transcendentalist and ultra-idealistic terms. However, apart from the soul's pre-natal contemplation of the Ideal Forms "beyond the heavens," there is in Plato's various writings also an interest in the way in which "copies" of the Ideal Forms are immanently embodied in the particular existents of this world of space and time, where they become available to be perceived and known, even if in a now "remembered," "reflected," or "shadowy," and therefore partial, kind of way.[37] It is at this point that they coalesce with Stoic seminal notions or conceptions/preconceptions (*ennoiai/prolepseis*) that were said to be intellectually derived empirically through the natural order.

It is certainly true that the unchanging and timelessly eternal Ideal Forms were regarded by Plato as real, and the particular instantiations of them in their shadowy

---

35. This is an emphasis that is already present in the way Antiochus blended Platonic and Stoic terms.

36. Indeed, he critiqued the theory himself fairly intensively in *Parmenides*.

37. Interestingly enough, the Platonic works where this is found, *Phaedrus* and *Timaeus*, are the very works which feature most noticeably in the writings of Philo. Eudorus commented on *Timaeus*; Philo wrote a commentary on it; Cicero made a translation of it, and so on.

appearances in the particularities of space and time were thought to be less than real, for this is a world that "comes to be and passes away, but never really is."[38] However, he was in fact nevertheless challenged by the way in which the Forms were actually perceived and known, precisely as they were encountered, "embodied," as it were, in the passing and ephemeral world of particular material things.

In the account of creation in *Timaeus* 51a, Plato speaks of the initial need of the yet-to-be-formed, neutral, and pristine immaterial "substance" to be void of all the Forms. He thought of this pristine substance as "invisible and unshaped" while it waited to be fitted to receive the copies of all things intelligible and eternal (the Forms). Only so could this primordial "substance" be receptive to the impression of a specific Form in a particular existent thing of time and space. But Plato hardly exudes confidence in his speculative musings about all this; he confesses that the particulars of space and time partake "in some most perplexing and most baffling way" in the intelligible Forms. An understanding of the mysterious manner in which the timeless Forms could be perceived by the senses insofar as they were "impressed" in historical particulars seems to have eluded him. It defied a single clear exposition, but the bare fact of it meant that there is a sense in which Plato's philosophy could be read in such a way as to suggest that he positively resisted the temptation to disengage entirely from the world. This is certainly the way in which Plato came to be read by the Middle Platonists from Antiochus onwards. It is not insignificant therefore that *Timaeus* was among the most read of his works in this period.

The same theme is found in *Phaedrus*. In *Phaedrus* 249d Socrates acknowledges that the philosopher "separates himself from human interests, turning his attention towards the divine." Ordinary folk in the world "consider him mad." There are few in number who "when they see here any likeness of the things of that other world, are stricken with amazement and can no longer control themselves."[39] Nevertheless, it is precisely within the physical world that it is possible to recognize a likeness to the reality of remembered Ideal Forms; this recognized likeness is "a 'constitutive representation' of that in which it 'participates.'" Clearly, for Plato, flickering glimpses of the ideal perfection of the eternal Forms were somehow perceived from within the imperfect world of particular material and physical things. There is thus in Plato a regular foray into the empirical, fed by a fascination with the way in which particular instances of things in this passing world of space and time "participate" in the eternal intelligible Forms and trigger the remembrance of them.

It is refreshing to find that, contrary to the usual all-too-stereotypical presentation of the idealism of Plato, Catherine Pickstock has very helpfully pointed out "that Plato did *not* wish to drive a wedge between form and appearance."[40] In *Phaedrus*, the participation of the Forms of the "good" and the "beautiful" within particulars of this

---

38. *Timaeus* 28a.
39. *Phaedrus* 250a.
40. Pickstock, *After Writing*, 14–15.

world, for example, permits a flickering acquaintance through these immanent copies of the Forms which "shine out" from within the *onta* of this world (the sum of the particular things of the created order). Thus, Pickstock makes the point that, for Plato, the perception of particular instances of the good and the beautiful is what triggers the philosopher's "mad" pursuit in quest of the divinely transcendent reality of "the good" and "the beautiful" in their Ideal Forms. But, vice versa, particular instances of the good and the beautiful may be understood to "participate" in their corresponding Ideal Forms. She therefore concludes her assessment of Plato by declaring that ". . . the strongly positive view of *methexis* (participation) in the *Phaedrus* frees him from the charge of otherworldliness and total withdrawal from physicality . . . ."[41] On the contrary, it was the reflection of "goodness" and "beauty" perceived in the passing world of space and time that triggered the "madness" of desire[42] for the eternal and changeless Ideal Forms of the good and the beautiful.[43] Thus, the apprehension of the shadowy "copies" of Forms that were understood to be immanent in particulars was essential to the contemplative desire to pursue them.

Thus in *Phaedrus*, no less than *Timaeus*, we have the genesis of the notion of "immanent ideas." It is possible that this notion was also in Plato's mind at the end of *Phaedo*, but even if not, later Middle Platonists certainly understood Plato in this kind of way.

This concentration of interest in the reflection of the Forms in particulars, or to put it in another, perhaps even more Platonic way, the "*methectic*" participation of the particulars of this world *in* the eternal Forms, came to command the attention of Middle Platonism in large part because (ironically) the Middle Platonists approached the reading of Plato from a more empirical perspective inherited from the monism of Stoicism. Generally speaking, Plato's theory of the pre-existing soul's acquaintance with the eternal Forms had been left behind in epistemologies from Epicurus onwards. Instead, philosophies, of which Stoicism is the classic example, thought of the unconscious acquisition of the knowledge of intelligible "conceptions" (*ennoiai*), and "preconceptions" or "anticipations" (*prolepseis*), that were said naturally and unreflectively to be generated in humans. Thus, by contrast with Platonic "innate Ideas" as triggers of the remembrance of the eternal Forms, the "conceptions" and "preconceptions/anticipations" (*ennoiai* and *prolepseis*), as the Stoics continued to refer to them, were unreflectively acquired by regular and repeated empirical acquaintance.

---

41. Pickstock, *After Writing*, 14.

42. *Phaedrus* 249d.

43. Pickstock, *After Writing*, 14. It may also be noted that in the *Symposium*, the contemplation and experience of beauty through the world of appearances, gives the soul sight of an eternal and changeless beauty. This suggests a positive use of the material world.

However, the kind of coalescence or "harmonization" of Platonic "innate Ideas" and Stoic "conceptions and preconceptions," such as we see already beginning in Antiochus, was in a sense inevitable. Especially under the increasing transcendental thrust of the Neopythagorean interests promoted by Eudorus, Middle Platonism once again even began to think of the eternal and transcendental nature of the Forms of which the "immanent ideas" were copies, as "thoughts" in the "mind of God."[44] In the process of this development, the Stoic notions of "conceptions" and "preconceptions" could be "gathered up" into a kind of synthetic amalgam with these resurgent Platonic ideas, even if these two philosophies disagreed over the issue of the manner in which the Ideas and conceptions/preconceptions were acquired.

In the emerging world of Middle Platonism, we know that this side of Plato's reflection on the Forms did not escape the interest of those who we normally think of as Stoics.[45] In Paul's own day, for example, Seneca appears to have borrowed, if not from Plato himself, then from a platonic source.[46] In his famous *Letters 58* and *65*, Seneca, among other things, apparently equates Platonic Ideas with the Stoic seminal principles of reason, the "conceptions" or "preconceptions," which were brought to the identification of things in the material world in making claims to knowledge. Certainly, Seneca speaks in Platonic fashion of the Ideas as the "eternal exemplar of things which are brought into being in accordance with nature." By way of illustrative example, he uses the paradigm of a human face that is used by an artist in painting a portrait, the portrait being a "copy," which embodies the "form" of the face.[47] Then he goes on to draw an important distinction between the transcendent eternal Ideas, and the immanent "form" or "shape" of them that is found in their counterparts in the material world. By contrast with the feminine *Idea*, what is discerned of it in its embodiment in a particular thing is denoted by the neuter *Idos*; a term, as it happens, that is already used by Plato himself in *Timaeus* 51a. Here we have evidence of the growing Stoic interest in the notion of the "immanence" of transcendental Platonic Ideas, which is in a sense a bridge between the undisputed dualistic poles of Platonic ontology. Clearly, it is a mistake to speak, as Engberg-Pedersen does, of a dichotomy that allegedly "distinguishes sharply between the world of the senses and the world of

---

44. An emphasis that bulks large in the writings of Philo; but already for Antiochus of Ascalon, the Ideas in their transcendent and objective aspect are referred to as "the thoughts of God." For the role of Antiochus in the identification of the Demiurge and World Soul of the *Timaeus* with the Stoic *Pneuma-Logos* see Dillon, *The Middle Platonists*, 95.

45. For Cicero's use of Plato, see Schofield, "Cicero's Plato."

46. Seneca (4 BC—AD 65) seems to have thought that he was reliant upon Plato himself, and it has to be said that it is certainly possible to find resonances of what he has to say in Plato's dialogues; however, it may be that he is dealing with Plato at second hand.

47. Seneca, *Letter 58*, secs. 16–22.

ideas." In the interaction between Stoicism and Platonism, this alleged distinction was not always quite so sharply dawn.

Interestingly, in Seneca's *Letter 65*, the eternal transcendent Idea (by contrast with its reflected embodied *Idos* in a particular reality of space and time, which in turn may be said to "participate" in it), is understood to reside in the mind of God in exactly the way that had already been embraced by a number of Middle Platonists. It is likely that Eudorus of Alexandria already thought of Platonic ideas as "thoughts in the mind of God."[48] Similarly, these "paradigmatic exemplars" or Ideas, says Seneca, "God contains within himself," while their copies (the "immanent ideas") were encountered in material things. The location of eternal ideas "in the mind of God" was to become an often-repeated strategy of Middle Platonists. This is especially so of Philo[49] who, by coalescing the Ideas into a composite unity, was therefore able to speak of the eternal Word in a way that anticipates the prologue of St. John's Gospel, with its theology of the divine Word, through which "all things came into being."[50] As a consequence, it may be quite a challenge to try to unscramble Stoic and Platonic input in John's theology of the Word.

It must be clearly said, therefore, that the notion of the "immanence" of Ideas in material and physical things, or conversely, the "participation" of material and physical things in eternal Ideas (whether clearly formulated by Plato himself, or imagined by his Middle Platonist successors to have been entertained by him), means that we are ill-advised to draw a sharp dichotomy in this period between an alleged Platonic idealism and the empirical materialism characteristic of the Stoics. The difference between Plato's alleged idealism and Stoic empiricism was almost certainly much more blurred in the world of Middle Platonism than Engberg-Pedersen is inclined to allow. In this period, it is therefore a mistake to over-focus on the eternal and transcendental nature of Plato's Ideas, so as then to draw a dichotomy between Platonism and Stoicism, at the expense of an appreciation of Plato's fascination with their immanent embodiment in material things. Rather, if anything, the "*methectic* bridge," between "immanent ideas" and their transcendental eternal paradigms, makes this schema of Plato more sympathetic to the Jewish view of God and of God's ultimate transcendence, even when God is immanently engaged in dealing with the world, than to Stoicism's quasi-animism or pan-en-theism.

The hybridizing kind of epistemology, which equates Platonic immanent Ideas with Stoic conceptions and pre-conceptions, demonstrates the capacity of Middle Platonists to avoid a chaotic eclecticism by consciously selecting only specific aspects

---

48. See Dillon, *The Middle Platonists*, 128.
49. Dillon, *The Middle Platonists*, 159.
50. John 1:3.

of Stoic thought that could be integrated with the resurgent Platonism or vice versa. This means that, while the more empirical face of Middle Platonism's reading of Plato makes for the possibility of "harmonization" with the empirical thrust of Stoic epistemology, the ultimate transcendence of the Platonic Forms is nevertheless retained. In other words, the notion of intelligible "preconceptions" or "anticipations" (*prolepseis*) which Stoicism inherited, ultimately from Epicurus, as universal notions that were believed to be acquired naturally and unreflectively and then brought to the knowledge of particular things, could, in the world of Middle Platonism, coalesce with Platonic "immanent Ideas" through their various embodiments in the physical and material order. On the other hand, the perception of them within the particulars in the world of space and time could be interpreted as the "shadow of God" in the world, the revelation of the divine creative activity.[51] This in turn resonated with monistic Stoic notions of the all-pervading divine presence in the natural world, specifically through the divinely intelligible Spirit, the *logos-pneuma*. But from a Platonic point of view, the perception of the Ideas in the particulars of space and time ignited the contemplative quest for the elusive eternal originals in which they "participated."

Now, this "*methectic*," or participative, bridge between timeless transcendental Ideal Forms and their concrete embodiment in the material and historical existents of particular things in space and time, may be more important for our understanding of Paul than a concentration of interest on Stoic terminology and patterns of thought alone will allow. It is this understanding of the relation of God to the world that appears to be presupposed by Paul himself in Rom 1:20, when he castigated those in the pagan world who were "without excuse," for "Ever since the creation of the world [God's] eternal power and divine nature, invisible though they are, have been understood and seen through the things he has made." This natural theology, with modifications, could clearly be shared not only with his Stoic neighbors, but with those who had embraced (or who at least had been touched by) a Middle Platonic reading of Plato as well. However, from a Platonic perspective, this approach to epistemology nevertheless allows for a dual reference. In a sense, encounters with the Forms in their immanent embodiment in particulars of space and time may be understood to point "beyond themselves" to their transcendental exemplars, and thus to stimulate the earnest desire for them. But equally, it is implicit in Paul's argument in Rom 1 that it is epistemologically possible for humans willfully to focus upon the created order itself without attention to the "shadow" of God's invisible presence in and through it. This means that, in terms of

---

51. Philo speaks of the perception of the "shadow of God" as the "trace" left by the Logos as the active agent in creation; the Logos being the sum total of the "Ideas in activity." It is easy to see how Platonic "Ideas in activity" could be equated with seminal reason-principles (*logoi spermatikoi*) borrowed from the Stoics.

thought, it is possible to focus either on one or the other, the material face of physical reality or the ideal exemplary paradigms that are constitutive of it, and indeed to contrast one with the other. On the other hand, it is possible at the same time to speak of the continuity of the one with the other; from a Platonic point of view, the "memory" of the Ideal Forms being reactivated by their perceived immanent embodiments—or, in Paul's language, the "eternal power and divine nature" of God, though invisible, in their embodiments are "seen through the things he has made."

This duality is actually also exemplified by Paul in his references to the experience of the Spirit. If we read St. Paul with an eye to discerning the "epistemic dynamics" apparently presupposed by him, Paul often works with a pattern of thought in which he draws a distinction between the Spirit of Christ which he concretely experienced while he was "in the body" (and in a sense "away from the Lord" in *this* world), and the possibility of a more clear seeing of Christ "face to face" in the heavenly life—whether after his death, or at the Eschaton, should this arrive prior to his death (the question of timing is not a material concern at this point).[52] In a sense, as in the case of Plato's acquaintance with the good and the beautiful in this world, which he says in *Phaedrus* ignites the "mad" desire of the philosopher to pursue their Ideal Forms, so the partial seeing of the reflected image of Christ in the power of his Spirit in concrete experiences of space and time, ignites Paul's yearning to be "with Christ" and to see Christ "face to face." His yearning desire is to be "away from the flesh" and "with Christ," "for that is far better." This becomes the object of his hope beyond death, or beyond life in this world should the *parousia* and the end of the world occur prior to his death. Clearly, a kind of platonic ontological dualism underpins all this. In this way, Platonic epistemological presuppositions operate within Paul's inherited Second Temple eschatological hope.

Moreover, there is a kind of continuity between one of the polarities with which Paul works and the other, for the concrete experience of the Spirit is the promissory guarantee which grounds this hope of greater clarity to come.[53] Thus, as St. Paul himself says, as a consequence of Christ's Resurrection, we may abound in hope "in the power of the Holy Spirit."[54] In this way, Paul marries an epistemology of faith with his forward looking Jewish eschatological trust towards the future, but the dual polarity, of the perceived activity of the Spirit of Christ in space and time, and the transcendent Christ (who is located in heaven "at the right hand of the Father" and who is yet to be fully known), is retained. Indeed, Paul appears to presuppose a dualistic ontology insofar as he speaks of "what is seen" and "what is unseen," and observes that in the condition

---

52. It is clear that in Paul's statements about it being better to be "with Christ" than to "live in the flesh," he is contemplating the possibility of his own death, as in Phil 1:20–23. The same may be said of the parallel thought in 2 Cor 5:8, where being "away from the body" and "at home with the Lord" does not seem to be associated exclusively only with the *parousia*.

53. 2 Cor 5:5.

54. Rom 15:13.

of his temporary afflictions in this world we "look not at what can be seen but at what cannot be seen."[55] In fact, he helpfully draws out the ontological implications of this epistemological duality: "what can be seen is temporary" and "what cannot be seen is eternal."[56] Clearly, Paul does not just inhabit a world that is monistically Stoic. The epistemology presupposed by all this seems unmistakably Platonic.

Now, let us bring this feature of Middle Platonic epistemology into association with what Paul has to say about the perception of the Spirit, and with his understanding of the relation between the "life-giving Spirit of Christ," and the Raised Christ himself. In one sense, Paul works with an apparently simple identification of the Spirit and Christ himself, so that it is possible for him to speak of the "Spirit of Christ," and then quite simply of "Christ," as two ways of referring to the same experienced reality (as in Rom 8:9–10). However, on other occasions Paul draws a distinction of epistemological importance between "the life-giving Spirit" of Christ (or "the Spirit of life in Christ Jesus" in which faithful disciples *participate*, and therefore claim to know in actuality), and the transcendent Christ whom Paul hopes to see "in person," as we would say today, or "face to face" to use his own idiom. It is because of the radical ontological hiddenness of the raised and exalted Christ in heaven that Paul could say, "we walk by faith, *not* by sight."[57] However, given the eschatological framework of Second Temple Judaism, Paul nevertheless interpreted what he did perceive and identify in faith as the "life-giving Spirit," as the guarantee or first-fruits of what is to be directly and more clearly encountered in the time to come.[58] This has important epistemological significance. We do not hope for what we already see, but the experiential ground of faith and hope does in fact provide a partial or ambiguous (dare we say "shadowy"?) and indistinct cognitive access to Christ. Clearly, there is a kind of epistemological dualism here, which is presupposed by Paul whenever he enters this kind of discourse about the nature of faith and eschatological hope. Moreover, it is clear that he is not just making a distinction of a temporal kind, between "now" and "then"; present and future. To some degree he has knowledge of the reality of the *pneuma* of Christ, yet it points to the more full knowing of a realty that, in terms of its present heavenly existence, remains radically hidden until its revealing on "the day of the Lord." In a sense, the distinction is not just temporal but quantitative; he hopes to see more in the time to come than he does at present. In this case, there is continuity between what is empirically known in experience, even if partially, *as* the Spirit of Christ embodied in

---

55. 2 Cor 4:18.
56. 2 Cor 4:18.
57. 2 Cor 5:7; italics added.
58. 2 Cor 5:5; Rom 8:23; also 15:13.

the community life of the baptized, and what is transcendent and hidden (in heaven), and therefore yet to be fully known at its ultimate revealing.

In a sense, the empirically experienced reality of the Spirit of Christ is perceived and identified insofar as it is an embodied *participation* (*methexis*) in the life and love of the transcendent reality of the heavenly Christ who, in the radical hiddenness of heaven, retains his invisible "otherness." In this way the heavenly Christ, through the gift of his Spirit, endows the community of faith with its distinctive form and identity. Or, conversely, the community of faith has its distinctive form and identity insofar as it "participates" in the eternal reality of the life of Christ. In other words, Paul's epistemological distinctions between the present partial perception of the living Spirit of Christ's *pneuma*, known in and through the life of the church, and the clarity of sight to come at its heavenly and transcendent fulfillment, are almost certainly to be understood in broadly Platonic dualistic terms, rather than in Stoic monistic terms. It is from this epistemological perspective that we can grasp something of the "participative" dynamics of Paul's "in Christ" and "Body of Christ" language.

In all this, Paul's language of the knowing of the Spirit in faith, while allowing for a degree of unknowing that is logically implicit in expressions of the hope of knowing more to come, echoes the Platonic epistemological doctrine that Ideas cannot be fully grasped in our lifetime, and are themselves so transcendent as not to be objects of exact knowledge. This was in fact one of the bones of contention between Platonists and Stoics, for Stoics happily grounded the possibility of knowledge on the inductively arrived at conceptions/preconceptions (*ennoiai/prolepseis*), whereas the transcendent elusiveness of the Platonic Ideal Forms seemed to them to deny the very possibility of knowledge. Nevertheless, the Platonists steadfastly held to the view that, because only God can know the "thoughts of God" perfectly, in this life only a qualified knowing of them is humanly possible. In a similar way, Paul's hope is grounded in his perception of the Spirit, but this is necessarily only a partial seeing; we do not hope for what we already fully see. A more full seeing is yet to come; then he will know even as he is himself fully known by God, but in this life a full knowledge of ideal reality is impossible. It remains hidden and transcendent.

The Platonist's view that human beings do not have direct access to the intelligible and divine realm persisted through the Middle Platonic world of Paul's time and into the third-century AD. Even in the century after Paul, for example, Albinus (Alcinous) in *Didaskalikos* (c. AD 145) was still speaking of the pursuit of wisdom in terms of striving to achieve a likeness to the divine through the contemplation of the divine and the thoughts of the divine, even though its full achievement remained beyond human grasp in this world.[59] Indeed, it was a novel epistemological innovation when, well into

---

59. *Didaskalikos* 28: quoting Plato's *Theaetetus*, Albinus says "assimilation to God is to be prudent,

the third-century AD, Plotinus affirmed the possibility that the soul was capable of pure and direct contemplation of the Ideas in this life. That the transcendent Ideas were beyond human grasp in this world is an obverse example of the "mad" pursuit of ideal Forms that *Phaedrus* says is triggered by the reactivated "memory" of them by acquaintance with their immanent embodiments in the this-worldly particulars of space and time. Albinus indicated that this desire initiates a "movement towards" the ideal, not its full possession.[60] In the light of this, we can appreciate Paul's declaration that here we see, but only as in a mirror, dimly.[61]

It is also noteworthy that, in speaking of the partial knowing of the divine love that is appropriate to faith, Paul employs the Platonic image of "a reflection"—as in the polished metal mirrors of his day. Likewise, in 2 Corinthians, Christ is even himself thought of as the "image," or *eikōn* of God.[62] This is language that we tend today to interpret in a thorough-going dualistic way, as though a reflection or *eikōn* were somehow entirely separate from that which it represents. However, if it is understood *methectically* to "participate" in its Ideal Form, then an *eikōn* enjoys a kind of continuity similar to that which Seneca discerned between a portrait and the human face of which it is a "copy." As the *eikōn* of God, understood in a Platonic and *methectic* sense, Christ himself "participates" in the divine and heavenly reality of God; he has his true identity *from* God and thus truly *reveals* God as his "express image." Likewise, the church itself, as the Eucharistic community of those baptized *into* Christ, may be understood as a particular entity of this world that, as the Body of Christ, has its distinctive identity by means of its *(methectic) participation* in the heavenly reality of Christ himself through the constitutive gift of the Spirit of Christ.

In this way, Plato's idea of *methexis*, the participation of the particulars of space and time in transcendental reality, provides the broad pattern which helps explain Paul's thought in relation to his life of "participation" (through the "life-giving Spirit *of* Christ") in the life of Christ *himself*, and his interpretation of this in faith as a partial or incomplete knowing. In the perspective of Second Temple eschatology, this is the knowing that therefore becomes the basis of his eschatological hope of a more clear knowing of the transcendent exalted Christ in the time to come. Once again, whether this epistemic fulfillment happens for individuals immediately after death, or in the form of the earthly manifestation of his heavenly reality when Christ returns at the *parousia*, is (epistemologically speaking) immaterial. Likewise, the participation of baptized Christian believers through faith in the *pneuma* of Christ, actively by grace *helpinging them conform* to

---

just and holy"; "to become like God is to be righteous and holy and wise" . . . "therefore we ought to try to escape from earth to the dwelling of the gods as quickly as we can." Note also his emphasis on the unknowable ineffability of God in *Didaskalikos* 10.

60. See *Didaskalikos* 4. What is within a divine power is "impossible for a human being"; it is "completely incomprehensible to us."

61. 1 Cor 13:12: "For now we see in a mirror, dimly, but then we will see face to face. Now I know only in part; then I will know fully, even as I have been fully known."

62. 2 Cor 4:4.

the pattern of Christ himself (thus to be, "like him," as it were, as "copies" of his ideal form, with the hope ultimately of becoming "as he is"), also resonates with the Platonic *methectic* model of the "participation" of earthly material and physical particulars in a normative transcendent heavenly reality.

It is clearly a mistake to underestimate the possible influence of Plato behind Paul's understanding of things, simply on the basis of the popular view of Platonism that trades exclusively in the allegedly ethereal abstractions of pure idealism—as though Platonic Forms are always only plucked from the miasma of abstract thought. Even in a world that was in many important respects still Stoic, Plato's theory of the reality of transcendental eternal Forms or Ideas, and the immanence of the participation of the particulars of the passing world of space and time in them (even as the "shadowy" and imperfect representations or appearances of them), cannot be shuffled off stage and out of view. In the very mixed and fluid world of first-century philosophy, it is therefore a mistake to draw a rigid distinction between Platonism as a dualistic ontology and Stoicism as a monistic one. Equally it would be a mistake to interpret Paul from the perspective of Stoicism alone and to ignore the possible influence of Platonism.

These epistemological considerations have profound implications for the understanding of the ontology of the Spirit as Paul thought of it. It certainly means we cannot be at all sure that Paul slavishly followed Stoicism by conceiving of *pneuma* in straightforwardly materialistic and physical terms which presuppose an ontological monism. While Engberg-Pedersen opts for a Stoic understanding of Paul's conception of the alleged material and physical nature of the Spirit, it would be preferable to say that the Spirit as Paul conceives of it is experienced as something that, though understood to have been *concretely* known as something with which the early Christians were actually acquainted (particularly as the animating Spirit of the community of faith), was nevertheless *not* itself simply a material or physical reality, but rather a non-material, spiritual, and ultimately transcendent reality. Despite the fact that, in this life, the Raised Christ could not therefore be fully known, or clearly, distinctly, and literally described, the Spirit of Christ was perceived as a reality concretely known by acquaintance, for it was through the Spirit that the baptized were privileged to *participate* in the transcendent life of the Raised Christ himself. Insofar as the material bodies of the baptized themselves "participated" in the Spirit of Christ, Christ himself could therefore be understood to "shine through them" so as to establish them in their baptismal identity, just as God was able "to give the light of the knowledge of the glory of God in the face of Christ."[63] Despite the resonance of this language of "shining" with Stoicism, a dualistic cosmology is nevertheless sustained. As the earthly manifestation within material and physical human lives of an essentially heavenly and otherwise

---

63. 2 Cor 4:6.

Ideal and hidden reality, the Spirit retains both a this-worldly and, at the same time, an otherworldly reference. This means that, though we may appropriately describe the Spirit as a "concretely experienced" reality that is actually known in faith by acquaintance, it is a mistake to go on to conclude that the Spirit is itself to be thought of monistically as a straight-forward "physical" or "material" reality. Thus, the Spirit, precisely as the object of *faith*, though concretely perceived within this world of space and time, does not lose its ontologically transcendental character.

Not least, it is of theological importance to resist a purely Stoic reading of Paul with an implicit Stoic understanding of the ontology of the Spirit, so as to resist the suggestion that it is somehow independent of God. By appreciating the capacity of a broadly Platonic dualistic ontology to open the way to understanding the Spirit as a concretely experienced and cognitively perceived reality, which nevertheless does not lose the transcendent and otherworldly reference of the ultimately unknowable heavenly Form in which it itself participates and which gives it its specific identity, we can understand how it was that Paul could call it, not just the "Spirit *of* Christ," but the "Spirit *of* God."

13

Belief and Behavior

Having the Mind of Christ

FAITH IN THE RESURRECTION of Christ has an immediate impact on human behavior. Even the most fleeting acquaintance with the epistles of St. Paul will indicate that he spent a good deal of his time and mental energy encouraging and exhorting the communities for which he exercised a concerned pastoral care to live according to standards of behavior that to him appear to have been unequivocally clear. Generally speaking, Paul encouraged people to observe the law of ordered civil society in which they found themselves; they were to submit to governing authorities for "those authorities that exist have been instituted by God."[1] They were to be good law-abiding citizens. Within the home, household codes prevailed: young men were to take notice of the wisdom of older men; slaves were to obey their masters; children their parents; and wives were to be submissive to their husbands. All this was par-for-the-course in an ethical environment in which Stoic ideals of living in accordance with what nature was believed to have intended was the norm. All this could be discerned by the prudent exercise of reason and with a degree of common sense.

Whether Paul would have counseled that Christian people should obey the governing authorities in Nazi Germany during the 1930s, or pursue the business ethic of modern western competitive individualism, let alone commend the "headship" of husbands over their wives in the context of domestic violence, is quite another matter. However, generally speaking, Paul believed people should live according to and within the law, for the law provided the basic ordering necessary for society to hold together. But Christians "are not under the law but under grace."[2] While, as far as possible, they might live by the law, the gospel of Christ calls them to live according to a standard over and above what the law requires. The law may require them to pay their taxes; the gospel calls them to generosity of spirit and to the sharing of their resources to ensure the well-being of others. This means living in accordance, not just with what is naturally appropriate when judged by the exercise of ethical reasoning (let alone

---

1. Rom 13:1.
2. Rom 6:14.

acquiescing in a host of objectionable anti-human practices in the monistic world of modern secular materialism), but rather in accordance with what is appropriate to the relationship they enjoyed in faith with Christ, and the values of his dawning Kingdom. This means that, while Paul was a man of his time, who was furnished with a vocabulary and ways of ethical argument that were identifiably Stoic, he brought to it a new and uniquely distinctive norm insofar as the Raised Christ himself thenceforth provided the standard of judgment.

Troels Engberg-Pedersen has very convincingly demonstrated the role of Stoic language and patterns of argument in the ethical (*parenetic*) passages of Paul's major epistles.[3] His extensive use of Stoic language is remarkably clear, for example, in Philippians, where it seems that Paul found this language very serviceable for his purpose and put it to good use, even if he may not necessarily have been particularly conscious of its Stoic antecedents.[4] Among terms with a Stoic resonance are *prokopē* ("progress" in 1:12, 25), *ta diapheronta* ("things that really matter" in 1:10) as the obverse of *adiaphora* ("things indifferent"), *autarkēs* ("self-sufficient contentment" in 4:11), *chara* ("joy," which first comes up in 1:4) and, very importantly, "living or conducting oneself as a citizen" (*politeuomai* in 1:27) and the concept of *politeuma* ("citizenship" in 3:20).[5]

However, as Engberg-Pedersen points out, this comes with the important rider that Paul substitutes "Christ" for "reason" in the discernment of appropriate norms of ethical behavior. Whereas Stoic ethical theory promoted the need to live in accordance with laws intended by nature, and that were held to be intelligible to reason, Paul substituted the notion of belonging to Christ, and of living in a manner appropriate to this relationship. This is clearly exemplified in Philippians.[6] By contrast with the reasoning of his non-Christian Stoic neighbors, in ethical matters it was "the mind of Christ" that informed the life of Christian believers. Hence Paul's exhortation: "Let the same mind be in you that was in Christ Jesus."[7] In Philippians, having the "mind of Christ" is therefore substituted for a set of ethical norms of the kind that Stoicism sought to discern in the natural order through the exercise of reason.

---

3. Engberg-Pedersen, "Stoicism in Philippians." See also his *Paul and the Stoics* for a more extensive analysis of Philippians, as well as Galatians and Romans.

4. Perhaps in seeking to communicate to a philosophically educated audience, Paul had no hesitation in embracing the use of this language, though not all commentators are comfortable with this suggestion. See Fee, *Paul's Letter to the Philippians*, 427–35.

5. While earlier interpreters, who were often nervously anxious to keep the flag of the Biblical Theology Movement flying, sought to keep "Greek" influence at a distance by trying to argue that Paul actually transforms the Stoic meanings so that he remains untainted by Greek conceptions, the general tendency to disparage these Stoic terms is now a lost cause and entirely unnecessary.

6. See Engberg-Pedersen, "Stoicism in Philippians."

7. Phil 2:5.

On the other hand, it is hard to see that Paul could have reached this position without the help also of Plato. Apart from the appearance in Philippians of characteristically Stoic terms, there is the near *hapax*[8] of *morphē* that appears significantly in the key Christ-hymn of Phil 2:5–11, concerning Jesus, who "though he was *in* the form (*morphē*) of God," did not think of God-likeness in terms of snatching at status and power, but "emptied himself," and being found in human likeness took "the form (again, *morphē*) of a slave." As we shall see, this use of *morphē* appears to have had a Platonic origin. Given the obvious importance of this passage for Paul's understanding of what appears to have been, for him, a defining norm of Christian behavior, it is important to pause to examine it carefully.

The fact that the Septuagint only uses *morphē* very rarely (nine times), and then that it is used to translate a number of Hebrew and Aramaic words, but is never used in reference to the "form of God," makes it clear that there is really no LXX warrant for the use of this kind of language by Paul.

Some have argued in the past that Paul's use of *morphē theou* is actually synonymous with the "image of God" (*eikōn theou*) of Gen 1:27 in the LXX. In this case, the reference is to Jesus' status as a child of Adam, "made in the image of God." David Steenburg has shown, however, that it is very unlikely that *morphē* and *eikōn* were used synonymously,[9] and Larry Hurtado has very convincingly argued that, while *eikōn* is used in making a linkage or contrast of Jesus with Adam, *morphē* is never used elsewhere in an allusion to Adam. Furthermore, Hurtado points out that Phil 2:6–8 includes no other allusion to the Genesis story of the creation (and fall) of Adam that might lead readers in the direction of making such a connection.[10] Certainly, it seems clear enough, that more is at stake in Phil 2 than the statement that Jesus was made "in the image of God" in the way any other human being, as a child of Adam, is made "in the image of God." Paul's sense seems to be that, "being in the form (*morphē*) of God" is something uniquely memorable about Jesus, rather than something he shared with all other humans, and even that, though Jesus was the (humanly unique) "image of the invisible God" (in the sense of being *the* expression of the nature, will, and purpose of God), he (astonishingly) "did not regard equality with God" in terms of grasping at

---

8. The only other occurrence of *morphē* in the New Testament is in the reconstructed additional ending of Mark at 16:12, where the Raised Jesus is said to have been manifested "in another form (*morphē*)," apparently to the travelers on the way to Emmaus. The verbal form *morphōthē* is certainly a *hapax legomenon* (Gal 4:19 where Paul says he works until "Christ be formed in you"); the noun *morphōsis* is found twice—in Rom 2:20 and 2 Tim 3:5.

9. Steenburg, "The Case against the Synonymity of *Morphē* and *Eikōn*," 77–86.

10. Hurtado, *How on Earth Did Jesus Become a God?* 99. See also *Lord Jesus Christ*, 121–23. James Dunn finds numerous allusions to Adam insofar as Christ, unlike Adam, does not grasp at "being like God" (Dunn, *The Theology of Paul the Apostle*, 281–87"). Alas, allusions to Adam Christology may, however, be illusory in this passage.

power, but lived a life of self-effacing humility, "taking the form (*morphē*) of a slave," and so on. All this appears to refer uniquely to the remembered Jesus.

In any event, the lack both of direct LXX verbal precedent and of clear Genesis allusions to Adam in Phil 2, frees us to think of the meaning of *morphē* in much more neutral mixed Stoic-Platonic epistemological terms within the general linguistic context of the world of Middle Platonism. If the use of *morphē* was, as most scholars seem to agree, almost certainly already incorporated into this text when Paul himself received it, it could well have been a term that was picked up at a previous time from the popular contemporary linguistic environment. Here the road leads inexorably back to Plato. Though Plato himself did not use *morphē* a great deal, it is a term that assumed an undeniable Platonic pedigree, and that actually went out of use under the influence of Stoicism.[11] The remnant survival (or perhaps revival) of *morphē* that we see in Philippians certainly appears to preserve a Platonic resonance, which we should note is primarily epistemological in nature, rather than speculatively metaphysical or cosmological. In its original Platonic use, *morphē* signifies the inherent characteristic or distinctive identity or essence of some person or thing, not so much in the abstract, but as the essential identifying form in which something appears as actually subsisting *in* an objective individual person or thing. The distinctive *morphē* of a person or thing is that by which that person or thing may be identified and known. It is thus to be understood unmistakably as an epistemological term having to do with the dispositional characteristics by virtue of which an identity is known, rather than something speculatively metaphysical. In other words, as "the Form in which something appears," *morphē* is close to an "immanent Idea" or *Idos* of the kind that so occupied the mind of the Middle Platonists.[12] When encountered in space and time, the *morphē* of a particular person or thing could be understood to reactivate the "memory" of an Ideal Form. This epistemological meaning of the term seems most appropriate in its use in Philippians. Larry Hurtado rightly observes that the phrase "being in the form

---

11. See Behm's entry under μορφή in Kittel and Friedrich, *Theological Dictionary of the New Testament*, iv, 742–59. Behm insists that ". . . there is no trace of a Hellenistic philosophical understanding of μορφή in this passage" (Phil 2), 752. In support of this he cites Lightfoot, *Saint Paul's Epistle to the Philippians* (1927), 132, and Lohmeyer who, he says, "rightly says that it is impossible to see in μορφή a philosophical term, however attenuated" (*Die Briefe an die Philipper, Kolosser und an Philemon*, 1964). This general kind of attempt to distance Paul from Hellenistic philosophical influence is characteristic of the Biblical Theological Movement. However, a distinction is to be dawn between metaphysics and epistemology. The actual reasons given by Behm indicate that he is thinking in metaphysical terms rather than in epistemological terms. He relies upon the view that the Jewish God is conceived in personal and ethical terms, whose transcendence resists "any attempt at a sensual objectification of the divine form" (749). This, however, fails to make the distinction between the transcendence of God as God is in God's self, and the epistemological importance of God's revelation in immanent form as God makes his presence known in faith to finite human perception. The incarnational "objectification of the divine form" in Christ may certainly be known by faith through the senses, as was argued in chapter 5.

12. As was discussed in the previous chapter.

of God" in Philippians "gives little encouragement for metaphysical speculation."[13] Rather, it signals something that can be perceived by the senses and thus known.

It has to be conceded, however, that the interpretation of Phil 2, and the kenotic (self-emptying) Christology that has been dogmatically erected upon it, has in the past been dominated by metaphysical considerations. It has been traditional to interpret this passage to refer to Jesus' alleged enjoyment of divine status and powers as a "divine being" in a pre-existent heavenly life, *prior* to his birth as a human being.[14] Even Larry Hurtado, who thinks Paul's reference to Jesus' "being in the form of God" gives no encouragement for metaphysical speculation, does not hesitate to think in metaphysical terms of Jesus' pre-existence, so that "equality with God" is said to be something enjoyed by Jesus *prior* to his becoming human: this means "being in some way 'divine' in status and mode and then becoming a human being."[15]

A heavily speculative metaphysical reading of Phil 2 suggests that the reference to Jesus' "being in the form (*morphē*) of God" but not regarding "equality with God" as something to be grasped or held on to, means that the self-emptying or condescending act was essentially a self-abnegation of divine powers that was necessary if the pre-existing divine person was to become a man. The act of condescension or self-emptying thus becomes the divine act of becoming human.

In the subsequent kenotic Christology that has been built upon this reading of Philippians, it has even been suggested that divine and heavenly powers (especially of omnipotence, omniscience, and omnipresence) were thus "left behind" in heaven, as it were, in this act of self-abnegation in the interests of Jesus' appearing on earth as a truly human person. Alternatively, it has been suggested that by becoming human, or "putting on a human form," these divine powers were withdrawn from view or hidden beneath Jesus' humanity.[16] Because they were "kept in reserve" during the course of Jesus' incarnate life, they were not brought publicly into play.[17] These suggestions have

---

13. Hurtado, *How on Earth Did Jesus Become a God?*, 96.

14. See for example, Marshall, *The Epistle to the Philippians*, 50, and Witherington, *Jesus the Sage*, 263: "The choice being described in Philippians 2 is the choice to take on human flesh, a choice only a pre-existent one could make." See also Byrne, "Christ's Pre-Existence." The attribution of this emphasis on pre-existence to Paul almost certainly goes beyond what is warranted by Philippians 2. Note James Dunn's cautious account of the pre-existent wisdom of God, with which Jesus came to be identified, rather than the pre-existence of Jesus himself. Dunn says: "That Paul intended an allusion to the preexistent Christ's self-abasement in incarnation must be judged unlikely" (Dunn, *The Theology of Paul the Apostle*, 292).

15. Hurtado, *How on Earth Did Jesus Become a God?*, 101.

16. In the manner of the withdrawal of the undercarriage of an aircraft during the course of flight.

17. As though Rafael Nadal were to conceal his true prowess and power as a tennis player, in an act of self-abnegation, by putting on a heavy army great coat, so as to play at the level of his less expert opponents.

raised no end of theological problems relating to an unavoidable change in the Godhead at the time of the incarnation, insofar as they imply the abandonment by Jesus of some formerly possessed divine powers.[18] Alternatively, the concealing of divine powers beneath the outward appearance of Jesus in human form, seems to lead directly into the cul-de-sac of Docetism by suggesting that Jesus was a "pre-existent" divine being who only outwardly "appeared" to be a man. In other words, this particular reading of Philippians leads directly into the suggestion that Jesus, as a pre-existing divine being, was not truly human but only appeared to be so (a heresy).

These dogmatic problems alone might cause us to hesitate before a too ready acceptance of the proposition that Paul's use of the phrase concerning Jesus "being in the form of God" implies Jesus' pre-existence. Still less might we be prepared to accept the proposition of Larry Hurtado that "well before the epistle the idea of Jesus' 'pre-existence' had become part of Christian belief."[19] Indeed, Hurtado is even prepared to speculate that Paul entertained notions of Jesus' "pre-existence" in anticipation of the full-blown incarnationalism of John's Gospel. Thus, he says that Paul is to be read in the light of John 1:1–18, and of the words John places on the lips of Jesus in John 17:5. However, it is one thing for John to speak of the pre-existence of the Word "through whom all things were made" and to associate Jesus, as "the Word Incarnate," with this divinely creative Word of God, but it is quite another thing to contend that Paul already anticipated this by thinking of *Jesus* as a pre-existing divine being who humbled himself by becoming human. That a Johannine type incarnationalism is already present in Paul's mind, as Hurtado suggests, in 1 Cor 8:6[20] and 2 Cor 8:9,[21] is surely clutching at straws.[22] It is just possible, in a broadly platonic environment in which the consolidation of eternal Forms, as "ideas of God," into the unitary pre-existing Eternal Word (as in Philo), combined with the basic platonic belief in the reality of the Ideal world over against the passing and shadowy world of time, could also accommodate the belief that Jesus might have been thought of as pre-existing his human birth "in the mind and foreknowledge of God" with an appropriate degree of realism attaching to the Platonic

---

18. Thus contravening the fundamental incarnational principle of the Fathers that at the incarnation "what he was he remained, what he was not he assumed." As Hans Frei pertinently observed, the view that "in the incarnation the Word of God divested himself deliberately and self-consciously of omnipotence over the world" is a "literalistic, simple-minded, speculative, and rather incredible heresy." This remark will be found in his essay "Theological Reflections on the Accounts of Jesus' Death and Resurrection," which the publishers have included as an Appendix in the 2013 Kindle edition of *The Identity of Jesus Christ*, at Loc.3665.

19. *How on Earth Did Jesus Become a God?* 101. See also, the earlier discussion of Jesus alleged "pre-existence" in *Lord Jesus Christ*, 118–26.

20. "Yet for us there is but one God, the Father, from whom are all things and for whom we exist, and one Lord, Jesus Christ, through whom are all things and through whom we exist."

21. "For you know the generous act of our Lord Jesus Christ, that though he was rich, yet for your sakes he became poor, so that by his poverty you might become rich."

22. Hurtado, *How on Earth Did Jesus Become a God?*, 102.

Ideal world.[23] However, I suspect that to read a fully blown incarnationalism involving the pre-existence of Jesus as "a divine being" back into the thought of Paul is probably an anachronistic speculative bridge too far. Indeed, the metaphysical reading of notions of Jesus' pre-existence into Phil 2 renders a logically noxious blow to the entire passage, given Paul's fundamental purpose for citing this ancient christological hymn in the first place. At the very outset, Paul exhorts the Philippians to "let the mind of Christ be in them" as a behavioral norm, and thus to act as Christ acted. As Hurtado himself is rightly prepared to say, being divine and choosing to become human "is obviously not a choice that mere mortals can replicate!"[24]

However, if in the general context of the thought-world of Middle Platonism, *morphē* is understood in a more clearly epistemological and less metaphysical way, speculative abstractions of this kind become unnecessary and inappropriate. Without this kind of speculative metaphysical complication, what the Philippians are exhorted by Paul to emulate is the perfectly reasonable, and behaviorally possible, earthly human life of servanthood, such as was remembered to have been lived out by the historical and human Jesus in obedience to his calling, even unto death on the Cross. Unlike Adam, at least in this behavioral sense, Jesus did not grasp at "equality with God," but instead accepted his fate in faithfulness to his mission. It was for this reason that God "highly exalted him."[25]

This means that, instead of the kenotic act of self-humbling being the heavenly act of a pre-existing divine being who was allegedly prepared not to cling on to an already possessed heavenly "equality with God" in terms of divine status and power, it may well be, as C. F. D. Moule and Piet Schoonenberg have forcefully argued,[26] that the "equality with God" that Jesus did not grasp at, or attempt to appropriate to himself, may be understood to be an ever present *future* possibility for the human Jesus as he lived his human life. Instead of something already possessed and enjoyed in a pre-existent life, prior to his birth and human life, it was a human possibility for him from which he steadfastly turned away and refused to take advantage of for himself during his human lifetime. In this resolve he was steadfast, even unto death. In this case, the sense of Phil 2:5–11 is that "even though Jesus came in the 'form' (*morphē*) of God, and thus was the expression of the nature, will and purpose of God, he (astonishingly and ever so impressively) did not reckon 'equality with God' or 'Godlikeness,' in terms of grasping at power and exalted status." That is to say, he did not think of Godlikeness as men and women normally think of Godlikeness. Self-aggrandizement

23. In a similar way in which the Raised Christ could be said, in the second-century *Odes of Solomon*, to be in the "mind" and "thought" of God.

24. Hurtado, *How on Earth Did Jesus Become a God?*, 104.

25. Phil 2:9.

26. See Schoonenberg, "He Emptied Himself," and "The Kenosis or Self-Emptying of Christ," and Moule, "Further Reflections on Philippians 2:5–11," and "The Manhood of Jesus in the New Testament." See also Macquarrie, "Kenoticism Reconsidered"; and Murphy-O'Connor, "Christological Anthropology in Phil. II, 6–11."

was not what he was remembered to have exhibited. Rather, just the contrary, "being found in human form, he humbled himself" and took "the form of a slave. . ." This is the "mind of Christ" that Paul exhorts the Philippians to emulate in their own lives, in a way that is not only legitimate but *humanly possible* for them to actualize. The kenotic self-effacing choice thus becomes the decision to embrace a distinctive style of humanity; it was the human choice of the human Jesus to "empty himself" and take on the lowly role of a servant. Thus, we are brought by an epistemological, rather than a metaphysical, reading of Phil 2 into direct contact with a controlling image of the way in which Jesus was remembered.

Despite his support for the notion that Phil 2 contains an implicit reference to early metaphysical belief in Jesus' divine pre-existence, Larry Hurtado correctly sees that, in declaring that Jesus did not seek to exploit equality with God, Paul's allusion is really to the steadfast refusal of the human Jesus to succumb to "a common expression of vain human hubris."[27] By contrast with the foolish efforts of humans to achieve self-inflated and exalted status, Jesus' self-humbling is to be seen as precisely the opposite of this: instead of the arrogant and self-inflated grasping at status and power of worldly leaders and the "foolish human hubris (especially exhibited by human rulers who sought to be treated as divine),"[28] Jesus exhibited divinity in the lowly *morphē*, or Form, embodied in the unique unsubstitutable[29] particularity of his character as servant of all.

This means, however, that the kenotic act was not one of a "divine being" humbling himself by taking human form in such a way as to camouflage or conceal a hidden divinity, but rather, that the remembered acts of the human historical Jesus who did not snatch at divine status and power, but humbled himself in taking on the form of servant-humanity, actually disclosed the true nature of divinity. In other words, the theological significance of Jesus' humanity is that this uniquely remembered and specific form of the servant-humanity of Jesus is revelatory of the nature, will, and purpose of God for Paul. In this way, Jesus' definitive expression of the human form (*morphē*) of a specific style of humanity, in his lowly life as servant of others, thus does not replace or conceal the alleged powers of divinity (formerly exercised in an alleged pre-existent life), but actually *reveals* the form (*morphē*) of God. A particular *form* of humanity—lowly, self-effacing, and self-humbling servant-humanity—is precisely what by a paradox reveals his divinity. Jesus' faithfulness to his mission even unto death is therefore the cause whereby "God highly exalted him, and gave

---

27. Hurtado, *How on Earth Did Jesus become a God?*, 100.
28. Hurtado, *How on Earth Did Jesus become a God?*, 105.
29. To use Hans Frei's much favored term.

him the name that is above every name. . ."[30] Far from abandoning divinity, or concealing divinity (as in traditional late-nineteenth and early twentieth-century kenotic Christology), the humanity Jesus lived out actually revealed the true nature of divinity in a theologically significant and definitive way that was understood to be unique to him. This is what injects the humanity of Jesus with its abiding theological significance and unique importance. This, indeed, is the abiding meaning of Jesus' humanity for Christian faith in God.

Furthermore, a platonic perspective on the meaning of *morphē* invites the suggestion of the *methectic* embodiment or participation of the Forms both of "divinity" and "servant-humanity" in the embodied historical particularity of Jesus' life. In terms of the epistemology of faith, this allowed for the re-definition of God via the specifics of the kind of humanity for which Jesus was remembered. Or perhaps better, it signaled the full "participation" of the historical Jesus, in the particularity of his embodied historical life, in the Forms both of "divinity" and human "servanthood." In this case, Paul's use of *morphē* suggests that the embodied Form, or "immanent Idea" (*Idos*), both of "divinity" and of human "servanthood," came to expression in the life of the historical Jesus as he was concretely experienced and known. By using *morphē* in relation to the concepts both of "divinity" and "servanthood," Paul conveys the sense that Jesus could be identified by the definitive Form of "divinity" that paradoxically was revealed through the form of human "servanthood." In other words, these are not antithetical, but mutually illuminative concepts;[31] both were actually understood in faith to be present as constitutive identifiable qualities of Jesus' remembered historical life.

We may refer to this as "neo-kenotic Christology." It follows that in Christ there was a kind of coincidence of the divine with a specific style of human identity of such a kind that the latter threw a definitive interpretative light on the former. "Though he was rich, for our sakes, he became poor"[32] in this sense. The particular form of the humanity Jesus lived out in his historical life, and for which he was remembered by his faithful disciples, may therefore be said thereby to have *revealed* divinity, not in terms of arrogantly snatching at some kind of supreme power over others (in the way that humans usually think of divine status and power), but in terms of serving them, loving them, and caring for them. This is how Jesus was thus known "*in human likeness*"[33] even unto death, and this was the reason for which God highly rewarded him. This was thus precisely what was so impressive and therefore uniquely memorable about him. Hence the abiding significance of the humanity of Jesus for revealing the *true*

---

30. Phil 2:9.
31. As stated by Behm in his article on μορφή cited above.
32. 2 Cor 8:9.
33. Phil 2:7.

nature of divinity. If we wish to speak of monotheism in the wake of the Christ-Event as "christological monotheism," this is the nub of it.

I think it is clear that in the Middle Platonic context of an intellectual environment in which Stoicism continued to be an active influence, it is nevertheless hard to appreciate how Paul could so easily appeal to the behavioral model of the person of the Raised Jesus Christ, as a substitute for the exercise of reason, without this kind of help from Plato. Whereas, through the exercise of reason, Stoic ethical argument sought to discern appropriate norms of behavior that were in accordance with *what nature intended*, Platonists as a regular practice further conceived the ethical quest in terms of the discernment by contemplation of the Ideal Forms, most notably of "the good," or "the just," as "divine thoughts," or "the ideas of God." In Plato's *Timaeus*, for example, it is God himself, who establishes himself through his relational and providential aspect (the Demiurge) to the world as the model of human virtue, for "He desired that all should be, so far as possible, like unto Himself."[34] When viewed through a Platonic lens, the grasp of ethical norms therefore came with an additional twist in the form of an ultimate transcendental reference, and insofar as ethical principles were perceived to be an indication of "the mind of God," they opened the way to the human possibility of being "like God."

Given his resurrection faith, in Philippians Paul introduced a significant permutation on this tradition by pointing to the having of the "mind of Christ," so as to be "like Christ," as that which determines the quality of Christian behavior, rather than simply the more abstract discernment of the "mind of God" and "being like God." Even though this was the pattern of behavior defined in the life and witness of the historical Jesus, who was remembered to have taken the form of a servant, there is in fact no discontinuity between Paul and the transcendental theistic sensibilities of Middle Platonism that were becoming increasingly current at this point. As we have seen, though traditional kenotic interpretations of Philippians have suggested that the kenotic self-abnegation of the incarnation involved the concealing of infinite and exalted divine powers by the assumed humanity of the incarnate Jesus with all its finite limitations, or (worse) even the surrender of divine powers in the interests of becoming fully human (both of which unfortunately introduce the idea of change into the Godhead), Paul's real point is that the particular form (*morphē*) of the humanity lived out historically by Jesus as the humble servant of others, far from concealing the true nature of divinity or even abandoning it, was in a sense coincident with it and therefore actually revealed it. Access to "the mind of God" was thus effectively gained via "the mind that was in Christ Jesus."

---

34. *Timaeus* 29e.

Moreover, the Christ whose mind was to be pursued was, by virtue of his Resurrection, now understood not just as the remembered historical servant figure of the past, who was obedient unto death, but the Raised and exalted one who, like God, was now known in faith in the present. Access was now gained to the intelligible "mind of God" as an eternal presence through "the help of the Spirit of Jesus Christ."[35] Among other things, this meant, as Paul made clear in 1 Cor 2, that those baptized into Christ and who were in receipt of the gift of the Spirit now partook of its divine communicative powers: "no one comprehends what is truly God's except the *pneuma* of God." Therefore, Christians have received "the *pneuma* that is from God" so that they "might understand the gifts bestowed on [them] by God."[36] Paul makes it clear that this facilitates a kind of "spiritual discernment" that is denied to the "natural man" who does not possess the *pneuma* of God.[37] As a consequence, as "pneumatic people," the baptized "critically judge all things" (but are themselves critically judged by no-one)[38]: "For who has known the mind of the Lord so as to instruct him?"[39] But, says Paul, "we have the mind of Christ."[40] Essentially the same idea is found in Romans where having the "mind-set" (*phronēma*) of the Spirit is contrasted with having the mind-set of the flesh.[41]

Apart from the fact that natural "reason" and ethical argument was replaced by the person of Christ as the "master model" of the desired behavior appropriate to Christian belonging, Paul also parted company with contemporary Stoicism insofar as he well knew that merely ethical or moral striving after virtue was of itself insufficient to account for the life and witness of Christians. In a sense, this Stoic option was no better than works of the Jewish law. As the baptized sought to describe the unique quality of their post-Easter experience, they pointed to something more. Hence the importance of their belief that the Raised Christ who, as a consequence of the Resurrection (and of the response of trusting faith in him), actually distributed the gift of his Spirit in the community life of baptized believers. The consciousness of this "giftedness" was not an occasion therefore of self-congratulation, but of thankfulness to God.

If Christ was in the Form (*morphē*) of God, and if Christ himself thereby provided the "master model" of appropriate moral and ethical behavior that was deemed

---

35. Phil 1:19.
36. 1 Cor 2:10–13.
37. 1 Cor 2:14.
38. 1 Cor 2:15.
39. 1 Cor 2:16. See also Rom 11:34: "For who has known the mind of the Lord? Or who has been his Counselor?"
40. 1 Cor 2:16.
41. Rom 8:5–6.

appropriate to this relationship with him, then the role of the Spirit was actually to *form* the image of the divine life of Christ in the baptized in such a way that it could be "made visible" and proclaimed in the world with confidence and integrity. The earnest goal of Paul's ministry among the communities in his care, was therefore to sustain them in faith, and in the life of the Spirit, in the hope that Christ might be brought to birth and "formed" in them: "My little children, for whom I am again in the pain of childbirth until Christ be formed (*morphōthē*) in you."[42] Once again, this is essentially epistemological and moral language, but it has ontological implications. Christian lives are actually changed and transformed by the gift of the Spirit of Christ.

This means that Christian moral behavior is not just the result of an *imitatio*. Nor does it just come down to a matter of trying. Rather than Christ himself just providing the abstract model behaviour for its achievement by human effort, the desired moral transformation of humanity is effected on earth through "the help of the Spirit of Jesus Christ."[43] This was what ensured that Christ was "formed" in them. In this case, the point of human striving to live in accordance with the "mind of Christ" is thus to facilitate the revealing in the wider world of the divinely given reality of Christ's Spirit that was known by faith in concrete experience. Paul was therefore well aware that the success of his mission, particularly in the face of adverse opposition and suffering, could only be achieved through the prayers of the Philippians and with "the help of the Spirit of Jesus Christ." It was not so much a matter of trying as of trusting—trusting in the continuing supply of the promised gift of the life-transforming *pneuma* of Christ. Hence the emphasis that Luther rightly found in the Pauline theme of faith alone, and grace alone, rather than on works of the law.

It has already been noted that the same dual earthly/heavenly polarity of a Platonic-style epistemology, which, beginning with the perception of shadowy "copies" of Ideal Forms in the world, leads to the contemplation of the perfection of their hidden heavenly originals, finds an echo in Paul's focus on the concrete knowledge of the Spirit of Christ, which simultaneously points beyond itself to the Ideal heavenly and exalted life of the Raised Christ himself. The other side of this penny is that, by having the "mind of Christ" it was possible for baptized believers themselves to reveal the otherwise hidden and heavenly Christ in the world. This is because believers, by their (*methectic*) participation in the life of Christ through baptism and the gift of the Spirit, thereby receive their own true or distinctive identity, which in a similar way then also points "beyond itself." Paul thus exhorted the Corinthians to live in such a way that "the life of Jesus may be made visible in our mortal flesh."[44] The way in which the baptized participate in

---

42. Gal 4:19.
43. Phil 1:19.
44. 2 Cor 4:11.

the life of the Spirit in this world, which allows them to interpret it in faith, and in hope as the down payment of a clearer vision to come, therefore also possesses a Platonic resonance insofar as, in the interim while they awaited its full eschatological revealing at the parousia, they were conscious at the same time of participating already in the heavenly transcendent reality of the Raised Christ himself, and this in such a way as already to reveal him in the world.

In all this, Christ is not just the "master model" or "exemplar" for them to emulate but, as I would myself prefer to say, "the constitutive form" or "generative image" which is actually given to the baptized by the gift of his Spirit. It seems clear enough that Paul's reference to Christ being formed in believers means that the active presence of the "Spirit of life in Christ Jesus" or the "life-giving Spirit" of Christ in them, rather than just being an abstract paradigm which they themselves might seek to emulate or imitate, actually ensured that they received their baptismal identity from him. All these terms—"master model," "exemplar," or "constitutive form" and "generative image"—trigger remarkably "Platonic" resonances with the idea of eternal transcendent Forms in which the particulars of space and time have their identity by a kind of "participation" (*methexis*).

In urging the Philippians to have "the mind of Christ" and to live, not by coercively lording it over others, but more humbly as the servants of others, Paul was holding up the vision of the ideal community to which the Philippians were urged to aspire. At the beginning of his argument in Phil 1:27, he thus enjoined the Philippians to "live as citizens" (*politeuesthe*) in the harmony and peace of "one spirit and one soul."[45] In other words, as he was to say elsewhere, they were to live in the harmony of inter-personal communion (koinonia) with one another.[46] Now, it is highly significant, and entirely in accord with the dual polarity characteristic of the epistemological sympathies presupposed by Paul, that his point of reference for the ideal model of this kind of community life is thought of in transcendental heavenly terms. In Phil 3:20, he places this ideal model of citizenship (*politeuma*) "in heaven." This contrasts with the usual Stoic emphasis on living as a natural citizen of an earthly city. It is no coincidence that Paul speaks of the "heavenly" or "upward" call of God in relation to this: "I press on towards the goal for the prize of the heavenly call of God in Christ Jesus."[47] In other words, a Platonic voice can once again be heard in Paul's otherwise Stoic sounding language.

---

45. The connection here with the Stoic interest in political and ethical "citizenship" (*politeuma*) does not escape us.

46. 2 Cor 13:13.

47. Phil 3:14.

It is also not surprising that, by Paul's time, Stoic models of the ideal city of the kind that had originally been described by Zeno of Citium (c. 335—c. 263 BC), with a focus on the achievement of harmony, friendship, and freedom by a law-abiding citizenship in an actual discrete city-state, had long since begun to be pulled in an ideal or "platonic" direction.[48] As a consequence of the reformation of Stoicism initiated by Chrysippus (c. 280—c. 207 BC), the ideal community had already become not so much a model city-state of a matter-of-fact or natural kind, operating in actual practice in this world according to a Stoic political/ethical blueprint, so much as the ideal community of all morally good people, who may in fact be found across the particular city-states of the entire world. As Troels Engberg-Pedersen has himself clearly pointed out, this model city-state transcends a merely local perspective. For Chrysippus, the ideal city was a "cosmic city": "If we ask where the 'cosmic city' is to be found, the answer, as we can now see, should be, in people's minds. It is the 'place' created by or made up of people who have the attitudes that go into Stoic virtue."[49] In this respect, the Stoic Chrysippus sounds suspiciously Platonic. However, when we remember (via Diogenes Laërtius)[50] that Chrysippus seems deliberately to have levelled out the hierarchical model of the divine Being/Demiurge/World-Soul that he found in Plato's *Timaeus* into one unified active principle, and that ethical and political virtue involved the alignment of human reason with a providential and immanent divine pure reason that permeated the cosmos, it is clear that Chrysippus' "cosmic" city still belongs in a monistic schema. But, very significantly, Paul lifts the "cosmic" city on to a transcendental plane: his model of the ideal community is in heaven. For Paul, in the genuinely ideal community of heaven virtuous citizens are reconciled, not just among themselves but also with God, for this reconciliation is already established in heaven through the work of the Raised Christ. This heavenly reality in turn provides the model for achieving the authentic inter-personal communion of the baptized in the churches of the cities of this world. Indeed, by faith, baptism, and the gift of the Spirit, the members of these communities could well have understood themselves to participate (precisely in a Platonic *methectic* way) in this heavenly paradigm. We see here the presupposed dual focus of Paul's understanding of such things: the communion of the local church does not just "reflect," but actually "participates in," the heavenly reality of a citizenship which is "in heaven" through the gift from heaven of the Spirit of Christ. This is a form of reconciled inter-personal communion established, not only humanly on earth of a kind that might be achieved among the baptized by human striving, but by the action of God; it is a communion with the God of heaven through the reconciliation won by Christ himself, who is now understood to be "at God's right hand." Indeed, it is an inter-personal communion that can be achieved on earth only because it has already been achieved by Christ with God in heaven.

48. For example, Plato's speculation on the form of the ideal city in the *Republic*.
49. Engberg-Pedersen, "Stoicism in Philippians," 272.
50. Diogenes Laërtius, *Lives and Opinion of Eminent Philosophers*, 7.87–88.

This at once illustrates the apparent dual polarity of the epistemological and ontological presuppositions implicit in so much of what Paul has to say, and also explains how a double linguistic reference is possible—sometimes with the focus being on the earthly reality which "participates" in a heavenly exemplar, and sometimes the focus being in more transcendental terms on the heavenly exemplar itself.

A purely Stoic monism which invites the suggestion that the Spirit, as Paul understood it, was somehow of a piece with the natural order (though divine), and ontologically an integral element within the natural world in a kind of pan-en-theism (so that it is itself also "material and physical"), does not seem to account for the more mysterious nature of the Spirit that is only partially and ambiguously known in faith in this world, and that points beyond itself to the transcendent reality of its source in the exalted Raised Christ himself. Just as surely, this epistemic dualism points to a kind of ontological dualism. The fact that Christ is not met in person (or face to face) in this life so as to be fully known, points to his hidden heavenly existence, which is yet to be eschatologically revealed.

Likewise, from this same generally platonic perspective it is possible to think of each particular local church, not as "part of the Body of Christ," but as a particular manifestation *of* "the Body of Christ," the multiplicity of local churches in cities scattered around the Mediterranean all having their distinctive life and identity by "participation" in the life of the universal Christ of heaven through the gift of his Spirit. Each local church thus enjoys a "completeness in itself" (to use Westcott's phrase), as the local manifestation of the Body of Christ, with the universal worldwide church of space and time being the sum of all the churches, with earthly structures to facilitate the maintenance of unity between them, and to facilitate common action in the world.

Obviously, we cannot claim to know with absolute certainly that this Platonic/Stoic mixture of presupposed ideas was what was conditioning Paul's thought or not by pointing to quite explicitly quoted Platonic sources. We can only point to similarities of epistemological pattern and their ontological and behavioral implications, and speak in terms of interpretative possibilities. What is certain, however, is that Troels Engberg-Pedersen's more dominant and exclusively Stoic reading of Paul's epistemological and ontological commitments of an unequivocal monistic kind, in which Platonic influences become more superficially linguistic resonances only, cannot be allowed to go unchallenged. A more positively Platonic reading of Paul seems, both historically and theologically, a more attractive option.

14

Postscript

IN HIS SEMINAL STUDY of Paul's use of the phrase "in Christ,"[1] C. F. D. Moule noted that many have found difficulty not only in coming to terms with Paul's original meaning, but in fathoming how this phrase might be meaningfully understood today. Moule also observed that, though Paul's more characteristic language is of believers being "in Christ," he sometimes speaks also of "Christ" being "in them." On the other hand, however, while Paul does use this language of Christ being "in them," he actually speaks more often of the Spirit being "in them." Indeed, in numerical terms, he preferences talk of the Spirit being "in them" over references to them being "in the Spirit." As a consequence, despite some variation, Paul's most regular language pattern is to speak of the faith experience of believers as life "in Christ," with "the Spirit in them."

In this study I have endeavored to unpack the epistemological structure of faith, so as to understand just how the presence of the Spirit may be perceived as the constitutive animating Spirit in the community of the baptized, and specifically how it is possible to claim not just to know this "Spirit of life in Christ Jesus" by actual acquaintance, but also, in faith, to identify it *as* the living Spirit of the *Jesus* who lived and taught in first-century Palestine and who died upon the Cross and was raised from the dead. At the same time, I have sought to defend a transcendentalist understanding of the ontology of the Spirit of Christ so as to release our understanding of it from an over-association with a Stoic perspective on the Spirit in the purely monistic "material and physical" sense of "warm breath." By contrast, the empirical experience of the Spirit points ontologically in a more dualistic sense towards the hidden and heavenly reality of the Raised Christ himself, "at the right hand of the Father," whose gift of the Spirit is most characteristically known as Christ's Spirit of self-giving love. Even if the actual experience of the Spirit was in other ways akin to the nature of the experience of *pneuma* in the Stoicism with which the world of Paul was familiar, instead of being thought of as the all-pervading "warm breath," it henceforth was identified and

---

1. In *The Origin of Christology*.

known in Christian faith by reference to the remembered character of Jesus himself, as his self-giving gift of love.[2]

Given that the Spirit continues to be understood as the constitutive and animating Spirit of the Christian community, it seems to follow that those who today claim to perceive and know its presence in faith as "the Spirit of the Raised Christ," and commit themselves to a life of obedient discipleship and moral integrity appropriate to their newfound relation with him, also feel justified in speaking of this, using Paul's language, as being "in Christ," or being members of the "Body of Christ." Ever since Deissmann late in the nineteenth-century, however, Christian theologians have wrestled with the question of exactly what Paul intended to convey by his use of the phrase "in Christ."[3] Even though St. John, who seems to have had access to this theological tradition expressed by Paul, had no apparent qualms in extending this kind of language in uninhibited exuberance—when, for example, he has Christ speak of himself as being "in the Father" and the Father "in him," and of his disciples being "in them" both[4]—this is a phrase that continues to raise questions about how exactly one person can somehow really be said to be "in" another. What contemporary sense does it make to speak of one person somehow being "in" another person, and how is it that both Paul and John are apparently entirely untroubled by this?

References to believers' participation in the life of Christ, through incorporation by baptism into the "Body of Christ," have been found just as troublesome. As we noted in chapter 1, in recent years, E. P. Sanders, though highlighting the importance of this participative language to an understanding of Paul, nevertheless expresses his puzzlement about exactly what Paul's talk of "participation" might amount to, and confesses that he has enormous difficulty in explaining exactly what it can mean.[5] Neither Bultmann's contention that it can be reduced to a matter of existential self-understanding without any descriptively objective meaning, nor the alternative of a more traditional naïve description of a kind of "magical"[6] transfer of Christ into believers, is judged to be at all convincing. From Sanders' point of view, neither is an acceptable explanation of Paul's meaning. Further, he confesses that just what "participation" in the life of another can actually mean for us today eludes him.

Even though the background philosophical mix of Stoicism and Platonism, in the Middle Platonism of the Hellenistic Judaism of Paul's day, may help to throw light on how he conceived the life-giving Spirit, no doubt there will be endless attempts to try to express what Paul seems to have been getting at in a more modern idiom. In chapter 1 of this book, I raised the possibility, at least with regard to Paul's references either to Christ or the Spirit being "in believers," of following the lead provided by the

---

2. Rom 5:5.
3. Originally, this was raised by A. Deissmann as long ago as 1892.
4. As in John 17.
5. Sanders, *Paul and Palestinian Judaism*, 518–23; see the initial discussion of this in chap. 1 above.
6. Sanders' word, following Bultmann.

dyothelite insights of Maximus the Confessor. Insofar as Maximus argued for belief in two wills in the Incarnate Jesus—the one a general divine and eternal will, and the other the outworking of this same will in the time-bound and particular decisions of his historical existence—he provides a model of what we might speak of as a divine/human "coincidence of willing." Using this paradigm, it is possible for us today to think of the will of the living Raised Christ actually operating together with our own wills. The idea of the coincidence in our experience of the moral pressure of a divinely eternal and changeless will, and the exercise of our own wills in historical time in conformity with it, is surely a thinkable thought. In this way, we may think today of the eternal and changeless divine will of God as revealed historically in Christ, but still operative in our human attempts to act in accordance with that will in the temporal thread of our own human activities and behaviors. Despite Bultmann, no magical transference of Christ and his will into us, in a way that might obliterate our own human willing, is envisaged.

Having now, in the previous two chapters, explored some of the implications of the Platonic kind of epistemology that Paul appears to have presupposed, we are in a position to contemplate the possibility that Paul's view of the "participation" of the baptized in the life of Christ, so as to admit the Pauline claim to be "in Christ" and "members of the Body of Christ" through the gift of his Spirit, may be understood by appealing to the Platonic notion of *methexis*.

Epistemologically speaking, for Paul, as a representative figure typical of the intellectual world of Middle Platonism, to be "in Christ" (or to be members of the "Body of Christ," as the baptized live in faith through the gift of the Spirit of Christ), is to "participate" in the life of Christ in a way roughly analogous to the way in which, Platonically speaking, red particulars of this world "participate" (*methectically*) in the eternal and Ideal Form of "redness." The Ideal reality is what gives the earthly particular its specific constitutive identity as a red object, regardless of its geographical location in space and time, and in the face of the multiplicity of red objects that in other respects may all be quite different from one another even while sharing the same quality of "redness." Somehow, for Plato, the immanent Form of "redness" was constitutively present in the red particulars of this world, in the sense of actually making them red. This way of conceiving reality generally helps us to grasp how it was that Paul could so easily speak of the earthly experience of participating in the life of the heavenly and exalted Raised Christ. It provides a kind of epistemological and ontological underpinning of his many references to being "in Christ," or being a member of "the Body of Christ." This means that, from a *methectic* point of view, Paul was not just using a metaphor or figure of speech. He understood each baptized Christian, and each local Christian community, to enjoy through the gift of the Spirit a kind of constitutive identity by virtue of their actual "participation" in the life of the transcendent and eternal Raised Christ.

These same epistemological considerations that take their place within the broader context of a set of dualistic cosmological and ontological presuppositions of a broadly Platonic kind, also help us to appreciate the underpinning of the *dyothelite* proposals of Maximus—the coincidence of an eternally changeless divine will which is played out in time and space in the historical human willing of the incarnate Jesus. An echo of the same kind of dualism may be heard in Paul's exhortation to the Philippians: "Let this mind be in you that was in Christ Jesus." In other words, this same platonic-type dualism, which appears to have transformed Paul's reception of Stoicism, may be discerned in the way in which he developed his understanding of how a grasp of the mind and will of God by having "the mind of Christ" might inform human behavior in this world. Clearly, this contrasts very remarkably with a Stoic appeal to reason in discerning modes of behavior that were simply believed to be in accordance with "what nature intended."

Though today we may not be Platonists, we might nevertheless seek to remain true to this model insofar as we insist that when we, using the same language, speak of being "in Christ," or of being "members of the Body of Christ," we also do not just understand ourselves to be speaking metaphorically. This "in Christ" language is not just a way of saying we have faith in Christ, or that we belong to Christ in some purely abstract and entirely notional sense. We are not just engaging in "a manner of speaking." Nor is our talk of being members of the "Body of Christ" to be understood in the metaphorical sense that we are a body of people who happen to understand their identity by some kind of notional reference to Christ. Rather, because our faith in the Raised Christ is based on our actual acquaintance with his life giving Spirit, which we perceive in faith essentially as a gift, informing and transforming our lives, we are constrained to say that we have a sense of sharing in his Raised and exalted life in such a way that we are thus ontologically changed and given a new human identity. The gift of the Spirit is the constitutive identifying element of our Christian existence. From the Platonic idea of *methexis*, we thus draw some insight into the constitutive realism of the experience of participation "in Christ," and of being members of the "Body of Christ." This Platonic insight permits us to insist that, to be true to our Easter experience, we are obliged to claim to know the presence of an objective life-transforming reality in our own lives of a kind that is constitutive of our Christian identity and determinative of our Christian behavior. One important implication of this is that it is not something which we achieve by our own effort. We have a distinct sense of "receiving" the Spirit of Christ's love with the objective reality of a gift, which "blows where it wills," and is positively and unmistakably known in reconciled human unity with others, and with God, in the unmistakable actuality of the communion of the church. This is something in which we are conscious of "participating," and for which, as the Eucharistic community, we are dispositionally prone always to "give thanks."

Another possibility that is open to us is to explore the notion of *methexis* with its original meaning as it was used in ancient Greek theatre, even prior to its philosophical use by Plato. In the context of ancient drama, *methexis* referred to the impromptu participation of the audience in the creation of the action of the drama being played out in front of them. This invites the idea of the alignment of Christian believers in faith with the exalted Christ, who "ever lives to make intercession for them,"[7] in the continuing work of redemption. In other words, a more dynamic understanding of *methexis* allows us to think of participating in the "drama of redemption" after the manner of audience participation in ancient Greek theatre. This, by contrast with usual "in Christ" and "Body of Christ" language, is less static and ontological and much more dynamic and functional. In this case, to be "in Christ," and to be members of the "Body of Christ," would be to be drawn into the drama of Christ's redemptive work, conceived by describing the active participation of faithful Christian disciples by their intentional temporal insertion in the eternal pleading of the sacrifice at Calvary of the Raised and Exalted Christ in payer and worship "at the right hand of the Father." In the traditional formula, this is something we actually participate in "through him, with him, and in him" in worship.

On the other hand, while we may not actually be card-carrying Platonists, we understand ourselves in diachronic communion with St. Paul and other members of the primitive Christian church, because the essential elements of what they described, employing their own Stoic/Platonic idioms, are still recognizable by us today in our own concrete experience of faith. We fully recognize that their intellectual world was radically different from ours, and that their attempts to describe this experience were made in the context of the eschatological hopes of Second Temple Judaism, while at the same time they necessarily utilized (even if unwittingly) a set of conceptual tools belonging to the popular epistemology and ontology of the intellectual world of Middle Platonism.[8] However, even though we may seek to describe and communicate our faith experience (as best we can) in the language of today, against the background of a quite different set of cosmological considerations, and by using epistemological

---

7. With a focal reliance on the Epistle to the Hebrews.

8. Many readers will appreciate the theological ingenuity of Pieter Craffert in seeking to overcome the historical and cultural gulf between that ancient world and the world with which we are familiar. See Craffert, *Life of a Galilean Shaman*.

tools that have long since undergone considerable critical development, we nevertheless discern the continuity of our fundamental experience with that spoken about by Paul and other primitive Christians in the making of their faith claims. Indeed, even though we are conscious of living in a different intellectual environment with entirely different cosmological presuppositions, we continue to be able to use much of the same language. We receive such words as "God," "Christ," "Spirit," "Grace," "Love," and "Communion," and make them our own as we seek meaningfully to describe our own concrete religious experience.

There is obviously a danger in trying to modernize Paul. It seems much better to allow him to speak in his own Hellenized Jewish idiom and then try to stand in his shoes, and to see things as far as possible as he saw them, difficult though this may be. Nevertheless, there comes a time when all of us must accept the constraints, not just of time and energy, and the difficulties of thinking exactly as characters of the ancient past thought, but the constraints and difficulties that are imposed on us by the limitations of language itself. If theology is the attempt to say something about what by definition is "beyond words"—transcendent, ineffably sublime, and, indeed, ultimately incomprehensible and unknowable to humankind by description—then we are confronted by the inevitability of the constraints and limitations that are part and parcel of the verbal expression of all religious belief. Even when God is revealed, it is not as though a riddle is thereby solved; rather, God is revealed as mystery—as a transcendent reality that is apprehended but never comprehended. Theology is the valiant attempt to say something about the Infinite in a language tailored for use with respect to finite things. In terms of pure description, it is destined to fall short of its goal. From this perspective it must work with a clear consciousness of its own quite unavoidable limitations.[9] This must also apply specifically to the theology of the Resurrection of Christ as the supreme moment of the revelation of the divine in the "Jesus Christ whom God raised from the dead": his presence among us transcends our capacity to express it in mere words.

Wittgenstein once said that "a nothing would serve just as well as a something about which nothing could be said."[10] It is perfectly understandable that some take the ultimately nihilistic route of opting for negativity. The rising tide of darkness, in the form of an avowed atheism, means calmly accepting the fact that life is without ultimate meaning, and that human living is without ultimate purpose or hope. On the other hand, others of us insist that it is not so much that "nothing can be said," but that in theological pursuit something is said, though, by a paradox, in the first instance using negative terms—in-finite, im-material, a-temporal, un-changing, im-

---

9. Following Mansel, *The Limits of Religious Thought*.
10. Wittgenstein, *Philosophical Investigations*, para. 304.

passible, and ontologically in-dependent. This *apophatic* route simply clears a blank screen upon which positive images of a metaphorical and analogical kind, such as we find regularly in the stories of the Bible, are then projected. But then that screen has to be scrubbed clean again, erasing those humanly projected images, by resort once again to a series of *apophatic* "but not" phrases. If God is thought of as a Father, a King, a Shepherd, a Judge, a Rock or a Wind, and so on, God is *not* to be thought to be like any of those things in a literal sense. None of these images can be unpacked and explained in a straightforward clear and distinct literal specification. These are all irreducible metaphors and analogies. A clear and distinct specification of their meaning eludes us, for an infinite and transcendent God is by definition always "beyond" all such images of him. In the Hebrew/Christian tradition, "nobody can see God and live." This resonates with the contention that is found in the thought of Plato from the very beginning and through Middle Platonism, that in this life nobody can have a direct knowledge of the Ideal Forms. As Rudolf Bultmann at least in one sense rightly said, "God can be addressed but not expressed."

Likewise, in the Resurrection tradition of the New Testament we necessarily work with a set of graphic images: the empty tomb, various and sometimes conflicting narrative accounts of the first appearances, and Paul's often-repeated attempts to describe the distinctive quality of human life transformed by the gift of the living Spirit of Christ. As in the theology of God, the experience of the presence of the transcendent, Raised, exalted, and glorified Christ, "at the right hand of the Father," but concretely known in human experience as "a life-giving Spirit," must be acknowledged to be ultimately beyond all our attempts to express it in the words and concepts of a finite language. We rightly rehearse the New Testament resurrection traditions, with their halting attempts to expresses something of the experience of Christ's post-Easter appearances and continuing presence in the life of the community of faith, but we wisely resist any attempt to preserve them as though in aspic. It is a mistake to treat the textual record as a kind of fetish. On the contrary, we remember John's assurance that it is those who do not see in the apparently clear and distinct way that Thomas is said literally to have done in the gospel story[11] who at the end of the day will be counted "blessed." Significantly, John does not go on to spell out the details of this "blessed" option. This is of a piece with the *apophatic* course taken by the church's first systematic theologian, St Mark, insofar as he steadfastly resisted the temptation even to try to conjure up a verbal image of a visual "appearance" of the Raised and exalted Christ at the end of his gospel. Rather, using the words of the angel, he was content to point towards a possibility: "He is going ahead of you to Galilee; there you will see him."[12] Thus, though Mark shows . . . he does not tell.

Try as we may to paint a verbal picture of "what happened at Easter," and to express something of our own Easter experience of the continuing presence of the Raised

---

11. In the story of John 20.
12. Mark 16:7.

Christ through the medium of the Spirit of his self-gift in the communion of the church, there comes a time when we must all acknowledge that words ultimately fail us. Even in our best attempts to express something of the experience of the mystery that grounds the perception of the presence of Christ in faith, not least as the animating Spirit of the Christian community that is constitutive of its communion, we acknowledge from start to finish that mere words are inadequate to the task.

This should not surprise us, for we face analogous challenges from day to day even when we try to describe even utterly mundane experiences—as, for example, our stammering efforts accurately to describe even the taste of lychees, or the subtle bouquet and smooth flavor of a Margaret River shiraz. Similarly, if in fact much more so, in our endeavor to express something of our experience in faith of the perception of the Raised Christ as "a life-giving Spirit," we have to acknowledge that ultimately we have to do with a transcendent and essentially heavenly reality which is by definition therefore "beyond words." As we have already seen, this is par-for-the-course in relation to explaining the actual experience of being "in Christ," or participating in the new life of Christ in the "Body of Christ."

It is at this point that the challenge of endeavoring to speak further of the Easter mystery must necessarily be set aside. What we need at this point is not more words—whether it be more Theology or more Christology. Rather, we are instead necessarily constrained to *do* something. Shocking though it may sound to those brought up with an acute consciousness of the importance of "faith not works," at this point we need works rather than words alone. More important than persisting with the theological and christological task of wrestling with what Paul and the gospel writers seem to have been getting at, and what it can all possibly mean for us today in terms of our concrete experience, it becomes necessary to enter more deeply into the latent possibilities of our own actual experience of Christian faith through praxis. This is to say, we have to enter more deeply into the experiential life of faith, rather than abstract theorizing. It is a matter of ceasing to speak in order to act and to do, for at this point, to use a phrase borrowed from Catherine Pickstock,[13] we are constrained to bow to the "liturgical consummation of philosophy."[14] This means forsaking the forensic study of the ancient textual traditions and the constant wrestle with their meaning, so as simply to hear them again in living rehearsal, and then, when words begin to fail us, to turn to the "invisible words" of the church's body language, the paradigms of its sacramental tradition: we "greet one another with a holy kiss"[15] and break the bread and share the cup.

---

13. Pickstock, *After Writing*.
14. Where "liturgy" is understood as "something done"; "a work."
15. 2 Cor 13:12.

This is not to suggest, of course, that what we do together "in Christ," as members together of the "the Body of Christ," or in the "Communion of the Spirit," can be imagined to be contained within the four walls of a church building. Though this may be a kind of epicenter where Christ becomes functionally available to us through his Body—the "Body of Christ" on the altar and gathered around it—when we hear the Word of God, and perceive Christ's presence in faith, we know also that beyond those ecclesial walls we are humanly called to a set of behavioral norms: to love and serve one another, to care for one another, to heal the sick, to visit prisoners, and bind up the broken-hearted. We hear God's call to nurture little children, and to take care of the frail aged, to welcome strangers, and accommodate refugees. Just as the timelessly eternal God makes time for us, we make room for those whose only fault is to seek to escape poverty and persecution by helping them find their feet and forge a new form of life. Likewise, we are to struggle for justice and peace, and for a fair distribution of the resources of the earth. In other words, motivated by our perception of the presence of the Spirit of Christ, and the insights of faith, and hearing the call to Christian discipleship informed by the self-sacrificial values of the Gospel, we go into the "place of mission." All the while, we go as persons who are conscious of striving to have the "mind of Christ" as befits the discipleship of the servants of others, being sealed with the Spirit of "the saints of God." All this goes on in the hope of a greater eschatological outpouring of Christ's Spirit in the world in time to come. When mere words fail us in our efforts to describe our Easter experience of new life "in Christ," we prosecute Christ's mission by actively going into the "Galilee of the nations"—the place of mission. And we go in the trusting faith that Christ will be faithful to his promise to be present with us always. We "Go into Galilee"—in the trusting faith that "there we shall see him."

Bibliography

Primary Sources

Albinus (alias Alcinous). *Didaskalikos*. www.esonet.org/the-didaskalikos-of-albinus-145-ad/.

Aquinas, Thomas. *Summa Theologiae*, 55: *The Resurrection*. Translated by C. Thomas Moore, OP. London: Eyre & Spottiswoode, 1976.

Augustine. *Confessions*. Translated by Henry Chadwick. Oxford: Oxford University Press, 1991.

———. *Sermons* in *The Works of Saint Augustine*. Translated by Edmund Hill, OP, edited by John E. Rotelle, OSA. Hyde Park, NY: New City, 1997.

The Babylonian Talmud. Edited by Isidore Epstein. London: Soncino, 1990. Conveniently at: http://www.come-and-hear.com/talmud/.

Besant, Walter, and Henry James. *The Art of Fiction*. 1885. Reprint, Naperville, Il: Allenson, 1959.

Calvin, John. *Institutes of the Christian Religion*. 2 vols. Translated by Henry Beveridge. 1846. Reprint, Grand Rapids: Eerdmans, 1975.

Charlesworth, James H., ed. *The Old Testament Pseudepigrapha*. 2 vols. Garden City, NY: Doubleday, 1983–85.

Diogenes Laërtius. *Lives and Opinions of Eminent Philosophers*, Book VII: The Stoics. https://en.wikisource.org/wiki/Lives_of_the_Eminent_Philosophers.

Eudorus of Alexandria. *Collection of Fragments* by C. Mazzarelli, "Raccolta e interpretazione delle testimonianze e dei frammenti del medioplatonico Eudoro de Alessandria" in two parts:
  "Parte prima: Testo e traduzione delle testimonianze se dei frammenti sicuri." *Rivista di filosofia neoscolastica*, 77 (1985) 197–209.
  "Parte seconda: Testo e traduzione delle testimonianze non sicure," *Rivista di filosofia neoscolastica*. 77 (1985) 535–55.
  For studies, see the bibliography in John Dillon, *The Middle Platonists, 80 B.C. to A.D. 220*, 417–18. Ithaca: Cornell University Press, 1977. Also, the chapter on Eudorus by Paul Moraux, *Der Aristotelismus bei den Griechen*. Berlin: de Gruyter, II (1984) 509–27.

Evagrius of Pontus. *The Greek Ascetic Corpus*. Oxford Early Christian Studies. Translated by Robert E. Sinkewicz. Oxford: Oxford University Press, 2003.

Gregory the Great. *On the Song of Songs*. Translation and introduction by Mark DelCogliano. Collegeville, MN: Liturgical, 2012.

Gregory of Nyssa. *Commentary on the Song of Songs*. Translated by Casimir McCambly. Brookline, MA: Hellenic College, 1987.

———. *The Life of Moses*. Translated by Abraham J. Malherbe and Everett Ferguson. New York: Paulist 1978.

———. *On the Soul and the Resurrection*. Nicene and Post-Nicene Fathers II/5. Edited by Philip Schaff and Henry Wace. Edinburgh: T. & T. Clark 1892. https://www.ccel.org/ccel/schaff/npnf205/.

The Holy Bible, with the Books called Apocrypha: Revised Version with Revised Marginal References. Oxford: Oxford University Press, [1898].

The Holy Bible, Containing the Old and New Testaments with the Apocryphal/Deuterocanonical Books: New Revised Standard Version. Oxford: Oxford University Press, 1989.

Hugh of St Victor. *Hugh of Saint Victor On the Sacraments of the Christian Faith*. Translated by Roy J. Deferrari. 1951. Reprint, Eugene, OR: Wipf & Stock, 2007.

Hume, David. *Dialogues Concerning Natural Religion and Other Writings*. Edited by Dorothy Coleman. Cambridge: Cambridge University Press, 2007.

Josephus. *Works*. 9 vols. LCL. Edited by H. St. J. Thackeray et al. Cambridge: Harvard University Press, 1929–65.

Kant, Immanuel. *Critique of Practical Reason*. Translated and edited by Mary Gregor, with an Introduction by Andrews Reath. Cambridge: Cambridge University Press, 1997.

———. *Critique of Pure Reason*. Translated by Norman Kemp Smith. London: Macmillan, 1929.

Kierkegaard, Søren. *Concluding Unscientific Postscript to Philosophical Fragments*. Translated by Howard V. Hong and Edna H. Hong. Princeton: Princeton University Press, 1992.

———. *The Sickness unto Death: A Christian Psychological Exposition for Upbuilding and Awakening*. Princeton: Princeton University Press, 1941. http://www.naturalthinker.net/trl/texts/Kierkegaard,Soren/TheSicknessUntoDeath.pdf.

King, William. *The Right Method of Interpreting Scripture, in what Relates to the Nature of the Deity and His Dealings with Mankind Illustrated in a Discourse on Predestination*, Sermon before the Irish House of Lords in 1709, edited by Richard Whately. London: Murray, 1821.

Maximus the Confessor. Scholia on the Church Hierarchy, (Dionysius the Areopagite). *Patrologia Graeca*. Paris: Migne, 1857, 4.

———. "Two Hundred Texts on Theology and the Incarnate Dispensation of the Son of God." In *The Writings of Maximus the Confessor*. Translated by R. P. Pryne. Philadelphia: Great Library Collection, 2015.

Menander. *Menander*. Translated by W. G. Arnott. LCL. Cambridge: Harvard University Press, 1979. https://www.loebclassics.com/view/menander_comic_poet dyskolos_peevish_fellow/1979/pb_LCL132.207.xml

The Mishnah: Translated from the Hebrew with Introduction and Brief Explanatory Notes. Edited and translated by Herbert Danby. Oxford: Oxford University Press, 1933.

Origen. *De perfectione spirituali*, (J. E. Weis-Leibersdorf, Leipzig, 1912). New edition, E. de Places, *Diadoque de Photice. Oevres spirituelles*. Sources Chretien 56. Paris, 1955, 84–163.

———. *Contra Celsum*. Translated by Henry Chadwick. Cambridge: Cambridge University Press, 1953.

———. *On First Principles* (*De Principiis*). Foreword by John C. Cavadini. Introduction by Henri de Lubac. Notre Dame: Ave Maria, 2013.

Otto, Rudolph. *The Idea of the Holy: An Inquiry into the Non-rational Factor in the Idea of the Divine and Its Relation to the Rational*. Translated by John W. Harvey. Oxford: Oxford University Press, 1923. 2nd ed. 1950.

Pascal, Blaise. *Pensées*. Edited and translated by Roger Ariew. Indianapolis: Hackett, 2004.

Philo of Alexandria. *Philo of Alexandria: An Annotated* Bibliography. 3 vols. Edited by Roberto Radice and David T. Runia, 1937–86, 1987–96, and 1997–2006. Supplements to Vigiliae Christianae 8, 57 and 109. Leiden: Brill, 1992, 2000, 2011.

———. *Works*. Translated by F. H. Colson. LCL. Cambridge: Harvard University Press, 1929–62.

———. *The Works of Philo: Complete and Unabridged*. Translated by Charles Duke Yonge. (1854–1855). http://www.earlyjewishwritings.com/philo.html.

Plato. *Complete Works*. Edited by John M. Cooper. Indianapolis: Hackett, 1997.

Pseudo-Macarius. *Patrologia Graeca 34*. Edited by J. P. Minge. Paris: Imprimerie Catholique, 1857–66.

Seneca, Lucius Annaeus. "Letters 58 and 65." In *Seneca's Letters from a Stoic*. Translated and edited by Richard Mott Gummere and Chandran Prasad. Lexicos, 2011.

Spinoza, Baruch. "Letter XXIII to Oldenburg." In *On the Improvement of the Understanding/The Ethics/Correspondence*. Translated by R. W. Elwes. Mineola, NY: Dover, 1955.

Stoicorum Veterum Fragmenta. Edited by H. von Arnim. Stuttgart: Teubner, 1903–24.

Tertullian. *Tertullian's Treatise on The Resurrection*. Translated by Ernest Evans. London: SPCK, 1960. http://www.tertullian.org/articles/evans_res/evans_res_04english.htm

Toland, John. *Christianity not Mysterious* (1697). Introduction by John Valdimir Price. London: Routledge/Thoemmes, 1995.

Secondary Sources

Alston, William P. *Perceiving God: The Epistemology of Religious Experience*. Ithaca, NY: Cornell University Press, 1991.

Argyle, M. *Bodily Communication*. London: Methuen, 1975.

Aune, David E. "Anthropological Duality in the Eschatology of 2 Cor 4:16–5:10." In *Paul beyond the Judaism/Hellenism Divide*, edited by Troels Engberg-Pedersen, 215–39. Louisville: Westminster John Knox, 2001.

Bailey, Kenneth E. "Informal Controlled Oral Tradition and the Synoptic Gospels." *Asia Journal of Theology* 5 (1991) 34–54.

———. "Middle Eastern Oral Tradition and the Synoptic Gospels." *ExpT* 106 (1995) 363–67.

Barr, James. *The Garden of Eden and the Hope of Immortality*. 1993. Reprint, Eugene OR: Wipf & Stock, 2003.

Barrett, C. K. *A Commentary on the First Epistle to the Corinthians*. London: A. & C. Black, 1971.

Bauckham, Richard. *Gospel Women: Studies of the Named Women in the Gospels*. Grand Rapids: Eerdmans, 2002.

———. *Jesus and the Eyewitnesses: The Gospels as Eyewitness Testimony*. Grand Rapids: Eerdmans, 2006.

Baxter, Anthony. "Historical Judgement, Transcendent Perspective and 'Resurrection Appearances.'" *Heythrop Journal* 40 (1999) 19–40.

Becker, Carl. "Detachment and the Writing of History." *The Atlantic Monthly*, cvi, 1910, 524–36.

Behm, J. "μορφή." In *TDNT* 4 (1967) 742–59.

Bergson, Henri. *Matter and Memory*. Translated by Nancy Margaret Paul and W. Scott Palmer. London: Allen & Unwin, 1962.

Bockmuehl, Markus. "Resurrection." In *The Cambridge Companion to Jesus*, edited by Markus Bockmuehl, 102–18. Cambridge Companions to Religion. Cambridge: Cambridge University Press, 2001.

———. "Whose Memory? Whose Orality? A Conversation with James D. G. Dunn on Jesus and the Gospels." In *Memories of Jesus*, edited by Robert B. Stewart and Gary R. Habermas, 31–44. Nashville: Broadman & Holman, 2010.

Bonazzi, Mauro. "Eudorus of Alexandria and Early Imperial Platonism." In *Bulletin of the Institute of Classical Studies Supplement*, Greek and Roman Philosophy 100 BC–200 AD, II, edited by R. W. Sharples and R. Sorabi, 94 (2007) 365–78.

———. "The Platonist Appropriation of Stoic Epistemology." In *From Stoicism to Platonism: The Development of Philosophy: 100 BCE–100 CE*, edited by Troels Engberg-Pedersen, 120–41. Cambridge: Cambridge University Press, 2017.

Boring, E. G. "A New Ambiguous Figure." *American Journal of Psychology* 42 (1930) 444–45.

Botwinick, Jack. "Husband and Father in Law—a Reversible Image." *American Journal of Psychology* 74 (1961) 312–13.

Broad, C. D. *The Mind and Its Place in Nature*. London: Kegan Paul, 1925.

Browne, Peter. *A Letter in Answer to Christianity not Mysterious* (by John Toland, 1697), with an introduction by John Valdimir Price. London: Routledge/Thoemmes, 1995.

———. *Things Divine and Supernatural Conceived by Analogy with Things Natural and Human*. London: Innys & Manby, 1733.

Bryan, Christopher. *The Resurrection of the Messiah*. Oxford: Oxford University Press, 2011.

Buber, Martin. *I and Thou*. Translated with Prologue and Notes by Walter Kaufmann. New York: Scribner, 1970.

Bultmann, Rudolf. *Essays: Philosophical and Theological*. Translated by J. C. G. Greig. London: SCM, 1955.

———. *Faith and Understanding*. Edited with an introduction by Robert W. Funk. Translated by Louise Pettibone Smith. London: SCM, 1969.

———. *The History of the Synoptic Tradition*. 2nd ed. Oxford: Blackwell, 1968.

———. *Theology of the New Testament*. Vol. 1. Translated by Kendrick Grobel. London: SCM, 1952.

Burridge, Richard A. *Four Gospels One Jesus?: A Symbolic Reading*. 1994. Reprint, London: SPCK, 2013.

———. *What Are the Gospels? A Comparison with Graeco-Roman Biography*. Grand Rapids: Eerdmans, 2004.

Byrne, Brendan. "Christ's Pre-Existence in Pauline Soteriology." *Theological Studies* 58 (1997) 308–30.

Byrskog, Samuel. "A New Perspective on the Jesus Tradition: Reflections on James D. G. Dunn's *Jesus Remembered*." *JSNT* 26 (2004) 459–71.

———. *Story as History—History as Story: The Gospel Tradition in the Context of Ancient Oral History*. WUNT 123. Tübingen: Mohr/Siebeck, 2000.

Campenhausen, Hans von. *Tradition and Life in the Early Church: Essays and Lectures in Church History*. Translated by A. V. Littledale. London: Collins, 1968.

Carnley, Peter. "John Henry Newman and the Demea Tradition in Anglican Theology." In *The University and the Church: Essays in Honor of William Alexander Johnson*, edited by James Proud and Karl Johnson, 187–217. New York: Hudson, 2008.

———. "The Poverty of Historical Scepticism." In *Christ, Faith and History*, edited by Stephen Sykes and J. P. Clayton, 165–89. Cambridge: Cambridge University Press, 1972.

———. *Resurrection in Retrospect: A Critical Examination of the Theology of N. T. Wright*. Eugene, OR: Cascade Books, 2019.

———. *The Structure of Resurrection Belief*. Oxford: Clarendon, 1987.

Coakley, Sarah. "Is the Resurrection a 'Historical' Event'? Some Muddles and Mysteries." In *The Resurrection of Jesus Christ*, edited by Paul Avis, 85–115. London: Darton, Longman & Todd, 1993.

———. "The Resurrection and the 'Spiritual Senses': On Wittgenstein, Epistemology and the Risen Christ." In *Powers and Submissions, Spirituality, Philosophy and Gender*, 130–52. Oxford: Blackwell. 2002.

Coleridge, Samuel Taylor. *Biographia Literaria*. London: Everyman, 1906.

Collingwood, R. G. *The Idea of History*. 1946. Reprint, with an introduction by Jan van der Dussen. Oxford: Oxford University Press, 1993.

Collins, Adela Yarbro. "The Empty Tomb in the Gospel according to Mark." In *Hermes and Athena*, edited by E Stump and T. P. Flint, 107–40. Notre Dame: Notre Dame University Press, 1993.

———. *Mark: A Commentary on the Gospel of Mark*. Hermeneia. Minneapolis: Fortress, 2007.

Congar, Yves, OP. *Tradition and Traditions: An Historical and a Theological Essay*. Translated by Michael Naseby and Thomas Rainborough.. London: Burns & Oates, 1966.

Conzelmann, Hans. *First Corinthians: A Commentary on the First Epistle to the Corinthians*. Translated by J. W. Leitch. Edited by George W. MacRae. Hermeneia. Philadelphia: Fortress, 1988.

Craffert, Pieter F. *The Life of a Galilean Shaman: Jesus of Nazareth in Anthropological-Historical Perspective*. Matrix 3. Eugene, OR: Cascade Books, 2008.

Cranfield, C. E. B. *The Gospel according to Saint Mark: An Introduction and Commentary* (1959). Cambridge: Cambridge University Press, 1966.

———. "The Resurrection of Jesus Christ." In *The Historical Jesus in Recent Research*, edited by James D. G. Dunn and Scot McKnight, 382–91. Winona Lake, IN: Eisenbraun, 2005. Reprinted from *ExpT* 101 (1989–90) 167–72.

———. "St Mark 16:1–8." *Scottish Journal of Theology* 5 (1952) 282–298, 398–414.

Creed, J. M. "The Conclusion of the Gospel according to Saint Mark." *JTS* 31 (1930) 175–80.

Croce, Benedetto. *Aesthetic as Science of Expression and General Linguistic*. Translated by D. Ainslie. London: Farrar, Straus, 1922.

Dahl, Nils. A. "Promise and Fulfillment." In *Studies in Paul: Theology for the Early Christian Mission*. 1977. Reprint, Eugene, OR: Wipf & Stock, 2002.

Danove, Paul. *The End of Mark's Story: A Methodological Study*. Biblical Interpretation Series 3. Leiden: Brill, 1993.

Darwin, Charles. *The Expression of the Emotions in Man and Animals*. London: Murray, 1872.

Davis, Stephen T. "James D. G. Dunn on the Resurrection of Jesus." In *Memories of Jesus*, edited by Robert B. Stewart and Gary R. Habermas, 225–66. Nashville: Broadman & Holman, 2010.

———. "'Seeing' the Risen Jesus." In *The Resurrection: An Interdisciplinary Symposium on the Resurrection of Jesus*, edited by Stephen Davis et al., 126–47. Oxford: Oxford University Press, 1997.
Deissmann, Adolf. *Die neutestamentliche Formel "in Christo Jesu."* Marburg: Elwert. 1892.
———. *Paul*. Translated by William E. Wilson. New York: Harper, 1957.
———. *St. Paul: A Study in Social and Religious History*. Translated by Lionel R. M. Strachan. 1912. Reprint, Eugene, OR: Wipf & Stock, 2004.
Dewey, Joanna. "The Gospel of Mark as Oral/Aural Event: Impressions for Interpretation" in *The New Literary Criticism and the New Testament*, edited by Elizabeth Struthers Malbon and Edgar V. McKnight, 145–63. JSNTSup 109. Sheffield: Academic Press, 1994.
Dillon, John. *The Middle Platonists: 80 B.C. to A.D. 220*. Ithaca, NY: Cornell University Press, 1977. Reprint, 1996.
Dryer, D. P. *Kant's Solution for Verification in Metaphysics*. London: Allen & Unwin, 1966.
Dunn, James D. G. "2 Corinthians III.17—'The Lord is the Spirit.'" *JTS* n.s. 21 (1970) 309–20.
———. "Eyewitnesses and the Oral Jesus Tradition." *Journal for the Study of the Historical Jesus* 6 (2008) 85–105.
———. "In Grateful Dialogue: A Response." In *Memories of Jesus*, edited by Robert B. Stewart and Gary R. Habermas, 287–323. Nashville: Broadman & Holman, 2010.
———. *Jesus and the Spirit: A Study of the Religious and Charismatic Experience of Jesus and the First Christians as Reflected in the New Testament*. London: SCM, 1975.
———. *Jesus Remembered*. Christianity in the Making 1. Grand Rapids: Eerdmans, 2003.
———. "On History, Memory and Eyewitnesses: In Response to Bengt Holmberg and Samuel Bryskog." *JSNT* 26 (2004) 473–87.
———. *The Theology of Paul the Apostle*. Grand Rapids: Eerdmans, 1998.
Ebeling, Gerhard. *The Word of God and Tradition: Historical Studies Interpreting the Divisions of Christianity*. Translated by S. H. Hooke. Philadelphia: Fortress, 1968.
Engberg-Pedersen, Troels. *Cosmology and Self in the Apostle Paul*. Oxford: Oxford University Press, 2010.
———, ed. *From Stoicism to Platonism: The Development of Philosophy, 100 BCE–100 CE*. Cambridge: Cambridge University Press, 2017.
———. *John and Philosophy: A New Reading of the Fourth Gospel*. Oxford: Oxford University Press, 2017.
———. *Paul and the Stoics*. Edinburgh: T. & T. Clark, 2000.
———, ed. *Paul beyond the Judaism/Hellenism Divide*. Louisville: Westminster John Knox, 2001.
———, ed. *Paul in His Hellenistic Context*. Minneapolis: Fortress, 1994.
English, Donald. *The Message of Mark*. Downers Grove, IL: InterVarsity, 1992.
Evans, C. F. "I will go before you into Galilee." *JTS* n.s. 5 (1954) 3–18.
———. *Resurrection and the New Testament*. SBT 2/12. London: SCM, 1970.
Farrer, Austin M. *A Study in St. Mark*. Oxford: Oxford University Press, 1952.
Fee, G. *Paul's Letter to the Philippians*. New International Commentary on the New Testament. Grand Rapids: Eerdmans, 1995.
Fenton, John. "The Ending of Mark's Gospel." In *Resurrection: Essays in Honour of Leslie Houlden*, edited by Stephen Barton and Graham Stanton, 1–7. London: SPCK, 1994.
Frankenberg, Wilhelm. *Evagrius Pontus*. Berlin: Weidmann, 1912.
Frege, Gottlob. "On Sense and Reference." In *Translations from the Philosophical Writings of Gottlob Frege*, edited by Peter Geach and Max Black, 56ff. Oxford: Blackwell, 1952.

Frei, Hans W. *The Identity of Jesus Christ: The Hermeneutical Bases of Dogmatic Theology.* 1975. Reprinted, with a new introduction by Joshua B. Davis, foreword by Mike Higton, and edited by Mark Alan Bowald. Eugene, OR: Cascade Books, 2013. Kindle ed., with an appended essay, 2013.

Frisch, Karl von. *The Dance Language and Orientation of Bees.* Cambridge: Harvard University Press, 1967.

Fuller, Reginald H. *The Formation of the Resurrection Narratives.* London: SPCK, 1972.

Gerhardsson, Birger. *Memory and Manuscript: Oral Tradition and Written Transmission in Rabbinic Judaism and Early Christianity.* Acta Seminarii Neotestamentici Upsaliensis 22. Lund: Gleerup, 1961.

———. *Memory and Manuscript: Oral Tradition and Written Transmission in Rabbinic Judaism and Early Christianity; with Tradition and Transmission in Early Christianity.* Biblical Resource Series. Grand Rapids: Eerdmans. 1998.

———. *The Origins of the Gospel Traditions.* Translated by Gene J. Lund. Philadelphia: Fortress, 1979.

———. *The Reliability of the Gospel Tradition.* Peabody, MA: Hendrickson. 2001.

———. *Tradition and Transmission in Early Christianity.* Coniectanea Neotestamentica 20. Lund: Gleerup, 1964.

Gregory, Andrew F. "An Oral and Written Gospel? Reflections on Remembering Jesus." *ExpT* 116/1 (2004) 7–12.

Guy, Harold A. *The Origin of the Gospel of Mark.* London: Hodder & Stoughton, 1954.

Habermas, Gary R. "Remembering Jesus' Resurrection: Responding to James D. G. Dunn." In *Memories of Jesus*, edited by Robert B. Stewart and Gary R. Habermas, 267–86. Nashville: Broadman & Holman, 2010.

Hadas, Moses. "Plato in Hellenistic Fusion." *Journal of the History of Ideas* 19 (1958) 3–13.

———. *Hellenistic Culture: Fusion and Diffusion.* Norton Library 593. New York: Norton, 1989

Hanson, K. C. "How Honorable! How Shameful: A Cultural Analysis of Matthew's Makarisms and Reproaches." *Semeia* 61 (1994 [96]) 81–111.

Harvey, Anthony. "'They discussed amongst themselves what this "rising from the dead" could mean' (Mark 9.10)." In *Resurrection: Essays in Honour of Leslie Houlden*, edited by Stephen Barton and Graham Stanton, 69–78. London: SPCK, 1994.

Hays, Richard B. *The Faith of Jesus Christ: The Narrative Substructure of Galatians 3:1—4:11.* 2nd ed. Biblical Resource Series. Grand Rapids: Eerdmans, 2002.

———. *First Corinthians.* Interpretation. Louisville: Westminster John Knox, 2011.

Hengel, Martin. *The Four Gospels and the One Gospel of Jesus Christ.* Translated by John Bowden. London: SCM, 2000.

———. *Judaism and Hellenism: Studies in Their Encounter in Palestine during the Early Hellenistic Period.* 2 vols. Translated by John Bowden. Philadelphia: Fortress, 1974.

Hermann, Ingo. *Kyrios und Pneuma: Studien zur Christologie der paulinischen Hauptbriefe.* Studien zum Alten und Neuen Testament 2. Munich: Kösel, 1961.

Herrmann, Wilhelm. *The Communion of the Christian with God, Described on the Basis of Luther's Statements.* Translated by J. Sandys Stanyon. Revised by R. W. Stewart. London: Williams & Norgate, 1906.

Hewitt, J. Thomas, and Matthew V. Novenson. "Participationism and Messiah Christology in Paul." In *God and the Faithfulness of Paul*, edited by Christoph Heilig et al., 393–415. WUNT 2/413. Tübingen: Mohr/Siebeck, 2016.

Hick, John. *Faith and Knowledge*. London: Macmillan, 1967.

———. *Philosophy of Religion*. Prentice-Hall Foundations of Philosophy Series. Englewood Cliffs, NJ: Prentice Hall, 1963.

Hofer, Walther. "Towards a Revision of the German Concept of History." In *German History: Some New German Views*, edited by Hans Kohn. Boston: Beacon, 1954.

Holmberg, Bengt. "Questions of Method in James Dunn's *Jesus Remembered*." *JSNT* 26 (2004) 445–57.

Hooker, Morna D. *The Gospel according to St Mark*. Black's New Testament Commentaries. London: A. & C. Black, 1991.

Hooker, Richard. *Laws of Ecclesiastical Polity: A Critical Edition with Modern Spelling*. Edited by Arthur Stephen McGrade. Oxford: Oxford University Press, 2013.

Hoskyns, E. C. "Adversaria Exegetica." *Theology* 7 (1923) 147–55.

Houlden, Leslie. *Backward into Light*. London: SCM, 1987.

———. *Connections*. London: SCM, 1986.

Hurtado, Larry W. *How on Earth Did Jesus Become a God?* Grand Rapids: Eerdmans, 2005.

———. *Lord Jesus Christ: Devotion to Jesus in Earliest Christianity*. Grand Rapids: Eerdmans, 2003.

———. "YHWH's Return to Zion." In *God and the Faithfulness of Paul*, edited by Christoph Heilig et al., 417–38. WUNT 2/413. Tübingen, Mohr/Siebeck, 2016.

Jenson, Robert W. *Systematic Theology*, Vol. 1: *The Triune God*. Oxford: Oxford University Press, 1997.

———. "The Praying Animal." In *Essays in Theology of Culture*, 117–31. Grand Rapids: Eerdmans, 1995.

Jewett, Robert. *Romans: A Commentary*. Hermeneia. Minneapolis: Fortress, 2008.

Johnson, Aubrey R. "Hebrew Conceptions of Kingship." In *Myth, Ritual and Kingship: Essays on the Theory and Practice of Kingship in the Ancient Near East and in Israel*, edited by S. H. Hooke. Oxford: Clarendon, 1958.

———. *Sacral Kingship in Ancient Israel*. Cardiff: University of Wales Press, 1967.

Kähler, Martin. *The So-Called Historical Jesus and the Historic, Biblical Christ*. Edited and translated by Carl E. Braaten. Fortress Texts in Modern Theology. Philadelphia: Fortress, 1964.

Käsemann, Ernst. *Commentary on Romans*. Translated and edited by Geoffrey W. Bromiley. Grand Rapids: Eerdmans, 1980.

———. *Perspectives on Paul*. Translated by Margaret Kohl. Philadelphia: Fortress, 1971.

Kelber, Werner H., and Samuel Byrskog, eds. *Jesus in Memory: Traditions in Oral and Scribal Perspectives*. Waco, TX: Baylor University Press, 2009.

Kendall, Daniel, SJ, and Gerald O'Collins, SJ. "The Uniqueness of the Easter Appearances." *Catholic Biblical Quarterly* 54 (1992) 287–307.

Kooten, George van. "Paul's Stoic Onto-Theology and Ethics of Good, Evil and 'Indifferents': A Response to Anti-Metaphysical and Nihilistic Readings of Paul in Modern Philosophy." In *Saint Paul and Philosophy: The Consonance of Ancient and Modern Thought*, edited by Gert-Jan van der Heiden et al., 133–64. Berlin: de Gruyter, 2017.

Knox, John. *Christ the Lord: The Meaning of Jesus in the Early Church*. Chicago: Willett, Clark, 1945.

———. *The Church and the Reality of Christ*. London: Collins, 1963.

———. *Criticism and Faith*. London: Hodder & Staughton, 1953.

———. *The Death of Christ*. 1958. Reprint, London: Collins/Fontana, 1967.

———. *The Early Church and the Coming Great Church*. London: Epworth, 1957.

———. *The Humanity and Divinity of Christ: A Study of Pattern in Christology*. Cambridge: Cambridge University Press, 1967.

———. *On the Meaning of Christ*. New York: Scribner, 1947.

Kümmel, Werner Georg. *Introduction to the New Testament*. Translated by A. J. Mattil Jr. London: SCM, 1966.

Lampe, G. W. H., and D. M. MacKinnon. *The Resurrection*. London, Mowbray, 1966.

LaNave, Gregory F. "Bonaventure." In *The Spiritual Senses: Perceiving God in Western Christianity*, edited by Paul L. Gavrilyuk and Sarah Coakley, 159–73. Cambridge: Cambridge University Press, 2012.

Leyden, W. von. *Remembering*. London: Duckworth, 1961.

Lewis, C. S. *The Four Loves*. New York: Harcourt Brace, 1960.

Long, A. A., and D. N. Sedley. *The Hellenistic Philosophers*. Cambridge: Cambridge University Press, 1987.

Lightfoot, R. H. *The Gospel Message of St. Mark*. Oxford: Clarendon, 1950.

———. *Locality and Doctrine in the Gospels*. London: Hodder & Stoughton, 1938.

Lindars, Barnabas. *New Testament Apologetic: The Doctrinal Significance of the Old Testament Quotations*. London: SCM, 1961.

Lohmeyer, Ernst. *Die Briefe an die Philipper, an die Kolosser und an Philemon*. Kritisch-exegetischer Kommentar über das Neue Testament 9. Göttingen: Vandenhoeck & Ruprecht, 1964.

——— *Das Evangelium des Markus*. Kritisch-exegetischer Kommentar über des Neue Testament 2. Göttingen: Vandenhoeck & Ruprecht, 1951.

——— *Galiläa und Jerusalem*. Forschungen zur Religion und Literatur des Alten und Neuen Testaments NF 34. Göttingen: Vandenhoeck & Ruprecht, 1936.

Louth, Andrew. "The Greek Tradition." In *The Orthodox Christian World*, edited by Augustine Casiday, 3–14. Routledge World. New York: Routledge, 2012.

Macan, Reginald W. *The Resurrection of Jesus Christ: An Essay in Three Chapters*. London: Williams & Norgate, 1877.

Mack, Arien, and Irvin Rock. *Inattentional Blindness*. Cambridge: MIT Press, 1998.

Mack, Burton L. *A Myth of Innocence: Mark and Christian Origins*. Philadelphia: Fortress, 1988.

Macpherson, Fiona, "Ambiguous Figures and the Content of Experience." *Noûs* 40 (2006) 82–117.

Macquarrie, John. "Kenoticism Reconsidered." *Theology* 77 (1974) 115–24.

McCormack, Bruce L. "What's at Stake in Current Debates over Justification? The Crisis of Protestantism in the West." In *Justification: What's at Stake in the Current Debates*, edited by Mark Husbands and Daniel J. Treier, 81–117. Downers Grove, IL: Inter-Varsity, 2004.

McDonald, James I. H. *Kerygma and Didache: The Articulation and Structure of the Earliest Christian Message*. Society for New Testament Studies Monographs Series 37. Cambridge: Cambridge University Press, 1980.

McKnight, Scot. "Telling the Truth of History: A Response to James D. G. Dunn's *Jesus Remembered*." In *Memories of Jesus*, edited by Robert B. Stewart and Gary R. Habermas, 45–58. Nashville: B&H, 2010.

Magness, J. Lee. *Sense and Absence: Structure and Suspension in the Ending of Mark's Gospel*. Society of Biblical Literature Semeia Studies. Atlanta: Scholars, 1986.

Malcolm, Norman. "A Definition of Factual Memory." In *Knowledge and Certainty: Essays and Lectures*, 222–40. Englewood Cliffs, NJ: Prentice-Hall, 1965.

———. "Three Forms of Memory." In *Knowledge and Certainty: Essays and Lectures*, 203–21. Englewood Cliffs, NJ: Prentice-Hall, 1965.

Mandelbaum, Maurice. "Objectivism in History." In *Philosophy and History*, edited by Sidney Hook, 43–56. New York: University Press, 1963.

Mansel, H. L. *The Limits of Religious Thought*. Bampton Lectures 1858. London: Murray, 1859.

Marcus, Ralph. "Divine Names and Attributes in Hellenistic Jewish Literature." *Proceedings of the American Academy for Jewish Research* 3 (1931–32) 43–120.

Marguerat, Daniel. *The First Christian Historian: Writing the "Acts of the Apostles."* Translated by Ken McKinney, Gregory J. Laughery, and Richard Bauckham. Society for New Testament Studies Monograph Series 121. Cambridge: Cambridge University Press, 2002.

———. *La Première Histoire du Christianisme: Les Actes des Apôtres*. Lectio divina 180. Paris: Cerf, 1999.

Marxsen, Willi. *Mark the Evangelist: Studies on the Redaction History of the Gospel*. Translated by James Boyce. Nashville: Abingdon, 1969.

———. "The Resurrection of Jesus as a Historical and Theological Problem." In *The Significance of the Message of the Resurrection for Faith in Jesus Christ*, edited by C. F. D. Moule, 15–50. London: SCM, 1968.

———. *The Resurrection of Jesus of Nazareth*. Translated by Margaret Kohl. Philadelphia: Fortress, 1970.

Marshall, I. Howard. *The Epistle to the Philippians*. Epworth Commentaries. London: Epworth, 1992.

Mascall, E. L. *The Secularisation of Christianity: An Analysis and a Critique*. London: Darton, Longman & Todd, 1965.

———. *Theology and the Future*. Charles A. Hart Memorial Lectures. London: Darton, Longman & Todd, 1968.

Metzger, Bruce M., ed. *A Textual Commentary on the Greek New Testament*. London: United Bible Societies, 1975.

Michel, Otto. "Μιμνῃσκομαι." In *TDNT* 4 (1967) 675–83.

Michaelis, W. "ὁράω." In *TDNT* 5 (1967) 315–82.

Mill, J. S. *A System of Logic, Ratiocinative and Inductive*. 1843. Reprint, London: Longmans Green, 1872.

Minear, Paul S. "Review of John Knox's *The Death of Christ*." *Religion in Life* 27 (1958) 610–11.

Mishkin, David. *Jewish Scholarship on the Resurrection of Jesus*. Eugene, OR: Pickwick, 2017.

Moffatt, J. *Love in the New Testament*. London: Hodder & Stoughton, 1929.

Moore, G. E. *Philosophical Papers*. London: Allen & Unwin, 1959.

Morgan, Robert. "Flesh is Precious: The Significance of Luke 24:36–43." In *Resurrection: Essays in Honour of Leslie Houlden*, edited by Stephen Barton and Graham Stanton, 8–20. London: SPCK, 1994.

Morgan, Teresa. "Narratives of Πίστις in Paul and Deutero-Paul." In *Saint Paul and Philosophy*, edited by Gert-Jan van der Heiden, et al., 165–87. Berlin: de Gruyter, 2017.

Moule, C. F. D. "Further Reflections on Philippians 2:5–11." In *History and the Gospel*, edited by W. Ward Gasque and Ralph P. Martin, 264–76. Exeter, UK: Paternoster, 1970.

———. "The Manhood of Jesus in the New Testament." In *Christ, Faith and History*, edited by S. W. Sykes and J. P. Clayton, 95–110. Cambridge: Cambridge University Press, 1972.
———. *The Origin of Christology*. Cambridge: Cambridge University Press, 1977.
———. *The Phenomenon of the New Testament : An Inquiry into the Implications of Certain Features of the New Testament*. SBT 2/1. London: SCM, 1967.
———. "St Paul and Dualism: The Pauline Conception of Resurrection." *New Testament Studies* 12 (1966) 106–23.
Murphy-O'Connor, Jerome. "Christological Anthropology in Phil. II, 6–11." *Revue Biblique* 83 (1976) 22–50.
Newman, John Henry. *An Essay in Aid of a Grammar of Assent* (1870), with an introduction by Nicholas Lash. Notre Dame: Notre Dame University Press, 1979.
Nineham, Dennis. "Eyewitness Testimony and the Gospel Tradition." *JTS* 9/1 (1958) 13–25; 9/2 (1958) 243–52; and 11/2 (1960) 253–64.
———. *The Gospel of St. Mark*. Pelican Gospel Commentaries. Harmondsworth, UK: Penguin, 1963.
Noë, Alva. *Action in Perception*. Cambridge: MIT Press, 2004.
O'Collins, Gerald, SJ. "The Appearances of the Risen Christ: A Lexical-exegetical Examination of St Paul and Other Witnesses." *Irish Theological Quarterly* 79 (2014) 128–43.
———. *Believing in the Resurrection: The Meaning and Promise of the Risen Jesus*. Mahwah, NJ: Paulist, 2012.
Ong, Walter J., *Orality and Literacy: The Technologizing of the Word*. London: Metheun, 1982.
———. *The Presence of the Word: Some Prolegomena for Cultural and Religious History*. 1967. Reprint, Minneapolis: University of Minnesota Press, 1981.
Pannenberg, Wolfhart. "Did Jesus Really Rise from the Dead?" *Dialog* 4 (1965) 128–35.
———. *Jesus—God and Man*. Translated by Lewis L. Wilkins and Duane A. Priebe. Philadelphia: Westminster, 1968.
Pelikan, Jaroslav. *The Christian Tradition: A History of the Development Doctrine*, Vol. 2: *The Spirit of Eastern Christendom (600–1700)*. Chicago: University of Chicago Press, 1974.
Perkins, Pheme. *Resurrection: New Testament Witness and Contemporary Reflection*. Garden City, NY: Doubleday, 1984.
Perrin, Norman. *The Resurrection Narratives: A New Approach*. London: SCM, 1977.
Pickstock, Catherine. *After Writing: On the Liturgical Consummation of Philosophy*. Oxford: Blackwell, 1998.
Plummer, Alfred. *A Critical and Exegetical Commentary on the Second Epistle of St Paul to the Corinthians*. International Critical Commentary. Edinburgh: T. & T. Clark, 1915.
Rahner, Karl. "The 'Spiritual Senses' according to Origin." In *Theological Investigations*, vol. 16, 81–103. New York: Seabury, 1979.
Ramsey, A. M. *The Resurrection of Christ: An Essay in Biblical Theology*. London: Bles, 1945.
Ramsey, Ian. *Christian Empiricism*. London: Sheldon, 1974.
Rawlinson, A. E. J. *The Gospel according to St Mark*. London: Methuen, 1925.
Reist, Benjamin A. *Towards a Theology of Involvement: A Study of Ernst Troeltsch*. London: SCM, 1966.
Richardson, Alan. *Christian Apologetics*. London: SCM, 1947.
———. *History, Sacred and Profane*. London: SCM, 1964.
Richardson, Cyril C. "Love: Greek and Christian." *Journal of Religion* 23 (1943) 173–85.

Riley, Gregory J. *Resurrection Reconsidered: Thomas and John in Controversy*. Minneapolis: Fortress, 1995.

Robinson, H. Wheeler. "The Hebrew Conception of Corporate Personality." In *Werden und Wesen des Alten Testaments: Vorträge gehalten auf der internationalen Tagung alttestamentlicher Forscher zu Göttingen vom 4–10 September 1935*, edited by Johannes Hempel, et al., 49–62. Beihefte zur Zeitschrift für die alttestamentliche Wissenschaft, 66, Berlin: Töpelmann, 1936.

Robinson J. A. T. *The Body: A Study in Pauline Theology*. SBT 1/5. London: SCM, 1952.

Rogerson, John W. "The Hebrew Conception of Corporate Personality: A Re-examination." *JTS* 21 (1970) 1–16.

Rose, Herbert Jennings. "Herakles and the Gospels." *Harvard Theological Review* 31 (1938) 113–42.

Russell, Bertrand. *The Problems of Philosophy*. London: Williams & Norgate, 1912.

———. *The Analysis of Mind*. Muirhead Library of Philosophy. London: Allen & Unwin, 1921.

Ryle, Gilbert. *The Concept of Mind*. 1949. Reprint, Harmondsworth, UK: Penguin, 1966.

Sanders, E. P. *Paul and Palestinian Judaism: A Comparison of Patterns of Religion*. Minneapolis: Fortress, 1977.

Schofield, Malcolm. "Cicero's Plato." In *From Stoicism to Platonism: The Development of Philosophy, 100 BCE–100 CE*, edited by Troels Engberg-Pedersen, 47–66. Cambridge: Cambridge University Press, 2017.

Scholla, Robert W., SJ. "Recent Anglican Contributions on the Resurrection of Jesus (1945–1987)." PhD diss., Rome: Gregorian University, 1992.

Schoonenberg, Piet. *The Christ*. Translated by Della Couling. London: Sheed & Ward, 1971.

———. "'He Emptied Himself': Philippians 2:7." *Concilium* 1/1 (1965) 47–66.

———. "The Kenosis or Self-Emptying of Christ." *Concilium* 1/2 (1966) 27–36.

Schreiber, Johannes. "Die Christologie des Markus." *Zeitschrift für Theologie und Kirche* 58 (1961) 154–83.

Schweitzer, Albert. *The Mysticism of Paul the Apostle*. Translated by William Montgomery. London: A. & C. Black, 1953.

Schweizer, Eduard. "Resurrection—Fact or Illusion?" *Horizons in Biblical Theology* 1/1 (1979) 137–59.

Searle, John R. "Proper Names." In *Philosophical Logic*, edited by P. F. Strawson, 89–96. London: Oxford University Press, 1967. Originally published in *Mind* 67 (1958) 166–73.

———. "Proper Names and Descriptions." In *Encyclopedia of Philosophy*, edited by Paul Edwards, 6:487–91. London: Taylor & Francis, 1967.

Shiner, Whitney, *Proclaiming the Gospel: First Century Performance of Mark*. Harrisburg, PA: Trinity, 2003.

Shutt, R. J. H. "The Concept of God in the Works of Flavius Josephus." *Journal of Jewish Studies* 31 (1980) 171–87.

Smith, Daniel A. *Revisiting the Empty Tomb: The Early History of Easter*. Minneapolis: Fortress, 2010.

Stauffer, Ethelbert. "Words for Love in Pre-Biblical Greek," in the entry for "ἀγαπάω, ἀγάπη, ἀγαπητός," by Gottfried Quell and Ethelbert Stauffer. In *TDNT* 1 (1964) 35–38.

Steenburg, David. "The Case against the Synonymity of *Morphē* and *Eikōn*." *JSNT* 34 (1988) 77–86.

Sterling, Gregory E. "Hellenistic Philosophy and the New Testament." In *Handbook to Exegesis of the New Testament*, edited by Stanley E. Porter, 313–58. New Testament Tools and Studies 25. Leiden: Brill, 1997.

———. "The Love of Wisdom: Middle Platonism and Stoicism in the Wisdom of Solomon." In *From Stoicism to Platonism: The Development of Philosophy, 100 BCE–100 CE*, edited by Troels Engberg-Pedersen, 198–213. Cambridge: Cambridge University Press, 2017.

———. "Wisdom or Foolishness? The Role of Philosophy in the Thought of Paul." In *God and the Faithfulness of Paul: A Critical Examination of the Pauline Theology of N. T. Wright*, edited by Christoph Heilig, et al., 235–53. WUNT 2/413. Tübingen: Mohr/Siebeck, 2016.

Stewart, Robert B., and Gary R. Habermas, eds. *Memories of Jesus: A Critical Appraisal of James Dunn's Jesus Remembered*. Nashville: Broadman & Holman, 2010.

Stowers, Stanley. "The Dilemma of Paul's Physics: Features Stoic-Platonist or Platonist-Stoic?" in *From Stoicism to Platonism: The Development of Philosophy, 100 BCE–100 CE*, edited by Troels Engberg-Pedersen, 231–53. Cambridge: Cambridge University Press, 2017.

Strawson, Peter. "Proper Names." In *Philosophical Writings*, 39–70. Oxford: Oxford University Press, 2011.

Streeter, B. H. *The Four Gospels*. 4th rev. ed. London: Macmillan, 1930.

Swete, H. B. *The Gospel according to St Mark* (1898). London: Macmillan, 1902.

Swinburne, Richard. *The Resurrection of God Incarnate*. Oxford: Clarendon, 2003.

Taylor, Vincent. *The Formation of the Gospel Tradition: Eight Lectures*. London: Macmillan, 1957.

Troeltsch, Ernst. "The Dogmatics of the 'religionsgeschichtliche Schule.'" *American Journal of Theology* 17 (1913) 1–21.

———. "Empiricism and Platonism in the Philosophy of Religion." *Harvard Theological Review* 5 (1912) 401–22.

———. *Gesammelte Schriften*. 4 vols. Tübingen: Mohr Siebeck, 1912–1925.

———. "Historiography." In *Encyclopaedia of Religion and Ethics*, edited by James Hastings, 6:716–23. Edinburgh: T. & T. Clark, 1913.

Vansina, Jan. *Oral Tradition as History*. Madison: University of Wisconsin Press, 1985.

Wedderburn, A. J. M. "Some Observations on Paul's Use of the Phrases 'In Christ' and 'With Christ.'" *JSNT* 8 (1985) 83–97.

Weiss, Johannes. *Die Schriften des Neuen Testaments*. Göttingen: Vandenhoeck & Ruprecht, 1909.

Westcott, B. F. *The Gospel of the Resurrection: Thoughts on Its Relation to Reason and History* (1866). 4th ed. London: Macmillan, 1913.

———. "The Resurrection of Christ—A New Revelation." *Contemporary Review* 30 (Nov. 1877) 1070–87.

———. *The Revelation of the Risen Lord*. London: Macmillan, 1881.

Windisch, Hans. *Der Zweite Korintherbrief*. Kritisch-exegetischer Kommentar über das Neue Testament 6. Göttingen: Vandenhoeck & Ruprecht, 1924.

Witherington, Ben, III. *The Gospel of Mark: A Socio-Rhetorical Commentary*. Grand Rapids: Eerdmans, 2001.

———. *Jesus the Sage: The Pilgrimage of Wisdom*. Minneapolis: Fortress, 1994.

Wittgenstein, Ludwig. *Culture and Value*. Translated by Peter Winch. Chicago: University of Chicago Press, 1980.

———. *Philosophical Investigations*. Translated by G. E. M. Anscombe. Oxford: Blackwell, 1958.

Wright, N. T. *The Climax of the Covenant: Christ and the Law in Pauline Theology*. Edinburgh: T. & T. Clark, 1991.

———. *Paul and the Faithfulness of God*. 2 vols. Christian Origins and the Questions of God 4. Minneapolis: Fortress, 2013.

———. *The Resurrection of the Son of God*. Christian Origins and the Questions of God 3. Minneapolis: Fortress, 2003.

———. *Who Was Jesus?* Grand Rapids: Eerdmans, 1992.

Zahrnt, Heinz. *The Question of God: Protestant Theology in the Twentieth Century*. Translated by R. A. Wilson. London: Collins, 1969.

Zizioulas, John. *Being as Communion: Studies in Personhood and the Church*. London: Darton, Longman & Todd, 1985.

———. "On Being a Person: Towards an Ontology of Personhood." In *Communion and Otherness: Further Studies in Personhood and the Church*, 99–112. London: T. & T. Clark, 2006. Also in *Persons, Divine and Human*, edited by C. Schwoebel and C. Gunton, 33–46. Edinburgh: T. & T. Clark, 1992.

Author Index

Alston, William P., 101n5, 137n35
Argyle, Michael, 117
Aune, David E., 243n5, 255n40

Bailey, Kenneth E., 199n5, n6
Barr, James, 257n47
Barrett, C. K., 3n9
Barth, K., 2, 5, 110–11, 153, 155
Barton, Stephen, 261n59
Bauckham, Richard, 42, 173, 178n19, 197n1, 198, 215–21, 225, 229
Baxter, Anthony, 101n4
Becker, Carl, 208n31
Behm, J., 292n11, 297n31
Bergson, Henri, 181, 185
Besant, Walter, 224n8
Bockmuehl, Markus, 41, 171n3, 175n13, 204n20
Bonazzi, Mauro, 271n14
Borg, Marcus, 225-26n11
Boring, E. G., 147
Bornkamm, Günther, 153n25
Botwinick, Jack, 148
Bousset, Wilhelm, 8
Broad, C. D., 182, 183n39, 185n45
Browne, Peter, 154n28
Bryan, Christopher, 43, 216n42
Buber, Martin, 123
Bultmann, Rudolf, 2, 5, 15–17, 19–20, 33, 110–11, 153, 171–72, 174, 177, 198, 201, 207, 305–6, 310
Burkitt, F.C., 32n12
Burridge, Richard, 173
Byrne, Brendan, 293n14
Byrskog, Samuel, 173n7, n9, 197n1

Calvin, John, 58n8, 106, 274–75n28
Campenhausen, Hans von, 181n31
Carnley, Peter, 3n7, n8, 5n14, 26n69, 41n41, 60n12, 86n37, 98n74, 135n33, 175, 181n32, 205n26, 228n18, n20, 245n14

Coakley, Sarah, 3n7, 108–9, 143–44
Coleridge, Samuel Taylor, 162
Collingwood, R. G., 20, 202, 208n32
Collins, Adela Yarbro, 36, 37n31, n33
Congar, Yves M.-J., OP, 181n31
Copleston, Edward, 135
Craffert, Pieter, 308n8
Cranfield, C. E. B., 3n9, 33
Creed, J. M., 33n17
Croce, Benedetto, 209
Crossan, John Dominic, 225-26n11

Dahl, Nils. A., 20
Danove, Paul, 37n33
Darwin, Charles, 116, 117n40, n41
Davis, Stephen T., 1n4, 30n1, 40, 112, 115, 129, 146n15, 175n13, 176n15, 189n66, 205, 211, 263
Deissmann, Adolf, 8, 15, 17, 19–20, 305
Dewey, Joanna, 43n54
Dibelius, Martin, 198n2
Dillon, John, 91, 269n4, 270n6, 280n44, 281n48, n49
Dryer, D. P., 141n3
Dunn, James D. G., 1, 3, 8n21, 29n77, 82n24, 107n27, 165, 172, 173n6, n9, 175–77, 180n30, 187, 188n56, 189–91, 195, 196n79, 197n1, 198, 199n6, 201–7, 210–14, 217, 219, 221, 225, 227, 230n24, 237n44, 240, 263, 291n10, 293n14

Ebeling, Gerhard, 153n25, 181n31
Engberg-Pedersen, Troels, 16, 62, 74–75, 77–80, 84–90, 92n57, 94, 96–97, 99, 112, 121, 271n12, 272n21, 273–76, 280–81, 287, 290, 302–3
Evans, Christopher, 35, 44, 46

Farrer, A.M., 46
Fee, G., 290n4

AUTHOR INDEX

Fenton, John, 33n18, 46n69
Frege, Gottlob, 231
Frei, Hans, 70n50, 132, 170n2, 174n11, 223–24, 230, 233–34, 240, 294n18, 296n29
Friedrich, Gerhard, 292n11
Frisch, Karl von, 129n15
Fuchs, Ernst, 153n25
Fuller, Reginald H., 44
Funk, Robert W., 225–26n11

Gerhardsson, B., 173n7, 197n1, 199n4
Gregory, A. F., 175n13
Gunkel, Hermann, 198n2
Guy, H. A., 41n39

Habermas, Gary R., 173n9, 175n13, 176n15, 189n66, 197n1, 198n3, 263n66
Hadas, Moses, 269n4
Harvey, Anthony, 251n33
Hays, Richard B., 73n1, 247–48
Heiden, Gert-Jan van der, 79n15
Hengel, Martin, 216n41, 269n2
Hermann, Ingo, 61n14, 82n24
Herrmann, Wilhelm, 171, 207n29
Hewitt, J. Thomas, 17n46
Hill, William Ely, 147–48
Hick, John, 101n5, 134n32, 137–38, 142–43, 149, 161
Hofer, Walther, 209
Holmberg, Bengt, 173n9
Hooker, Morna D., 42
Hooker, Richard, 274n28
Hoskyns, E. C., 35n29
Houlden, Leslie, 50–51, 53–54
Hume, David, 135, 154n28, 193
Hurtado, Larry W., 63, 64n24, 89, 90n44, 291–96

James, Henry, 224
Jenson, Robert W., 127n10, 128n14, 240–41n50
Jewett, Robert, 70
Johnson, Aubrey R., 6n17

Kähler, Martin, 176, 223–24, 229n22
Kant, Immanuel, 25, 141, 150–51, 157, 168, 194
Käsemann, Ernst, 10, 61, 153n25, 166n60
Kelber, Werner H., 173n7
Kendall, Daniel, SJ, 130–31
Kierkegaard, Søren, 51, 171n4, 235
King, William, 154n28
Kittel, Gerhard, 292n11
Knox, John, 173–82, 185–96, 197, 199–205, 212–15, 221, 223, 225, 229n23, 230, 233, 235
Knox, W. L., 42n51
Kooten, George van, 79n15

Kümmel, Werner Georg, 33n18

LaNave, Gregory F., 106n21
Leyden, W. von, 184
Lewis, C. S., 233
Long, A. A., 80n20
Lightfoot, R. H., 33n17, n18, n20, 34, 292n11
Lindars, Barnabas, 38n36, 58, 64n26
Lohmeyer, Ernst, 33n18, 34, 292n11
Louth, Andrew, 107n26

Macan, R. W., 2
Mack, Arien, 145n13
Macquarrie, John, 295n26
Magness, J. Lee, 42
Malcolm, Norman, 181–89, 193
Mandelbaum, Maurice, 208
Mansel, H. L., 55n100, 154n28, 309n9
Marcus, Ralph, 89n43
Marguerat, Daniel, 42n44
Marshall, I. Howard, 293n14
Marxsen, Willi, 33n18, 34, 131–32, 202
Mascall, E.L., 179, 192
McCormack, Bruce L., 70
McKnight, Scot, 198n3
Metzger, Bruce M, 31n8
Michaelis, W., 130–31
Mill, J. S., 194n76
Minear, Paul S., 229
Moffatt, J., 233n32
Moore, G. E., 184n44
Morgan, Robert, 261n59
Morgan, Teresa, 73n1
Moule, C. F. D., 8, 27n70, 228n19, 244, 295, 304
Murphy-O'Connor, Jerome, 295n26

Newman, John Henry, 25, 133–43, 229
Nineham, Dennis, 32n12, 42n51, 216n41
Noë, Alva, 145, 160n34
Noth, Martin, 198n2
Novenson, Matthew V., 17n46

O'Collins, Gerald, SJ, 37n33, 130–31
Ong, Walter J., 43n54
Otto, Rudolph, 109–10, 114, 144

Pannenberg, Wolfhart, 1, 3, 55n99, 61
Pascal, Blaise, 163
Pelikan, Jaroslav, 22n62
Perkins, Pheme, 130
Perrin, Norman, 35, 45
Pickstock, Catherine, 43, 278–79, 311
Plummer, Alfred, 243n6

AUTHOR INDEX

Quell, Gottfried, 233

Radice, Roberto, 91n55
Rahner, Karl, 105–7
Ramsey, A. M., 244, 255n42, 261–62
Ramsey, Ian, 101n5
Rawlinson, A. E. J., 32n12
Richardson, Alan, 208–9
Richardson, Cyril C., 233n32
Robinson, H. Wheeler, 6n17
Robinson, John A. T., 6n16, 8–10
Rock, I., 145n13
Rodriguez, Rafael, 173n8
Rogerson, John W., 6n17
Rose, H. J., 39n37
Runia, David T., 91n55
Russell, Bertrand, 181–82, 183n40, 185
Ryle, Gilbert, 182, 183n41, 184, 190, 215n39, 235, 236n42

Sanders, E. P., 16–17, 19, 305
Schleiermacher, Friedrich, 109
Schofield, Malcolm, 280n45
Schoonenberg, Piet, 295
Schreiber, Johannes, 44
Schweitzer, Albert, 8, 29
Schweizer, Eduard, 262–63
Searle, John R., 194, 231
Sedley, D. N., 80n20
Shiner, Whitney, 43n54
Shutt, R. J. H., 89n43
Smith, Daniel, 35n27, 36–39
Spinoza, Baruch/Benedict, 230n25
Stanton, Graham, 261n59

Stauffer, Ethelbert, 233
Steenburg, David, 291
Sterling, Gregory E., 91n56, 92n57, 272n20
Stewart, Robert B., 173n9, 175n13, 176n15, 189n66, 197n1, 198n3, 263n66
Stowers, Stanley, 98m75
Streeter, B.H., 32n12, 33n13
Swete, H. B., 32n12
Swinburne, Richard, 4

Taylor, Vincent, 216n41
Toland, John, 154n28
Troeltsch, Ernst, 70n46, 197, 205, 207, 212

Vansina, Jan, 216n43

Whately, Richard, 135
Wedderburn, A. J. M., 6n17, 20
Weiss, Johannes, 35n29
Wellhausen, Julius, 33
Westcott, B. F., 1, 2, 3n7, 33, 261, 267, 303
Windisch, Hans, 255n40
Witherington, Ben, III, 42n48, 293n14
Wittgenstein, Ludwig, x, 11, 109, 139, 141–45, 150–52, 194, 309
Wright, N. T., 1, 3, 18–20, 24, 33, 40, 60–65, 70, 71n56, 74n2, n3, 81n21, 83n27, 90n45, 92n57, 112, 129, 130n21, 138, 164, 176n16, 205n26, 219, 228, 242n1, 244n10, 245n14, 246–57, 259

Zahrnt, Heinz, 111n35, 155
Zizioulas, John, 13–14, 127

Subject Index

Achilles, 36, 218
Albinus (alias Alcinous), 53, 90–91, 94, 95, 108, 285–86
   Didaskalikos, 91, 108, 285, 285–86n59, 286n60
Ambiguity, in perception, 112n36, 158–61
   of Paul's "partial knowing" of the Spirit, 165–66
   of puzzle pictures, 141–43
   of resurrection appearance narratives, 164–65
   (*see also under* Freedom in perception)
Analogy, 154n27, 179n22 (*see also under* Metaphor)
   of father's love for children, 234
   of Origen and Gregory of Nyssa on river and drops of water, 260
   of Origen's image of wood turned to smoke, 259
   Paul's image of body and members, 262
   of seed planted in ground, 245
   Troeltsch's "principle of," 70n46 (*see also under* Troeltsch)
Andronicus, 7
Anglican Liturgical tradition, 261
Antiochus of Ascalon, 76, 269, 270, 277n35, 278, 280, 280n44
Apophatic (negative) language, 9, 41, 53, 90–91, 94, 154n28, 155n29, 310 (*see also under* Metaphor)
Apollodorus, 37
Aquinas, Thomas, 19n54, 104, 120, 240n50, 259
Aristobulus of Alexandria, 269
Aristotle, 128
Augustine of Hippo, 113n38

Basil of Caesarea, 27n71, 126–27
Behavioral obligations (of relation to Christ), 17–18, 23–24, 28, 64, 66, 69, 79, 126, 289–91, 295–300

Biblical Theology Movement, 74n3, 233, 242–44, 257, 290n5
Blindness, as theme in Mark, 47
   of Bartimaeus, true disciple, 35, 47, 48n81
   conceptual blindness, 141–45, and faith, 152–53
   conceptual blindness in thought of Kant, 150–51, 155–57, 168–69
   following and seeing (of Raised Christ), 48
   "inattentional/aspect blindness," 145–50, 168
   of man "who sees by stages," 47
   seeing and following (of historical Jesus), 47–48
Bodily resurrection, 241, 242–46, 249–50
   absence of concept of "body" in Hebrew thought, 256-57
   "body" by contrast with "flesh," 259–62
   body (*soma*), a Hellenistic concept, 257
   body "transformed not abandoned" (Wright), 250–55
   functional/relational view of "body," 262–64
   as instrument of location and inter-personal access, 259, 262–64, 267
Body of Christ, xi, 5–17, 21, 26, 67, 75, 78, 139
   in eucharistic sharing, 264–65, 266–67
   functional understanding of in Paul, 262–64
   as local church, complete in itself, 267 (Westcott), 302–3
   not located in heaven by Paul, 264
"Body language," 115–17, 122, 139, 311 (*see also under* Non-verbal communication)
Bonaventure, 105–6

Caligula, 270n11
Cappadocian Fathers, 89
Case, Shirley Jackson, 199n7
Celsus, *Contra Celsum*, 144n10, 260n53, n54, n55, n56
Chicago Divinity School, 173n10, 199

Christology, deductive and inductive approaches, 228–29
Cicero, 269, 277n37, 280n45
Conscience, 25, 135, 136–37
Constantinople, Third Council of, 22–23
Cranmer, Thomas, 261
Creed, Apostles' and Nicene, 261
Chrysippus, 302
Cyril of Jerusalem, 261

Demea, in Hume's *Dialogues,* 135
  in Anglican theology, 154n28
  in theology of John Henry Newman, 135n33
  (*see also under* Language, limits of theological language)
Demythologizing, 2, 111 (*see also under* Bultmann)
Diogenes Laërtius, 302
Dyothelitism, 22, 306
Doubt
  as reason for Mark's omission of appearance narrative, 31–32
  in Matthew's Gospel, 28:16–17, 145, 164–65
  in relation to faith and freedom, 112n36, 141–69
  (*see also under* Freedom in perception)
Duck/Rabbit (Wittgenstein), 141

Ecclesiology
  Knox's appeal to "memory of Jesus" as constitutive of ecclesial identity, 177
  Paul's reliance on constitutive presence of the Spirit of the Raised Christ for, 10, 12, 13n32
Eiffel Tower, as model of theological discourse, 155
Emotional intelligence, 114
Empiricism, 87, 101, 103, 120
  British (from Hume to Logical Positivists), 193
  in Stoicism, 275, 277, 281
Epicurus, 279, 282
Epistemology (*see under* Faith)
Eschatological hope
  actualized by "out-pouring of Spirit," 67–69, 83, 166
  not wishful thinking, 36
  "revealed" in "visitation of God", 258
  of Second Temple Judaism, 283–86, 308
Eudorus of Alexandria, 53, 76, 90, 91, 94–95, 270, 277n37, 280, 281
Evagrius of Pontus, 107–8
Eyewitness testimony, 120, 130, 171–73, 178n19, 198–99, 215–21, 225, 229–30

Faith
  alleged non-cognitive nature in Mark's view of (Houlden), 50–54
  apophatic approach in Mark, 41
  cognitive realism of Mark's view of, 51–55
  empirically grounded in the deliverances of physical senses, 102–4, 111–12, 119–22
  epistemology of, x–xi, 4–5, 8–9, 12, 15, 28–29, 49, 159, 195, 273, 297
  and "experiencing as" (Hick), 142–43
  as form of non-cognitive idealism (Dunn), 200–3
  importance of interpretative concepts for, 152–53
  as involving both hearing and seeing, 130–32
  as knowledge (*fides*), 4, 55, 70, 100, 124, 125, 133, 168, 200
  logical impossibility of trust without justifying grounds, 50–51, 55
  logical priority of *fides* in relation to *fiducia,* 125, 200
  in Mark's Gospel, 31–56, 310
  in Matthew's Gospel, 48–54
  not propositional belief, 65–67, 69–71, 100, 136–37
  as "remembering and knowing" in theology of Knox, 174 200, 203, 238
  as "right understanding" of significance of historical Jesus (Marxsen), 202
  and "seeing-as" (Wittgenstein), 141–42
  similarity of pattern of theistic faith in God, and resurrection faith, 101
  similarity of pattern with knowledge of persons and material things, 101–2, 114
  Spirit, as the object of faith and ground of hope, 54, 58–69, 72, 100–101, 121
  in theology of Barth, 110–11
  in theology of Bultmann, 110–11, 201
  as trust (*fiducia*), 4, 50, 55, 70, 100, 124–25, 133, 168, 200
  (*see also under* Blindness, and Illative sense)
"Flesh and blood," 246–49, 251–57, 258–61
Form criticism, 198–200, 215–16, 217
  its historical antecedents, 198n2
Freedom
  Augustine's view of, 162–63
  and "epistemic distance" (Hick), 161, 263
  Hugh of St Victor's view of, 163
  Pascal's view of, 163–64
  in perception, xi, 52, 112n36, 141, 157–58
  in religious perception and faith, 157–69
  Samuel Taylor Coleridge's view of, 162
  (*see also under* Ambiguity, Rubin Goblet, and Kanizsa Triangle)

SUBJECT INDEX

Galilee
- as origin of "universal mission," spelled out by Matthew, 31, 44
- as "place of discipleship" (Hooker), 42
- as "place of mission," 43–48, 312
- as place of rendezvous with Raised Christ as shepherd/leader, 30, 31, 34–36, 38, 41–42

Grace, 108, 140, 166, 289, 299–300
Gregory of Nazianzus, 126
Gregory of Nyssa, 108–9, 111, 120, 123, 126, 143, 157, 260–61
Gregory the Great, 107n24

Hellenization (of Jewish culture), 257, 269–74
Heracles, 36–37, 39
Herod Agrippa, 76n11
Historical Jesus, 5, 171–2, 174, 195–96, 197, 201, 223
Hitler, Adolf, 4
Historical skepticism, 171, 176n16, 197
- of James Dunn, 205–12

Hope
- of first Christians, grounded in continuing experience of Spirit, 36, 57, 60–64, 66–69, 78–79, 83, 100, 166
- of Paul to meet Raised Christ "face to face," 125, 166
- of Second Temple Judaism, 20
- not wishful thinking, 36, 68

Hugh of St. Victor, 163

Idealism
- in contemporary NT studies, 20–21, 202–3
- and faith, 43

Ignatius of Antioch, 267n83
Illative sense, 134–39, 143, 229
Immortality of the Soul, 81, 242–44, 246, 250–52, 258
- in Wisdom of Solomon, 243, 272
Intermediate state, 255

John Chrysostom, 260
John's Gospel
- "abundant Spirit" in, 4, 12, 62, 70–71, 100n2, 139, 203
- and Platonic/Stoic Philosophy, 276
- pre-existence of the Word in, 293–96
- Thomas episode in, not a paradigm of faith, 52, 57n1, 164, 310

John, First Epistle of, on love and Spirit, 62–63, 167, 234
Jerome, 260
Josephus, 76n11, 89n43, 90n48, 270n11
Junia, 7
Kanizsa Triangle, 160

Kenotic Christology (Phil 2), 293–98

Language
- limits of in relation to the exalted, Raised Christ, 156
- limits of theological language, 3, 11, 53, 55, 99, 135, 154, 309
- (*see also under* Metaphor)

Lavoisier, Antoine, 151

Mark's Gospel
- absence of appearance narrative, 30, 34, 36
- apophatic approach to faith, 41
- "disappearance" of Jesus" body, 35n27, 36–40
- hearing of (in context of worship), 42–43
- "lost" ending of, 32–33, 48
- Mark as systematic theologian, 41n39, 46–48, 219
- Mark's alleged belief in *parousia* rather than resurrection appearance, 34–36
- reader-response theory, 42

Mathews, Shailer, 199n7
Maximus the Confessor, 22–23, 24n64, 166n59, 306–7
Memory, three forms of, 181–85
- certainty of (in theology of Knox), 205, 212–13
- as "ecclesiastical psychology," 179, 192-94
- episodic and dispositional memory, 189–92, 213–22, 235–37
- epistemic function of, 195–96, 230–31, 238
- expressed in putatively factual statements, 189, 195, 230
- factual, 182–83
- knowing in faith as clarification of memory of Jesus, 238–40
- logical primitiveness of factual memory, 184–86
- ostensible and veridical, 197, 212–13
- perceptual, 181–82
- personal, 183–85
- presupposed by use of proper-names, 194-95
- relevance to Knox's view of "the church and her memory," 185–89
- "uniquely referring" memories, 195, 230–37

Menander, 33n19
Metaphor
- essential to religious language, 98, 140, 154–56
- of image of "Body of Christ," 5–11
- irreducible to prosaic specification, 97, 99, 154
- more than a metaphor, 10, 304–7, 310–11
- of "resurrection" (Dunn/Pannenberg), 3–4

Methexis (participation), *see under* Plato
Middle Platonism, x–xi, 38, 76–80, 91–94, 107–8, 268, 269–74, 277–82, 292
Mithridatic Wars, 269
Monothelitism, 22
Moses, 36, 269
Morphe, 291–93, 295–300
Mystery
    of God, 1, 5, 55, 93, 95, 97, 135, 154–58, 161, 168, 237, 309
    of resurrection, 3, 4, 41, 46, 53, 100, 242, 244, 245, 249, 311
    of the Spirit, 303
Mysticism (Schweitzer), 8, 22

Neoplatonism, 109n31, 120, 270
Neopythagorean transcendentalism, 270, 280
Noetic sciences, 105n17
Nero, 32n12
Non-verbal communication, 115–19
    and religious perception, 119-22

Origen, 105–9, 111, 113, 120, 123, 144, 159, 259–62

Papias of Hierapolis, 178, 217
Paralinguistic communication, *see under* Non-verbal communication, Body language
Participationism:
    Christ/Spirit "in him," 23–25
    descriptive of concrete experience, 21
    Paul's "in Christ" participative language, 5–12, 15–17, 25–29
    Platonic "*methectic*" view of, 279, 281, 286–87, 297-98
    in thought of Adolf Deissmann, 8, 15, 17, 19, 20
    in thought of E. P. Sanders, 16–17, 19, 305
    in thought of R. Bultmann, 15–17, 19, 20
    in thought of Troels Engberg Pedersen, 16
    its verbal sources, 17, 20–21
    Wright view of as "incorporative messiahship," 20
    (*see also under* Plato/"*methexis*")
Paul
    his acquaintance with Wisdom, 94–96, 243, 272–73
    his (*parenetic*) ethical passages, 18, 65–67, 79, 288–90
    his Stoic language and patterns of ethical argument, 74, 77, 290
    Stoic underpinning of his understand of Spirit, 74–75
    his view of God, 88–96
    his view of transcendence of Spirit, as against "material and physical" Spirit (Engberg-Pedersen), 93–98
    love as defining characteristic of Spirit, 98–99
Person
    as distinct from individual, 14, 90n46, 125
    as one who addresses another and is addressed by another, 124–29
    persona, in civic affairs of Roman world, 126
    prosopon in Greek tragedy, 89, 125
    in Trinitarian theology of Cappadocian Fathers, 126-27
    as the "praying animal," distinct from all other animal creatures, 128–30
Philo of Alexandria, 6, 53, 76, 90, 91, 92n57, 93, 94, 95, 243n5, n7, 244n10, 248n29, 270, 273, 276, 277n37
    as contemporary of Paul, 76n11, 270
Plato
    growing ascendancy of, over Stoicism in Middle Platonism, x, 76–79, 90–94, 269
    "immanence" of Ideal Forms in Middle Platonism, 107–8, 280–84, 287
    influence on Paul (minimized by Engberg-Pedersen), 274–76, 303
    input into ethical thought, 281, 290, 298, 299, 301
    "*methexis*," 107, 279–87, 297, 300–2, 306
    "*morphe*," 291–93, 295–99
    ontological dualism of, 77, 276, 283, 303
    pre-natal acquaintance with Ideal Forms, 270, 277
    Cratylus, 244n10
    Gorgias, 244n10
    Parmenides, 277n36
    Phaedo, 243n5
    Phaedrus, 107, 277n37, 278, 279, 283, 286
    Republic, 243n7, 277, 302n48
    Statesman, 269n3
    Theaetetus, 270n7, 285n59
    Timaeus, 107, 269, 277n37, 278, 279, 280, 298, 302
Plotinus, 80n19, 108, 109n31, 270, 286
Plutarch, 6, 269n5
Presence of Christ, as "life-giving Spirit," 29, 61, 68, 70n50, 84–85, 132, 139, 166, 239, 241, 311
Proper-names
    role in interpretation of experience, 138
    logic of, 192, 194, 231
Pseudo-Macarius, 108
Pythagoras, 269

Rad, Gerhard von, 198n2

Redaction criticism, 30, 171
Resurrection, as historical event, 1, 3
   historiographical reliance on Gospels of John and Luke, 30
   Mark's belief in, 31–32
   in Mark's Gospel, 41, 46
   in theology of Pannenberg, 1, 3, 55n99, 61
   in theology of B. F. Westcott, 1, 2, 3
   as transcendental "mystery of God," 1, 3, 4–5, 100, 135, 154–56, 158, 161, 168, 237, 242, 244–45, 249, 309–11
Romulus, 36–37
Rubin Goblet, 158–59

Sabellius, 126
Scheele, Carl Wilhelm, 151
Schmidt, Karl Ludwig, 198n2
Self-giving of Jesus, 26, 54, 119, 162, 192, 214, 226, 227–28, 230–38, 240n50, 304–5
   Cross as symbol of, 188, 191–92, 232
Seneca, Lucius Annaeus. 6, 280–81, 286
Septuagint (LXX), 33, 89, 257, 291–92
Socrates, 269
Spinoza, Baruch/Benedict, 230n25
Spirit of Christ, x, 4, 5, 6–15, 16–17, 21, 57, 58–72
   as allegedly "material and physical" (Engberg Pedersen), 75–99, 273–75, 303, 304
   as an essentially "personal" presence, 131–32
   gift of the Spirit, 7, 10, 11, 18, 19, 26, 29, 44, 58–59, 62, 66, 68, 70, 117, 140, 166, 168, 234, 246–48, 258, 265, 268, 286, 299-300, 304, 306, 307
   "spiritual body," 83n27, 245–47, 260–61, 263
Spiritual senses
   interpreted with linguistic concepts and proper names, 102–3
   in view of Origen, 105–9, 111, 113, 120, 123
   in view of Bonaventure, 105–6
   in view of Evagrius of Pontus, 107
   in view of Diadocus Photicus, 105, 108
   in view of Pseudo-Macarius, 108
   in view of Gregory of Nyssa, 108–9, 111, 120, 123
   in view of Sarah Coakley, 108–9, 143–44
   in view of Ludwig Wittgenstein, 109, 143–44
Stalin, Joseph, 4
Stoicism
   and "citizenship," 126, 290, 301–2
   empirical acquisition of conceptions/preconceptions, 270, 277, 280
   as ingredient of Middle Platonism, 269–70
   its use of metaphor of "body," 6
   Stoic approaches to religious perception, 120–21
   Stoic monism, 75–77, 91–93, 273, 276, 279, 287, 303
   Stoic understanding of "warm breath" (*pneuma*), 26, 75–76, 80–88, 92, 97–98, 121, 132, 270n6, 304
sturmfreies Gebiet, 2, 171, 178, 213, 225
Suchet, David, 43n52
Syro-phoenician woman, 45

Temple, a place of prayer "for all nations," 45
   as image of dwelling place of God/Spirit, 266
Tertullian, 127, 259, 261
Theology, as "grammar of God," 102, 152–3
Tiberius Julius Alexander (Philo's nephew), 76n11
"Total person," 242 (*see also under* Biblical Theology Movement)
Totus Christus, 13, 267
Transcendence of God, 90, 95–97, 154–55, 162, 270, 281, 292n11
   (*see also under* Language, and Metaphor)
"Transphysical" restoration (Wright), 246-52
Trinity, inter-relatedness of "persons" of, 23, 89, 126–28, 240n49, n50

Vasse Felix, 237

Wisdom of Solomon, 94, 243, 272–73
Word theology (of Barth and Bultmann), 2–5, 174

www.ingramcontent.com/pod-product-compliance
Lightning Source LLC
Chambersburg PA
CBHW080923300426
44115CB00018B/2921